Torah To *Telos:*
The Passing of the Law of Moses:
Volume #2

The Resurrection of Daniel 12:2:
Fulfilled or Future?

Did Daniel 12:2 Foretell the Consummative Resurrection of the Dead, or, Events Simply Foreshadowing the "Real" End – The End of the Current Christian Age?

© 2016 JaDon Management

All rights reserved. No part of this book may be reproduced or transmitted in any form or by any means, electronic or mechanical, including photocopying, recording, or by any information storage and retrieval system, except for brief quotations for the purpose of review or comment, without the expressed written permission of the author or publisher, except where permitted by law.

ISBN - 978-1-937501-15-0 1-937501-15-9

Logo Design: Joseph Vincent

Cover Design by:
Jeffrey T. McCormack
The Pendragon: Web and Graphic Design
www.the pendragon.net

Foreword
by William Bell

Daniel 12 by Don K. Preston, is the kind of book you write after years of being a warrior in many debates. From his first encounter with Bill Lockwood to his last encounter with Dr. Michael Brown, (as of this writing) Preston has been writing this book. The breadth and depth of his argumentation demonstrate why he is the hardest working man in the "eschatology business."

The logic is precise, lucid, more refined, extremely thorough and undeniable. Men express such keenness of skill after being battle tested.

What we have here is an anthology of apologetics on the resurrection. It is a complete dismantling of futurist eschatology of all sorts, a death choke-hold around the necks of Dominionists, Postmillennialists Amillennialists and Dispensationalists. No longer need it be said that resurrection is the last stronghold to be tackled in pursuit of understanding Covenant Eschatology. With this work on Daniel 12, resurrection can now be the starting point. Generations to come will be indebted to Preston's exegetical labors.

This book is a Handbook for refuting futurism. It should be required reading for every Preterist who not only needs a thorough and correct approach to meeting the sophistry of all forms of futurism, but to build the confidence needed to face any foe.

The validity of Consistent Preterism is no longer in doubt. The term "hyper" is now extinct and obsolete. The Emperors of futurism, -- Kenneth Gentry, Gary Demar, Joel McDurmon, Sam Frost, Thomas Ice, Keith Mathison, Dr. Michael Brown, N.T. Wright, Jonathan Seriah, et. al, have no clothes. They can no longer hide under the cloaks of partial preterism in any of its forms. To continue to peddle futurism from this point forward may reveal they have other agendas to which they assign a higher priority than truth.

There is but one refrain to appropriately describe the fate of futurism from this publication forward: *MENE, MENE, TEKEL, UPHARSIN*. To all futurists, God has numbered your kingdom, and finished it. You have been weighed in the balances and found wanting; Your kingdom has been divided and given to destruction. Futurist eschatology is bankrupt.

This book thoroughly exposes the doctrine of prominent futurists - leaving them "without excuse. It remains to be seen how they respond to the grace of the gospel that has been laboriously extended on their behalf. Silence is not an option. Nothing short of an (attempted) refutation or full embrace of these arguments is acceptable.

This book demonstrates that there is no further doctrinal reason to reject the resurrection of the dead as having been fulfilled in 70AD, as the hope of Israel in connection with the downfall of the Jewish temple.

Preston documents the radical change of views by Dominionists who seem oblivious to the consequences of their more recent acknowledgment that the resurrection of Daniel 12 and the Messianic Banquet of Matthew 8:11-12 were both fulfilled in A.D. 70. They can no longer deny the land promise to Abraham has been fulfilled.

Preston's stunning and persuasive development of the role of John the Baptist, as a herald of the end and covenant wrath of God, though overlooked by most commentators, cannot be disputed. This argument is an axe laid to the root of the tree of futurism leaving the ground trembling from the fall of that great oak.

Postmillennialists such as Gentry, Mathison, Seriah, etc. who continue to adopt non-creedal AD 70 views, while still claiming faithfulness to the creeds, expose their desperate and futile attempt to labor outside a Consistent Preterist paradigm while falling into a cavern of contradictions.

Don's exposure of Joel McDurmon's shoddy scholarship and specious attempt to dismiss history's scholarship on the controversial resurrection text of Job 19:25 is more than revealing - and extremely powerful. Regardless of which fork in the road McDurmon took, Job's resurrection teaching led him to the last day, back to Daniel 12, 1 Cor. 15, Matt. 8:11-12, Revelation 20 - and directly to AD 70!

Gary Demar and Kenneth Gentry's admission that Daniel 12 and Revelation 10-11 refer to AD 70AD nailed them to the wall. Neither of these men can afford to continue to avoid public debate if they are to retain any integrity in their handling of the word of God on eschatology.

Daniel 12 is shown likewise to refute the resurrection of the bodies of saints in Matthew 27:52 as a viable option for the eschatological resurrection to eternal life at the last day.

John Noe, Joel McDurmon and Sam Frost are given a primer on the resurrection and the eschatological Spirit. The work of the Holy Spirit is proof that the end time resurrection has occurred. Daniel 9, and "seal up vision and prophecy" has sealed the arguments of these men and silenced them.

Dispensationalists' contradictions on the Abomination of Desolation as Mosaic Covenant wrath on Israel come back to bite them.

Dr. Michael Brown cannot waive a wand with his favorite - but misguided - phrase, "That has not happened yet," after viewing the evidence on *pateo* in Luke 21:21-24 and the correlations from Isaiah 24-29 and chapter 59. The Great Tribulation and the Abomination of Desolation have tripped all these men in their views of futurism. Arguing for a type of the types is no longer possible on any resurrection text.

More could be said about the 144,000, i.e. the remnant of Israel as the first-fruits, Mt. Zion, the heavenly city of Isaiah 65, and the festal gathering in Hebrews 12, the martyr comparison of Daniel 12, Matthew 23 and Revelation 6. Commenting further on the thoroughness and logical presentation of this material would be a detraction of their merit. Read it, study it and if you cannot refute it, embrace it and teach it.

The research is fully documented, with extensive quotes from scholarship as well as all detractors so they have no eye-sight problems in seeing their own self-contradictory statements.

Much more could be said, but chances are, you won't believe until you read it. This book is another outstanding contribution of scholarship to the Consistent (true) Preterist community and the world.

Table of Contents

Introduction:

A Brief History of the Interpretation of Daniel 12, A Look at Modern Dominionism and Daniel 12: Some Initial Observations

Point #1 – Page 35f

If Abraham and the martyred Worthies of Hebrews 11, including the prophets, received their eternal kingdom reward through the resurrection in AD 70 – as posited by the Dominionists – then undeniably, that resurrection to eternal life did not involve the raising, restoration and resuscitation of their long decayed biological bodies!

Point #2 - Page 41f

If Abraham, Isaac, Jacob, the martyrs of Hebrews 11, and the prophets received their kingdom reward through the resurrection to eternal life in AD 70 – as posited by the Dominionists – then clearly, they received their eternal reward 2000 years prior to New Covenant believers who are, per the Dominionists, still waiting for our resurrection to eternal life.

Point #3 - Page 44f

Abraham, Isaac, Jacob, the Martyrs of Hebrews 11 and the Prophets Did Not Receive Their Resurrection Reward to Eternal Life During Jesus' Ministry, at the Cross, or at the ascension of Christ.

Point #4 - Page 55f

The Resurrection to Eternal Life Is Comprehensive. Thus, the Resurrection of Daniel 12 Is the "General Resurrection."

Point #5 - Page 71f

The Resurrection to Eternal Life of Daniel 12 Would Be the Judgment of the "Living and the Dead."

Point #6 - Page 108

The Resurrection of the Just and the Unjust: Daniel 12 and Acts 24:14f.

Point #7 - Page 118

Daniel 12 and 1 Corinthians 15 - Is the Resurrection of Daniel 12 the Same Resurrection as Predicted by Paul in Corinthians?

Point #8 - Page 145

Daniel 12, Revelation 6 and the End of the Intermediate State.

Point #9 - Page 158

Daniel 12 – Resurrection and the Great Tribulation: In Scripture The Great Tribulation Immediately Precedes the Resurrection.

Point #10 - Page 231

Was Daniel 12:2 Fulfilled in Matthew 27:51-52?

Point #11 - Page 245

Is the Resurrection of Daniel 12 the Resurrection of Job 19?

Point #12 - Page 268

Daniel 12, the Vindication of the Martyrs and the Millennium.

Point #13 - Page 303

The Salvation of the Remnant and the Final Salvation.

Point #14 - Page 329

The Last Days Presence of the Spirit and the Resurrection.

Point #15 - Page 367

Was Daniel 12 Written About the Time and Events of Antiochus Epiphanes - And Does that Matter?

Point #16 - Page 377

Is Daniel the Resurrection of "Many" But Not *All*?

Summary and Conclusion - Page 388f

Preface

> Let me state at the outset: If Daniel 12 predicted the "final" resurrection of 1 Corinthians 15, 1 Thessalonians 4 and Revelation, then all futurist eschatologies are falsified.
>
> In this book, we will prove, with a wealth of powerful, textual, thematic, contextual evidence that Daniel 12 did in fact predict the same end time events as Corinthians 15 and Revelation 20.

This is the second volume in a series of books on the passing of the Law of Moses. The most commonly held view is that the Law of Moses was nailed to the cross. However, this series of books is setting forth strong proof that this view is incorrect, even though I personally accepted it for many years. It is my firm belief that the Law of Moses endured until the end of God's covenant dealings with Israel in AD 70. My thesis is that the Law of Moses ended only at the eschatological consummation: i.e. *From Torah To Telos*.

But this book is also about the resurrection foretold in Daniel 12. Amazing changes are taking place in the theological world today, in regard to Daniel 12. Commentators who once insisted that Daniel foretold the resurrection of decomposed corpses at the end of human history have abandoned that view. They now teach that Daniel foretold a spiritual resurrection / restoration of the corporate body of Israel at the end of the Old Covenant age in AD 70. They tell us, however, that AD 70 was typological of the "real" resurrection at the end of history. This is a stunning, remarkable change.

Scholars and commentators throughout the centuries have agreed that Daniel 12:2 foretold the "final resurrection" at the end of the age, which they posit as the end of human history, the end of time. This is indeed the "creedal" view. While many of the "higher critical" school see Daniel as predictive of the Antiochan period, nonetheless, among more conservative scholars it has and continues to be held that Daniel foretold the consummative resurrection.

So, this book is focused on Daniel 12 and what it says about not only the end of the Law of Moses, but eschatology, and particularly the resurrection of the dead. My purpose is to demonstrate three things:

1.) That Daniel foretold the "final" eschatological resurrection of the dead.

2.) To show that the resurrection foretold by Daniel was to be at the end of Torah, the Law of Moses. After all, the Old Testament foretold the resurrection and the OT could not pass until that consummation. Thus, once again: *From Torah To Telos*.

3.) To expose the radical changes in regard to Daniel 12 that are taking place particularly in the Dominionist (i.e. Postmillennial) and even the Amillennial, world of eschatology. These changes are nothing short of astounding.

So, a good bit of this book will focus on establishing that Daniel 12 did predict the "final" resurrection because as just suggested, some radical changes have been taking place in the evangelical world in regard to this marvelous prophecy of the resurrection.

As noted, Daniel 12 has historically been considered one of the clearest of all OT prophecies of the last days "final" resurrection. While occasional commentators have applied Daniel's prophecy to other events, without doubt, the consensus of church history and the creedal statements applied Daniel to the eschatological consummation.

The purpose of this work is to vindicate that historical, "traditional" belief. *Not because it is historical* or creedal, but because I believe it to be the proper Biblical view. In addition, as just suggested, I will demonstrate that the resurrection foretold by Daniel 12– the consummative resurrection - occurred at the end of the Old Covenant age, at the destruction of Jerusalem, in AD 70.

As just stated, with the rise and spread of Covenant Eschatology,[1] changes – *radical changes* - are afoot in regard to Daniel 12, and especially in the Dominionist (Postmillennial) camp. These developments are almost unbelievable – not to mention fatal to their futurist eschatology. While some in the Amillennial world are adopting the same changes, the shift is not as pronounced as in the Dominionists world. Thus, our focus here, in regard to examining the extreme changes that are taking place, will be on the Postmillennial world.

This work is somewhat polemic. I will document from the works of leading Dominionists how they are now in violation of the creeds that they claim to honor. They now contradict their own writings. And more importantly, their view of eschatology has no foundation in scripture.

---

[1] Covenant Eschatology, also known as the full preterist view of eschatology, is the view that all Biblical prophecy was fulfilled in the first century, in the fall of Jerusalem. The "end of the age" is seen as the end of the Old Covenant age of Israel (thus, "Covenant Eschatology"), and has nothing to do with the end of human history (i.e. historical eschatology.

Acknowledgments

A work such as this is the result, in many ways, of the contributions from many sources. I cannot even name all of those who have assisted in the production of this work, but I will list some of them.

I must of course, as always, express my profound love and appreciation for my wife. To say that she is my "Rock" does not do justice to the role that she plays, every day, in every way, in my ministry. Her patience and understanding of my "obsession" with study, research and writing, that takes so much of my time, is incredible. On many occasions, as we are riding along, she will ask, "Where are you? You seem so far away!" My response is normally, as just recently when I was deep in thought on this book: "Trying to finish my book," and she said, "That is what I thought," and that was satisfactory to her. For years she has supported, encouraged and supported me in every way. Words fail to proper express my appreciation and my love for her.

There were several who volunteered to proof read and edit this book, including Stephen Temple, Jim Wade and my wife, of course. I truly appreciate their help in making this book better. Any remaining errata are my own doing!

Jeff McCormack designed the cover and did his fine outstanding job.

My special thanks to Sam Dawson, who once again volunteered to create the indices. I know that not only I, but the readers of this work surely appreciate this very helpful aid. His patience with my continual editing and revising is greatly appreciated!

To the many people who have encouraged me to address this topic, I express my thanks. I would even thank those who reject the idea that Daniel 12 foretold the final resurrection. Those objections provoked me to re-study the issue. Iron sharpens steel, as the saying goes, and as I have encountered objections to the full (true) preterist view, and specifically objections to the view espoused in this book, those objections have provoked deeper analytical thought. I hope the result of that study and research will be to the greater glory of God.

HISTORY, DOMINIONISM AND DANIEL 12

SOME INITIAL OBSERVATIONS

This initial segment will present a "Reader's Digest" version of what I will develop more extensively in the body of the work. I hope it does not seem too redundant, but I want to give a "taste" of what is to come and how important it is.

I could give literally reams of citations from the commentaries to support the statement that historically there is a broad based consensus that Daniel 12 foretold the end of human history and the raising of decomposed human corpses out of the dirt. Rather than belabor the point I will give only a few citations that demonstrate that consensus.

Commentators such as Matthew Henry gave three "applications" of Daniel. He nonetheless concluded on v. 2:

> "It must be meant of the general resurrection at the last day: The multitude of those that sleep in the dust shall awake, that is, all, which shall be a great many. Or, Of those that sleep in the dust many shall arise to life and many to shame. The Jews themselves understand this of the resurrection of the dead at the end of time; and Christ seems to have an eye to it when he speaks of the resurrection of life and the resurrection of damnation (John v. 29); and upon this the Jews are said by St. Paul to expect a resurrection of the dead both of the just and of the unjust, Acts xxiv. 15." (Christian Ethereal Library: http://www.ccel.org/study).

Interestingly, Henry applied the resurrection of v. 2 to two different "spiritual" resurrections, i.e. the restoration of Israel from captivity and the Maccabean vindication, but then made it refer to a literal raising of individual human bodies! So, per Henry, the same verse spoke of two spiritual, corporate resurrections,[2] but then, to a literal, physical, end of time resurrection of individual corpses. That is an awful lot of resurrections in one verse!

John Peter Lange (circa 1876), said, "It is manifest that the last and general resurrection is here intended." Interestingly, Lange notes that a "majority" of scholars of his day believed that the resurrection of Daniel 12 was limited to strictly Israel and did not refer to the final resurrection. Lange clearly rejected that view.[3] Demonstrating a shift in scholarly consensus, Schmisek says: "J. J. Collins sums it up best by saying, 'there is virtually unanimous agreement among modern scholars that Daniel was referring to the actual resurrection of individuals from the dead, because of the explicit language of everlasting life. This is, in fact, the only generally accepted reference to resurrection in the Hebrew Bible."[4]

The highly respected commentators Keil and Delitzsch viewed Daniel 12 as the source of Jesus' resurrection doctrine saying that Jesus quoted from Daniel in John 5:28-29.[5]

---

[2] As an exception to the Dispensational view of Daniel 12, Ironside said: "The second verse does not, I believe, speak of an actual physical resurrection, but rather of a moral and national one." It is the same kind of language that is used both in Isaiah 26:12-19 and Ezekiel 37, to describe Israel's national and spiritual revival." (H. A. Ironside, *Daniel the Prophet,* (Neptune, N. J., Loizeaux Brothers, 1969) 231-232.

[3] John Peter Lange, *Commentary on Ezekiel and Daniel*, (Grand Rapids, Zondervan, modern reprint date unknown)262.

[4] Brian Schmisek, *Resurrection of the Flesh or Resurrection From the Dead,* (CollegeVille, Min. Liturgical Press, 2013)54).

[5] Keil and Delitzsch, *Commentary on Ezekiel and Daniel*, Vol. IX, (Grand Rapids, Eerdmans, 1975)482

In modern times, Richard Middleton says, "The most explicit mention of resurrection in the Old Testament occurs in the book of Daniel, the only full-fledged apocalypse in the Hebrew canon. According to Daniel 12, a time of future distress and trouble is coming; but beyond the distress there will be deliverance for Israel (v. 1). This deliverance is then described in explicit language of resurrection."[6] It is more than a little perplexing how Middleton - along with most scholars - ignores verse 7, and then, Jesus' application of Daniel to the events surrounding the judgment of Jerusalem in AD 70 (Matthew 24).

James Montgomery Boice says Daniel 11-12 jumps from a discussion of the persecution under Antiochus "to the time of great persecution at the end of history and the end of that age by a general resurrection of all persons and the final judgment."[7]

C. Marvin Pate says: "Judaism... assigned the resurrection of the body and the coming of the Spirit to the end of time (Ezekiel 37; Daniel 12:1-3; Enoch 62:15; 2 Enoch 22:8; 4 Ezra 2:39, 45)."[8]

Greg Beale sees Daniel 12 as a prophecy of the "final" resurrection. He says Daniel 11-12 serve as the source of Revelation 7 and the 144,000 who go through the Tribulation. He demonstrates several direct verbal and thematic parallels and correlates it all to the Messianic Woes. He then says, (p. 211, n. 41) that John 5:24-29

---

[6] Richard Middleton, *A New Heaven and a New Earth*, (Grand Rapids, Baker Academic, 2014)138.

[7] James Montgomery Boice, *An Expositional Commentary, Daniel*, (Grand Rapids, Baker, 1989)119.

[8] C. Marvin Pate, *The End of the Ages Has Come, The Theology of Paul*, (Grand Rapids, Zondervan, 1995)231.

sees the resurrection of the saints predicted in Daniel 12:2 as inaugurated in Jesus' ministry."[9]

Brant Pitre, says, "According to the OT, the resurrection itself would be preceded by a period of great tribulation"... Daniel 12, which is the most explicit prophecy of resurrection in the Hebrew books of the Old Testament. Strikingly, this description of the resurrection is preceded by the Great Tribulation"[10]

Below, I will document how some of the leading Dominionists have traditionally seen Daniel 12 as a prediction of the consummative resurrection, but as a result of the growth of Covenant Eschatology have now radically changed their views.

This sampling of commentators should be more than sufficient. We could multiply quote on top of quote but anyone *even vaguely familiar* with church history knows that it is indisputably true that Daniel 12 has almost always been applied to the final resurrection at the end of the current Christian age.

It is therefore, amazing that some modern Postmillennialists, those who (ostensibly at least) claim to honor church history and the creeds, are now almost flippantly, without so much as even a nod to church history and the creeds, rejecting that earlier, universal testimony. All the while, of course, *they claim that they are faithful to the creeds and church history!* In fact, we are told that we should not be even slightly concerned that all of the previous commentators failed to get Daniel 12 right! It does not matter that they were wrong, we are told, because now, these commentators, ever so faithful to church history, will straighten them out! This is laughably self-contradictory and patently false. It is in fact, shoddy scholarship to make such claims. This is so remarkable in light of

---

[9] C. Marvin Pate, *The End of the Ages Has Come, The Theology of Paul,* (Grand Rapids, Zondervan, 1995).

[10] Brant Pitre, *Jesus, Tribulation and the End of Exile*, (Grand Rapids, Baker Academic, 2005)187.

the fact that the Dominionists list the unhistorical, non-creedal position of the preterist paradigm as one of the key reasons for rejecting it.

Kenneth Gentry, wrote an article giving his reasons for rejecting the true preterist eschatology and for his refusal to formally debate the issue. What was his very first reason? Here it is:

> "First, hyper-preterism is heterodox. It is outside the creedal orthodoxy of Christianity. No creed allows any second Advent in A. D. 70. No creed allows any other type of resurrection than a bodily one. Historic creeds speak of the universal, personal judgment of all men, not of a representative judgment in A. D. 70."[11]

The irony here is incredible.

Gentry rejects the true preterist view because it is not creedal. But watch this: "No creed allows any other type of resurrection than a bodily one," says Gentry. Yet, Gentry posits a resurrection in AD 70, a resurrection decidedly not in the creeds! Furthermore, he posits a resurrection of corporate Israel – a concept not found in even one creed. But of course, we are supposed to believe that Gentry is creedal!

Gentry likewise says: "Historic creeds speak of the universal, personal judgment of all men, not of a representative judgment in A. D. 70." Oh, but wait! Gentry has a redemptively significant judgment of the living and the dead in AD 70 that was representative of a future judgment! But of course, we are to believe that Gentry is creedal!

---

[11] http://www.reformed.org/eschaton/index.html?mainframe=/eschaton/gentry_preterism.html

Finally, it should be noted that Gentry's is on record saying that he will not engage in formal debate with preterists.[12] He refuses to engage *because full preterism is not creedal*. Here is the irony, he has engaged in formal debates with Dispensationalists and yet, as he notes, Dispensationalism is not creedal!

So, Gentry, Mathison, Seriah and a host of other Dominionists appeal to church history and a consensus of scholarship that stands against preterism. Yet, these same men have no problem at all affirming positions that church history and scholarly consensus stand against. For instance, Schmisek, citing Collins, says the unanimous consensus of scholarship is that Daniel 12 refers to the raising of corpses out of the ground.[13] Yet, Gentry and other Dominionists feel free to differ from that "unanimous agreement" of scholarship not only on Daniel, but for instance the dating of

---

[12] Gentry has been invited *many* times - as recently as 2016 - to meet me in formal public debate but has adamantly refused to do so.

[13] Brian Schmisek, *Resurrection of the Flesh or Resurrection From the Dead*, (CollegeVille, Min. Liturgical Press, 2013, p. 54) – "J. J. Collins sums it up best by saying, 'there is virtually unanimous agreement among modern scholars that Daniel was referring to the actual resurrection of individuals from the dead, because of the explicit language of everlasting life. This is, in fact, the only generally accepted reference to resurrection in the Hebrew Bible."

Revelation[14] and even other issues. *They* can reject church history and scholarship, but heaven help the preterist for doing so!

So there you have it! Covenant Eschatology is not creedal, it is not historical, it differs with scholarship and it is therefore wrong. And yet, now, these same "creedalists"[15] are applying the very verses that those hallowed creeds, church history and scholarship utilizes and appeals to as proof of that "universal, personal judgment of all men" and they are applying them to AD 70! Although they are at *radical* odds with the creeds in the application of those prophecies

---

[14] For instance, Gentry takes note that his position on the dating and application of Revelation (with which I largely agree) lies outside the historical view of the church, but defends his position: "The view that I shall present and defend below is contrary to what the vast majority of Christians believe today. Almost certainly you have been taught a radically different view at some point in your Christian journey. You may even be tempted to scoff at its very suggestion at this point. Nevertheless, I challenge you to bear with me as we wade through the evidence on this matter in Revelation. I am convinced that you will find the flood of evidence becoming a river 'that no man can cross.'" (Kenneth Gentry, *The Beast of Revelation*,(Powder Springs, Ga, American Vision, 2002)18.

[15] It is refreshing to read Gary DeMar's comments on the creeds in a recent article addressing the almost blind allegiance to the authority of the creeds by the Reformed Amillennial camp of Prof. David Engelsma. DeMar reminds his readers that even the Westminster Confession of Faith rejects the "authority" of the creeds. DeMar notes: "The Westminster Confession of Faith Chapter 31 says as much: 'III. All synods or councils, since the apostles' times, whether general or particular, may err; and many have erred. Therefore they are not to be made the rule of faith, or practice; but to be used as a help in both.'" - See more at: http://americanvision.org/10080/anti-postmillennialist-makes-weak-case/#sthash.uBxb4eCL.7yC38cNe.dpuf

of the resurrection, they insist that they are faithful to the creeds, church history and scholarship.

As an example of this remarkable departure, notice the change in Kenneth Gentry, widely considered to be one of the leading apologists for the modern Postmillennial world.

Gentry historically applied Daniel 12:2 to the "end of the world."[16] Now, however, he says, "Daniel appears to be presenting Israel as a grave site under God's curse; Israel as a corporate body is in the dust (Daniel 12:2; cp. Ge. 3:14, 19). In this he follows Ezekiel's pattern in his vision of the dry bones, which represents Israel's 'death' in the Babylonian dispersion (Ezekiel 37). In Daniel's prophecy many will awaken, as it were, during the great tribulation to suffer the full fury of divine wrath, while others will enjoy God's grace in receiving everlasting life."[17] Reformed Amillennialist James Jordan, with whom I had a formal debate in 2003 takes the same basic view.[18]

So, Gentry now applies Daniel 12 to AD 70. This is, needless to say, a *radical* change from his earlier view and yet, he has given no indication noting that change.

Side Bar: Interestingly, in his revised *Dominion*, (2009, 495, n. 45) Gentry takes note that Dispensationalist Dwight Pentecost had significantly altered his views over the years, yet had not indicated those changes in his later writings. He says Pentecost's "radical

---

[16] Kenneth Gentry, *The Greatness of the Great Commission*, (Tyler, Tx., Institute for Christian Economics, 1993)142.

[17] Gentry, *He Shall Have Dominion*, (Draper, VA., Apologetics Group, 2009)538.

[18] James Jordan, *Handwriting on the Wall*, (Powder Springs, GA., American Vision, 2007) 617+.

shift" in his application of some key eschatological texts, "does not seem to him to compromise his eschatological system."

Well, Gentry has made an astoundingly "radical shift" in his application of one of the key eschatological texts and yet, has not indicated that change in his writings so far as we can determine. He has *done* what he chides Pentecost for doing!

Gentry's, Jordan's and the view of other Dominionists put them at odds with the huge majority of scholarship, church history, the creeds and other Postmillennialists. Jonathin Seriah for instance, says Daniel 12.2 – "Clearly refers to physical death and burial of the body," and that it, "does not mention, 'any reference to a national resurrection (as per many pantelists)'"[19] This is clearly Seriah versus Gentry.

I think it is beneficial for our study to illustrate even more graphically how the Dominionists of the day differ so radically from the creeds on critical eschatological texts and doctrines, all the while condemning true preterists for being non-creedal. The list below is not comprehensive, but the reader will quickly notice how vital the doctrines are to the eschatological narrative and the irony of how the Dominionists can hold these non-creedal views while claiming to be faithful to the creeds.

Postmillennialists and the Creeds – Per modern Postmillennialists the Creeds were wrong on the following:

✔The resurrection of Daniel 12 was in AD 70 - Gentry, DeMar, McDurmon.

✔ Matthew 13 / 24 and the end of the age was in AD 70 - DeMar, McDurmon, Leithart, etc..

✔ Matthew 22 / Luke 20- The Age to come – in AD 70 (DeMar, McDurmon).

---

[19] Jonathin Seriah, *The End of All Things*, (Moscow, Idaho, Canon Press, 1999)117.

✔ Matthew 24– The parousia and end of the age – in AD 70 – Gentry, DeMar, McDurmon.

✔ Anti-Christ - Gentry, DeMar, McDurmon Leithart, Mathison, Seriah, etc. all posit the anti-Christ in the first century.

✔ Romans 11:25-27– AD 70 – DeMar, McDurmon, Jordan (Reformed Amillennialist). Gentry still takes the traditional Reformed view insisting that there is yet to be a conversion of national Israel at the end of the current age.

✔ 1 Corinthians 15– Reformed Amillennialists James Jordan, in our formal debate, said 1 Corinthians 15 had "a fulfillment in AD 70," but we are still looking for final fulfillment. Likewise, Joel McDurmon in our formal debate said the same thing. To say this is non-creedal is a stunning understatement!

✔ The Last Days = Israel's last days, not the last days of time – DeMar, McDurmon, Leithart, Seriah, etc..

✔ 2 Peter 3– the destruction of heaven and earth – in AD 70 - Jordan- DeMar, McDurmon.

✔ The Early Dating of Revelation - Gentry, DeMar, McDurmon Leithart, Mathison, Seriah, etc..

✔ Identity of "Babylon" in Revelation as Old Covenant, first century Jerusalem – Gentry, DeMar, McDurmon Leithart, Mathison,[20] Seriah (*End*, 1999, 88), etc.).

✔ The Wedding of Christ was in AD 70– Gentry, McDurmon, etc.

✔ New Creation of Revelation 21– in AD 70 - Gentry, DeMar, McDurmon Leithart, Mathison, Seriah, etc..

---

[20] In *Postmillennialism*, (1999, 153) Mathison identified Babylon as Jerusalem. But, in *Age to Age*, (689) he now says Babylon was Rome.

Make no mistake. *None* of the creeds agree with the modern Dominionists on these issues. All of this raises a very serious question: If the Creeds were wrong on these key, fundamental eschatological texts and tenets, then why must we conclude that they had to be right on 1 Corinthians 15 / 1 Thessalonians?

This should be deeply troubling to anyone and everyone that reads the Dominionist literature when they attack true preterists for being non-creedal and in violation of the beliefs of the historical church.

I am personally convinced that the on-going controversy with what Gentry disparagingly calls "hyper-preterism" has spawned his radical departure from tradition. After all, if these men continue to hold that Daniel 12 did in fact foretell the "final resurrection" then since Daniel 12:7 unequivocally posits that resurrection at the time of the destruction of Old Covenant Israel (AD 70 by their own admission) then *this would totally falsify their futurist eschatology*. So, rather than accept the text, they accept a view at complete odds with their own creeds. But it needs to be noted that this change, as revolutionary and as desperate as it patently is, *actually involves these commentators in an inescapable and fatal contradiction*. And one of the purposes of this book will be to expose those contradictions in the Dominionist camp.

Note that Gentry, Jordan, now also Sam Frost, all admit that Daniel 12 foretold the events of AD 70 – as the resurrection of the just and unjust. This demands that there was *a resurrection to eternal life in AD 70*. By the very nature of the case, if Daniel 12 foretold the resurrection of "the living and the dead" in AD 70, then that was the time of the "solution" to the question of the Intermediate State of the Dead. After all, are we not told that the dead are waiting on the resurrection to eternal life?

So, the Dominionists are now telling us that the elect, the righteous remnant – including the righteous *dead* - were raised to eternal life in AD 70. As we will see, this is *hugely problematic* for these commentators, but they clearly do not see the problem, or if they do see it, *they are not telling anyone*!

Let me pose a question: Was the resurrection of the righteous remnant in AD 70 inclusive of the dead righteous saints in Hebrews 11? The Dominionists tell us that those dead saints, "have received what was promised." So, yes, if they – the dead Worthies of Hebrews 11 - "received what was promised," then patently, the resurrection to eternal life that the Dominionists agree occurred in AD 70 involved the dead saints. I suggest therefore, that the Dominionist admission that Daniel 12 was fulfilled in AD 70 is a *prima facie* falsification of the Postmillennial eschatology.

Consider that those in Hebrews 11 were all considered *martyrs*. And the span of time covered by that list of martyrs extends from Abel-Moses, and right up to the contemporary audience of the book that was, like all the foregoing saints, suffering for their faith. There is an organic unity in the suffering saints. There is no dichotomy between "Old Testament" martyrs and "New Testament" martyrs.

And what did that audience long for? What was their (one) hope (Ephesians 4:4)? Well, that honor roll of faith, from Abel onward, longed for the heavenly city. They longed for a "father land" (Greek, *patrida*, 11:14) that was "heavenly" (*epouraniou, v. 16*). We are justified in saying, by combining their desire for a "fatherland" and "a heavenly," that they longed for a "heavenly fatherland," and, they longed for the "better resurrection."

(The fact that they longed for a "heavenly fatherland," falsifies McDurmon's claim in our formal public debate (July 2012) that Abraham looked ultimately for *a physical fatherland*, i.e. earth. During the debate, McDurmon sought to mitigate the spiritual, heavenly aspect of Abraham's hope. He went so far as to claim that the translation of "heavenly country" is anachronistic and unjustified. He insisted that while Abraham had received in Christ the *spiritual* aspect of the promises YHVH made to him, he was still waiting on the earthly *physical* aspect.[21] His claim about the

---

[21] See our discussion below *of First that Which Is Natural*, Then the *Spiritual*. McDurmon and the futurists reverse the order of God's *modus operandi* that has always

translation is patently desperate and specious when one combines v. 14 with v. 16. The book of that formal debate is available from me).

So, notice that those in Hebrews 11 were martyrs and they longed for "the better resurrection." Are these part of the righteous remnant that Gentry, Jordan, etc. say would be resurrected in AD 70, in fulfillment of Daniel 12?

N. T. Wright, commenting on Daniel 12:2 identifies, "those in the dust of the earth" who were to be raised, as *martyrs*: "There can be little doubt who these persons are: they the righteous who have suffered martyrdom on the one hand, and their torturers and murderers on the other. The rest– the great majority of humans, and indeed of Israelites, are simply not mentioned."[22]

Okay, so, once again, those in Hebrews 11 are *martyrs* and they longed for *the better resurrection*. Those in Daniel 12 were *martyrs* and like those in Hebrews 11, they looked forward to the resurrection, *the resurrection to eternal life*. We thus have irrefutable testimony of both Daniel 12 and Hebrews 11 confirming that the (better) resurrection that the martyrs longed for would involve *those who were biologically dead; and it would be resurrection to eternal life*. Again, this is the end of the Intermediate State of the Dead.

This means that it cannot be argued that the resurrection of the elect that is the focus of Daniel 12 or Hebrews simply or exclusively related to some kind of deliverance for the living saints. This resurrection involved both "the living and the dead." This is *critical*, so hang onto it as we proceed.

Another point to garner from this, as suggested just above, is that the better resurrection anticipated in both Daniel and Hebrews involved the "heavenly fatherland," the heavenly city that was part

---

been that the natural always pointed to the spiritual.

[22] N. T. Wright, *Resurrection of the Son of God*, (Minneapolis, Fortress, 2003)110.

and parcel of the Abrahamic hope. This is nothing less than the promise of the New Creation (cf. Isaiah 65). There is simply *no way* to temporally divorce the better resurrection of Hebrews 11:35f from the heavenly fatherland and city. There is no gap of millennia between the reception of the better resurrection and the heavenly fatherland and city.[23] What kind of eschatology would seek to divorce *resurrection* from the heavenly city and heavenly fatherland?

Okay, so when was that resurrection promise fulfilled? Well, these Postmillennialists tell us it was fulfilled *in AD 70*. But then, when we start looking at their additional comments, we begin to see the huge problems that they present for themselves.

Frost for example, in an extremely confused and confusing article, alludes to Daniel 12:3 and the righteous shining forth as the stars. He queries, "Who was leading many to righteousness at the time of Jesus? Well, Jesus for one. The 'many' of Israel that heard his words either passed from death to life, or rejected his word and went to judgment (Hades)."[24] Frost clearly does not see the problem he has created for himself.

If Daniel 12:2-3 was being fulfilled in Jesus' ministry– i.e. at the time of John 5:24f - then of necessity, the Great Tribulation (and therefore, of necessity, the Abomination of Desolation) *had already begun*. (Much more on this below).

Pitre correctly observes: "According to the O. T., the resurrection itself would be preceded by a period of great tribulation."... "Daniel

---

[23] In my debate with McDurmon, I noted the direct similarities between what he was saying and the Dispensational paradigm. He vehemently denied this, but it is undeniably true. I documented many of those parallels in a series of articles that can be found on my websites: www.eschatology.org; www.donkpreston.com.

[24] Sam Frost, "The Problem with Daniel 12:2" article. Posted on Reign of Christ website Nov. 18, 2011.

12, which is the most explicit prophecy of resurrection in the Hebrew books of the Old Testament. Strikingly, this description of the resurrection is preceded by the Great Tribulation."[25] A simple reading of the text shows that this observation is undeniably true. Virtually all scholarship concurs in this assessment.[26] Incidentally, Frost ostensibly agrees with this pattern of occurrence in his article.

So, Daniel said the Great Tribulation (and again, by logical extension, the Abomination of Desolation) *would precede the resurrection of v. 2*. But wait, Frost says the resurrection of v. 2 had already begun in John 5 - in the personal ministry of Jesus! The argument here is simple and destructive for Frost:

The Abomination of Desolation and Great Tribulation of Daniel 12 would precede the resurrection of Daniel 12:2.

But the resurrection of Daniel 12:2 had begun in John 5:24f – Frost.

Therefore, the Abomination of Desolation and Great Tribulation of Daniel 12 had already preceded the resurrection of John 5:24f.

This is logically inescapable and textually undeniable.

Would Frost therefore argue that Abomination and Tribulation had already appeared prior to John 5? No, and such an argument would be absurd. Yet, textually and contextually Frost must, based on his argument that Daniel 12:2-3 was in the process of fulfillment in John 5 claim that the Abomination and the Tribulation had begun at some point prior to John 5. That would fly in the face of Jesus' prediction and application of Daniel 12 in Matthew 24:15f. There, the Abomination and ensuring Tribulation had patently not occurred

---

[25] Brant Pitre, *Jesus, The Tribulation and the End of Exile*, Grand Rapids, Baker Academic, 1975)187.

[26] Cf. Emile Schurer, *The History of the Jewish People in the Times of Jesus Christ*, Vol. II, (Edinburgh, T and T Clark, 1979)514f.

when he spoke. Furthermore, the Abomination and Tribulation would demand the flight of the disciples from Judea. That patently had not happened in John 5.

To say that Frost's position is specious and untenable is to dramatically understate the case. His claim about the relationship between Daniel 12:2 and John 5 negates his entire article. (There are several other *major* problems with Frost's article / position that we will not address here. But this single problem is sufficiently devastating as a negation of his claims).

But there is far more that is problematic for the Dominionists who are now (finally) admitting that Daniel 12 was fulfilled in AD 70 and that is that they are positing (implicitly, but of logical necessity) that the Old Covenant saints, i.e. all of those from Abel forward, have been raised to eternal life and that they received their eternal reward:

1.) Without *being raised out of the ground* in restored, resuscitated physical bodies! Needless to say, this is devastating to any futurist view of the resurrection.

2.) And that they received their eternal reward separate and apart from New Covenant saints!

In other words, the Dominionists claim that *no one today has received resurrection to eternal life – except "forensically."* We have to wait until the "end of history" for *our resurrection to eternal life, our* reward and the reception of *our* inheritance, we are told. (Cf. again Seriah). By positing the fulfillment of Daniel 12 in the first century – at AD 70 – and by then positing our resurrection to eternal life at the end of human history, the Dominionists have created a truly aberrant eschatology. They have imbibed deeply at the well of the "gap theory" positing a so far 2000 year gap between the reception of eternal life by the OT saints and a yet future, who knows when, reception of eternal life by saints today.

Consider the righteous dead of Hebrews 11. Remember that we are discussing all of the righteous martyrs– *the dead saints*– from Abel onward. They longed for *the better resurrection*, the heavenly fatherland / city, what Hebrews 10: 34f would describe as "a better and an enduring substance", the "great reward", "the promise", etc.. And once again, we find total confusion and illogic on the part of the Postmillennialists.

Keith Mathison, commenting on Hebrews 11-12 says: "That which the Old Testament believers looked for in faith has come, and they have now received what was promised."[27] He also says: "Christians are now experiencing the fulfillment of the eschatological hopes of Israel."[28]

However, after affirming that the OT saints have received what was promised to them and after stating that Christians now enjoy the fulfillment of Israel's eschatological hopes and promises, Mathison claims that, "the fullness of the blessing is yet future, because we await the consummation." This is unmitigated double-speak.

If the OT saints have received what was promised to them, then they have received the heavenly fatherland, the City made by YHVH and *the better resurrection*. In other words, they have received and entered into the New Creation. So, just how much of that inheritance have they not received, if the fullness is still to come? Have they only received *some* of the better resurrection? Have they received partial "eternal life"? Do they (we) live in the outskirts of the heavenly city – or perhaps - do we live in the slums? Not according to Joel McDurmon.

In an article responding to a writer who affirmed that Christians are now pilgrims, wandering through this world, waiting for the

---

[27] *Keith Mathison, Postmillennialism: An Eschatology of Hope*, (New Jersey, P&R Publishing, 1999)135.

[28] Keith Mathison, *Age to Age: The Unfolding of Biblical Eschatology*, (Phillipsburg, NJ, 2009)625.

establishment of a future literal Zion, McDurmon categorically rejected this view:

> "When the argument of faith and pilgrimage in Hebrews 11 finally does turn to "us" it notes a complete change of status. While all of those Old Testament pilgrims died and "did not receive what was promised," New Testament believers are different: "God had provided something better for *us*" (Heb. 11:40). So, we are categorically *not* like them. We are in a better position than they. The promised Kingdom has indeed come, it is given to us. We are not exiles waiting to receive the promise. Indeed, the author tells the first-century believing Jews in the very next chapter, as a continuation of the argument in Hebrews 11, "you have come to Mount Zion" (Heb. 12:22). They were no longer exiles; they had arrived!
>
> This arrival verse is very important. Horton refers to the Christians as pilgrims. He denies we have arrived, or downplays it in any meaningful sense. He constantly refers to Zion as a future destination: the "path to Zion," "this journey to Zion," "Marching to Zion." But Hebrews makes it absolutely clear that New Testament believers "have come to Zion." This is in the past tense. Horton says nothing about this verse, and yet it is the culmination of the argument the author began in Hebrews 11."[29]

In addition to the above, in his *Jesus V Jerusalem*, McDurmon wrote: "Zion" has been "spiritualized," if you will, and, "revealed to be fulfilled in the person of the ascended Christ: 'But you have

---

[29] http://americanvision.org/4445/the-great-omission.

come to Mount Zion and to the city of the living God, the heavenly Jerusalem, and to the innumerable angels in festal gathering."[30]

You might be led to think, based on McDurmon's claims, that he believes Abraham and the faithful of Hebrews 11 have received what was promised. That is what he said about Matthew 8 – Abraham, Isaac and Jacob received the kingdom. And, he says above and in his book that the Zion promises have been... "spiritualized" and "fulfilled in Christ." Christians, "have (past tense) received the kingdom," and we are not pilgrims. We are in a better position than those OT saints. So, it *sounds* like he believes "promises fulfilled," right? Well, a closer look reveals some major, inherent contradictions in his view and that of the other Dominionists. We will discuss those contradictions below.

The question is, *Are we (really) in a better position than them?* McDurmon *says* we are. Yet, while he says the Zion prophecies are fulfilled, he then cites Zion texts and says they are *not fulfilled*. We and *even the OT saints* stand together in waiting for the fulfillment of these texts. Should we ignore such blatant self-contradiction?

Make no mistake, McDurmon says Abraham and the Worthies in Matthew 8 have in fact received the kingdom. They have sat down at the Messianic Banquet. This happened in AD 70: "The kingdom will be populated by Abraham, Isaac and Jacob, when the rebellious would be cast out. The kingdom population would also include 'all the prophets' (13:28)" (2011, 64). When does McDurmon posit the, "sons of the kingdom" being cast out"? In AD 70.

So, Abraham and the OT Worthies populated the kingdom, at the Messianic Kingdom Banquet, when the sons of the kingdom were cast out.

---

[30] Joel McDurmon, *Jesus V Jerusalem,* (Powder Springs., GA, American Vision Press, 2011)178. The book is available from my websites.

The sons of the kingdom (Old Covenant, unfaithful Israel), were cast out in AD 70 – McDurmon.

Therefore, Abraham and the OT Worthies populated the kingdom, at the Messianic Kingdom Banquet, in AD 70.

Follow me here. Abraham and the OT Worthies populated the kingdom, at the Messianic Kingdom Banquet, in AD 70. This kingdom, resurrection banquet of Matthew 8 is nothing different from the heavenly fatherland, the heavenly city and the "better resurrection" in Hebrews 11. So, if Abraham and the Worthies received that kingdom, that City, the fatherland and the resurrection in AD 70, and if, as Joel claims to believe, Christians today have received what they looked for, then how in the name of reason can it be affirmed that, "We are in a better position than those OT saints"? This is a glaring self-contradiction and fatal to the Dominionist paradigm.

In our debate McDurmon openly stated, in line with Mathison, that in fact, Christians – and Abraham himself - are still waiting for the real – the *physical* – fulfillment of the promises to Abraham. Of course, if Abraham - and we – are waiting for the fulfillment of the physical city – Zion - that claim is disingenuous to say the least.

The author, Horton, said Christians are "marching to Zion", waiting for physical Zion. McDurmon said this is wrong. We have received fulfillment of Zion, spiritually, in Christ. Oh, but wait, says McDurmon when debating me, we *are* in fact waiting for the physical promises made to Abraham to be fulfilled in Zion after all! And of course, if we are still waiting on Zion and those physical promises, McDurmon's claim that we are not pilgrims, that Zion is fulfilled and that we stand in a better position than the OT saints, is just so much verbiage, shoddy logic, poor scholarship and self-contradiction.

As you can see, there is gross confusion in the Dominionist camp in regard to Matthew 8, Hebrews 11 and the promises made to the Fathers. Their self-contradictions are compounded by their sudden and recent admissions that Daniel 12 was fulfilled in AD 70. This confusion is the result of a false eschatology, not from what the text says.

Let's look closer now at the problems inherent in the Dominionists' claims about Daniel 12, Matthew 8, Hebrews 11 and the resurrection.

Remember that Daniel 12, Matthew 8 and Hebrews 11 are patently speaking of the reward / inheritance of *the dead saints* – not simply the living. In other words, they are discussing *the end of the Intermediate State of the Dead*. These texts speak of the reception of the anticipated reward, the resurrection to eternal life at the time of the end. At this juncture, let's take a closer look at Matthew 8, another key text that deals with *resurrection and reward*.

In the famous story of the "faith full" Centurion, we find this: "When Jesus heard it, He marveled, and said to those who followed, "Assuredly, I say to you, I have not found such great faith, not even in Israel! And I say to you that many will come from east and west, and sit down with Abraham, Isaac and Jacob in the kingdom of heaven. But the sons of the kingdom will be cast out into outer darkness.[31] There will be weeping and gnashing of teeth."

Notice that like Hebrews 11, we are dealing here with the promises made to *Abraham and the faithful*. Just like Hebrews 11 says the "better resurrection" was the hope of Abraham, Matthew 8 is

---

[31] This text is full of prophetic irony. Israel had always been and considered themselves to be the true "sons of the kingdom" and the "sons of light." Yet, Jesus here posits the true "sons of the kingdom" as those who follow him in faith. At the same time, the historical "sons" are cast out! This is parallel to Acts 3:23 where Peter, citing Deuteronomy 18, spoke of Christ the fulfillment and said that those who rejected him would be, "cut off out from among the people" (my translation). In other words, "the people" would be the followers of Christ; they would be the true Israel of God.

clearly discussing the resurrection.[32] How else could Abraham, Isaac and Jacob sit down at the banquet, since they were all dead, but Jesus is discussing the time of them sitting down at the great banquet in the kingdom. Yes, this is patently resurrection - as virtually all commentators agree.

What is interesting is that, as usual, the Dominionists entrap themselves on Matthew 8 without perceiving the problem.

As we saw just above, McDurmon, commenting on Matthew 8, says, "The kingdom would be populated by Abraham, Isaac and Jacob when the rebellious would be cast out. The kingdom population would also include "the prophets' (Luke 13:28)." (2011, 64; cf. p. 62-63 also). Take particular note of the fact that McDurmon posits the Banquet at the time Abraham would inherit the kingdom, along with the prophets' reception of their reward. This is correct and ties Matthew 8:11 (par. Luke 13:28f) in with Daniel 12 and Hebrews 11-12.

One could not help but draw this very conclusion from McDurmon's comments given above. If the Messianic promises concerning Zion have been "spiritualized" and "fulfilled in Christ" then *of necessity* Isaiah 25, Matthew 8 and 1 Corinthians 15 have been fulfilled. I argued this point repeatedly in our formal debate and McDurmon then claimed that there was in fact "a fulfillment" of 1 Corinthians 15 in AD 70, but not the "final" fulfillment. As we shall see below however, the fact that the Dominionists affirm the fulfillment of Daniel, Matthew 8 and Hebrews 11-12 denies any additional, future fulfillment.[33]

---

[32] Here is another example of how the Dominionists so flippantly reject "church history" and the creeds. Matthew 8 is widely taken as the "final resurrection." Yet Gentry, DeMar, McDurmon, Leithart, et. al, reject that historical view and admit that Matthew 8 was fulfilled in AD 70.

[33] See my book *AD 70: A Shadow of the "Real" End?* for a total refutation of the idea set forth by McDurmon

Remember that Gentry offered this on Matthew 8:11f – "In fact, the dark clouds of the 'day of the Lord' in AD 70 hang over much of the New Testament. God is preparing to punish His people Israel, remove the temple system, and re-orient redemptive history from one people and land to all peoples through the earth (Matthew 8:10-11– 21:43)." (2009, 342).[34]

Mathison says (2009, 408f) says that in Luke 13:22f, (the parallel of Matthew 8, Jesus was preparing his disciples for the coming imminent judgment, the fall of Jerusalem. Jesus warned his disciples and Israel that ethnicity would no longer matter.

So, what we have is the affirmation that Matthew 8:11 was fulfilled in AD 70. Lamentably these commentators fail to see the significance of the fact that the "sons of the kingdom" being cast out, is synchronous with Abraham, Isaac and Jacob sitting down *at the Messianic Banquet* - the time of the resurrection per Isaiah 25:6-8. (Jesus' parallel words recorded in Luke 13 make this connection even more graphically and powerfully). Logically and contextually, when the Dominionists agree that Matthew 8:11 was fulfilled in AD 70 they are affirming the fulfillment of *Isaiah 25*. Let me illustrate.

---

and other Dominionists that AD 70 foreshadowed the real, "final" end of the age. This is a specious claim. There is not a syllable of Biblical proof for it.

[34] Many Amillennialists differ with the Dominionist view of Matthew 8 and insist that it refers to the "end of time." Kim Riddlebarger, *A Case for Amillennialism*, (Grand Rapids, Baker Academic, 2003)111, He dismisses any connection between the text and the judgment of Israel. He applies the casting out of the "sons of the kingdom" to unbelievers, generically speaking. To ignore the referent to the "sons of the kingdom" and simply refer it to "unbelievers" being cast out, is to ignore the *sitz em leben* in which Jesus spoke and "moralize" the text in an entirely inappropriate way. Audience relevance flies out the window.

Jesus' reference to the Banquet in the kingdom is taken directly from Isaiah 25:6-9:

> "And in this mountain The Lord of hosts will make for all people A feast of choice pieces, A feast of wines on the lees, Of fat things full of marrow, Of well-refined wines on the lees. And He will destroy on this mountain The surface of the covering cast over all people, And the veil that is spread over all nations. He will swallow up death forever, And the Lord God will wipe away tears from all faces; The rebuke of His people He will take away from all the earth; For the Lord has spoken. And it will be said in that day: "Behold, this is our God; We have waited for Him, and He will save us. This is the Lord; We have waited for Him; We will be glad and rejoice in His salvation."

Isaiah foretold the coming Banquet that would be established "in this mountain" i.e. Zion. And of course, "Zion" is seen in Hebrews 11-12 as the consummation of the hope of Abraham (Hebrews 12:21f). The connection between Zion and the resurrection cannot be denied.

As we have seen, Isaiah 25 is one of the foundational texts for Paul's resurrection doctrine in Corinthians (1 Corinthians 15:54-56). In other words, *the resurrection that Paul anticipated was the resurrection foretold by Isaiah 25.* Let me express again the connections that are so important to see:

The resurrection foretold by Isaiah 25 would be at the time of the Messianic Banquet (the time of the resurrection of 1 Corinthians 15).

The Messianic Banquet would be when Abraham, Isaac and Jacob sat down in the kingdom.

Therefore, the time when Abraham, Isaac and Jacob would sit down in the kingdom would be at the time of the resurrection (the resurrection of 1 Corinthians 15).

> **I am unaware of any commentator - in history - who has argued that Abraham, Isaac and Jacob would sit down at the Messianic Banquet *in Hades*.**
>
> **Matthew 8 is about those faithful Worthies sitting at the Messianic Banquet – promised in Isaiah 25 – at the end time "final" resurrection. Thus, of necessity, Matthew 8 is the (final) resurrection to eternal life, in the kingdom.**
>
> **What is so stunning is that the Dominionists claim to believe that Matthew 8 was fulfilled in AD 70!**

Few would doubt that the time under consideration in Isaiah 25 and 1 Corinthians 15 is the time of *the final resurrection to eternal life*. It is the end of the Intermediate State of the Dead.[35] But this means that *Matthew 8:11f* likewise foretold the "final resurrection." So, let me put it like this:

The Messianic Banquet would be when Abraham, Isaac and Jacob sat down in the kingdom.

---

[35] Incredibly, McDurmon, in our debate, argued that simply because the word "final" is not found in Isaiah 25, it cannot be argued that Isaiah actually predicted the, well, "final resurrection." Such was his desperation to defend a futurist eschatology *on the absence of one word*! He repeated that same hermeneutical fallacy in his *Changed* book (2012, 62) in his comments on 1 Corinthians 7.

The time when Abraham, Isaac and Jacob would sit down in the kingdom would be at the (general) resurrection (Isaiah 25:6-8; the resurrection of 1 Corinthians 15) - the end of the Intermediate State of the Dead.

(Important note: I am unaware of any commentator who argues (or who has *ever* argued) that the Patriarchs would sit down at the Messianic Banquet, in the kingdom, in *Hades*.)

But Abraham, Isaac and Jacob would sit down in the kingdom at the Messianic Banquet when, "the sons of the kingdom" were cast out in AD 70 (Gentry, McDurmon, DeMar, etc.).

Therefore, Abraham, Isaac and Jacob sat down in the kingdom at the Messianic Banquet, in the final resurrection, (the resurrection of Isaiah 25:6-8; 1 Corinthians 15) when the sons of the kingdom were cast out in AD 70.

Matthew 8 is patently about the fulfillment of the Abrahamic resurrection promises.[36] We cannot fail to note that Matthew 8 and Hebrews 11 are parallel in their discussion of the Abrahamic resurrection promise. Both are discussing the end of the "Intermediate State" of the dead, since they discuss the resurrection to eternal life. Likewise, we remind you that the Dominionist posit Daniel 12 as synchronous with Matthew 8 – AD 70. As we have seen, they also posit the fulfillment of Hebrews 11-12 in AD 70. So, from the Dominionist keyboards, we find the following connections: Daniel 12 = Matthew 8 = Hebrews 11-12.

To drive home the point here, because it is so critical, is that what simply cannot be missed or dismissed is that the fulfillment of Abraham's resurrection promise / hope in Matthew 8 is nothing less than the fulfillment of Isaiah 25 – and thus, of 1 Corinthians 15. It is the fulfillment of Romans 4:13 as well!

---

[36] The connection between the Messianic Banquet, the resurrection and Matthew 8:11 is widely – almost universally - held in critical scholarship.

If Matthew 8 is the fulfillment of Isaiah 25, this is *prima facie* demonstration that logically the Dominionists have affirmed the fulfillment of 1 Corinthians 15. You cannot divorce Matthew 8 from the resurrection of Isaiah 25 *and Isaiah 25 foretold the resurrection of 1 Corinthians 15*. So, again, to posit the fulfillment of Matthew 8 in AD 70 is an undeniable declaration of the fulfillment of 1 Corinthians 15.

You cannot, as an increasing number of Postmillennialists now attempt to do (e.g. Gentry, McDurmon, etc.) say that AD 70 was a typological fulfillment of Isaiah 25 and 1 Corinthians 15. This is a theological fabrication without a syllable of Biblical proof.

This is just another example of the "double talk" emanating from the Dominionist camp. Gentry and others want to make the AD 70 resurrection of Daniel 12 typological of the greater, final resurrection. Yet, he denies that any of the other eschatological elements of the same chapter are typological of future events.

Gentry teaches that a theory of "double fulfilling" AD 70 fulfillments in the book of Revelation, for example, is "pure theological assertion" that has "no exegetical warrant."[37] In fact, when debating against the Dispensationalists, the Dominionists are adamant that the concept of "Double Fulfillment" is un-Biblical and without warrant.

Gary DeMar, who has done some wonderful work on Matthew 24 and says this about the attempts to see a Double Fulfillment of Matthew 24 and other eschatological elements:

> "Either the Olivet Discourse applies to a generation located in the distant future from the time the gospel writers composed the Olivet Discourse or to the generation to whom Jesus was speaking; it can't

---

[37] Kenneth Gentry, *Four Views on the Book of Revelation*, ed. C. Marvin Pate (Grand Rapids, MI: Zondervan, 1998)43–44.

be a little bit of both. As we will see, the interpretation of the Olivet Discourse in any of the synoptic gospels does not allow for a mixed approach, a double fulfillment, or even a future completion. Matthew 24:34 won't allow for it."[38]

As I point out in my book *AD 70: A Shadow of the "Real" End?* the Dispensationalists are increasingly claiming that the appearance of John as Elijah, the appearance of the "anti-Christs" in 1 John 2:18, the Abomination of Desolation and the Tribulation did in fact occur in the first century, but those first century events were fore-shadowings of the real end.

What is the Dominionists' response?

Responding to Millennialist Marvin Pate, who argued that the anti-Christs of 1 John 2:18 are predictive of the final anti-Christ, Gentry says: "Pate specifically notes that the mark of the beast, 'can be understood as pointing a guilty finger at those Jews in the first century.' Why, then, should we look for further fulfillments beyond this most relevant first century one?"[39]

McDurmon, in a 2011 speech at the American Vision Prophecy Conference, spoke on the Double Fulfillment hermeneutic of Dispensationalism. His lesson was entitled "Double Fulfillment: Double Cross." He said that hermeneutic is false.

Also, in McDurmon's book, *Jesus –V- Jerusalem* McDurmon, he continued his attack on the Dispensational hermeneutic, especially as it relates to the anti-Christ. Millennialists claim that the first century "anti-Christs" that John spoke of in 1 John 2:18 as already present - in fulfillment of prophecy by the way - "pre-figure" the

---

[38] Gary DeMar, *The Olivet Discourse: The Test of Truth*, http://www. americanvision.org/blog/?p=190.

[39] Kenneth Gentry, *Four Views of Revelation*, (Grand Rapids, Zondervan, 1998)45.

"final, greater" end times anti-Christ. McDurmon said this "double fulfillment" hermeneutic "distorts the scripture."[40]

However, in 2012 I had a formal public debate with McDurmon.[41] In that exchange, McDurmon took the position that prophecy is not only fulfilled *twice*, but it is fulfilled, "multiple times." So, the Dispensationalists are wrong to posit a double fulfillment of prophecy but the Postmillennial (Dominionist) *demand* a *multiple* fulfillment scheme!

When it comes to the Abomination of Desolation and the ensuing Great Tribulation, the Dominionists are almost indignant at the suggestion that those things were typological of yet future events. Gentry says, "Copious, clear and compelling evidence demonstrates that the great tribulation occurs in the first century" (2009, 356). Mathison likewise says: "There is no end time tribulation. Jesus' prophecy about tribulation in Matthew 24 was fulfilled between AD 30 and AD 70." *(*1995,144).

So, the Dominionists reject the Dispensational claims that the events of the first century were typological. Yet, they then carefully pick out the resurrection and end of the age themes and say these events *were* typological! How Gentry is able to slice, dice, delineate and dichotomize the text of Daniel 12 and say that only the resurrection of that prophecy was / is typological is a mystery. He does not inform of us of his hermeneutic nor do any of the other Postmillennialists.

Dominionists are arbitrary and capricious in their application of "typology" to the end of the age events of the first century. They simply dismiss some events (i.e. John as Elijah, the anti-Christs, the

---

[40] Joel McDurmon, *Jesus -v-Jerusalem*, (Powder Springs, GA., American Vision, 2011)185.

[41] The book of the debate is available at www.bibleprophecy.com, or, www.eschatology.org. It is also available on Kindle, Amazon and other retailers.

Abomination) as fore-shadowings, while insisting that other elements (the World Mission, the judgment, resurrection and parousia) were in fact typological. What is their proof? They give none and their failure to even try to give such evidence is telling indeed.[42] We will discuss this even more fully below.

While we will examine the text more in-depth below, I want to call your attention now to Revelation 10-11.

> "The angel whom I saw standing on the sea and on the land raised up his hand to heaven and swore by Him who lives forever and ever, who created heaven and the things that are in it, the earth and the things that are in it, and the sea and the things that are in it, that there should be delay no longer, but in the days of the sounding of the seventh angel, when he is about to sound, the mystery of God would be finished, as He declared to His servants the prophets."

Mathison comments on these verses: "Israel's judgment has come in response to the cries of the martyrs (6:10). With the destruction of the temple, the mystery will be finished (cf. Ephesians 3:4-6)."[43] In an incredible bit of self-contradiction, however, Mathison applies Daniel 12 – *which is the source of Revelation 10* – to an end of history event! (2009, 281).

Gentry emphasizes the language of imminence in Revelation 10 as well as chapter 11:15f and in his commentary his emphasis on

---

[42] See my *AD 70: A Shadow of the "Real" End?* book for more. This book has quickly become one of my best-selling titles, as more and more people are seeing the insurmountable problems with the Dominionist and Amillennial claims.

[43] Keith Mathison, *Postmillennialism: An Eschatology of Hope*, (New Jersey, P & R Publishing, 1999)151f.

imminence is focused on the impending judgment of Old Covenant Jerusalem.[44]

McDurmon, commenting on Luke 18 and the prayer of the saints for vindication of their suffering, ties that prayer and God's promise of vindication in AD 70 to Revelation 11: "We learn that the first century saints did in fact pray constantly in heaven to be *avenged* (Revelation 6:10). God's answer to that prayer would, thus, be the great judgment he had just described (Luke 17:26-37; see also Revelation 11:18)" (2011, 114–his emphasis).

The Postmillennialists are not alone in seeing the influence of Daniel 12 on Revelation[45] and particularly chapters 10-11. Beale comments on this influence in his massive (and helpful) *Commentary on the New Testament Use of the Old Testament*.[46]

So, the Dominionists make the connection between the completion of the mystery of God at the sounding of the seventh trumpet and the judgment of Revelation 11:15f. That connection is undeniable since Revelation 10:5f is about the sounding of the seventh trump and chapter 11:15f is about the sounding of the seventh trump. Thus, any attempt to divorce these texts from one another is futile. What the Postmillennialists fail to point out to their audience

---

[44] Kenneth Gentry, *Before Jerusalem Fell*, (Fountain Inn, SC, Victorious Hope Publishing, 1998)134, note.

[45] Andrew Perriman, *Coming of the Son of Man*, (London, Paternoster, 2005)34, 185, 205), comments on the fact that Daniel 12:7 refers to the destruction of Jerusalem. He says that the seals of Revelation are the fulfillment of Daniel's prediction and that, "John is given the unsealed scroll at the beginning of the period of the shattering of the power of the holy people" (Daniel 12:7) – in other words, at the beginning of the period of the judgment of Jerusalem."

[46] Greg Beale, (Grand Rapids, Baker Academic, 2007)1116+.

however, is the devastating implications of their admissions about that application.

To understand this read Revelation 11:15-18:

> "Then the seventh angel sounded: And there were loud voices in heaven, saying, "The kingdoms of this world have become the kingdoms of our Lord and of His Christ He shall reign forever and ever!" And the twenty-four elders who sat before God on their thrones fell on their faces and worshiped God, saying: "'We give You thanks, O Lord God Almighty, The One who is and who was and who is to come, Because You have taken Your great power and reigned. The nations were angry Your wrath has come the time of the dead, that they should be judged that You should reward Your servants the prophets and the saints those who fear Your name, small and great should destroy those who destroy the earth."

Note the constituent elements of this text that are parallel to the texts we have already examined:

☛ Revelation 11 patently echoes the promise of Daniel 12, when the righteous would shine in the kingdom. This is the time of the full arrival of the kingdom when Abraham would sit down at table in the kingdom. Revelation 11 is about the full arrival of the anticipated kingdom that cannot be shaken – Abraham's resurrection hope (Hebrews 11-12).

Remember that McDurmon says the kingdom was populated by Abraham and the Worthies (who were all dead of course) and the prophets. And he says that occurred in AD 70. Well, Revelation tells us of the resurrection, the time of the rewarding of the dead (Abraham and the Worthies), the time of the prophets receiving their reward, at the full establishment of the kingdom! Thus, the correspondence between Matthew 8 is established and the AD 70 resurrection to eternal life in the kingdom is demonstrated.

☛ This is the time of the resurrection, the time of the dead that they should be judged – the termination and consummation of the Intermediate State of the Dead. This agrees perfectly with what we have seen. In Matthew 8, the promise of necessity entails the judgment / reward of Abraham, Isaac, Jacob. They were biologically dead, but Matthew 8 depicts their reward – the "better resurrection." Likewise, Hebrews 11-12 of necessity entails the judgment / rewarding of the long dead faithful. And this is what Revelation clearly affirms. The connections are too clear to deny.

☛ Revelation 11 is the vindication of the martyrs. As we have seen, this is the story of Daniel 12, Matthew 8 (parallel Luke 13) and Hebrews 11-12. Remember that Mathison said the judgment of Revelation 11 is the answer to the martyrs' prayer of Revelation 6.

☛ Revelation is about the time of the rewarding of the prophets. This brings us directly back to Daniel 12, where Daniel was told he would die and rest until the time of the end, when he would rise to his inheritance (12:2, 12-13). That inheritance would be, of course, *the resurrection to eternal life* of vs . 2. Once again, keep in mind that McDurmon and the Dominionists say that not only did Abraham, Isaac and Jacob sit down in the kingdom when the sons of the kingdom were cast out in AD 70, McDurmon says, commenting on Luke 13: "The kingdom population would also include "the prophets' (Luke 13:28)." (2011, 64; cf. p. 62-63 also).

Very clearly, Revelation 11 cannot be divorced from the texts we have examined. So, let me frame my thoughts in simplified form:

The prophets (of necessity, *the dead prophets*) would receive their reward of eternal kingdom life at the time of *the resurrection to eternal life* (Daniel 12:2-13; Matthew 8; Luke 13; Hebrews 11-12; Revelation 11).

The prophets (of necessity, *the dead prophets*) would receive their reward of eternal kingdom life when the sons of the kingdom were cast out in AD 70 – (Daniel 12; Matthew 8; Luke 13:28f; Hebrews 11-12; Revelation 11:15-18).

But the prophets (of necessity, *the dead prophets*) would receive their kingdom reward – through *resurrection to eternal life* – in AD 70, in fulfillment of Daniel 12, Matthew 8, Luke 13, Hebrews 11-12, Revelation 11– *the Dominionists agreeing*.

This argument alone is more than sufficient to demonstrate the utter fallacy and desperation of the Dominionist and Amillennial camps in their current application of Daniel 12 and these other texts, to AD 70.

So, we have documented not only the history of the church's view of Daniel 14, but we have shown how *the Dominionists agree in their application of Daniel and other resurrection and kingdom texts to AD 70*. What I want to do now, in the main body of this book, is to develop in depth the logically necessary facts to be derived from all of this.

Point #1

IF ABRAHAM AND THE MARTYRED WORTHIES, INCLUDING THE PROPHETS, OF HEBREWS 11 RECEIVED THEIR ETERNAL KINGDOM REWARD THROUGH THE RESURRECTION IN AD 70– AS POSITED BY THE DOMINIONISTS– THEN UNDENIABLY, THAT RESURRECTION TO ETERNAL LIFE DID NOT INVOLVE THE RAISING, RESTORATION AND RESUSCITATION OF THEIR LONG DECAYED BIOLOGICAL BODIES!

As we noted above, the promise of Daniel 12, Matthew 8, Hebrews 11-12 and Revelation 11 is clearly the promise of the resurrection to *eternal life*. So, if all of the faithful martyrs received eternal life through resurrection in AD 70, *then what further resurrection – to eternal life – do they need?* After all, the promise of the texts we have examined is the promise of eternal life. It is eternal life through *resurrection*. It is eternal life *in the everlasting kingdom*. But it patently was not the raising of corpses out of the ground. A serious issue is raised here.

Dominionists, as a general rule, believe that man possesses an eternal, incorruptible spirit. Even the Westminster Confession of Faith (The *real* Bible of many in the Reformed world), speaks of man: "The bodies of men, after death, return to dust see corruption; but their souls (which neither die nor sleep), having an immortal subsistence, immediately return to God who gave them."[47]

If man possesses an immortal soul, (and I am not affirming a position, simply making the argument) then of necessity, *that soul already possesses "eternal life"* since it is "an immortal subsistence." This being true, then the resurrection to eternal life promised in Daniel cannot refer to life (simply unending existence) being given to the spirit of man, for the spirit already possess that eternal, incorruptibility per the Dominionists / Reformed!

---

[47] The Westminster Confession, Chapter 32 - "Of the State of Man After Death of the Resurrection of the Dead."

In our debate, Joel McDurmon affirmed that there was "a fulfillment" of 1 Corinthians 15, in AD 70. I noted that this meant that *incorruptibility and immortality was given in AD 70*. I challenged McDurmon to show how or why there must be another, future resurrection to eternal life, incorruptibility and immortality if those things were given in AD 70. I asked repeatedly what the difference might be between the eternal life given then and the eternal life that is supposedly yet to come. Not a word of response - little wonder why.

This is hugely problematic for the Dominionists. You cannot admit that there was a resurrection to eternal life in AD 70– which of necessity involved the living and the dead – and then say that there must be, of necessity, another, yet future resurrection to eternal life!

If the dead saints, all the righteous of Hebrews 11-12 – *which extends back to Abel!* – received their kingdom resurrection to eternal life reward in AD 70, then *they patently do not need another resurrection, of biological bodies,* to everlasting kingdom life. After all, for instance, 1 Corinthians 15 foretold the resurrection, to eternal life, in the kingdom. So, how precisely is *that* resurrection to eternal life in the kingdom different from that promised in Daniel 12?

If Abraham, Isaac and Jacob are currently sitting at the Messianic Banquet, then they have been resurrected – *period*! The Intermediate State of the Dead has ended. If they are currently sitting at the Messianic Banquet in the kingdom, then Isaiah 25 has been fulfilled. And if Isaiah 25 has been fulfilled, then 1 Corinthians 15 has been fulfilled. After all, Paul said the resurrection to eternal life in the kingdom would be when Isaiah 25 would be "brought to pass" (from *genetai*, 1 Corinthians 15:54-55). What more could they possibly need that is *better* than *eternal life in the everlasting kingdom*?[48] This raises another serious problem.

---

[48] Interestingly, Jonathin Seriah makes a statement that I think many Dominionists would find disturbing, yet, in practicality, they believe it is true. Seriah says, "You don't

As we have shown, the Dominionists say that the faithful martyrs were resurrected to kingdom life, *eternal life*, in AD 70. Yet, at the same time, they claim that New Covenant saints (who they wrongly divorce from the OT saints) have not been resurrected to eternal life in the everlasting kingdom.

Of course, I can hear cries of "Foul" at this time. Dominionists claim that believers today are "resurrected," and that we do have, at least *forensically*, eternal life. We are "raised" in our conversion by faith (Ephesians 2:1f). But catch this. The texts we have examined are about the end of the age resurrection to eternal life of the dead saints. The resurrection to eternal life in the kingdom of Matthew 8, Hebrews 11, Revelation 11 is about the time when the power of the blood of Christ was applied for "those under the first covenant" (Hebrews 9:15) at his parousia.

Those texts predicted the objective, true rewarding of the dead, not just in some "legal" anticipatory sense, but in the consummative sense.

Daniel 12 is the end of the age, climactic resurrection. The Messianic Banquet of Matthew 8 (Isaiah 25 / 1 Corinthians 15) is the resurrection of Isaiah 25, which Paul places at "the end." The same is true in Revelation 11.

> have to be resurrected to go to heaven." (Jonathin Seraiah, *The End of All Things,* (Moscow, Idaho, Canon Press, 1999)167, n. 32. Of course, the statement is patently false, because per Daniel 12, the resurrection had to take place for eternal life to be given! Likewise, in Matthew 8 Abraham and the Worthies sit at the Banquet, but according to Isaiah 25 the Messianic Banquet takes place *at the time of the resurrection*. The obvious truth, to restate Seriah's comment is: "You do not have to be raised out of the dirt to go to heaven!" But of course, the Dominionists claim that you *do* have to be raised out of the dirt to receive the "real" salvation in heaven.

There are at least three facts that militate against the direct link between the "resurrection of conversion" and that depicted in these texts.

#1 - First is the temporal factor. The resurrection of Daniel 12 would, as we have seen, take place after the appearance of the Abomination of Desolation and the Great Tribulation. Those events belong exclusively to the first century – they are not ongoing realities. This is an incredibly important fact that neither Frost or any of the other Dominionists – or futurists[49] – either seem to grasp or to accept. We will develop this more below.

#2 - The resurrection in these texts, certainly Daniel, Matthew 8, Hebrews 11-12 and Revelation 11 is directly related to the final vindication of the dead martyred saints. And that final vindication of the martyrs is posited by John in Revelation as *at the end of the millennium*. See our study below on the vindication of the martyrs and the millennium.

Like the appearance of the Abomination and the Tribulation, the avenging of the blood of the martyrs was restricted temporally to the parousia of Christ in AD 70. According to Jesus, all of the righteous blood, of all the righteous, from Abel to Zecharias, (Another way of saying all the martyrs "from A-Z" in other words) was to be avenged in his generation, in the judgment of Jerusalem. This avenging of the blood is irrefutably not a reference to personal conversion (resurrection) through faith in Christ.[50]

---

[49] Dispensationalists do recognize the link between the Tribulation and the parousia / resurrection, but they rip it out of its temporal context, i.e. the first century. They likewise divorce the Great Tribulation from the *judgment on Israel* see Israel as an "innocent victim" delivered from that Tribulation by Christ at his parousia. More on this below.

[50] Notice also the direct link between Matthew 23 and Hebrews 11. The list of martyrs begins at Abel in both texts. See my lengthy discussion of the connection between Matthew

#3 - As we have seen, the resurrection depicted in these texts involves *the biologically dead saints*. However, their "resurrection to eternal life" is not, nor can it be, their "conversion."[51] Abraham and the prophets receiving their inheritance centuries after their biological death is not related to the time of their personal conversion. Their reception of eternal life, the kingdom, the heavenly fatherland and city, *is the final reward of their faith*, not the moment of their conversion by faith.

Let me close this section by reiterating our opening remarks: If Abraham, Isaac, Jacob, the martyrs of Hebrews 11 and the prophets received their kingdom reward through the resurrection to eternal life in AD 70 – as posited by the Dominionists – then clearly, that resurrection to eternal life did not involve the raising, restoration and resuscitation of their long decayed biological bodies. And, if this is true, if they received their resurrection to eternal kingdom life in AD 70, without being raised out of the dirt of the earth, then clearly, those entering Christ today do not have to be raised out of dirt to receive eternal life in the kingdom. This is devastating to all futurist views of eschatology.

23, 1 Thessalonians 4 and Hebrews 11 in my book *We Shall Meet Him In The Air, The Wedding of the King of kings*.

[51] By their "conversion" I mean that those deceased OT Worthies did not, in their post-mortem state, hear the gospel preached to them, ponder whether they believed it or not, and then decide they believed in Christ and accepted him. The scripture is clear that those OT Worthies lived by faith in the One that was coming. When Christ died "for the remission of the sins that were under the first covenant" their faith was joined to the power of Christ's death and resurrection, resulting in their soteriological "resurrection." But, this is not how I am using the word "conversion" since in modern evangelical thought, the word conversion means a receptive response of unbelievers to the preaching of the gospel of Christ.

If Abraham, Isaac, Jacob, the martyrs of Hebrews 11 and the prophets received their kingdom reward through the resurrection to eternal life in AD 70 – *as posited by the Dominionists*– then clearly, that resurrection to eternal life did not involve the raising, restoration and resuscitation of their long decayed biological bodies!

If *they* received *their* resurrection to eternal kingdom life in AD 70, *without being raised out of the dirt of the earth*, then clearly, those entering Christ today do not have to be raised out of dirt to receive eternal life in the kingdom.

This falsifies all futurist eschatologies!

Point #2

IF ABRAHAM, ISAAC, JACOB, THE MARTYRS OF HEBREWS 11 AND THE PROPHETS RECEIVED THEIR KINGDOM REWARD THROUGH THE RESURRECTION TO ETERNAL LIFE IN AD 70 – AS POSITED BY THE DOMINIONISTS – THEN CLEARLY, THEY RECEIVED THEIR ETERNAL REWARD PRIOR TO – 2000 YEARS AND COUNTING SO FAR – NEW COVENANT BELIEVERS WHO ARE, PER THE DOMINIONISTS, STILL WAITING FOR OUR RESURRECTION TO ETERNAL LIFE. THIS IS A DIRECT VIOLATION OF HEBREWS 11:39-40.

"And all these, having obtained a good testimony through faith, did not receive the promise, God having provided something better for us, that they should not be made perfect apart from us."

It should be remembered that McDurmon claims that Christians today stand in a better position than the OT saints. He claims to believe that we have received the kingdom, whereas the OT saints didn't. Oh, wait, remember that he also says Abraham, Isaac and Jacob did, after all, receive the kingdom the resurrection to eternal life – in AD 70, when the sons of the kingdom were cast out.

Then, however, we must remember that the Dominionists claim that the better resurrection – the resurrection to eternal life in the everlasting kingdom – has not truly taken place yet. So, *how in the name of reason* can Dominionists, claim, as we have documented that they do, that the resurrection of Daniel 12, Matthew 8, Luke 13:28f; Hebrews 11-12, Revelation 11:15f *has taken place* - yet, New Covenant Christians "stand in a better place" than those OT saints? How does that work?

The OT Worthies were resurrected. ✔ We are resurrected. ✔

They were resurrected to eternal life. ✔ We are resurrected to eternal life. ✔

They were resurrected to the Messianic Kingdom Banquet. ✔ We are in the Messianic Kingdom and sit at the Banquet. ✔

-41-

So, once again, exactly how is it that we today "stand in a better place" than they?

McDurmon claimed in our debate that there was "a resurrection" in AD 70 in fulfillment of 1 Corinthians 15. I challenged him to demonstrate, exegetically and contextually, the difference between the incorruptibility and immortality that arrived in that AD 70 resurrection and the incorruptibility and immortality that is supposedly coming at the end of human history resurrection. McDurmon offered not a word of explanation. The reason is simple, there is no difference.

Since New Covenant Christians[52] have not truly been raised to eternal life in the everlasting kingdom, per the Dominionists, but the Old Covenant saints have been, *are they not in a better position than us?* If Abraham, Isaac and Jacob have sat down at the Messianic Banquet in the kingdom - in fulfillment of Isaiah 25 / 1 Corinthians 15 - but New Covenant saints are still waiting on the resurrection in fulfillment of 1 Corinthians 15 / Isaiah 25 then, undeniably those OT saints have in fact received the promises and they did so "without us" in violation of Hebrews 11:39f. *They* are, therefore *in a better position than us!*

According to Hebrews 11:39-40 those OT saints, Abraham, Isaac, Jacob, etc., could not receive the heavenly fatherland, the heavenly city, the better resurrection "without us" – the first century "last days," "first fruit" generation of believers. Reception of those blessings, by both OT and NT saints, was to be synchronous.

---

[52] I am not suggesting that the OT saints could not receive their reward before us *today*. I am saying that the first century saints, *the first fruits* and the OT saints would receive their reward at the end of the age (Matthew 13). The resurrection motif has to do with the resurrection / harvest of that Old Covenant age, not the harvest of the Christian age. Evangelism in the New Covenant age is an on-going, unending reality.

Note that 1 Thessalonians 4 Paul said the New Covenant saints would not "precede" those attending Christ at his parousia – the dead saints. There would be *synchronicity* in the reception of the kingdom and eternal life.

So, when the Dominionists and some Amillennialists, posit the fulfillment of Daniel 12, Matthew 8, Hebrews 11 and even Revelation 11 in AD 70, and say that the OT saints received the reward promised in those prophecies, this is a fatal admission that the "final resurrection" has occurred.

When / if they affirm that those OT saints, "have received what was promised" but that we today have not yet received eternal life, they are denying the words of Hebrews 11:39f and 1 Thessalonians 4. The "harvest" at the end of the age, was to bring God's eschatological schema to perfection – at the same time.

And yet, as we have seen, on the one hand the Dominionists claim that those OT saints received their inheritance, to eternal life around the Messianic Banquet. But we today have not received those same blessings. We do not sit at the Messianic Banquet, because Isaiah 25 and 1 Corinthians 15 has supposedly not been fulfilled. Not *really*. Then, however, the same commentators claim that we today have received what those OT saints did not receive! We are supposedly in a better position than they are, yet they received the "better resurrection" reward around the Messianic Banquet in the eternal kingdom, of the heavenly fatherland and city, but, *we are somehow still waiting*! This is an unmitigated theological *mess*!

Point #3

ABRAHAM, ISAAC, JACOB, THE MARTYRS OF HEBREWS 11 AND THE PROPHETS DID NOT RECEIVE THEIR RESURRECTION REWARD TO ETERNAL LIFE DURING JESUS' MINISTRY, AT THE CROSS, OR AT THE ASCENSION OF CHRIST.

We noted above how Frost ties Daniel 12 to the public ministry of Jesus. In other words, Daniel 12 began to be fulfilled through the preaching of Jesus. Those responding in faith were, "raised from the dead." Then, Frost – claiming to agree with my writings - likewise applies Daniel 12 to Jesus' ascension when (it seems) the righteous in Hades were taken by him to the heavenly realm.

So, per Frost, Daniel 12 was fulfilled in the personal ministry of Jesus and in his ascension. The problem with this is, as suggested above, both Jesus' ministry and Jesus' ascension occurred prior to the Abomination of Desolation and the ensuing Great Tribulation. Thus, once again, the Dominionist view is revealed to be anachronistic in its application of Daniel and the resurrection.

> Daniel 12 cannot refer to the righteous being removed from Hades at Christ's ascension, because Daniel 12 posits the resurrection *after the Great Tribulation and Abomination!* Thus, the resurrection of Daniel 12 was not fulfilled at Christ's ascension. The Dominionist application is anachronistic.

In addition, if the *righteous dead* were taken out of Hades at the ascension, one has the right to ask why the wicked were not likewise removed from Hades at the same time. After all, per Daniel, the resurrection included both righteous and unrighteous. And, Frost includes the unrighteous in the fulfillment of Daniel 12 in Jesus' ministry by saying that those who heard Jesus' words but rejected them were raised to condemnation.

So, Frost on the one hand has Daniel 12 being fulfilled both in the time / space realm and in the unseen realm of the dead (Hades) for the righteous. But, he does not say – so far as we can determine – that Daniel 12 was fulfilled in the *unrighteous* dead being removed from Hades. This is disingenuous to say the least and has no merit in the text.

If Daniel 12 involved the resurrection of the righteous dead from Hades at the ascension, then it likewise included *the resurrection of the unjust* from Hades. If the righteous dead were raised out of Hades, to eternal life in the kingdom, around the Messianic Banquet, then as we have noted, they were resurrected without needing for their corpses to be raised out of the ground, restored and revived. But of course, this is destructive to the futurists, so they either ignore the issue or they simply wave their hand at it.

> If the righteous dead were raised out of Hades – *which is where Abraham, Daniel all the Worthies would be* - to eternal life in the kingdom, around the Messianic Banquet in AD 70, as affirmed by Dominionists, then as we have noted, they were resurrected *without needing for their corpses to be raised out of the ground, restored and revived*! But of course, this is destructive to the futurists, so they just ignore the issue,

Jesus' application of Daniel 12 likewise forbids the view that it referred to Jesus' personal ministry. In Matthew 13, Jesus predicted the harvest, which is patently the resurrection. He said the harvest – when both righteous and unrighteous as mentioned by Daniel – would occur at the end of the age, the time of the judgment.

In Matthew 13:40-43 Jesus spoke of the end time harvest, the sending forth of the angels for the gathering of the elect into the "barn" and the casting of the tares into the fire. That event, the harvest / resurrection, would occur at the end of the age. That patently was not at the cross or at the ascension.

In Matthew 13:40 Jesus used a very distinctive Greek term *sunteliea aenaeus* (consummation of the age). This term is only used a few times in the NT does not refer to Jesus' preaching ministry, but, to the end of the age at his parousia. It is the term found in Matthew 24:3 when the disciples asked about the end of the age that was to occur with the destruction of Jerusalem and the temple.[53] It is the term found in Hebrews 9:26 and this is where we find one of the multitudinous inconsistencies in the Dominionist camps.

Gentry on *sunteleia* claimed: "Matthew uses *sunteleia* (which appears in the phrase 'the end of the age' only for the end of the world: Matthew 13:39, 40, 49; 24:3; 28:20."[54] But, his claim cannot be sustained.

In Matthew 13 Jesus draws directly from Daniel's prediction of the end of the age harvest. The end of the age resurrection of Daniel was to be fulfilled, "when the power of the holy people (Old Covenant Israel and Torah) were destroyed (Daniel 12:7). This is how Jesus was applying that distinctive Greek term. It had nothing to do with "the end of the world" or human history.

Gentry ignores that and says the end of the age Jesus predicted in Matthew 13 is the end of time. But, where did Jesus indicate such a radical redefinition of *sunteliea aionos*?

So, Jesus applied Daniel's prophecy of the resurrection / harvest to the end of the age (which Daniel does as well (12:4) which was to be the time of the destruction of the power of the holy people (Daniel 12:7) the time of the destruction of Jerusalem and the temple (Matthew 24:3). This precludes the suggestion that the resurrection of Daniel applied to the preaching of Jesus and the acceptance / rejection on the part of his living audience.

---

[53] See my book *Into All the World, Then Comes The End*, for an extensive discussion of this Greek term.

[54] Kenneth Gentry, *The Olivet Discourse Made Easy*, (Draper, VA. Apologetics Group, 2010)46, n. 7.

As we have noted Dominionists are, at least those who are now acknowledging the fulfillment of Daniel 12 in the first century, likewise linking that fulfillment with Matthew 8 and Hebrews 11. That means, as we have seen, that Daniel 12 involved the judgment / resurrection of both *the living and the dead*. If Daniel 12 involved the reception of eternal life in the kingdom, around the Messianic Banquet, for Abraham and all the OT Worthies, then it clearly cannot be restricted to the living individuals that heard Jesus' message and accepted or rejected it.

Daniel 12 presents this view. The resurrection of v. 2 would be at the time of the end (v. 4). That resurrection would be to eternal life. In verse 12-13 Daniel was told that he would die "sleep" until the time of the end, when he would arise to his inheritance.

So, per Daniel, the time of the end was the time of the resurrection to eternal life and it was the time for rewarding the prophets with their inheritance. This is precisely what Matthew 8, Hebrews 11-12 and Revelation 11 foretold. We must impress on the reader's mind that the Dominionists, at least those we have cited, agree that Matthew 8, Hebrews 11-12 and Revelation 11 were all fulfilled in AD 70.

McDurmon says the OT Worthies have received the kingdom, fulfilling Matthew 8 (2011, 64) and Hebrews 11. Gentry tells us that Revelation 10-11 spoke of the impending judgment of AD 70. Mathison says the OT saints received what was promised them.

The point that cannot be missed in this is that the application of these texts to AD 70 precludes the application of Daniel 12 to the removal of the righteous saints from Hades at Jesus' ascension.[55]

---

[55] I do not deny that something awesome happened in regard to the righteous dead in the Hadean realm, at the ascension of Jesus. I am simply focusing on the fact that when Frost and others claim that Daniel 12 was fulfilled at that time, that this of necessity demands that the unrighteous were likewise resurrected at that time - and the Dominionists do not believe that to be the case.

These other texts patently draw on Daniel's prophecy of the end times resurrection and Jesus applied Daniel to the time of his parousia and the judgment.

The fact that Daniel 12 serves as the fountain from which Matthew 8, Hebrews 11 and Revelation 11 flows precludes the application of Daniel 12 to Jesus' personal ministry and the preaching of the gospel. It excludes the application to the removal of the righteous from Hades at the ascension, to the exclusion of the wicked.

Daniel's prophecy explicitly includes the resurrection of the wicked. Since the resurrection, per Jesus' application of Daniel, would be at the parousia and judgment of the unrighteous (the tares) at the end of the age, this definitively refutes the idea that Daniel 12 referred to Jesus' preaching ministry or the ascension. Daniel 12 foretold resurrection of both *the living and the dead at his parousia.*

It is interesting that Frost, commenting on an article by Gentry, in which Gentry[56] applied Daniel to AD 70, talks about the preterist hermeneutic, claiming it is false. Strangely though, he gave not one word of textual, hermeneutical evidence for why the preterists approach is wrong. Just verbiage and ridicule, which is hardly becoming. Here is Frost's attempt to negate preterism's take on Daniel as predictive of the "final resurrection":

"Since timing controls virtually every facet of Hyper Preterist interpretation, they cannot allow for any other precident (sic) setting matter to contol (sic) the NATURE of resurrection. The NT simply is read as repeating (not EXPANDING, not UNVEILING, not ELABORATING) the OT. So, when we quote Paul as saying, "I preach NOTHING other than the Law and the Prophets", this is taken to mean, literally, that no-thing in the NT is original. Nada. No thing. No idea. No expansion. No further revelation. We might

---

[56] http://postmillennialism.com/2012/03/daniel-12-tribulation-and-resurrection/#GPbse12THK7IYKDq.99

as well call the NT "MOT": More Old Testament."⁵⁷ (His emphasis).

Did you notice that Frost did not attempt to *negate* the preterist emphasis on "timing" or the hermeneutic of honoring Paul's emphatic words that he preached nothing but the hope of Israel? It should be noted that in an excellent article on 1 Thessalonians 4, Frost stated this very principle:

> "Paul's doctrines, so he claimed, were 'nothing aside' from what is found in the Tanakh. Luke's Greek reads, 'nothing outside' (*ouden ektos*) what was written. This provides us, then, with a logical parameter and a rule for reading Paul: Everything Paul taught is to be found and taught from the pages of the Tanakh. Anything not found in the Tanakh cannot be found in Paul."⁵⁸

The question is, *what is wrong with honoring the time statements?* What is wrong with accepting and applying the fact that Paul said, "I preach no other thing than that which Moses and all the prophets said should come to pass"? How would Frost now support his rejection of Paul's emphatic declarations about the source of his eschatology? He never tells us. All he does is ridicule this principle.

Of course, Frost's current comments are at odds with his earlier adherence to a hermeneutic *that actually honors time statements*:

---

⁵⁷ Found at: http://postmillennialism.com/2012/03/daniel-12-tribulation-and-resurrection/#GPbse12THK7IYKDq.99

⁵⁸ The article by Frost, "1 Thessalonians 4: A Textual and Theological Excursion Into Resurrection Life" was sent to me by Michael Bennett, via email, dated April 26, 2011.

"The timing of the resurrection of the dead determines the **NATURE** of the resurrection of the dead."[59] (His emphasis).

You will note that Frost now makes no attempt to explain how or why timing is no longer important in Biblical hermeneutic. He implies, very strongly, that there is something wrong with accepting the time statements, but he does not – and cannot – explain what is fallacious about accepting those divine statements.

In addition, Frost makes the almost unbelievable claim that preterists do not allow for the NT writers to "expand" or "explain" OT prophecies. *This is a ridiculous and blatantly false claim.* I know of no preterist guilty of this. Frost's claim makes one wonder if he believes the NT writers could change the time and framework for the fulfillment of say, Daniel 9:24f, without doing harm to the divine prophecy? If not, why not?

What Frost would have to prove with exegetical and hermeneutical *proof* (not just ridicule) is that the NT writers radically altered the time reference in Daniel 12. The prophet unequivocally posited that resurrection, the end time resurrection, at the time when the power of the holy people would be completely shattered (and again, note how an increasing number of Dominionists are honoring this).

So, could the NT writers change the time from the end of the Old Covenant age to the end of the Christian age, without doing violence to the time set in Daniel, by YHVH Himself? If so, how could they have done so? And to reiterate: if you read Frost's comments, you will notice that he offered *not a syllable of proof* to justify his implication that the NT writers did alter the OT prophecies in regard to time. All he did was scoff at the idea that we should honor time statements. What is also ironic is that Frost actually tries to honor the temporal delimitation of Daniel 12 by

---

[59] Frost in a written debate with a disputant named Tim, 9-25-2003. The debate was carried on Sovereign Grace website. I do not currently have a link to that article, but have a printed copy in my possession.

applying it to the first century, all the while now ridiculing preterists for honoring time statements. That is hardly a scholarly approach to Biblical interpretation.

Preterists do honor the OT texts that set the time for the fulfillment of the eschatological predictions. We also honor the fact that the NT writers said they were living in the time foretold by those OT prophets. Again, *what is wrong with that hermeneutic?*

What preterists also do, which is fatal to Frost's paradigm, is to honor the fact that when the NT writers do "expand and explain" the OT prophecies, they almost invariably interpret those OT prophecies *spiritually and not literally or physically!*[60] Let me illustrate.

The NT writers expand and explain that the OT temple was a type of the spiritual, New Covenant Temple, the body of Christ.

The NT writers explain that the Old Covenant priesthood foreshadowed the greater spiritual priesthood of Christ and all believers.

The New Testament writers explain how the physical circumcision of the Old Covenant anticipated the spiritual circumcision of Christ.

The NT writers explain that the promised "land" and the Old Covenant City, etc. were typological of the "dwelling place" that is "in Christ."

What is so important is that absolutely no where do the NT writers ever suggest or imply that the spiritual resurrection out of bondage, presented as being "dead" and in the "graves" in the OT, is now to be suddenly "expanded" and explained to foreshadow a literal raising of corpses out of the dirt.

---

[60] See my *Like Father Like Son, On Clouds of Glory*, for an extensive discussion of this hermeneutic in the NT writers.

I am unaware of any OT prophecy that the NT writers "re-worked" or "expanded" into a discussion of physical realities, such as a literal, physical resurrection. And if Frost cannot demonstrate that they did, his futurism is actually a "past tense" reality.

> Frost says preterists do not allow for the NT writers to expand and explain the OT prophecies. **This is blatantly false!** Preterists affirm, clearly, that the NT writers show how the OT realities, the cultic practices, even the land, the city and the Temple, were types of *the spiritual realities of Christ*. **What Frost refuses now to see is that not one time do the NT writers explain how the "spiritual," non-physical events of the OT must be fulfilled physically!**

What Frost and many of other Dominionists do is to radically alter God's *modus operandi*. God has almost always operated from the natural to the spiritual,[61] even from the physical to the spiritual. But, what do the Dominionists now do? Well, you can witness that in my

---

[61] A common misconception is that in Scripture "natural" means physical, while "spiritual" means "non-physical." Likewise, it is assumed that "flesh and blood" refers to the human physical body, but this is likewise not necessarily true. That is a misunderstanding, but I cannot develop it here. In a telling moment in my debate with McDurmon, he was asked how he could affirm the physical resurrection in light of Paul's statement that "flesh and blood cannot inherit the kingdom." He responded that "flesh and blood" does not refer to the physical body, but rather to life under the Old Covenant system! I immediately responded by noting that this demands that the resurrection of 1 Corinthians 15 had to have been fulfilled in AD 70 with the passing of the "flesh and blood" body of Torah! McDurmon's admission is a fatal one.

debate with Joel McDurmon, where he acknowledged that the OT physical cultus and praxis were typological of the spiritual things in Christ. But then, amazingly, he argued that the current spiritual things of Christ actually point forward to the coming physical fulfillment of what the spiritual things point to. Thus, in Dominionist hermeneutic the physical pointed the spiritual, *which points to the physical.*

I challenged McDurmon several times to justify that hermeneutic exegetically, but got no response.[62] The reason is simple. No NT writer ever says, suggests, hints at, or says in any way that what was happening in the first century anticipated or foreshadowed something greater, something physical.[63] On the contrary, they affirmed, repeatedly in numerous ways, that what was happening in their generation was the culmination, the glorious climax, of all prophetic expectation.[64]

I could continue with this, but, let me summarize the point under consideration: Daniel 12 and the other prophecies we have examined cannot be referent to the removal of the righteous saints

---

[62] The book of that debate is available here: http://www.store.bibleprophecy.com/end-times-dilemma-fulfilled-or-future/. It is also available on Kindle, Amazon other retailers.

[63] See my *AD 70: A Shadow of the "Real" End?* for a complete refutation of the hermeneutic suggested by McDurmon and hinted at by Frost other Dominionists. Their claims are without merit.

[64] See my discussion of 1 Corinthians 10:11 in which Paul affirmed that the goal of all previous ages had arrived in the first century. Paul's language falsifies any idea that he or the other apostles looked beyond the contemporary fulfillment of the OT prophecies to something different, something better in the far distant future. That discussion is in my *AD 70: A Shadow of the "Real"* End? which can be found on my websites, Amazon, Kindle other retailers.

out of Hades to some other Intermediate State, where they would continue to wait, for who knows how long.

> According to the Dominionist view, Abraham and the Worthies were raised out of the Intermediate state and given their place at the resurrection, eternal Kingdom Banquet.
>
> **Oh, but wait...**
>
> They then tell us that those Worthies were simply raised from one Intermediate State into *another* Intermediate State since they are (ostensibly) still waiting on their "real" reward, their real resurrection, in the real kingdom?

Daniel 12, Matthew 8, Matthew 23, Hebrews 11-12, Revelation 11 and the other texts examined are about the rewarding of the righteous with eternal life, life in the everlasting kingdom, at the end of the age, the time of the harvest. None of these motifs fit the idea of a removal of the righteous from Hades, at the ascension, into another interim place, where, although they received eternal life and their inheritance in the kingdom, they still have had to wait, so far for 2000 years, for another resurrection, another end of the age, another harvest, another Messianic Banquet, etc.. How many intermediate states are there, anyway? Daniel 12 has nothing to do with such an un-Biblical view.

Point #4

THE RESURRECTION TO ETERNAL LIFE IN THE TEXTS WE HAVE EXAMINED IS COMPREHENSIVE. SINCE THESE TEXTS ARE PARALLEL TO DANIEL, THE RESURRECTION OF DANIEL 12 IS THE "GENERAL RESURRECTION."

Frost tries desperately to deflect application of Daniel 12 to the "final" resurrection basing his argument on the fact that Daniel 12 says "many of those who sleep in the dust." He emphasizes the word "many" or "some" insisting that it must be limited therefore cannot refer to the "general resurrection when the "all" will be raised, per his view of John 5:28f. This is a specious argument and there are a variety of ways to demonstrate that.

As we have shown, the Dominionists clearly link Daniel 12 to Matthew 8, Hebrews 11-12, 1 Peter 4 and Revelation 11. What they fail to see is that this is a fatal admission because all of these texts are reference to the comprehensive resurrection of "all" men.

Of course, it should be noted that the Dominionists, ostensibly followers of Calvin, *reject his view of Daniel 12*:

John Calvin on Daniel 12:

> "The angel seems here to mark a transition from the commencement of the preaching of the gospel, to the final day of the resurrection, without sufficient occasion for it. For why does he pass over the intermediate time during which many events might be the subject of prophecy? He unites these two subjects very fitly and properly, connecting the salvation of the Church with the final resurrection and with the second coming of Christ. Wheresoever we may look around us, we never meet with any source of salvation on earth. The angel announces the salvation of all the elect. They are most miserably oppressed on all sides wherever they turn

their eyes, they perceive nothing but confusion. Hence the hope of the promised salvation could not be conceived by man before the elect raise their minds to the second coming of Christ. It is just as if the angel had said, God will be the constant preserver of his Church, even unto the end; but the manner in which he will preserve it must not be taken in a carnal sense, **as the Church will be like a dead body until it shall rise again.** We here perceive the angel teaching the same truth as Paul delivers in other words, namely, **we are dead** our life is hidden with Christ; it shall then be made manifest when he shall appear in the heavens."[65] (My emphasis).

So, while claiming to be faithful to the Reformed history, the modern day Dominionists are undeniably at odds with that tradition – not to mention the creeds.

The Apostles Creed, which is supposedly a foundational text which the modern Dominionists pledge allegiance to, undeniably says that Daniel 12:2 is the final, general resurrection.

In fact, a survey of commentaries quickly shows that the historical consensus, while noting that Daniel could be speaking of a corporate restoration of Israel, they nonetheless say that Daniel foretold the general resurrection. This is undeniable.

Frost, fully aware of all of this history, but in spite of his oft stated appeal to church history and the creeds, now flippantly says of that history and the creeds: "It matters not whether Calvin or whoever believed that it refers to the general resurrection or not. We can't fault expositors and commentators for getting details wrong to a

---

[65] Quote found at: (http://www.ccel.org/study/Daniel_12:2-7)

complex idea of eschatology."⁶⁶Very convenient indeed. For Frost and other Dominionists it matters not that they so often stand at odds with the historical church's view. It only matters that the preterists disagree with those historical views!

Of course, one has the perfect right to ask: If it is acceptable to reject the creeds and historical commentators because they overlooked something in the text like "some," then is it not equally acceptable to demonstrate – as it is so easy to do – that they overlooked the emphatic temporal framework that the God of heaven established in Daniel 12:6-7? In addition, is it not acceptable to take note of the fact – ignored by the commentators - that virtually every OT prophecy of the resurrection posits the resurrection in the framework of the time of judgment of Old Covenant Israel?⁶⁷

What is interesting is that Frost is forced by the time constraints to find a first century fulfillment of Daniel 12. So, accepting the time constraints, he seeks to escape the textual reality that Daniel merely

---

⁶⁶ Sam Frost article, "The Problem With Daniel 12:2," posted on Sovereign Grace website, Nov. 2011. Frost was once a full preterist but has since abandoned that view.

⁶⁷ In our debate, McDurmon sought to divorce Job 19:25 from the resurrection hope of Israel. Unfortunately for him, it is debatable whether Job 19:25 foretold the "end time" resurrection at all it is certain that he did not predict a "physical resurrection." N. T. Wright takes note of the tremendous translational problems of the text and says that few scholars today see in it a reference to "bodily life after death." (N. T. Wright, *The Resurrection of the Son of Man*, (Minneapolis, Fortress, 2003)98. McDurmon, in our debate, exhibited an unfortunate arrogance, claiming that the translational issues are actually "a piece of cake" and insisted that Job does predict a physical resurrection. McDurmon never justified his claims that the translational issues of Job– which scholars have debated for centuries– had suddenly become a "piece of cake" so easily dismissed or resolved by him.

uses a Hebraism (i.e. *some* for the all) to speak of that event which was in fact predicting the general resurrection, But, Frost and other futurists realize that to admit this, for even one nano-second, is to abandon their futurist eschatology. And this they seem unwilling to do.

> Frost says we should not be concerned that the historical church missed the "some" in Daniel 12, which, he claims, shows that Daniel did not predict the resurrection of "all." If it is acceptable to reject the entirety of church history on *this*, why is it not acceptable - even laudable – to note how the church throughout history has totally missed the undeniable reality that the Bible posits the resurrection at the end of the Old Covenant age of Israel? **Is it okay to note "some" oversight, but not "all" failures of the church to honor the context of scripture?**

The question before us now is whether Daniel 12 foretold the "general resurrection," expressing it in a Hebraism, or, whether he did predict something different. I believe a careful analysis of Daniel, especially in comparison with other predictions of the resurrection, (*analogia scriptura*) will demonstrate that Daniel 12 foretold the "general resurrection" at the end of the age and that he did not contemplate another, greater, different resurrection beyond that. For the moment, we will only examine one comparison and that will be the parallels between Isaiah 24-27 and Daniel 12. First of all, let's take a look at what Daniel 12 foretold.

What Daniel Predicted

Resurrection of those in the dust (v. 2).

Resurrection to eternal life (v. 2).

Resurrection into the kingdom (v. 3).

Resurrection at the end of the age (v. 4).

Resurrection at the reception of the inheritance (v. 12-13). Were - or will - the prophets be rewarded with eternal life, at a different end of the age resurrection?

Let's examine Daniel and Isaiah 24-27. I will show that Isaiah and Daniel foretold the same events. Thus, if, as is widely admitted, Isaiah predicted the "comprehensive resurrection" then if Daniel is parallel to Isaiah, the claim by Frost and others that Daniel is a "limited" resurrection is falsified.

Isaiah 24-27 and Daniel 12 – Out of the Dust

There is no question that Isaiah 24-27 serves as a major source for the NT doctrine of the (final) resurrection. Chapter 25:8 is quoted by Paul in 1 Corinthians 15 as one of his OT sources of his resurrection. A quick survey of chapters 24-27 reveals some amazing details that are directly related to Daniel 12.

☛ "Heaven and earth" is destroyed as a result of the violation of "the everlasting covenant" (24:1-5). From the following verses it is apparent that this a judgment on "the people" that inhabit "the city of confusion" (24:10) that rests "in the midst of the land" (24:13). This is a judgment on Jerusalem.

☛ YHVH shuts up the rebels and sinners for many days,[68] until the time in which He destroys heaven and earth then, "YHVH shall rule gloriously in Zion" (24:22-23).[69]

---

[68] Isaiah 24 is a prophecy of the millennium of Revelation 20. This view is supported by many scholars. See for instance, David Aune, *Revelation,* Vol. #52, (Nashville, Thomas Nelson 1998). Aune says Revelation 20 is drawn from Isaiah 24.

[69] The eschatological significance of "Zion" in Messianic prophecy cannot be over-emphasized. Zion was to be the locus of the resurrection, the eternal kingdom, salvation and every soteriological tenet imaginable. It is incredibly powerful therefore, when the writer of Hebrews said: "You

☛ It is at this time that the fortified city is desolated and the temple is turned to foreigners (25:2).

☛ "In that day" the Lord would make the Messianic Banquet (25:6). This is the Banquet anticipated by Abraham and the Worthies in Matthew 8 – the resurrection banquet. It is the Wedding Banquet of Matthew 22. It is the Wedding Banquet of the Lamb in Revelation.

Notice my argument here:

The Banquet of Isaiah 25 is the Banquet of Matthew 8.

The Banquet of Isaiah 25 is at the time when YHVH would destroy death (v. 8).

The time when YHVH would destroy death is the time of the "general resurrection" (1 Corinthians 15:54f).

Therefore, the Banquet of Matthew 8 is the time of the general resurrection.

Following on that is this:

The Banquet of Matthew 8 is the time of the general resurrection.

But, Matthew 8 was fulfilled in AD 70 per Gentry, McDurmon, DeMar, Jordan, etc., etc..

Therefore, the general resurrection was in AD 70.

Finally, notice this:

The time when Abraham, Isaac and Jacob sat down at the Messianic Banquet – the Banquet of Isaiah – is the time of the resurrection of Daniel 12 – (Dominionists).

---

have come to Mt. Zion!" See my discussion of this in my *Who Is This Babylon?*

But, the time when Abraham, Isaac and Jacob sat down at the Messianic Banquet would be the time of the general resurrection of the dead.

Therefore, the resurrection of Daniel 12, the time when Abraham, Isaac and Jacob sat down at the Messianic Banquet in fulfilment of Isaiah 25, was the time of the general resurrection.

Since the Dominionists posit both Daniel 12 and Matthew 8 as fulfilled in AD 70, since Matthew 8 is the time of the general resurrection of Isaiah 25 / 1 Corinthians 15, this logically demands that the general resurrection was in AD 70.

☛ "In that day" the Lord would destroy death (25:8). It goes without saying – or it should – that Isaiah 25 is the foundation for Paul's "general resurrection" doctrine in 1 Corinthians 15.

☛ "In that day" the time of the resurrection would be the time of the salvation of Israel (25:9f).

☛ "In that day" would be when the City of YHVH would be a city without walls, her walls would be salvation (26:1-3).

☛ That Day would be a time discerned by the righteous, but not "seen" by the wicked (26:10-11). This has tremendous implications for understanding *the nature of the resurrection*. Both the righteous and the unrighteous would see the same event. The righteous would see and understand that this was the work of the Lord. The wicked, seeing the same event, would not know what it was! This clearly cannot be describing an earth burning, time ending, descent of a 5' 5" Jewish man out of heaven, riding on a cloud.

☛ Israel is depicted as fruitlessly groaning in child pains achieving no deliverance (26:16f). This is, as Pitre has noted, a text anticipating the Great Tribulation inextricably tied to the resurrection.[70] And this is significant.

---

[70] Brant Pitre, *Jesus, The Tribulation the End of the Exile,* (Grand Rapids, Baker Academic, 2005)228+.

As Pitre notes, in the OT *the Tribulation is almost always linked with the resurrection!* It is certainly true in Daniel 12:1-2, serving to directly connect Daniel and Isaiah.

Pate agrees with this connection between the Tribulation and the Resurrection. Commenting on 1 Corinthians 2:6-10 he says: "The anti-God forces unwittingly crucified the Lord of glory, thereby sealing their own doom. The persecution / glory motif informing this statement stems from the Jewish apocalyptic belief that the people of God would undergo unparalleled suffering at the hands of God's enemies immediately prior to the coming of the kingdom of God on earth. Such affliction was expected to signal the end of this evil age and the beginning of the glory of the age to come."[71]

Of course, if the Great Tribulation is tied to the resurrection, as Pitre effectively demonstrates and as we will show below, then Jesus' prediction of the Tribulation for his generation is *prima facie* proof that Jesus posited the "general resurrection" for his generation. Furthermore, look at some additional information.

The resurrection of Isaiah 26 is the resurrection of Isaiah 25 (which of course is the resurrection of 1 Corinthians 15).

The resurrection of Isaiah 26 is at the time of the Great Tribulation.

But, the time of the Great Tribulation was to be in the first century, leading up to and climaxing in the destruction of Jerusalem (Matthew 24:15-21).[72]

---

[71] C. Marvin Pate, *The End of the Ages Has Come,* (Grand Rapids, Zondervan, 1995)47.

[72] Pitre takes note that in the OT, there is an invariable connection between the destruction of a city, *particularly Jerusalem*, and the birth pangs / Tribulation. See his work, p. 229f for numerous scriptural examples confirming this.

Therefore, the resurrection of Isaiah 25 – the general resurrection – was to be at the climax of the Great Tribulation, in the first century.

☛ In 26:19 we have the resurrection "out of the dust."[73] This clearly serves as a direct connection to Daniel 12 and commentators have long seen this connection. Unless one can demonstrate that the "dust" of Isaiah is a different "dust" from that in Daniel, then this connection stands firm. However, if one admits to the connection, then it presents a daunting challenge to the futurists, especially the Dominionists who are now viewing the "dust" of Daniel as a metaphorical reference to being defeated, humiliated, separated from YHVH.

If the "dust" of Daniel 12 is metaphoric language to describe Israel's separation from God (her covenantal death) and if the "dust" of Isaiah is the same death, then this clearly means that the resurrection of Isaiah is not being raised from biological death. But, if this is true, then since Isaiah 26 is the same resurrection as Isaiah 25 then Isaiah 25 cannot be a prediction of a resurrection of decomposed human corpses out of the dirt.

However, if the "dust" of Isaiah 26 and the "dust" of Daniel 12 is the same "dust," (covenantal death / separation) then since it is all but universally admitted that Isaiah 25-26 is the "general resurrection" this completely falsifies Frost's misguided attempt to say that Daniel's resurrection was not a prediction of the general resurrection. In other words, for the Dominionists to maintain their

---

[73] In Hebraic thought, to be "in the dust" was metaphoric language for being alienated from God, covenantally dead. To be cut off from the land was to be "dead." When one follows Isaiah's discussion of Jerusalem this is easily seen. However, in chapter 52:1f (and 62) Isaiah looks to the time of Jerusalem's redemption under Messiah and calls for Jerusalem to arise from the dust, put on her beautiful garments and rejoice that her days of mourning are over. Thus, Jerusalem was "in the dust" just as in Isaiah 26 and in Daniel. She was cast off, separated, alienated from the Presence of YHVH.

view that Daniel is not a prediction of the "final," general resurrection, they must definitively delineate between Isaiah 25-26 and Daniel 12.[74]

So, that leads me to this:

The resurrection "out of the dust" in Isaiah 25-26 is the same resurrection "out of the dust" of Daniel 12.

The resurrection out of the dust of Isaiah 25-26 is the general resurrection (it is the resurrection of 1 Corinthians 15).

Therefore, the resurrection "out of the dust" of Daniel 12 is the general resurrection (it is the resurrection of 1 Corinthians 15[75]).

This patently refutes all attempts at a woodenly literal interpretation of "some" in Daniel and shows the language to be a Hebraism.

It would take incredible theological gymnastics to delineate between Isaiah 25-27 from Daniel. The connection is firm.

☛ Isaiah 26:20-21 - The prophet foretells the avenging of the blood of the martyrs at the coming of the Lord. Is this the same avenging

---

[74] While some are attempting this now, it has been the general practice of Dominionists to tie Isaiah and Daniel together. Gentry, commenting on Isaiah 26, at one time claimed: "The general resurrection will be a resurrection of the body (Job 19:23-27; Isaiah 26:19; 1 Thessalonians 4:16) which is why it occurs at the place of burial (Daniel 12:2; John 5:28)." (*Dominion*, 1992, 283, 284). As we have shown, Gentry now says Daniel was fulfilled in AD 70. In his 2009 revision of *Dominion*, he still applies Isaiah 26 to the raising of dead corpses at the so-called end of time (2009, 288). He makes no attempt to justify his distinction between Isaiah and Daniel.

[75] See our discussion on the connection between Daniel 12 and 1 Corinthians 15. It is specious to divorce Daniel from Paul's resurrection doctrine in Corinthians.

of the blood of the martyrs discussed by Jesus in Matthew 23? If not, where is the evidence of the distinction? It is contextually without merit to delineate between this coming of the Lord for the vindication of the martyrs and the resurrection.

☛ In chapter 27:1f we are told that "in that day" which is the Day of the Lord's coming to avenge the blood of the martyrs in 26:20f, YHVH would destroy Leviathan, i.e. the Devil, that Great Serpent. Here is the promise of Revelation 12 and Revelation 20:11f!

So, the coming of the Lord in the vindication of the martyrs and to destroy Leviathan, is the time of the destruction of that Great Serpent, the Devil in Revelation 20. Thus, since Revelation is clearly the end of the millennium judgment, this means that Isaiah – which as we are seeing is directly parallel with Daniel 12 – would be fulfilled at the time of the "general resurrection" at the end of the millennium.[76]

As we suggested earlier, the connection between Isaiah 24-27, Matthew 23 and Jesus' teaching on the vindication of the martyrs should be determinative for our understanding of Isaiah's prediction of the resurrection. Note carefully the words of Jesus in Matthew 23:

> "Serpents, brood of vipers! How can you escape the condemnation of hell? Therefore, indeed, I send you prophets, wise men scribes: some of them you will kill and crucify some of them you will scourge in your synagogues and persecute from city to city, that on you may come all the righteous blood shed on the earth, from the blood of righteous Abel to

---

[76] I would suggest, as kindly as possible, that the view of Dominionists, that the NT envisioned "many" "crushings" of Satan is the height of desperation. This was McDurmon's claim in our debate, but, when challenged to demonstrate, exegetically, that this is true, he could not do it. That is because there is no evidence for it. There is only a presuppositional theory and theology, that is without merit.

the blood of Zechariah, son of Berechiah, whom you murdered between the temple and the altar. Assuredly, I say to you, all these things will come upon this generation" (Matthew 23:33-37).

The question arises: How localized was the judgment of AD 70 in the vindication of the martyrs? Some like to discount what happened there,[77] but, Jesus' words strongly refute the objection.[78]

That judgment, in vindication of the martyrs, *would go all the way back to creation*. It was not just a few, or even "some." Keep in mind that there were no "Jews" in the days of Abel yet, the blood of Abel cried out for vindication (Genesis 4). Jesus said his blood would be vindicated in the judgment of Jerusalem. This rather effectively negates the claim that the fall of Jerusalem was nothing more than the judgment of a backwater Jewish city.

---

[77] In 2008 I engaged in a formal public debate with Amillennialist John Welch in Indianapolis, Ind. In the debate, Welch constantly ridiculed the importance of the judgment of Jerusalem, by noting that Jerusalem was "hundreds of miles distant from Corinth, from Athens, etc.," and that the inhabitants of those far off cities would have no concern about the destruction of that insignificant city of Jerusalem. I responded by noting that Jesus' Passion was the same distance from those cities, and was known about by fewer people. I asked Welch if that meant Jesus' death-burial-resurrection was of no meaning to those far off cities – and even more so – to us. He never even attempted to answer the question. MP3s of that debate are available from me.

[78] Look at Jesus' language in Luke 21:25f as he describes that AD 70 judgment. His language is certainly "universalistic" and no limited. Furthermore, if one accepts that Revelation anticipated that judgment, then the "The Fall of Jerusalem was an insignificant, local event" is revealed as nothing but a desperate obfuscation of the significance of that age changing event.

Since Jesus said all of the blood of all of the righteous all the way back to creation would be vindicated, this demands that all of the Worthies of Hebrews 11 would be vindicated and rewarded in AD 70. This is the end of the Intermediate State. Incidentally, it also demands that the suffering martyrs in 1 and 2 Thessalonians would be vindicated and rewarded at the same time, thus demanding a first century fulfillment of those texts.[79]

Since the discussion here is about Daniel 12 and we have said that Daniel 12 must be viewed within the purview of that discussion, we want to explore that connection.

Daniel 12, The Vindication of the Martyrs

and Matthew 23

The connection between the resurrection of Daniel 12 and the vindication of the martyrs has been recognized by many leading scholars.

Wright, commenting on the resurrected righteous ones of Daniel 12:2 says: "There can be little doubt who these persons are: they the righteous who have suffered martyrdom on the one hand their torturers and murderers on the other. The rest – the great majority of humans and indeed of Israelites, are simply not mentioned."[80] Furthermore, many scholars believe that the resurrection doctrine sprang up in Israel from the hope of vindication for martyrdom.[81] One thing is for certain, in both OT and the New, there is in fact a direct link between resurrection and martyr vindication.

---

[79] See my *We Shall Meet Him In The Air, The Wedding of the King of kings,* for a full discussion of the interrelatedness of Matthew 23, Thessalonians and Hebrews 11.

[80] N. T. Wright, *Resurrection of the Son of God*, (Minneapolis, Fortress, 2003)110.

[81] John T. Carroll, *The Return of Jesus in Early Christianity,* (Peabody, Mas, Hendrickson, 2000)53.

There can be little doubt about the connection between Daniel and martyr vindication since Revelation 11 makes that connection firm. Revelation 11 and its prediction of the resurrection, the kingdom and the rewarding of the prophets is unmistakably drawing on Daniel 12. We have already seen how many Dominionists make the connection between Daniel and Revelation 10-11 so we need not go back over that material.

The thing to see here is that if Revelation 10-11 are, as just noted, drawing on Daniel 12, then since Revelation 11 undeniably posits martyr vindication at the resurrection of the dead and rewarding of the prophets, (and remember Daniel was told he would be rewarded at the resurrection, 12:12-13), then this ties the resurrection to martyr vindication.

This also completely negates the claim that Daniel 12 is speaking of the conversion of individuals, as posited by Frost. If Daniel 12 foretold the vindication of the martyrs – the vindication of Revelation 11:15f – then any claim that Daniel was predicting the "resurrection of conversion" is specious. Daniel and Revelation are speaking of the vindication and the rewarding of *the dead saints and the dead prophets* –at the end of the age resurrection / parousia.

> **If the resurrection of Revelation 11 is the resurrection of Daniel 12 – and most agree that it is – then any application of the resurrection of Daniel 12 to the "resurrection of conversion" is falsified. Revelation is about the vindication and rewarding of the dead – not the conversion of the living through the preaching of the gospel!**

This connection also speaks eloquently about the end of the Intermediate State. When Daniel died, he went to the Intermediate State, as all agree. But, he would arise to his inheritance at the time of the end. That inheritance would be at the resurrection per Daniel 12:2 and verse 12-13. That is where Revelation 11:15f places it.

This is very important to any understanding of the Intermediate State. Daniel, like Abraham, Isaac and Jacob, saw their inheritance "far off" in the time of Jesus. They saw Jesus' day and were glad. They were not glad because they realized they would now have to wait another two millennia or who knows how much longer! No, they were glad because they realized that when Jesus came, their vindication and the time of receiving that better resurrection, that eternal inheritance, that heavenly fatherland and heavenly city was near. Their time of waiting in the Intermediate State was almost over.

At least part of the significance of this is that if Revelation 11 is parallel with Revelation 20 and there is little doubt that they are,[82] we have powerful proof indeed that the resurrection of Daniel 12, being the vindication of the martyrs, was the "general" resurrection. Here is why.

Both Revelation 11 and 20 are focused on the kingdom / New Creation. Both are centered on the destruction of the enemies of the Father and Son. Both discuss martyrs. Both anticipate the vindication of the martyrs and Revelation 20 posits that at the end of the millennium - the arrival of the New Creation.

So, if Daniel 12 is = to Revelation 11 and if Revelation 11 is = to Revelation 20 in regard to the vindication of the martyrs, then since

---

[82] Note that Revelation 11 and 20 both speak of the judgment and the rewarding of the dead. So, unless one can demonstrate that Scripture posits two judgments of the dead, two arrivals of the kingdom, two days of the Lord's wrath, etc. in vindication of the martyrs, then Revelation 11 and 20 speak of the same event. And given the fact, as we have demonstrated, that the Dominionists apply Revelation 11 to AD 70, this becomes a (another) powerful example of the inconsistency of the Postmillennial eschatology. Simply stated, if Revelation 11is AD 70, then Revelation 20 is AD 70. Beale, *New International Greek Testament Commentary*, (Grand Rapids, Eerdmans, 1999)614, presents what he calls the "striking" parallels between chapter 11 and chapter 20.

Revelation 20 is, without controversy, the "general resurrection," and this fully establishes that Daniel 12 foretold the general resurrection.[83]

I would remind the reader again that historically, the almost universal consensus of scholarship has tied Daniel 12, Revelation 11 and Revelation 20 together.[84] A good example is Beale, in his commentary on Revelation 11. He explicitly links Daniel 12 and Revelation 11 to Revelation 20. He says the phrase in chapter 11: "the time of the dead that they should be judged...confirms without doubt that this passage is a description of the last judgment. The OT and Jewish writings expected the judgment of all dead unbelievers at the conclusion of history (e.g. Daniel 12). The parallel of Rev. 20:12-13 makes this interpretation explicit" (1999, 614).

Our next point will establish our case even more firmly.

---

[83] I will discuss more fully below the connection between the end of the millennium and martyr vindication. This is a profoundly important subject that is far too often given insufficient attention.

[84] Once again, we see the irony of those who divorce Daniel 12 from the general resurrection, all the while castigating preterists for being "non-creedal" and standing against the historical view of the church. Historically, the church has made the connection between Daniel and the "final resurrection." This is undeniable. But, the Dominionists especially, ostensibly staunch creedalists, now lightly reject that historical view, because they now realize that if one grants these connections, *all futurist eschatologies fall to the ground.* See again Frost's casual dismissal of the historical view of Daniel 12 yet, he claims to stand on the historical view of the church.

Point #5

THE RESURRECTION TO ETERNAL LIFE WOULD BE THE JUDGMENT OF THE "LIVING AND THE DEAD."

As we have shown above, the Dominionists posit Daniel 12 as the corporate salvation of Israel in obedience to Christ in the first century. Interestingly, Gentry gives no indication that he sees Daniel's prophecy applying to the dead saints. Of course, in his application of Matthew 8, of necessity, that text does refer to the dead saints because it involves Abraham, Isaac and Jacob.

But, as one surveys the literature it becomes obvious that the Postmillennialists have given little, if any, thought to the implications of admitting that Matthew 8, Hebrews 11 and Revelation 11 were fulfilled in the first century events climaxing in AD 70.

What the Dominionists are tacitly admitting in their application of Daniel 12 to the salvation of the living and by their application of the other texts cited to the dead saints, is that *the judgment of the living and the dead occurred in the first century.* In other words, they posit Daniel 12 as the judgment of the *living*. But, they apply Matthew 8 and Revelation 11 to the judgment and rewarding of the *dead*. Thus, Dominionists now say that the judgment of the living and dead occurred in the first century - in AD 70 - just as the full preterists.

If the judgment of "the living and the dead" occurred in the first century in the events reaching their full realization in AD 70, then it is the same as saying that the "final" resurrection occurred at that time. A quick survey of some of the key texts that speak of the judgment / resurrection of the "living and the dead" will quickly reveal that there is no doctrine of two such judgments and resurrections found in the Bible. Much more on this below.

Notice that in Matthew 23:29f, Jesus, while not using the specific terminology of "the living and the dead" nonetheless taught that the judgment of the living and the dead was to occur in his generation.

He spoke of the past martyrdom of the faithful. And what must be realized is that, contra those who wish to claim that the judgment on Jerusalem in AD 70 was a localized, almost insignificant destruction of a backwater city, Jesus said that all of the righteous blood, of all the righteous, all the way back to Creation would be judged and avenged in his generation. This stunning revelation undeniably involves the judgment of the dead.

What is significant is the connection between Matthew 23, which is almost universally admitted to be predictive of the judgment of Israel in AD 70,[85] when the righteous martyrs would be vindicated - and Hebrews 11. The connections are precise and powerful. Take a look at the chart delineating those parallels. Once we have established those connections, I will then briefly explore the relationship between Matthew 23, 1 Thessalonians 4 and Hebrews.[86]

---

[85] Even Dispensationalist Thomas Ice admits that Matthew 23 is "an undeniable reference to AD 70" (Kenneth L. Gentry and Thomas Ice, *The Great Tribulation Past or Future?*, (Grand Rapids, MI: Kregel Publications, 1999)103. Likewise, Amillennialist Riddlebarger admits that Matthew 23 predicted the AD 70 judgment (*Amillennialism*, (Grand Rapids, Baker, 2003)160.

[86] For an extended discussion of these connections see my book *We Shall Meet Him In The Air, the Wedding of the King of kings*. When one realizes that Thessalonians is directly parallel to Matthew 23 and Hebrews 11, there is no escaping the realization that the parousia and resurrection of Thessalonians occurred in the first century.

Matthew 23	Hebrews 10-11
Jesus discussed the martyrs	Hebrews discusses the martyrs
Discusses the past suffering of the saints	Discusses the past suffering of the saints
Martyrs beginning with *Abel*	Begins his discussion at *Abel* (11:4)
Martyrs including *Zecharias*	Martyrs including *Zecharias*[87]
Martyrs include the prophets	Martyrs include the prophets (11:32f)
Discusses the coming suffering of the saints (23:34f)	Discusses the *present* suffering of the saints (10:33f)
Judgment of persecutors / vindication / reward promised (v. 34-36)	Better resurrection – Abrahamic promise of the heavenly city and fatherland; vindication at the judgment (10:35-39)
Judgment of living and dead (34-36)	Judgment of living and dead i.e. "they / us"
This generation (23:36)	In a very, very little while (10:37)

---

[87] Lane (*Hebrews*, 1991, 390) says that, "Only one specific incident of such a stoning is reported in the OT. "Zechariah, son of Jehoiada the priest, had been stoned to death in the temple courtyard by order of king Joash." This is the Zecharias of Matthew 23, per Lane. It is clear that the Hebrews writer is on the same page as Jesus in regard to the martyrs.

Just as Jesus spoke of all of the blood shed on the earth all the way back to *Abel*, Hebrews 11 begins with *Abel*.

Jesus discussed the martyrdom of the *prophets*. Hebrews 11 likewise focuses on the blood of the *prophets*.

Jesus foretold the suffering of his *apostles*. The Hebrews brethren were partners in the suffering of the apostles (Hebrews 10:33f). The direct parallels between Jesus' martyr discourse in Matthew 23 and Hebrews 11 cannot be denied.[88]

It is significant that the author of Hebrews not only lists the very martyrs listed by Jesus i.e. prophets, Jesus, the apostles, but he does so in the context of the imminent vindication of those martyrs just as Jesus promised. Jesus said vindication of the martyrs would take place in the judgment of Old Covenant Jerusalem in his generation (Matthew 23:36). The writer of Hebrews said that promised vindication was coming "in a very, very little while."[89]

Given all of these parallels, let me make a point in regard to 1 Thessalonians 4, a key eschatological resurrection text.

---

[88] Commentators seldom comment on the link between Matthew 23 and Hebrews 11 in regard to eschatological fulfillment. Lane in an otherwise helpful section on the martyrs of Hebrews 11, does *mention* Matthew 23 a few times. However, he says not one word about the significance of that link in regard to the fulfillment of the Abrahamic promises, the *parousia* or the resurrection. This oversight is lamentable. The implications of the connections are profound.

[89] The Hebrews author had already stated that the judgment of the persecutors and the time of the rewarding of the faithful was coming in fulfillment of Deuteronomy 32 (Hebrews 10:33-37). The promise of the vindication of the martyrs was to occur in Israel's last days (Deuteronomy 32:20, 29, 43). This is critically important, but mostly overlooked.

The promise of the vindication and rewarding of the martyrs in Hebrews 11 would be fulfilled at the time of the "better resurrection."

But, the vindication and rewarding of the martyrs in Hebrews 11 is the same promise of the vindication of the martyrs in Matthew 23.

The vindication of the martyrs in Matthew 23 was to be fulfilled in Jesus' generation (Matthew 23:36).

Therefore, the "better resurrection" of Hebrews 11:35 was to be fulfilled in Jesus' generation.[90]

Let me make the connection with Thessalonians.

The better resurrection of Hebrews 11:35 is the resurrection of 1 Thessalonians 4 (and 1 Corinthians 15 of course).

The "better resurrection" of Hebrews 11:35 was to be fulfilled in Jesus' generation (Matthew 23/ Hebrews 11).

Therefore, the resurrection of 1 Thessalonians 4 (and of course 1 Corinthians 15) was to be fulfilled in Jesus' generation.

Notice the more specific parallels and argument:

The vindication and rewarding of the martyrs, *all the way back to Abel*, would be at the "better resurrection" of Hebrews 11:35.

But, Jesus said the vindication of all the martyrs, *all the way back to Abel*, would be in his generation.

---

[90] Remember that McDurmon, Mathison, Gentry, et. al, affirm that the saints of Hebrews 11 did in fact receive the kingdom – thus, the better resurrection - and they received it in AD 70. But then, of course, they turn around and say, "Not really!"

Therefore, the "better resurrection" of Hebrews 11:35 would be in Jesus' generation.

This agrees perfectly with the promise of Hebrews 10:37, as already noted, that judgment at Christ's coming was to be, "in a very, very little while" (*hosan, hosan micron*) and without delay.

Unless the salvation of the dead saints in Thessalonians has *nothing* to do with the time and context of the salvation of the martyrs in Hebrews and unless the vindication and rewarding of the saints in Hebrews has *nothing* to do with Jesus' promise in Matthew 23, then we have before us *prima facie* proof that Thessalonians was to be fulfilled in the first century generation.

Modern commentators are inconsistent in regard to Hebrews and the promises to Abraham. Mathison chronicles the promises listed in Hebrews 12:21f and insists: "Under the New Covenant we *have come* to Mt. Zion. We *have come* to the heavenly Jerusalem. We *have come* to the church of the firstborn. We *have come* to Jesus, the mediator of this glorious New Covenant.... That which the Old Testament believers looked for in faith has come they have now received what was promised" (*Hope*, 1999, 135 - his emphasis). However, in the very next paragraph Mathison affirms, "the fullness of the blessing is yet future, because we await the consummation."

If the promises of Hebrews 11-12 have become a reality and the Old Covenant faithful, "have now received what was promised," this *demands* that *the resurrection has occurred*. After all, those saints were waiting for the "better resurrection." They were not looking for some forensic declaration of God's approval of their faith, that would inform them, while they were in Hades, that one day, by and by, they would finally receive that "better resurrection."

Further, if one argues that these faithful martyrs were taken from Hades at Christ's ascension – which had occurred when Hebrews was written – the author is still affirming that they had not yet received their eternal reward as promised by Daniel. They had not yet been avenged as Jesus promised in Matthew 23. They had not yet sat down at the Messianic Banquet. They had not yet received their inheritance. Revelation posited that at the judgment of the living and the dead. But, they were on the verge of doing so. This means that their release from Hades at the ascension was not the "better resurrection."

The resurrection would occur on "Zion" per Isaiah 25:6f.[91] It was this resurrection that the faithful Worthies longed for (Hebrews 11:35). Thus, if the faithful Old Covenant saints have indeed received what was promised and Hebrews says the first century church had arrived at Zion, then of necessity the resurrection occurred in the first century.

Does Mathison not know that the heavenly Jerusalem promised to Abraham is the New Jerusalem promised in Isaiah 65 and Revelation 21:1f and that this heavenly city would only come after *the resurrection*?

I cannot emphasize this strongly enough: You cannot divorce the heavenly city and fatherland promised to Abraham from the better resurrection. That resurrection that he longed for was not an interim, typological, foreshadowing of the "real" resurrection. In prophecy *the consummative resurrection and Zion go hand in hand* (Isaiah 24:20-25:8). These are inseparable elements of the same promise. So, for Mathison (and other Postmillennialists and Amillennialists) to affirm the fulfillment of Hebrews 11-12 is tantamount, logically, to an declaration of the fulfillment of the resurrection.

---

[91] The importance of Zion in Old Testament prophecies of the end can hardly be overemphasized. Virtually all eschatological and soteriological tenets and blessings are linked with the "holy city." Zion would be the capital of the kingdom and from there the New Covenant would flow (Isaiah 2:2f). YHWH would rule in Zion (Isaiah 24:20f). In Zion the Messianic Banquet would be spread, when death was swallowed up in victory (Isaiah 25:6f). Thus, for the Hebrews writer to affirm that his first century audience had now come to Zion was a startling, thrilling and unabashed declaration that the eschatological consummation was now near.

Consider again the Abrahamic promise in light of Matthew 8:11f:

> "And I say to you that many will come from east and west sit down with Abraham, Isaac Jacob in the kingdom of heaven. But the sons of the kingdom will be cast out into outer darkness. There will be weeping and gnashing of teeth."

Here, the kingdom and the Messianic Banquet are presented as the goal of the Abrahamic promise. Almost all commentators recognize that the concept of Abraham at the Banquet is the story of the *resurrection*. It is the "better resurrection" of Hebrews 11:35. This fits Isaiah 25:6f perfectly, for the time of the Messianic Banquet is posited there as the time when YHWH would destroy death.

Note then the argument:

Abraham would sit at the Messianic Banquet at the time of the resurrection – the resurrection of 1 Thessalonians 4:13f.

The time when Abraham would sit at the Messianic Banquet would be when the sons of the kingdom, "you yourselves"(Luke 13:28f) were cast out.

Therefore, the time of the resurrection – the resurrection of 1 Thessalonians 4:13f – would be when "the sons of the kingdom" were cast out.

I want to remind you that Gentry and most Dominionists posit the fulfillment of Matthew 8 in AD 70 (Gentry, 2009, 234, 342). Gentry emphasizes that the sons of the kingdom were cast out at that time calling it a "dramatic redemptive-historical event." He claims however, without a word of corroborative proof, that, "AD 70 points to the end of history itself" (2009, 342). This is a theological invention without merit. Exactly how would the reception of the kingdom through resurrection to eternal life point to another kingdom, through resurrection to eternal life? How many resurrections to eternal life are there, anyway?

Gentry fails to honor the fact that the sitting at the table by Abraham and the faithful is the Messianic Banquet of Isaiah 25 – one of Paul's sources for his resurrection doctrine in 1 Corinthians 15:55-56. So, if Abraham sitting at the table would occur when the sons of the kingdom were cast out in AD 70, per the Dominionists and if Abraham sitting at the table is the time of the resurrection foretold by Paul (given that the Messianic Banquet is the time of the resurrection foretold by Paul) then clearly, the Dominionists cannot argue that AD 70 pointed to *anything* else!

To restate my questions from just above, what other resurrection did Abraham anticipate, that was to be better than that promised in Isaiah? What other Messianic Banquet did Isaiah predict?[92] The promise of sitting at the Messianic Banquet is the promise of the eschatological, end of the age resurrection, not the anticipation of another resurrection, another kingdom, at the end of another age. Since Gentry is clearly positing the Messianic Banquet at AD 70, this logically demands that the resurrection was in AD 70.

Let me express it like this:

The time when Abraham would sit at the table in the kingdom would be in AD 70 (Dominionists).

Abraham sitting at the table is the time of the Messianic Banquet of Isaiah 25:6f.

---

[92] Take note that just as Isaiah 25 foretold the establishment of the Messianic Banquet at the time of the destruction of the "city of confusion" (Isaiah 24:10f; 25:1-3) when the Temple would be turned over to foreigners, Isaiah 65 likewise predicted the time when YHVH's servants would *feast*, but OT Israel would be destroyed and God would form the New Creation (Isaiah 65:13-19). Matthew 8 agrees perfectly that the Kingdom Banquet would be at the resurrection, when the "sons of the kingdom" would be cast out. Gentry's admissions are fatal to his paradigm.

> **The Messianic Banquet of Isaiah 25:6f would be established at the time of the resurrection – when death would be destroyed (Isaiah 25:6-8).**
>
> **Therefore, the time of Abraham sitting at the Messianic Banquet would be at the time when death would be destroyed.**

Let me build on that with this:

> **The time of Abraham sitting at the Messianic Banquet in the kingdom[93] would be when death would be destroyed.**
>
> **But, the time of Abraham sitting at the Messianic Kingdom Banquet was in AD 70, when the sons of the kingdom were cast out (Gentry, McDurmon, DeMar, etc.).**
>
> **Therefore, death was destroyed - the resurrection of Isaiah 25 occurred – in AD 70.**

When would Abraham, Isaac and Jacob sit down at the Messianic Banquet? Notice again Matthew 8:11: "But the sons of the kingdom will be cast out into outer darkness. There will be weeping and gnashing of teeth." The time when Abraham would sit at the Messianic Banquet – *the time of the resurrection* – would be *when*

---

[93] Paul said the Thessalonians were suffering on behalf of the kingdom (2 Thes. 1:5). This is the kingdom (salvation and resurrection) of Matthew 8. As I show in my *We Shall Meet Him* book, this is the promise of Daniel 7 the time when the martyrs would be vindicated at the judgment of the persecuting power (Daniel 7:21f). And without doubt, the fulfillment of Daniel is confined to the days of the Roman empire.

the sons of the kingdom would be cast out![94] This was the time of the judgment of the living and the dead.

Notice the harmony between this and the rest of the NT testimony about the judgment of the "living and the dead."

In Matthew 23:29-36, Jesus foretold the vindication of all of the martyrs – *the dead* – in the judgment of Israel – the living. It is interesting, to say the least, how commentators all but ignore the significance of this text in eschatological discussions. While lip service is given to what Jesus said it is then all but ignored in later discussions in the epistles.

As we have just seen, the correlation between Matthew 23 and 1 Thessalonians 4 and Hebrews 11 is seldom discussed. Likewise, Paul's promise to the church at Thessalonica, being persecuted for their faith, is very often divorced from 1 Thessalonians 2:14f where Paul directly echoes Matthew 23. But, where is the justification for such a dichotomization?

In 1 Thessalonians 2 Paul is addressing the same church as in 2 Thessalonians 1. He speaks of the same problem, persecution. He makes the same promise, vindication. He posits that coming vindication when their persecutors are judged. He says that judgment of their persecutors was imminent.[95]

---

[94] See the even more graphic parallel in Luke 13:27f, where Jesus said Abraham would sit at the kingdom with those from the east and west, "and yourselves cast out." There is no question that Jesus was positing the time of the kingdom, the fulfillment of the Abrahamic *resurrection promise*, at the time when Old Covenant Israel would be cast out.

[95] See my *In Flaming Fire*, for an extended exegesis of 2 Thessalonians 1 and the correlation with Matthew 23 and 1 Thessalonians 2. In several formal debates, I have asked my opponents if Jesus came in the lifetime of the Thessalonians, in fulfillment of Paul's promise to give them relief at his parousia. Stunningly, my opponents, all of whom claim to

If Matthew 23 is the judgment of the living and the dead, then how is Matthew 23 not the time when Abraham, Isaac, Jacob would sit down at the Banquet in the kingdom – the time when the sons of the kingdom were cast out? Matthew 23 is the time when the sons of the kingdom were to be cast out, was it not? And, after all, Hebrews 11 posits these same identical faithful as martyrs.

So, Matthew 23 is the time of the judgment of the living and the dead, the time of the vindication of the martyrs, including Abraham, Isaac and Jacob – in AD 70.

Matthew 23 is the time when the sons of the kingdom would be cast out.

The time when the sons of the kingdom were cast out was to be the resurrection of Abraham, Isaac, Jacob, etc., when they would sit down at the Banquet in fulfillment of Isaiah 25:6f.

But, the time of the resurrection of Abraham, Isaac, Jacob, etc., when they would sit down at the Banquet in fulfillment of Isaiah 25:6f, is the time of the fulfillment of the resurrection of 1 Corinthians 15.

Therefore, the fulfillment of the resurrection of 1 Corinthians 15 was to be the resurrection of Abraham, Isaac, Jacob, etc., when they would sit down at the Banquet in fulfillment of Isaiah 25:6f the time when the sons of the kingdom were cast out – in AD 70.

We must take note again how the Dominionists agree that Matthew 23 was fulfilled in AD 70. They apply Matthew 8 to AD 70. They claim that the Old Testament saints received what they were promised, hoping perhaps, that their readers will not realize that what the OT saints (the martyrs) were promised was the better resurrection, when all of the blood, of all of the martyrs, all the way back to creation was vindicated, in the judgment of the living and the dead, in AD 70.

---

believe in the inspiration of scripture, have said, "No!"

The Postmillennial Dominionists have totally entrapped themselves by their own admissions and applications of these verses.

2 Timothy 4:1-2

"I charge you therefore before God and the Lord Jesus Christ, who will judge the living and the dead at His appearing and His kingdom."

Paul spoke here of the impending judgment of the living and the dead. Is this not the judgment of Acts 10:42, or Acts 17:30f? And is it different from the judgment of Matthew 23 and Hebrews 11?

It is interesting to read the comments of the Dominionists in regard to 2 Timothy 3.

Gentry, responding to the Amillennial view that things must get worse and worse in history, especially before the parousia, rejects this view by saying: "Paul is dealing with a particular historical matter in the first century. He is speaking of things that Timothy will be facing and enduring (2 Timothy 3:10, 14). He is not prophesying about the constant, long - term, unyielding prospects for all of history." (2009, 304).

However, in a bit of self-contradiction, he also says of 2 Timothy 3:1: "The NT suggests long "seasons" before Christ returns, (Mt. 25:5, 19; Acts 1:7; 2 Timothy 3:1; 2 Peter 3:4-9). Postmillennialism does not hold to the imminency of Christ's return." (2009, 225, n. 28).[96]

---

[96] Gentry's claim that the NT posits long seasons, perhaps many millennia, before the second coming is specious. Only his presuppositional theology can justify such a claim. It is not textual, grammatical, or linguistically justified. See my response to his claims in my *We Shall Meet Him In the Air* book, available from my websites, Amazon, Kindle other retailers.

So, per Gentry, we are to believe that Paul told Timothy to prepare *himself* for the "last days" dangers that he describes, but, we are to believe that "long seasons" are also involved in those words as well. This is, to speak bluntly, double talk.

What Gentry ignores is how chapter 4 has the, "I charge you *therefore...*" which of course means that Paul was telling Timothy to be prepared to face the last days events he was speaking about and drawing the conclusion of "therefore" to drive that point home.

McDurmon likewise emphasizes the first century application of chapter 3 and Paul's predictions about the "last days":

> "For Paul, everything he said about these decadent persons was meant to be immediately instructive to his audience *at that time*. It is fairly clear even in 2 Timothy that the references pertain to the rise of false teachers that had already come among them then (see 2 Timothy 2:16-17). Thus, his warnings about false teachers in 2 Timothy 3 have reference to problems the Church faced *already at that time*. Thus, 'the last days' pertained to *them* already.
>
> This grows even clearer from other Scripture references to 'the last days.' Hebrews 1:2 makes it absolutely undeniable that the last days were expiring then, at the time the letter was being written." (2011, 98).

So, in direct opposition to Gentry, who defines the last days as the entire period between Christ's incarnation and the end of human history,[97] McDurmon (and DeMar) say the last days referred to the

---

[97] Well, Gentry *sometimes* defines "the last days" as the Christian age. Sometimes, he defines it as the last days of the Old Covenant age! In his book, *The Beast of Revelation*, he defined the last days in the following way: "In A.D.70 the 'last days' ended with the dissolution of the temple and the sacrificial system" (*Beast*, p. 38). "The last days spoken of in

first century and the "last days" of the Old Covenant age, *not* the Christian age. And they tell us that the last days were about to expire at the fall of Jerusalem. Doesn't that mean that the "last day" of the "last days" occurred at the fall of Jerusalem?

Of course, if the last days referred to the first century and the end of the Old Covenant age, then, since the grammar of 2 Timothy 4 ties the judgment of the living and the dead to the climax of those last days, this demands that the judgment of the living and the dead was to be at the end of that Old Covenant age. Yet, DeMar, in a radio interview with Dr. Michael Brown, stated that he believes that the judgment of the living and the dead is still future.

It has to be asked, if we are to pay attention to the first century application of 2 Timothy 3, where is the contextual break between chapter 3 and 4. The grammar does not allow that, nor does the contextual flow. Where does Paul stop talking to Timothy about events that he must personally prepare to face and the promised judgment that he discusses?

The link between the first century application of chapter three and four is established by a careful look at the language of 4:1. Paul does not merely speak of the coming judgment of the living and the dead in some generic timeless manner. Instead, he says, (literally) that Christ was "about to (from *mello*[98]) judge the living and the dead." In other words, in perfect consistency with the first century emphasis that Gentry, McDurmon, DeMar place on the predictions

---

the New Testament were eschatological last days only for national Israel, not for the New Covenant church. The 'last days' were in fact the early days of the church of Jesus Christ." (*Beast*, 1989, xiv).

[98] *Blass-DeBrunner, A Greek Grammar of the New Testament and Other Early Christian Literature,* (Chicago, University of Chicago Press, 1961)181, says that *"mellein* with the infinitive (as in 2 Timothy 4:1, DKP) indicates imminence." Virtually all lexicons concur that *mello*, with the infinitive indicates something that was "about to be."

of chapter 3, Paul says Christ was "about to"[99] bring judgment on the living and the dead. There is no warrant for extrapolating that judgment into a far distant future.

There is another connection in 2 Timothy 4 that fully establishes the time of the judgment of the living and the dead, the judgment and the resurrection, to what we have seen about Abraham, Isaac and Jacob sitting down at the Banquet in the kingdom. Paul said in verse 8:

"Finally, there is laid up for me the crown of righteousness, which the Lord, the righteous Judge, will give to me on that Day not to me only but also to all who have loved His appearing."

---

[99] It is revealing to read the inconsistency of the Postmillennialists in regard to the word *mello*. In passage after passage – including Romans 8:18f!! by DeMar – it is affirmed that *mello* indicated imminence. Yet, when confronted with the indisputable fact that *mello* is used in passages affirming the "about to be" judgment and resurrection (Acts 17:30f; Acts 24:14f) all of a sudden, there is a thunderous silence, or in Gentry's case, a sudden abandonment of previous emphasis on the imminence contained in *mello*. I will not take the time here to document all of the texts in which Dominionists utilize *mello* to emphasize imminence but then, how they abandon it or ignore it in texts that they need to maintain their futurist eschatology. Suffice it to say that the Dominionists are totally inconsistent in their application of *mello*. The reader would be shocked at the gross inconsistency.

Paul anticipated his reward, the "crown of righteousness"[100] that he would receive on "that Day" from the righteous Judge. He here echoes the motifs of verse 1; Christ the judge, the Day of Judgment and the time of reward.[101] And of course, this "crown of righteousness" is nothing other than the "eternal life" and rewarding of the righteous promised in Daniel 12:2-3. But this is not all.

Notice that in verse 18, Paul continues:

"And the Lord will deliver me from every evil work and preserve me for His heavenly (*epouranion*) kingdom. To Him be glory forever and ever. Amen!"

Here, Paul anticipates his reward of righteousness, entrance into the "heavenly (*epouranion*) kingdom." We must remember that in Hebrews 11:16 Abraham longed for the heavenly (*epouraniou*) fatherland and city, which Mathison, Gentry, McDurmon all equated with the *kingdom*! Furthermore, we are reminded that these Dominionist representatives all say that Abraham and those OT Worthies inherited that kingdom – in AD 70.

McDurmon, remember, says the NT saints received the kingdom promised to those OT saints. And yet, incredibly, he actually then says NT saints are in a better condition / state than the OT saints, because we have received what was promised to them. (McDurmon did not address the fact that Hebrews 11:39-40 says the first century

---

[100] There is an echo of Paul's hope found in Galatians 5:5, where he said that he and the Galatians were eagerly longing for "the hope of righteousness." This hope is grounded in Daniel 9:24f where the eschatological Seventy Weeks would see the bringing in of "everlasting righteousness." The fact that Paul and the saints were still looking for the fulfillment of Daniel shows that the Seventy Weeks had not yet been consummated. See my *Seventy Weeks Are Determined...For the Resurrection,* for a fuller discussion.

[101] Need we observe also that the tenets that Paul mentions are the elements of Daniel 12?

saints and the OT saints would receive the inheritance at the same time. This indisputable fact falsifies the claim that Christians were / are in a better state than the OT saints).

So, we are supposed to believe that we have received what was promised to them and that we are in a better condition than they are. Yet, at the same time, we are asked to believe that Abraham and the Worthies have set down in the kingdom as promised! They have received eternal life. Just exactly *how* Christians are in a better state than Abraham and the Worthies who sat down at the Messianic Banquet in the kingdom in AD 70, is surely a great mystery that McDurmon never bothers to explain.

Like McDurmon, Mathison said the OT saints of Hebrews 11 received everything promised to them and he says Christians are now enjoying the fulfillment of the eschatological promises made to Israel. So, if the OT saints received the heavenly fatherland, i.e. the kingdom, this demands that Paul likewise entered the heavenly kingdom – at the Day of the Lord!

The Dominionists we have cited, the major representatives of the Postmillennial view today, all claim that Abraham, Isaac and Jacob sat down in the kingdom, in AD 70. In fact, Gentry says of Revelation 21 and the vision of the coming of the New Jerusalem (the heavenly city of Hebrews 11):

> "John sees the New Jerusalem coming down out of heaven to earth in the establishment of Christianity (Revelation 21:1-2). This was the heavenly city that Abraham ultimately sought beyond the temporal (and typical) Promised Land (Hebrews 11:10, 16). (2009, 147).[102] He adds: "The Heavenly Jerusalem

---

[102] So, Gentry says the literal land promise to Abraham was typological of the true spiritual promise to which Abraham actually looked – beyond the physical promises. However, in my 2012 formal debate with McDurmon, he insisted that the physical dirt was the real focus of Abraham's

is the bride of Christ that comes down from God to replace the earthly Jerusalem (Rev 21:2-5) in the first century (Rev 1:1, 3; 22:6, 10). With the shaking and destruction of the old Jerusalem in AD 70, the heavenly (recreated) Jerusalem replaces her" (2009, 367).

This is hugely problematic for the Dominionist followers. Abraham, Isaac and Jacob, indeed all the faithful OT saints, received the eternal heavenly kingdom in AD 70, these men tell us. Hebrews says they could not receive those promises in isolation from the last days, consummative generation[103] of the first fruit Christians. Thus, if they inherited that heavenly kingdom, then Paul entered into his reward at "The Day," the time of the judgment of the living and the dead, as well. Here is the argument, stated succinctly:

Abraham, Isaac and Jacob longed for the heavenly (*epouranou*) eternal kingdom (Hebrews 11).

Paul longed for the heavenly (*epouranou*) eternal kingdom (2 Timothy 4).

Abraham, Isaac and Jacob could not enter the inheritance of the heavenly kingdom in isolation from the NT first fruit saints (Hebrews 11:39-40).

But, Abraham, Isaac and Jacob entered into the eternal heavenly kingdom in AD 70, when the sons of the kingdom were cast out (AD 70 - Dominionism).

---

faith and hope and that the spiritual inheritance that Abraham received (the heavenly Jerusalem and land) typified the "real" hope of Abraham! Nothing could be more convoluted.

[103] In other words, the time of the harvest was to be the time when both OT saints and the first fruit NT saints entered into the everlasting kingdom (Matthew 13:39-40; 25:31-46).

Therefore, Paul entered into the heavenly kingdom, along with Abraham, Isaac and Jacob, in AD 70.

When Hebrews was written, Abraham and the Worthies stood on the cusp of receiving the "better resurrection" in the heavenly kingdom at the Messianic Banquet, because the time was near for the sons of the kingdom to be cast out. When Paul wrote 2 Timothy 3-4 he wrote of the judgment of the living and the dead and anticipated his own entrance into the heavenly kingdom. He said Christ was "about to judge" the living and the dead and provide him entrance into that eternal, heavenly kingdom.

So, Hebrews 11 and its prediction of the impending rewarding of the dead with entrance into the heavenly, eternal kingdom, is synchronous with 2 Timothy 3-4 and its prediction of the imminent judgment of the living and the dead and entrance into the heavenly, eternal kingdom. This was clearly the judgment of the living and the dead.

Paul expected to inherit the eternal, heavenly kingdom, "in that *the* Day," the time of the judgment of the living and the dead. The time of the inheritance of the heavenly kingdom was to be given at the "about to be" judgment. But, according to the Dominionists, the Worthies inherited the eternal heavenly kingdom, when the sons of the kingdom were cast out, in AD 70. This demands that the judgment of the living and the dead, at the appearing of Christ in his kingdom and the judgment, was in AD 70.

Did Paul long for a different heavenly kingdom from that which Abraham and the Worthies looked forward to? If so, would this not suggest that there were in fact two eschatological hopes, instead of one as Paul affirmed? It is simply wrong to make such a suggestion.

We have documented the Dominionist admissions that Daniel 12 foretold a spiritual resurrection in the first century. Look now at how Daniel 12 relates to the other texts we have examined.

Daniel 12 – Predicted the resurrection to eternal life, the time of the end, entrance into the (eternal) kingdom, the time of the eternal inheritance, the rewarding of the dead including the prophets.

Matthew 8 – We have the resurrection. We have the eternal kingdom. We have (of logical necessity) the judgment. We have the rewarding of the dead. We have the rewarding of the prophets (Abraham, Isaac, Jacob all being considered prophets) – all in AD 70 per the Dominionists.

2 Timothy 3-4 – To be fulfilled in the last days.[104] We have the "about to be" judgment of the living and the dead, the eternal heavenly (*epouranou*) kingdom.[105]

Hebrews 11 – Abraham and the Worthies anticipated the Better Resurrection. The promises undeniably related to the dead. And those faithful dead – including the *prophets* - longed for and were about to receive - the heavenly (*epouranou*) eternal inheritance – in AD 70.

---

[104] Remember that McDurmon says the last days is referent, not to the Christian age, but to the last days of Old Covenant Israel, consummating in AD 70. DeMar likewise says of the last days: "In AD 70 the 'last days' ended with the dissolution of the temple and sacrificial system. A similar pronouncement is made in 1 Peter 1: 20... "Gordon Clark writes of the meaning Peter gives to the 'last days'; 'The last days,' which so many people think refers to what is still future at the end of this age, clearly means the time of Peter himself. 1 John 2:18 says it is, in his day, 'the last hour.' Acts 2:17 quotes Joel as predicting the last days as the life time of Peter." (*Last Days Madness* (Powder Springs, GA., American Vision,1994)28.

[105] Notice that Paul said the things he was predicting would take place in the last days. Acts 2:17f, Hebrews 1:1f and 1 Peter 1:20 clearly state that the last days were the first century generation. This is a powerful delimitation for the time of fulfillment of the judgment of the living and the dead.

Revelation 10-11 - There, we have the consummation of what the prophets foretold. We have the time of the end (the last trumpet). We have the resurrection. We have the everlasting kingdom. (Which of course, is the eternal kingdom of 2 Timothy 4 and the heavenly fatherland of Hebrews). We have the rewarding of the dead, including the prophets. And remember that the Dominionists tell us Daniel 12 was to be fulfilled in the framework of the sounding of the seventh trumpet,[106] in AD 70.

Several things become abundantly clear in these comparisons.

If Daniel 12 is the same as Matthew 8 then Daniel was not fulfilled through the "conversion resurrection" i.e. by hearing the gospel obeying it and being raised to life, as posited by Frost. Paul had been converted long before he wrote Hebrews or 2 Timothy, where he was anticipating that resurrection to eternal life in fulfillment of Daniel at the "about to be" judgment of the living and the dead. *Furthermore, Matthew 8 is patently not about the conversion of Abraham and the Worthies!* It is, to be sure, the time of the application of the Atonement work of Christ (Hebrews 9:15), but, it is not Abraham's "conversion."

Daniel 12 is not a different resurrection, a different eternal kingdom, a different reward to eternal life, etc. from that in Matthew 8, Hebrews, 2 Timothy or Revelation 10-11. The biologically dead are involved in the resurrection in Matthew 8, Hebrews 11, 2 Timothy 4 and Revelation 11. Therefore, the resurrection of Daniel 12 involved the biologically dead – and thus

---

[106] See below for an extended discussion on the correlation between 1 Corinthians 15 and Revelation 10-11. The resurrection of 1 Corinthians would be at "the last trumpet" and the resurrection in Revelation would be at the sounding of the seventh – the last – trumpet, when all things foretold in the prophets would be fulfilled. The correlation is perfect. That discussion will be in our chapter on Daniel 12 and 1 Corinthians 15.

– it was not the "resurrection of conversion" through the preaching of the gospel.

Remember, the Dominionists we have cited posit fulfillment of each of these texts in AD 70. This means that *the resurrection to eternal kingdom life*, of Daniel 12 - at the judgment of the living and the dead - occurred in AD 70 - *but did not involve the raising of corpses out of the ground*. To say that this is devastating for all futurist views of the resurrection is a stunning understatement.

Matthew 8 is about the resurrection - the eternal kingdom reward – in fulfillment of Isaiah 25:6-8.
Matthew 8 was fulfilled in AD 70, when "the Sons of the Kingdom" were cast out – so say the Dominionists.
But, if that is true – and I concur wholeheartedly in this assessment – it proves beyond doubt that the resurrection to eternal life, the end of the Intermediate State, did not demand the raising of decayed human corpses out of the ground.
The Dominionists have completely falsified their own concept of the resurrection to eternal life by their application of Matthew 8!

It is specious to affirm the fulfillment of each of these texts, all of which are "resurrection texts," that foretold the resurrection to eternal life, in the everlasting kingdom, at the Judgment then say that there is another, even better, even greater resurrection to eternal life still to come. How much greater of a resurrection can there be than the resurrection to eternal life, in the everlasting kingdom? We will examine only one more text in our demonstration that the judgment / resurrection of the living and the dead was in fact the resurrection of Daniel 12 and occurred in AD 70.

1 Peter 4:5-17

"They will give an account to Him who is ready to judge the living and the dead. For this reason the gospel was preached also to those who are dead, that they might be judged according to men in the flesh, but live according to God in the spirit. But the end of all things is at hand; therefore be serious and watchful in your prayers. .... Beloved, do not think it strange concerning the fiery trial which is to try you, as though some strange thing happened to you; but rejoice to the extent that you partake of Christ's sufferings, that when His glory is revealed, you may also be glad with exceeding joy. If you are reproached for the name of Christ, blessed are you, for the Spirit of glory and of God rests upon you. On their part He is blasphemed, but on your part He is glorified. But let none of you suffer as a murderer, a thief, an evildoer, or as a busybody in other people's matters. Yet if anyone suffers as a Christian, let him not be ashamed, but let him glorify God in this matter. For the time has come for judgment to begin at the house of God; and if it begins with us first, what will be the end of those who do not obey the gospel of God?"

The strong parallels between Peter and Hebrews should strike us immediately. Just as Hebrews focuses on the suffering of the martyrs and their imminent vindication and reward, Peter discusses the identical motifs. And, just as Hebrews promised that the Worthies had arrived at Zion, the symbol of Messianic Prophetic expectation, Peter assures his readers that the end of all things, the time for receiving their eternal inheritance, "reserved in heaven for you" (1 Peter 1:5f) had arrived.

Hebrews says the OT Worthies were about to receive the promise of the eternal, heavenly kingdom. When the promise was originally given they knew it was "far off"(11:13-16). But in Paul's day, they were now "receiving" that eternal kingdom (12:28) and it was about to be fully manifested at the parousia that was coming in a "very, very little while" (10:37) – the time of receiving the great reward.

Peter says almost the identical thing. He spoke eloquently of the eternal inheritance to be received at the parousia that was near at hand (1:5-7). Just as Hebrews says the saints were "receiving a kingdom" (An *eternal* kingdom) Peter said his audience was, "receiving the end of their faith, the salvation of the soul" (1 Peter 1:9). What is so fascinating is that he says the OT prophets knew that the eternal inheritance they longed for and predicted was not for their day, (just like in Hebrews 11) but, it was being revealed in his, Peter's day (1:9-12). This is precisely what Hebrews 11 said.

Peter offers us some even more explicit language. He says that when he wrote, Christ was, "ready to judge the living and the dead." The word translated as "ready" (*hetoimos*) can mean morally prepared, or, coupled with that it can mean temporally on the point of doing something.

The Expositors Greek Testament, commenting on 1 Peter 4:5 says, "Greek readers would understand the imminent judge."[107] The New American Commentary likewise says the meaning of the verse is that the judgment was coming "very speedily."[108] J. N. D. Kelly says Peter is expressing the idea of the nearness of that judgment: "The End, as the writer is about to emphasize (4:7) is close at hand and will usher in the final judgment (the judge is even now **ready**)."[109] (His emphasis).

---

[107] Robertson Nicoll, *The Expositors Greek Testament*, Vol. V, (Grand Rapids, Eerdmans, 1970)71.

[108] Thomas Schriener, *New American Commentary*, 1, 2 Peter and Jude, Referenced in the Logos Bible Program.

[109] J. N. D. Kelly, *Black's New Testament Commentary, The Epistles of Peter and of Jude*, (London, A & C Publishers, Hendrickson, 1969)171.

Finally, of a host of commentators and sources that could be cited, the UBS Translators Handbook offers this on verse 5: "Since 'who is ready' emphasizes that the event of judging is to take place shortly, it may therefore be better to translate 'who will soon judge' rather than literally 'who is ready to judge.' The latter expression might mean simply 'he is prepared to judge.'"[110]

The point is that linguistically, 1 Peter 4:5 indicates that the judgment of the living and the dead (which of course is the time of the resurrection) was truly imminent. Christ was "ready," not only morally qualified, but, he was, as James expressed it, "standing right at the door" (James 5:9). Jesus had foretold that when the signs of the end appeared, they were to know that the end was "nigh, even at the door" (Matthew 24:32f). And that is what the disciples were expressing. But, Peter drives this point home in verse 7.

"The End of all things has drawn near" said Peter, almost 2000 years ago. What end would he have in mind other than the time of the end (1 Corinthians 15:23f), "the last day" (John 6:44, 54, etc.), the "last hour" (1 John 2:18)? The end Peter had in mind is, contextually, the judgment of the living and the dead of verse 5.

It is amazing to witness the Dominionist inconsistency in regard to the Biblical language of the end times. Many of them, DeMar, McDurmon, etc, as we have seen, insist that "the last days" is referent to the last days of the Old Covenant economy. McDurmon says, "Hebrews 1:2 makes it absolutely undeniable that the last days were expiring then, at the time the letter was being written." (2011, 198).

He also says, commenting on Hebrews 8, "As he wrote, in his time, the Old was becoming obsolete and was ready to vanish away. It has not yet been completely wiped out, but was certainly in its dying

---

[110] Daniel Arichea and Eugene Nida, *A Handbook on the First Letter From Peter*, (United Bible Society, 1994)– referenced in the Logos Bible Program.

moments. It died in AD 70, when the symbol and ceremonies of that Old System– the Temple and the sacrifices– were completely destroyed by the Roman armies. *This was the definitive moment when "this age' of Jesus and Paul ended and completely gave way to their 'age to come.'* This, of course, is exactly why Jesus tied 'the end of the age' to His prophecy of the destruction of the Temple." (2011, 47, My emphasis).

So, in Dominionist circles the last days, the end of the age, the last hour are all terms referring to the end of the Mosaic Age. And, that age had a "definitive moment" when it ended. However, without so much as a single contextual delineation or hint, when the term "the last day" is used, they tell us that term must refer to the end of human history, the end of the current age. Frost claims that the reference to "the last day" demands an end of time event because, "There are no days after this."[111] This is illogical and unscriptural and Frost's own view of Daniel 12 refutes the claim.

Frost does not believe that Daniel foretold the general resurrection of "the last day." To be honest, he is ambiguous and vague about when he thinks it was fulfilled, but, it cannot, he assures us, be the general resurrection because it is described as a resurrection of "some" and not all. We will address this claim below. But notice when the resurrection of Daniel 12 was to be. It was to be at "the end of the days."

So, the resurrection of Daniel 12 would be at *the end of the days*. If Frost's reasoning on John 6:44 is correct, then there could not be any days after "the end of the days," could there? How, per Frost's argument, do you get days after "the end of days?"

---

[111] Samuel Frost, *Why I Left Full Preterism*, (Powder Springs, GA, American Vision, 2012)23. As the title suggests, this book seeks to explain Frost's departure from the true preterist world. The sad thing is that Frost's explanation is embarrassingly illogical and devoid of exegetical documentation. It is a transparent and desperate attempt to hang onto "orthodoxy" at any cost.

Furthermore, Peter said "the end of all things has drawn near" (1 Peter 4:7). Per Frost's logic, there cannot be any "things" beyond the end of "all things." Thus, if the end of all things and the last day are synchronous - and how could they not be? - then the general resurrection on the last day had to have drawn near in 1 Peter 4. If not, why not? The point here is that when Peter said, "the end of all things has drawn near" (literal rendering) there is little doubt he was referring to the imminent termination of Israel's covenant age.

Have these men who appeal to John 6 and the "last day" not considered that the Old Covenant age that was coming to an end, had a "definitive last moment?" Have they not considered that since it had "the last hour" that this demanded that it had "the last day?"

I think Brooke caught the power of 1 John 2:18 and John's declaration that the last hour had arrived, quite well. And of course, the implications for understanding "the last day" are undeniable:

> "The Johannine teaching, whatever its origin may be, has taught us to spiritualize the New Testament expression of the doctrine of the last things. But the writer held firmly to the expectation of a final manifestation fo the Christ at 'the last day,' and he seems to have expected it within a few years of his own lifetime. When he uses the phrase 'the last hour' he clearly means the short period, as he conceived it to be, which still remained before the final manifestation of the last day. The phrase is found only here in the New Testament. The expression the last day occurs in the Gospel (seven times), and never without the article. Its use is confined to the gospel. The use of "hour" (hora) in connection with the coming of Christ is frequent in the Gospels, (Mt. 24:36 (Mk. 13:32) 24.42, 44, 50,;

25.13; Luke 12.40, 46. Cf. Romans 13.11; Revelation 3.3)."[112]

Brooke is pointing us to the fact that the consistency of John's use of "the last day" and "last hour" means he was speaking of the same eschatological consummation. The attempt by Dominionists to create two last times, two last days, two eschatologies is misguided.

There is nothing to suggest that Jesus or John had a different last day in mind distinct from "the end of days" of Daniel 12. And of course, it is particularly relevant to note that according to Jesus, those raised at the "last day" were to be raised to "eternal life" (John 6:54) which raises the question: Is this a different "eternal life" from that promised in Daniel 12? If so, in what way?

Just as Peter said the end of all things had drawn near, John said, "it is the last hour" (1 John 2:18). Now, surely, there can't be any "hours" after "the last hour," can there? Not per Frost's logic. Thus, we have "the end of all things," "the last hour," at the end of "the last days," all confined to the first century. Yet, to salvage his futurism, Frost insists that it is "the last day" referent that demands a future event. This is presuppositional (desperate) theology at work, and not exegesis.

Per Frost, Daniel 12 is not the general resurrection, and yet, it occurs at *the end of the days*. But, since John 6:44 occurs at "the last day" (after which there can be no days, per Frost) then that means that there was an "end of time" resurrection in fulfillment of Daniel 12 and there will be yet another end of time resurrection at some point of time in the future! Such are the consequences of bad logic and false claims.

The fact is that 'the last day" and "the end of days" is not a reference to the last day or the end of days of time *per se*, but, the

---

[112] Canon A. E. Brooke (D. D.), *The International Critical Commentary, The Johannine Epistles*, (Edinburgh, T & T Clark, 1957)51.

end of the Old Covenant age - the end of Old Covenant time. There were not any days of the Old Covenant age, after it had its critical, consummative last hour and last day in the first century. But, the last day of the Old Covenant age gave way to the unending kingdom of Jesus Christ, "age without end!"

And, once again, we find agreement with this among the Dominionists and even many Amillennialists.

Seraiah says, "It is true that the 'eschatology of the NT is predominantly preterist.'... 'The preterist interpretation is actually the most faithful to the Biblical text because it recognizes that Old Testament prophetic terminology was used by the New Testament authors. This recognition is helpful in distinguishing the prophecies of Christ's coming that were near, in the first century (Mt. 10:23; 16:28; 24:30; 26:64; 1 Thess. 5:2; 2 Thess. 1:7; James 5:7-9; 1 Peter 4:7; Rev. 1:3, 7, etc.) and thus fulfilled in AD 70, from those that were far (John 5:28-29; Acts 1:11; 17:31; 1 Cor. 15:23-24; 1 Thes. 4:16. 1 John 3:2; etc.) and thus not yet fulfilled even in our day." (*End*, 1999, 14).

The thing to be noted in the verses Seriah offers as proof of events "that were far off" is that *not one of them says those events were far off!* In fact, a closer examination of those texts will quickly reveal that they actually affirm the imminence of those eschatological elements.[113] It is only Seriah's preconceived, presuppositional theology that reads into those texts the idea of protraction and delay.

---

[113] See for instance my extensive discussion of Paul's "we who are alive and remain" in 1 Thessalonians 4:15, 17. It is unjustified to argue that Paul was using some vague, timeless "editorial we." Paul's language in Thessalonians was very "personal" and contemporary. My discussion is found in my *We Shall Meet Him In The Air, The Wedding of the King of kings*.

Like Seriah, DeMar admits that Peter looked to the imminent end of Israel's age: "One of the first things a Christian must learn in interpreting the Bible is to pay attention to the time texts. Failing to recognize the proximity of a prophetic event will distort its intended meaning. The New Testament clearly states that the 'end of all things' was at hand for those who first read 1 Peter 4:7; that is, the Old Covenant with its types and shadows was about to pass away." (*Madness*, 1994, 27).

Mathison, who has a tendency to "hedge his bets" and give an uncertain sound, nonetheless says: "It is possible that he (Peter, DKP) had in mind the words he heard Jesus speak thirty years earlier about the judgment that was expected within a generation. If that is the case, then the end Peter has in mind is not the end associated with the second coming of Christ and the final judgment. It is the end associated with the destruction of Jerusalem." (2009, 632).

Other sources could be cited, but, clearly, it is common for Dominionists to agree that Peter was anticipating the imminent coming of the Lord in AD 70. That being the case, I suggest that in verse 17 we have definitive proof that the judgment of the living and the dead, in fulfillment of the OT prophets, was truly near.

1 Peter 4:17

> "For the time has come for judgment to begin at the house of God; and if it begins with us first, what will be the end of those who do not obey the gospel of God?"

There are a couple of "bullet points" to be made here.

✶ When Peter speaks of "the time", he uses the definite article, indicating that he has a very specific, very well-known time of judgment in mind.

✶ When he speaks of the "time" he uses the word *kairos* which means a special, designated, appointed time. It is often a referent to God's appointed time for bringing about final salvation.

Gentry correctly apprises the significance of *kairos*, at least in some verses. Commenting on Mark 1:15, where Jesus said, "the time is fulfilled", Gentry said: "Christ asserts 'the time is fulfilled.' What is 'the time' to which he refers? The Greek term here is *kairos*, which indicates 'the fateful and decisive point' that is ordained by God.' This 'time' surely refers to the prophetically anticipated time, the time of the coming of David's greater Son to establish the kingdom, for he immediately adds: 'the kingdom of God is at hand.'" (2009, 218).

The noted scholar, F. F. Bruce, commenting on the same verses, said this: "These words express, among other things, the assurance that an ardently desired new order, long since foretold and awaited. was now on the point of realization."[114]

Peter's use of *kairos* in his first epistle is important. Notice his use in 1 Peter 1:10-11:

> "Of this salvation the prophets have inquired and searched carefully, who prophesied of the grace that would come to you, searching what, or what manner of time, (*kairos*) the Spirit of Christ who was in them was indicating when He testified beforehand the sufferings of Christ and the glories that would follow."

Notice first of all that Peter undeniably says in the very next verse that those OT prophets were informed that when they spoke of Messiah, his sufferings and the glories to follow (i.e. the salvation of the soul, v. 9) that they knew they were not speaking of their day and their time:

"To them it was revealed that, not to themselves, but to us they were ministering the things which now have been reported to you through

---

[114] F. F. Bruce, *The Time is Fulfilled*, (Exeter, Paternoster Press, 1978)15.

those who have preached the gospel to you by the Holy Spirit sent from heaven—things which angels desire to look into."

Peter's words raise an interesting point. If God does not, or perhaps cannot, communicate objectively and truthfully about the timing of events, because after all, "one day is with the Lord as a thousand years a thousand years is as a day" then how was it possible for the Lord to have clearly communicated to those OT prophets that the things they foretold were not for their day? Could it have been like when He told Daniel to seal the vision of the last days because fulfillment was far off? Could it have been like when Balaam said he envisioned the coming of the Messiah, but that coming was "not nigh"?

If one accepts those communications of temporal protraction, as normative and normal, it is clear that God did know how to communicate truthfully and objectively about the timing of events. Thus, when the Faithful Worthies were given the promise of the "heavenly fatherland", the city whose builder and maker was God the better resurrection saw those things "far off" (Hebrews 11:11-13) then God told them - truthfully – that those things were not near. They were not at hand in their day. They were not coming quickly.

This means that if God communicated truthfully that the salvation to come at the parousia was not for the days of the OT prophets, but Peter said, "the end of all things has drawn near" that we are to take the language seriously. After all, Peter says the Holy Spirit, sent from the Father, is the one instructing them to say that Day had now drawn near.

Notice again that the OT prophets desired to know *the time (kairos)* the *appointed* Day of Salvation, at the parousia. They were told it was not for their day. But, in 1 Peter 4:17 Peter declared "the time (*kairos*) has come for the judgment"!

The day– the *kairos*– longed for by the OT prophets, which was far off from them, was now near. Peter says that the, *kairos*, the appointed time had arrived! This is very significant. Look at the argument, simply stated:

The OT prophets longed to know the time (kairos) of the Day of the Lord and the attendant salvation (1 Peter 1:10-12).

The OT prophets were informed that their days were not the time (*kairos*) for the Day of the Lord and the attendant salvation.

Peter said that the time, the *kairos* anticipated by the prophets had arrived: "The time (*kairos*) has come for the judgment to begin" (1 Peter 4:17).

Therefore, the time (kairos) for the Day of the Lord and attendant salvation anticipated by the prophets had come.

There is no way, linguistically or contextually to divorce this discussion from the eternal salvation anticipated by Daniel. In fact, as the following chart will illustrate, there is a beautiful correspondence between Daniel and 1 Peter.

Daniel 12	1 Peter
Time of tribulation - Messianic Woes	Fiery trial is among you – sufferings of Messiah
Time of the end	These last days
resurrection to eternal life	eternal life
time of the inheritance	eternal inheritance
Vision was not understood	Revealed to us
Eternal life at resurrection	Eternal inheritance at the parousia
Revealed that it was not for them– far off	The end of all things has drawn near; The time has come;

The correspondence between these texts is striking. Daniel, just as Peter said, was informed that the time of the end, the resurrection to eternal life (i.e. salvation) was not for his day. But now, in Peter, the Spirit declared that the appointed time (*kairos*) had arrived. This means that the resurrection of Daniel 12 was about to take place at "the end" about which Peter said: "The End of all things has drawn near." Was "the end of all things" in Peter, when the incorruptible inheritance would be given, a different time of the end from Daniel, when everlasting life would be given? Is so, where is the evidence?

✶ Peter not only said "the time" had come, he said the time had come for "*the* judgment. Let me make a semi-technical point here from the Greek. When Peter used the term "*the* judgment" (*to krina*) he uses what is known as an *anaphoric article*.

The anaphoric article is, according to one of the leading Greek Grammars of the day, the preponderant use of the definite article in the Greek language.[115] One writer, drawing on Wallace, says, "An anaphoric reference, where the article indicates that the following substantive refers to another previously mentioned substantive. In providing this service, the article contributes to the meaning by helping the reader to associate the two substantives with each other, thus assists the reader in combining all the information about both substantives into one package."[116] Let me express this as simply as possible.

An anaphoric article is used by a writer or speaker when they are discussing a subject. After introducing the subject, they then add the article later to refer the reader back to their earlier discussion of that topic or subject. Let's apply that to 1 Peter 4.

---

[115] Daniel B. Wallace, *Greek Grammar Beyond Basics: An Exegetical Syntax Of The N.T.*, (Grand Rapids, Zondervan, 1996)218.

[116] http://inthesaltshaker.com/drills/article2.htm

In 1 Peter 4:5 the apostle introduced the subject of the judgment. It is the judgment of the living and the dead. In verse 5 he does not use the definite article at all (one reason being that he uses a verbal form). In verse 17 Peter brings up, again, the subject of the judgment. This time, to take the reader back to his earlier discussion of the topic of the judgment, he uses the definite article "the judgment." In other words, stated as simply as possible, the judgment of verse 5 is the judgment of verse 17.

Let me state the argument like this: (Based on the use of the anaphoric article in 1 Peter 4:17):

"The judgment" of 1 Peter 4:17 is the judgment of verse 5 - the judgment of the living and the dead.

The judgment of the living and the dead is the resurrection of the dead.

Therefore, the judgment of 1 Peter 4:17 is the resurrection of the living and the dead.

Following on this, take note:

The judgment of 1 Peter 4:17 is the resurrection of the living and the dead.

But, Peter said the time had arrived for "the judgment."

Therefore, the time had come for the resurrection at the judgment of the living and the dead.

We have already demonstrated that the judgment of the living and the dead is directly linked to Daniel 12. This connection best fits the evidence found in 1 Peter 1-5 indicating that the judgment, the parousia the end of all things was truly at hand. This being true, our thesis of *Torah to Telos* is fully confirmed; here is why.

As we have shown, the prediction of the resurrection was from "the law and the prophets" (Acts 24:14). So, since "the law" foretold, foreshadowed, the resurrection (it did so in types and shadows as well as overt prophecy) then Torah did not and could not pass until the resurrection, the judgment of the living and the dead, was fulfilled.

The modern, "orthodox" view of the resurrection taking place at the end of the New Covenant age is an overt denial - and distortion - of the Biblical truth that Torah would stand until the *Telos*, the resurrection of the dead.

Point #6

THE RESURRECTION OF THE JUST AND THE UNJUST:

DANIEL 12 AND ACTS 24:14F

Daniel foretold the resurrection of both the righteous and the unrighteous, i.e. the just and the unjust. It is, I think, significant that Daniel's prophecy is the clearest, most emphatic prediction of the resurrection of the "just and the unjust" in all of the Tanakh. Why is this significant?

As Paul stood on trial in Acts 24, for his hope of the resurrection, he said:

"But this I confess to you, that according to the Way which they call a sect, so I worship the God of my fathers, believing all things which are written in the Law and in the Prophets. I have hope in God, which they themselves also accept, that there will be a resurrection of the dead, both of the just and the unjust."

So, Paul said his doctrine of the resurrection of the dead came from "the law and the prophets," and that hope was that there was (literally) "*about to be* (from *mello*) a resurrection of the dead, both of the just and the unjust."

We want to emphasize the point that Paul repeatedly tells us that his one eschatological hope, his hope of the resurrection was, "nothing but the hope of Israel" (Acts 24; 26:6f; 21f; 28:16f). That hope was expressed in Moses, the law and the prophets.

Paul did not, in spite of McDurmon's claims in our debate, have a resurrection doctrine that was tied to Adam or Abraham and another, different, resurrection doctrine that belonged to Israel. To reiterate a point made in this book, if Paul had a doctrine of resurrection from Adamic death, or a doctrine of resurrection distinctively tied to Abraham *and not Israel*, then it is strange indeed that in his *magnum opus* on the resurrection Paul saw the solution to the Adamic death as tied to the fulfillment of God's Old Covenant promises made to Israel (i.e. Isaiah 25 / Daniel 12 / Hosea

13)! It is equally odd that in his discussion of the "redemption of creation" and the "adoption" that he said those promises belonged to "Israel after the flesh" (Romans 9:1-3).

This is deeply problematic for Frost and McDurmon. Frost argues for "three aspects of death" and says, "Two aspects have already been done away for the believer: estrangement and sheolic. Why then does physical death remain for the believer?" He proceeds to tell us that our physical lives are lived to Christ to manifest his life and death - meaning that we continue to live under the physical curse of Adam: "Jesus physically died as a penalty for becoming accursed for our account. We also die ('in Adam all die') due to the same penalty that came through Adam." (2012, 60). This is unmitigated confusion - it is bad theology. Look closer at what Frost's claims mean:

1. If we are delivered from alienation - i.e. we are forgiven of sin which ostensibly brings physical death - then why in the name of reason do we still die physically? Frost admits that this is a fair question, but his "answer" is totally unsatisfactory, for it leaves man under the Curse of Adam!

So, the wages of sin is (physical) death we are told. But, in Christ we have no sin - says Frost. Yet, we still have to experience the Adamic curse of physical death! It makes one wonder how effective Christ's work really is, does it not?

2. Frost is positing the "already but not yet" of resurrection, (in reality, Frost is positing an incredible "gap theory" of salvation) but refuses to deal with the indisputable fact that in the NT, the "not yet" is invariably posited as imminent. It is *never* far off.

3. Frost refuses to acknowledge that the resurrection - the final resurrection of 1 Corinthians 15 which is the deliverance from the Adamic physical death curse per Frost - was to be *in fulfillment of God's promises to Old Covenant Israel*. So, when Frost and McDurmon fail or refuse to deal with Israel and eschatology, they thereby tacitly admit their inability to do so. This is fatal to their eschatology.

4. Consider Frost's claim that the "Sheolic aspect" of death has been done away. Frost discourses on the trumpets and bowls of wrath in Revelation 16. According to Revelation 15, there could be no entrance into the Most Holy Place until the wrath of God was finished (consummated) in the judgment of Babylon and the sounding of the last trumpet and outpouring of the last bowl.[117] Frost has abandoned his view that Babylon was Old Covenant Jerusalem, because, he says, "If AD 70 was the *last* trumpet, then God *no longer acts* in history. His *last* act will be accompanied with the *last trumpet*" (2012, 33 - all emphasis his).

But, once again, Frost has entrapped himself. Keep in mind that the sounding of those trumpets and outpouring of those bowls would signal the opening of the Most Holy Place (Revelation 15:8). What is critical to understand about this is that *Hebrews 9:6-10 posits entrance into the MHP at the end of the Law of Moses!* That is, *at the fulfillment of God's promises to Israel found in Torah*. While Frost, McDurmon, etc. eschew Israel as critical and central to the eschatological narrative, they do so at the expense of truth.

So, if the trumpets and bowls have not been poured out, finishing the Wrath of God, then no man can enter the MHP, meaning that Torah remains binding. Sheolic death has not been truly conquered after all. But, that would mean that the Dominionist view of Matthew 8:11, Hebrews 11, and Revelation 11 would have to be jettisoned.

If the Sheolic aspect of death is ended, Abraham and the Worthies have received their eternal reward of the New Creation through the resurrection, as this work proves. If the Sheolic aspect of death has been destroyed, the last trump has sounded, the last bowl has been

---

[117] To abandon the view that Babylon was Old Covenant Jerusalem, and posit "Babylon" as some future entity puts Frost at odds with McDurmon, Gentry, DeMar, and most Dominionists. It also means he must now totally ignore, or mitigate the overwhelming imminence of the impending judgment of Babylon in Revelation.

poured out, and Frost's claim that God cannot be involved in history is false. Thus, by affirming the end of "sheolic" death, Frost inadvertently destroys his own claims and those of McDurmon as well.

Frost might seek to mitigate this argument by pointing out that the saints under the altar (Revelation 6) were no longer in Hades / Sheol. And I agree. But, this does not help Frost in any way.

While those under the altar were no longer in Sheol/ Hades, *they had patently not entered the MHP.* They were still in an "Intermediate State." They had not yet received their eternal kingdom reward; they had not yet been vindicated. Their reward and vindication would be at the Great Day of the Lord (Revelation 6:12f), when they would enter the New Creation promised to Abraham and the Worthies.

According to Jesus in Matthew 23, the vindication of all the blood of all the martyrs was to be judged and avenged in his generation in the judgment of Jerusalem (Matthew 23). So, for Frost to point to the souls under the altar as the victory over Sheol does not help him - it entraps him. The judgment of AD 70 had not yet taken place, thus, those souls had not yet been vindicated and rewarded by entrance into the MHP. *To be under the altar was not the full victory over Hades.* It was not to be in the MHP. That did not come until after the millennium when Hades was cast into the fire, per Revelation 20-22.

If Frost is correct to argue that Sheol has been destroyed this means that the millennium has ended. According to Revelation 20:10f Hades was not destroyed / overcome *until the end of the millennium.* Frost's claims are therefore specious, untenable and self-defeating. But, we return now to emphasize the unbroken chain of the "one hope" of the eschatological narrative.

The indisputable fact is that the Adamic problem was carried through Abraham, posited under and exacerbated by Torah, and it was to be "solved" at the end of Torah (1 Corinthians 15:54-56; Galatians 4).

Our point should be clear:

Paul said he had one hope of the resurrection.

That hope was the hope of Israel found in the law and the prophets.

He said that hope was the hope of the resurrection of the just and the unjust.

He said that hope was *about to be* fulfilled.

So, given these facts and the indisputable fact that Daniel 12 foretold the resurrection of *the just and the unjust at* the time of the destruction of the power of the holy people (AD 70) upon what basis would one argue that the resurrection of Acts 24 was not the resurrection foretold by Daniel 12?

Notice the direct correspondences:

The resurrection of Daniel 12 was the "hope of Israel."

The resurrection of Acts 24 was the hope of Israel.

Daniel 12 foretold the resurrection at the end of the age.

Acts 24 is patently the resurrection at the end of the age.

The prophecy of Daniel 12 would be fulfilled at the time of the judgment and destruction of Old Covenant Israel - in AD 70. When Paul spoke, that destruction was "about to be." It was "on the point of being."

The resurrection of Daniel would be the resurrection of the "just and the unjust."

The resurrection of Acts 24 would be the resurrection of the just and the unjust.

In my formal debate with Steve Gregg, (Denver, Co. 2013) I argued for the correspondence between Daniel 12 and Acts 24. Interestingly, Gregg concurred that Daniel 12 foretold the events of

AD 70. He also concurred that *mello*, with the infinitive, indicates imminence. However, he claimed that Acts 24 is about a "final" resurrection at the end of the current age. In response, I noted that AD 70 was near when Paul spoke the words in Acts 24. I noted that Daniel is the *only* OT prophecy that specifically foretold what Paul was anticipating. I noted that Paul was looking for the "about to be" resurrection of the "just and unjust" that Daniel foretold. In light of these facts, I asked Gregg how he could delineate between Daniel and Acts 24. He never offered a response.[118]

The pressing question is, given the perfect correspondences between Daniel and Acts 24, how would one go about delineating between these supposed two resurrections? How would one determine that Daniel foretold the corporate resurrection of the dead, corruptible body of Old Covenant Israel, transformed into the incorruptible body of Christ, but then, claim that Acts 24:14f must refer to the raising of decomposed, individual human corpses out of the ground? What is there about Acts 24 that demands the raising of corpses out of dirt?

Kenneth Gentry posted an article on the Internet commenting on Daniel 12. He posed the question: "Does Daniel teach that the eschatological, consummate resurrection occurs during the great tribulation in AD 70? No, he does not." He then proceeds to explain how Daniel 12 foretold the events of AD 70 and the resurrection of the corporate body of Israel into the body of Christ. (Of course, it should be noted that even in this scenario, the Tribulation and the resurrection are clearly inseparably linked). How does he delineate between Daniel and the "real" resurrection? He claims: "It appears that Daniel is drawing from the hope of the future, literal resurrection and applying it symbolically to the first century leading up to the tribulation in AD 70."[119]

---

[118] DVDs of that debate are available from my websites.

[119] You would be hard pressed to find a more glaring example of presuppositional theology than this. Gentry

So, Daniel believed in a future raising of corpses out of the dirt (But, where did he get that idea?) and somehow applied that physical resurrection spiritually to the corporate salvation of Israel in AD 70. We are supposed to see that the AD 70 resurrection foreshadowed the "real" resurrection of corpses. So, a "spiritual" resurrection foreshadowed a literal, physical resurrection; or, a future literal resurrection must be read backwards 2000 years to speak of a spiritual resurrection![120]

Former preterist Sam Frost once accepted the correspondence between Daniel and Acts 24. In the comment section of the article by Gentry, Frost offered a "critique" of the preterist hermeneutic he once espoused:

"Thus, please allow me to sum up the argument. First, since Acts 24 uses "just and unjust" and *"mello"* – then Acts 24 MUST be referring to Da 12.2 (first stated premise). Why? Because Da 12.2 uses "just and unjust" – supposedly (sic) the ONLY place where a resurrection of 'just and unjust' theme is used. Conclusion: Acts 24 must be referring to the "near" (*mello*) resurrection of Rev 20.11-15 (as well as Da 12.2); and this can be the ONLY resurrection

---

assumes, without giving a syllable of proof, the raising of human corpses out of the dust. Then, strangely, he claims that Daniel is drawing from that, to speak of the spiritual resurrection of the corporate body of Israel! Where is the evidence for this? Of course, Gentry fails to tell his audience how he has radically changed his views on Daniel. He fails to comment on how his views are at odds with the creeds. Gentry's article can be found here: http://postmillennialism.com/2012/03/daniel-12-tribulation-and-resurrection/#wwFIdYOUZSz1QDLK.99.

[120] See my book, *AD 70: A Shadow of the "Real" End?* for a thorough refutation of the claim that AD 70 was typological of the end of the current Christian age. The Dominionist eschatology depends, to a great degree on this idea yet, there is absolutely no proof for it.

fulfillment in the ENTIRE OT and NT. That's the Hyper Preterist argument." (All emphasis his).

As we noted above in response to Frost's ridicule of the time statements, *he gives not a syllable of evidence* to prove why the preterist hermeneutic is wrong. All he does is ridicule. This is hardly a scholarly way to deal with the argument and the logic. Ridicule is not refutation.

Frost says that as a true preterist, he argued that *mello* indicated the resurrection of Acts 24 was imminent. But, he says not a word about whether - or why - that is still valid.[121] No lexical evidence. No grammarian testimony to the contrary. No textual consideration. Nothing.

Frost admits that he once argued, "time determines nature" meaning that since the NT is so explicit and emphatic about the first century imminence of the Lord's coming and the resurrection that we must conform our concepts of the *nature* of the event with the stated *time* of fulfillment. He now rejects that principle. But he offered not a word to show how, or why, time statements are not legitimate exegetical and hermeneutical considerations. All he said was that preterists emphasize the Biblical time statements; *and that is true*. But, he gave no evidence for why that emphasis is wrong.

Frost says he argued that since Daniel 12 was the only specific prophecy of the resurrection of the "just and unjust" that this indicates the correspondence with Acts 24. But, he offered *not a*

---

[121] There are numerous websites that offer some excellent studies of the word *mello*. One can do a "Google" search and find a wealth of information. There is little justification for rejecting the imminence factor in the word. For just one website that investigates *mello*, see: http://www.biblicalfulfillment.org/id26.html. In fairness, we note that Frost did write an article attempting, *very weakly*, to explain away the imminence of *mello*. However, it appears that article has now been removed. I have been unable to find it following the link that I had.

word as to why we should not honor this fact. He did not offer other OT prophecies of the resurrection of the "just and unjust" that served as the source of Paul's resurrection doctrine. He didn't, because he can't.

And of course, Frost offered not a word of exegesis to explain the difference between the "resurrection to eternal life" in Daniel and the resurrection to eternal life that he posits at the so called end of time.

So, in other words, Frost, while a preterist, set forth a hermeneutic *that most scholars would recognize as sound, solid and logical, telling us that this is the preterist hermeneutic*. But he now rejects that hermeneutic *without giving a single exegetical or logical reason why*. That is less than convincing.

Consider these thoughts carefully and look closely again at the *perfect correspondence* between Daniel 12 and Acts 24.

The subject is the same - resurrection.✔

The subjects of the resurrection are the same: "the just and unjust."✔

The framework of the fulfillment of the hope of Israel is the same.✔

The timing is the same.✔

So, ask yourself the serious question: what is the *real evidence* for Gentry and Frost's attempt to apply those two texts to two totally different, disparate events, separated so far by 2000 years?

Daniel 12 patently does serve as the source of Paul's hope of the resurrection of the just and the unjust. Therefore, when one couples the fact that Daniel posited his resurrection prophecy at the end of Israel's covenant age with the fact that Paul said his resurrection hope was about to be fulfilled, this is powerful evidence indeed that Daniel 12 not only foretold the "final" resurrection, but, that it was in fact fulfilled in AD 70.

The correspondence between Daniel 12 and Acts 24:14-15 is perfect.

The subject is the same – resurrection.✔

The subjects of the resurrection are the same: "the just and unjust."✔

The framework of the fulfillment of the hope of Israel is the same.✔

The timing is the same.✔

There is, therefore, no justification for the claims of Gentry, Frost, et. al. to posit Daniel as AD 70 and Acts 24:14 as something totally different in time and nature from Daniel.

That is theological desperation.

Point #7

DANIEL 12 AND 1 CORINTHIANS 15

To my knowledge, there are no futurists who apply 1 Corinthians 15 *solely* to the events of AD 70. To do so would clearly be fatal to their futurist eschatology. As we have noted, both James Jordan and Joel McDurmon, in my debates with them, admitted that there was "a fulfillment" of 1 Corinthians 15 in AD 70.[122] Yet, they both nonetheless claimed that the "final" fulfillment of Corinthians lies in the future, at the end of the current age.

Of course, we can't help but comment again on how radical a departure this is from "historical, orthodox, Christianity" and the creeds. It is simply *stunning*!

While it is widely admitted and noted that the resurrection of 1 Corinthians 15 would be the fulfillment of Isaiah 25 and Hosea 13:14, it should be noted that lying behind Corinthians is also Daniel 9 and 12. We will focus here on the parallels between Daniel 12 and 1 Corinthians 15 which are numerous, specific and perfect. Take a look at the chart with the parallels and ask yourself, What is the difference between these two resurrection texts?

---

[122] Both men sought, desperately in my view, to escape the natural consequences of this admission by claiming that the events of AD 70 point to the final, ultimate fulfillment. When I challenged them to produce the contextual, exegetical evidence to support this historically unprecedented claim, neither man even attempted to do so. As I noted in the McDurmon debate, there is not one syllable in 1 Corinthians 15 to suggest another, greater fulfillment beyond the one to occur before all of Paul's audience died (1 Corinthians 15:50f).

Daniel 12	1 Corinthians 15
Hope of Israel	Paul's resurrection hope was nothing but the hope of Israel; "then shall be brought to pass the saying" (Isaiah 25 / Hosea 13/ Daniel 12)
Resurrection	Resurrection
Time of the end	Then comes the end
Some to eternal life	Some to eternal life
Eternal life	Incorruptibility
Kingdom	Kingdom
End of Torah / Israel	End of Torah

Paul is drawing directly from Daniel. Even though he quotes from Isaiah and Hosea, neither one of them mentions the, "time of the end," the resurrection to eternal life, entrance into the kingdom, etc..[123]

Let me make a few observations about some of these parallels.

---

[123] I would be the first to note that although these *specific words* are not used in Isaiah or Hosea, *the concepts and thoughts are absolutely present*. To the Hebraic mind, to mention resurrection was to include, among other things, temple, kingdom, Torah, eternal life, etc.. So, I am not employing McDurmon's hermeneutic in which the absence of specific words means the absence of a doctrine. I am simply pointing out that since Daniel does use the very words employed by Paul, that this indicates Paul's dependence on, or at the least, his reference to, Daniel.

✶ The resurrection as the hope of Israel

This is one of the greatest oversights in Amillennial and Dominionist circles. I have noted how in my formal debates with Amillennialists and Dominionists they have overtly denied that their eschatological expectation is based on and taken from the Old Covenant promises made to Israel.

The utter inconsistency of the Dominionist camp was graphically illustrated in my debate with McDurmon. I asked him when all of God's OT promises made to Old Covenant Israel were fulfilled and His covenant relationship with Israel terminated. He said that would not be until the "physical resurrection" at the end of the current age. However, he repeatedly tried to divorce the "final resurrection"– as the final solution to the Adamic death curse – from Israel, claiming it was not the focus of Paul's true eschatology.

So, on the one hand he affirmed the abiding validity of Israel as a covenant people – which of course, demands the continuance of the resurrection promises to the very end – but then said that those resurrection promises to Israel were not related to the final resurrection![124] This failure or refusal to focus on Israel and her promises is a fatal error in eschatological and "gospel" studies.

Wright takes note of this emphasis on Israel in Paul's theology: "His message for the world was the message that the God of Abraham, Isaac and Jacob had done at last what he had promised, providing the world its rightful Lord... Paul did not have to turn his back on engagement in the wider world in order to reaffirm his

---

[124] Of course, McDurmon's claim creates a "Two Covenant" Doctrine. God's Old Covenant with Israel remains valid until the end of the Christian age, but, at the same time, the Gospel Covenant is in effect. McDurmon would reject this, but logically, it is demanded by his own argument in our debate. It is logically impossible to affirm the continuance of God's covenant with Israel until the "end of time" and the gospel as well, without logically demanding the reality of a Two Covenant situation.

fundamental Jewishness. Genesis, Exodus, Isaiah and the Psalms, to look no further than some of Paul's favorite books, already affirm the whole world is to be claimed by Israel's God and is addressed by him precisely *through* what he is doing in and through and for Israel. ...Paul's engagement with his pagan context is precisely those deep-rooted Jewish understanding, just as the proper angle from which to examine those deep Jewish roots is his sense that now, in the messianic age, it is time to confront the world of the gentiles." (His emp., 2013, Vol I, 46f[125]).

Later in the same work, he offers this:

> "Insofar as Paul refers from time to time to Abraham he is simply a 'predecessor,' someone in the scriptures who had faith (or, the right kind of faith). Instead, I propose and shall now argue, that Paul's entire theology gains enormously in coherence and impetus if we see that he affirmed, even though he radically redrew, the particular second -Temple Jewish narrative,...; the story of God's people, of Abraham's people, as the people through whom the creator was intending to rescue His creation. This makes sense of so many passages in Paul's letters that it ought not to be open to doubt that Paul had this narrative in mind gave it substantially the same meaning it had within his native Judaism– except of course, for the radical re-description to which he had come through the shocking and totally unexpected way in which the story had in fact reached its denouement. But to

---

[125] See also Wright's presentation at Fuller Theological Seminary, found on YouTube: http://www.youtube.com/watch?v=NwXBo9Jvkb4.

> read the same story with new eyes as a result of its surprising ending is still to read the same story."[126]

The point is that the Abrahamic promises stand as the foundational key to understanding the Biblical narrative of theology and eschatology.[127] We cannot read the "story of Israel" in isolation from those Abrahamic promises. Nor should we read the story of the eternal Abrahamic inheritance into a supposed end of the Christian age, when Paul is emphatic that the inheritance belonged to the end of the Mosaic Covenant.

As Nanos correctly noted: " Judaism (i.e. Torah, DKP) was a faith which carried within itself the seeds of its own transformation. So Luke could console his fellow-Christians with the message that it was not they, but Jews still attending the synagogue who had abandoned the God of Abraham, Isaac and Jacob, of Moses and of David."[128]

This idea is found in Romans 3:21 where Paul said Torah itself testified of the time when righteousness "apart from the law" would

---

[126] N. T. Wright, *Paul and the Faithfulness of God*, Vol. I, (Minneapolis, Fortress, 2013)495.

[127] Space forbids a full discussion of the important Greek word *kleronomia* and its cognates. However, it needs to be noted that no other word carried so rich connotations in the story of Abraham, Israel and the eschatological consummation. It is related to the New Creation / resurrection promise of Hebrews 11. It related to the inheritance of "the land" in all of its consummated implications. It relates to the eschatological consummation (1 Peter 1:3f). So, when Paul said the inheritance was to come at the end of Torah, this is, in the purest sense *Torah to Telos*. It is at the same time a falsification of all futurist views that posit reception of the inheritance at the end of the Christian age.

[128] Mark Nanos, *The Mystery of Romans*, (Minneapolis, Fortress, 1996)268+, n. 83.

arrive. So, even Torah, which foretold the time of the fulfillment of the Abrahamic promises – which of course included the arrival of "the faith" and justification by the faith of Abraham (Galatians 3:6f) – posited that fulfillment at the time of the passing of Torah. This cannot be over-emphasized. Yet, all three futurist eschatologies all but ignore this critical and undeniable fact. Look closer at the Abrahamic Inheritance.

Abraham was promised the heavenly father land. He was promised the city, heavenly Zion. He was promised the better resurrection (Hebrews 11). These are the elements of the Abrahamic inheritance. Where do all futurist eschatologies posit the ultimate reception of those blessings? *At the end of the current Christian age.* But, that is *not* where Paul posited reception of the Abrahamic promises.

The Abrahamic promises - inclusive of the New Creation per Hebrews 11 - were given to him *prior to the creation of the nation of Israel* and *prior to the giving of Torah*. However, those promises became the "hope of Israel," assimilated into Torah and became part and parcel of the Abrahamic story. This is why Paul said in Galatians 3:

> "Brethren, I speak in the manner of men: Though it is only a man's covenant, yet if it is confirmed, no one annuls or adds to it. Now to Abraham and his Seed were the promises made. He does not say, "And to seeds," as of many, but as of one, "And to your Seed," who is Christ. And this I say, that the law, which was four hundred and thirty years later, cannot annul the covenant that was confirmed before by God in Christ, that it should make the promise of no effect. For if the inheritance is of the law, it is no longer of promise; but God gave it to Abraham by promise. What purpose then does the law serve? It was added because of transgressions, till the Seed should come to whom the promise was made; and it was appointed through angels by the hand of a mediator. Now a mediator does not mediate for one only, but God is one. Is the law

then against the promises of God? Certainly not! For if there had been a law given which could have given life, truly righteousness would have been by the law. But the Scripture has confined all under sin, that the promise by faith in Jesus Christ might be given to those who believe. But before faith came, we were kept under guard by the law, kept for the faith which would afterward be revealed" (15-23).

Notice not just the temporal priority, but the priority in importance that Paul places on the Abrahamic Covenant. First came the promise to bless the world through Abraham. (And keep in mind that according to Hebrews 11 that inheritance blessing was the nothing but the resurrection (v. 35). Later, added to that covenant promise, was Torah. But Paul is emphatic, that while Torah was good and served a divine purpose, *the inheritance of the Abrahamic promises was not to be through or by means of the Law*. Israel was kept under Torah *until* the time of the inheritance. This is, *prima facie*, *Torah to Telos. If the reception of the Abrahamic inheritance was the telos, the eschatological goal, then Paul affirmed in the clearest of terms that Torah would stand valid until the time of the inheritance.*

This is fatal to the views of Frost and McDurmon, and all who claim that Abraham must be raised from biological death to rule on earth. After all, the inheritance that Paul is discussing is not the limited land promise. That promise had been fulfilled long before, as we have demonstrated. No, *this inheritance is the heavenly city, the heavenly country and the better resurrection*. This is the promise that Abraham would "inherit the world" (Romans 4:13). This is the promise that in Abraham's Seed all the nations of the world would be blessed (Galatians 3:6-14). The fact that Paul undeniably posits the reception of that Abrahamic inheritance *at the end of Torah - not at the end of the Christian age -* demands that if Abraham and the Worthies have not entered into the New Creation inheritance, *via resurrection,* then Torah, every jot and every tittle, remains valid.

In a time-line then, we find Abraham and YHVH's promises to him. We find both the limited land promises and the "ultimate" land promise. We then have the founding of the nation of Israel, through whom and to whom the limited land promise was fulfilled. But, the "ultimate" promise was carried forward, with Torah as the "guardian" until the time of the inheritance of those Abrahamic promises (Galatians 4). But then, just as Paul said, Israel was only to be kept under Torah *until the time of the inheritance* – at the end of Torah – and the full arrival of "the faith" (Galatians 3:24f). At that time, Torah and her children, having served her divine purpose, would be cast out. The true children of Abraham – inclusive of the righteous remnant, but also anyone of faith - would receive the inheritance (Galatians 4:22f) bringing to a full reality the promise to Abraham, "In you and your seed shall all nations of the earth be blessed."

YHVH never intended for Torah to be the means of accomplishing or fulfilling those eschatological promises. Wright correctly apprises the "problem" of Torah itself:

> "We thus find Torah apparently preventing the Israel purpose from going ahead; the curse of Torah apparently prevents the intended Abrahamic blessing from reaching the world and brings wrath on God's people themselves, magnifying their 'trespass' so that the Adamic nature they share with the rest of humanity is writ large." (2013, Faithfulness, Vol. I & II, 507).

Torah became the "ministration of death" (2 Corinthians 3:5f). It was "the strength of sin" (1 Corinthians 15:55f). Neither perfection - or the inheritance - was through Torah (Hebrews 7:10f), but, would come through the New Covenant when the Old passed away (Hebrews 8:13). This is, in truth, what Daniel 12 affirms.

Let me put it like this:

The resurrection to eternal life - the Abrahamic promise of the "better resurrection" - would be when the power of the holy people was completely shattered (Daniel 12:2-7).

The power of the holy people was nothing less than Torah - the ground and basis of Israel's relationship with YHVH.

Therefore, the resurrection to eternal life, the reception of the Abrahamic promise of the "better resurrection" would be at the end of Torah.

This is quintessentially Torah To Telos! Since the Abrahamic Covenant promises of the New Creation and resurrection were to be given at the end of Torah, then if Torah was nailed to the cross, the resurrection of the dead and the New Creation had to have arrived at that time. While there is no doubt that the Abrahamic Covenant promises were initiated through the cross, there is likewise no doubt that the full arrival of those promises were to come at the parousia of Christ, to bring salvation (Hebrews 9:28*)*. And that was to be in "a very, very little while" (Hebrews 10:37).

What this means is that when one affirms a future resurrection they are in effect affirming the abiding validity of Torah – every bit of it. This means that when McDurmon maintained the abiding validity of the Mosaic Covenant until a proposed physical resurrection, he was in fact demanding that every jot and every tittle of Torah remains valid. Of course, he denied this in our debate, claiming - in direct violation of the emphatic words of Jesus in Matthew 5 - that *some* of the Law was removed, but some remains.

Torah - all of it - was to endure until the time of the inheritance of the Abrahamic promise - *Torah to Telos*. In Galatians, Paul did not say that some of the law was to remain until the time of the Inheritance. He simply stated that "the law" was the guardian until that time. The Abrahamic promise / inheritance was the resurrection. There was not to be an "interim" New Covenant age of waiting on the fulfillment of YHVH's promises to Abraham and the promise of the resurrection.

What futurism does is strange indeed. It posits *two ages* between Abraham and the fulfillment of the promise of the resurrection (the inheritance) that he longed for. According to the futurist paradigm, God gave the resurrection promise to Abraham (which itself was the promise hearkening back to Genesis). Then, 430 years after making that covenant with Abraham, YHVH gave Torah to Israel. Even though Paul is clear that the inheritance was to come at the end of Torah we are told by all futurist eschatologies that at the end of Torah, God did not give the inheritance, but rather gave the New Covenant. And now, under the New Covenant, we are still waiting for the *Telos*, the reception of the Abrahamic inheritance. This raises the question of Why?

Paul tells us that if the inheritance promised to Abraham - righteousness and *life* - could have been given through and by "law" then it would have been received by means of Torah (Galatians 3:20-21). But, Torah could not deliver from, "the law of sin and death" (Romans 8:1-3). So, if the Abrahamic inheritance could not be given by means of Torah, due to the ineffectiveness of Torah, then why is the Abrahamic Covenant not received by means of the Gospel of Christ, which came when Torah, (which prevented that inheritance from being received) was removed? In other words, if the inheritance was not received due to the weakness of Torah to give that inheritance, what is wrong with the Gospel since we ostensibly have to wait until the end of the gospel age to receive the Abrahamic promises?

So, Torah was "good"; it was *really* good at condemning man. But, God did not want to condemn man. He wanted to give man, through Abraham, the New Creation / better resurrection. As we have seen, in Galatians, Paul posits reception of the inheritance, not at the end of the Christian age, but *at the end of Torah*. This is where our investigation of Daniel 12 enters.

Daniel 12 foretold the resurrection to eternal life. Is this not the Abrahamic "better resurrection"? If it isn't, what is it? And if it is, then it is abundantly clear, as we have seen repeatedly, that Daniel posits reception of the Abrahamic resurrection promise at the time, "when the power of the holy people is completely shattered." This is Matthew 8:11 and agrees perfectly with Paul in Galatians - the Abrahamic Covenant promise of life and righteousness would be at the end of Torah. This is devastating to all futurist paradigms.

Every futurist view says that Torah - which prevented reception of the Abrahamic inheritance - ended long ago. In spite of the fact that Paul - and Daniel 12 - are clear that reception of the "better resurrection" and the New Creation anticipated by Abraham was to be at the end of Torah, they tell us we are still waiting for the reception of God's promises to Abraham and that will not happen *until the end of the Gospel age*. This is what Wright and others affirm when they speak of a future physical, renovated earth.[129]

The idea that YHVH removed Torah yet did not bring to realization that Abrahamic promise of the resurrection (i.e the inheritance) is specious. This is why we can confidently affirm that Daniel 12 foretold the "final" resurrection, the fulfillment of God's covenant promises to Abraham. Daniel 12:2 is the promise of eternal life – which is in no way different from the heavenly inheritance and resurrection of Hebrews 11 – and that promise would be fulfilled, "when the power of the holy people is completely shattered" (v. 7). Torah would endure until the *Telos*.

---

[129] See for instance Middleton, (2014, 71), who says, "When we attend to the basic thrust and movement of the biblical plot, it becomes abundantly clear that eschatological redemption consists of nothing other than the renewal of human cultural life on earth"). This raises a serious question. If, as Wright, Middleton, Pate and a host of similar minded men affirm, the "age to come" and the redemption has already begun, then why don't we see the beginning of the restoration of physical Eden? Why don't we have better "bugs, slugs and mosquitoes" to use one of my favorite terms. Why do we not see the human soma taking on the form of immortality? It is illogical to say that the restoration of "all things" has begun, yet to then say it is not necessary that we see radical changes in the earth - and man.

Whenever and whereever we posit the end of Israel's covenant relationship with YHVH, whether at the cross or AD 70 and yet affirm a yet future eschatology, we are forced, as witnessed by the quotes from Riddlebarger, Boettner, etc., to create another "New Testament," "New" eschatology that is foreign to and unknown to the Biblical writers.

The fact that both Daniel and Paul undeniably foresaw the resurrection as the fulfillment of Israel's promises (i.e. Abraham's promises incorporated into Israel's history) is *prima facie* falsification of all futurist eschatologies.[130]

✳ **The resurrection at "the end"**

Dominionists and many Amillennialists admit that there was "an end" in AD 70 and that it was "the end of the age."[131] But of course, they claim that the "real" end is the termination of the Christian age. They are forced to create two ends, of two ages. Worse, they are forced to affirm the end of what the Bible says is *endless* – the Christian age (Ephesians 3:20-21; Hebrews 12:27-28; Revelation 11:17f).

✳ **The resurrection to "eternal life"**

The Amillennialists and Dominionists have a *severe* problem here. Daniel said that in the resurrection that is the focus of his prophecy, *eternal life would be given*. So, if the Dominionists affirm - as we have shown that they do – that Daniel 12 was fulfilled in AD 70,

---

[130] The Dispensationalists emphasize Israel's key role in the end times. However, they join with the other two futurist schools in either denying or seeking to mitigate the first century imminence of the consummation of Israel's promises.

[131] See my book, *AD 70: A Shadow of the "Real" End?*, for a revealing listing of the eschatological tenets that the Dominionists admit occurred in AD 70. This includes the time of the Wedding, the (a) resurrection, the (a) parousia, the (an) end of the age, etc.!

then the question must be asked: what was the nature, what was the form, of the eternal life that was given to "the dead" when Daniel 12 was fulfilled?

Here is what I mean. The Dominionists as well as some Amillennialists who posit fulfillment of Daniel in AD 70, believe that believers now have eternal life by faith and that upon death they enter directly into heaven.[132]

Greg Beale says John 5:24-29 sees the resurrection of the saints predicted in Daniel 12:2 as "inaugurated in Jesus' ministry." (*Theology*, 2011, 210f, n. 41). Well then, what "part" of man currently enjoys eternal life? I ask this question because it is more than troublesome for those affirming the fulfillment of Daniel 12 and yet, they then turn around and say that eternal life is somehow, someway, off in the far distant, unknown future.

The Dominionists and Amillennialists widely believe that man possesses, already, *an eternal soul / spirit*. This is taught in the Creeds:

"The bodies of men, after death, return to dust to see corruption; but their souls (which neither die nor sleep), having an immortal subsistence, immediately return to God who gave them. The souls of the righteous, being then made perfect in holiness, are received into the highest heavens, where they behold the face of God in light and glory, waiting for the full redemption of their bodies; and the souls of the wicked are cast into hell, where they remain in torments and utter darkness, reserved to the judgment of the great day.

---

[132] On the reverse side of that coin are those Amillennialists who argue that we do not have eternal life now, except in promise, because if we possessed eternal life now, there could be no heaven and, we could not lose that life. This was affirmed by Michael Hatcher, in 2016, at the Bellview church of Christ lectureship. (You can Google that). Such illogical, unscriptural thinking is actually embarrassing, but it is still dominant in the fellowship in which I was raised.

Besides these two places for souls separated from their bodies, the Scripture acknowledgeth none."[133]

Well, if man's spirit is eternal, does it not possess "eternal life"?[134] And if, as Seriah claims, a person does not have to be resurrected to go to heaven, (1999, 167) what need is there for a future raising of corpses out of the ground? After all, the Confession just cited says the soul – the eternal soul - is already made perfect and is received into the highest heaven at death. While the Confession says there is more that must be done, this raises the question of *why*?[135]

If man's soul is already made perfect upon death and goes to the highest heaven,[136] then what "eternal life" was given in the

---

[133] The Westminster Confession Chapter 32 - "Of the State of Man After Death of the Resurrection of the Dead."

[134] Is the eternal life of Daniel "unending (quantitatively) life," or is it eternal life (qualitatively)? The Dominionists and Amillennialists are forced to basically redefine "eternal life" in Daniel by their affirmation that eternal life was given in AD 70. And yet, that very "redefinition" has tremendous theological implications.

[135] And take note that the Confession also says the wicked are already in hell! But if this is so, they most assuredly have been judged. They have received eternal damnation. Do they really need for their corpses to be raised in order to experience hell on a fuller, deeper level? This is all but ludicrous.

[136] Martin Luther vehemently denied the view espoused in the Confession: "As for the popular notion that the souls of the righteous have the full enjoyment of heaven prior to the resurrection, Luther whimsically remarked, "It would take a foolish soul to desire its body when it was already in heaven!" (D. Martin Luthers Werke, ed. Tischreden (Weimar, 1912-1921), p.5534, cited by Althaus, op. cit, p.417). He said further: "Now, if one should say that Abraham's soul lives with

resurrection of AD 70, in fulfillment of Daniel? It cannot be eternal (unending) life given to the soul, *for man already possesses that.* So, if man, *already in possession of "eternal life"* was *then given* eternal life in AD 70, does this not demand that man's "body" was given eternal life in AD 70? The implications of that are *stunning*! But we do not have space to develop this.

Daniel 12 and 1 Corinthians 15 spoke of eternal life, incorruptibility and immortality, being given at the resurrection at the time of the end. When the Dominionists and Amillennialists say Daniel was fulfilled, but we are still awaiting fulfillment of 1 Corinthians 15, they thereby posit a doctrine of two resurrections of the dead, two resurrections to eternal life. But for that, there is simply no Biblical support. These are empty claims with no exegetical support.

✷ Resurrection and the Kingdom

Daniel foretold the resurrection to eternal life and entrance into the kingdom (v. 2, 3). This is perfectly consistent with his prediction that at the time of the end, in the days of the fourth beast, the (persecuted) saints would be given the kingdom that would never pass away, never be destroyed (7:21f).

Likewise, Paul posited entrance into the everlasting kingdom at the resurrection, at the time of the end.

Keep in mind that the Dominionists openly say that Abraham, Isaac and Jacob – along with the prophets - entered into the *eternal inheritance of the kingdom* in AD 70. As we have seen, entrance into the kingdom for Abraham and the Worthies was entrance into the everlasting kingdom, in fulfillment of Isaiah 25, *the source of Paul's resurrection doctrine of 1 Corinthians 15.*

God but his body is dead, this distinction is rubbish. I will attack it. One must say, The whole Abraham, the whole man, shall live. The other way you tear off a part of Abraham and say, "It lives." (Table Talk, cited by Althaus, op. cit., p.447.)

So, Abraham and the Worthies entered into the everlasting kingdom – receiving their eternal inheritance – via resurrection to eternal life in AD 70 (Matthew 8:11). This resurrection to eternal kingdom life was in fulfillment of Isaiah 25 / 1 Corinthians 15. How then, in the name of reason can one claim that Daniel 12 is different from 1 Corinthians 15 – the final resurrection?

Is entrance into the kingdom as promised by Daniel 12 a different kingdom from that which was to be given the saints at the coming of YHVH in Daniel 7? Remember that the Dominionists, at least many of them, apply the coming of the one "like the Son of Man" in Daniel 7 – in vindication of the martyred saints – to AD 70, as we have shown.

If the coming of the one like the Son of Man in Daniel 7 is the time of the entrance into the kingdom of Daniel 12 (at the resurrection, of course) then one wonders if that is a different kingdom to be entered at the resurrection in 1 Corinthians 15. There is not a syllable of textual evidence to support such a dichotomization.

So, entrance into the kingdom in Daniel 7 was to be in the days of Rome and no later than that. Entrance into the kingdom in Daniel 12 was to be at the resurrection, when Israel was destroyed – which occurred in the days of Rome. And, entrance into the kingdom, at the resurrection was to be in Paul's generation: "Brethren, I tell you a mystery, we shall not all sleep" (1 Corinthians 15:51).[137]

✴ Resurrection and the End of Torah

In numerous formal debates, I have asked my Amillennial and Postmillennial opponents: "What was 'the law' that Paul defined as

---

[137] Other than presuppositional theology, there is nothing to suggest that Paul was using a generic "royal we" in 1 Corinthians 15. Unless the context, not preconceived ideas about the *nature* of the resurrection, demand that we view that personal pronoun in a generic timeless manner, then even the normal usage of the "royal we" is to refer to the speaker / writer and his contemporary audience.

'the strength of sin' in 1 Corinthians 15:55-56?" Almost invariably my opponents have responded: "The Law of Moses." And of course, Biblically this is undeniable. Yet, that undeniable, almost universally admitted fact, is fatal to any futurist view of 1 Corinthians 15 and any attempt to delineate between Daniel and Corinthians.

Let me put it like this:

The resurrection of 1 Corinthians 15 would be when "the law" that was "the strength of sin" was overcome and put away (1 Corinthians 15:55-56).

But "the law" that was the strength of sin, was Torah, the Law of Moses.

Therefore, the resurrection of 1 Corinthians 15 would be when Torah, the Law of Moses, was overcome and put away.[138]

Of course, this means that if the resurrection of 1 Corinthians 15 has not taken place, then the Law of Moses, every jot and every tittle, is still valid and binding today.

Notice - again - that the resurrection of Daniel 12 was to be fulfilled, "When the power of the holy people is completely shattered" (v. 7). This can be no other time than AD 70, when Torah came to an end. God's covenant relationship with Israel – her only true "power"- was broken, at the time when the people ate the flesh of their neighbor (Zechariah 11:8-9). This was in fulfillment, the consummate fulfillment, of the Law of Blessings and Cursings (Deuteronomy 28:53-57).

---

[138] I have yet to have a debate opponent give a substantive response to this argument. The normal "response" has been to either totally ignore it, or to say it can't be true because the resurrection of corpses out of the ground has not taken place. This is not "argument"; it is desperation.

Paul affirmed but one resurrection hope – the hope of Abraham carried through Israel and iterated in Moses, the Law and the prophets. That promise belonged to Israel "after the flesh" (Romans 9:3). Invariably, Paul and all other Bible writers, posited that resurrection at the end of God's covenant dealings with Israel. This is what we find in the comparison of Daniel 12 and 1 Corinthians 15.

The fact that both Daniel and 1 Corinthians 15 posit the resurrection *at the end of Torah* should be the definitive proof – for anyone – that the two texts foretold the same resurrection. This falsifies all attempts to make the resurrection of Daniel a "typological foreshadowing" of the "real" resurrection at the supposed end of human history.

Having established the perfect correspondence between Daniel 12 and 1 Corinthians 15, take a look now at the correlation between 1 Corinthians 15 and Revelation 11:15f. Why is this important? It is because Revelation 11 is widely admitted by the Dominionists to apply to the "resurrection" of Daniel 12 – i.e. AD 70.

1 Corinthians 15	Revelation 10-11
Resurrection	✔
Seventh (Last) trumpet	✔
Kingdom	✔
immortality	✔
Fulfillment of Israel's promises	✔
Eternal Inheritance	✔
End of Torah	✔

We have already documented how *many* Dominionists admit that Revelation 10-11 was fulfilled in the events of the close of Israel's age. Those same Postmillennialists see a direct connection between Daniel 12 and Revelation 10-11. This being the case, how can the connection between 1 Corinthians 15 be denied? How many times must scripture describe, define and delineate the topic of the resurrection before we as students honor what it is saying? And, if we are going to claim that there are different resurrections in view in these texts, is it not our responsibility to prove that case?

It has been my experience, in both formal debate, in written debate and in numerous private discussions that such evidence is never given. It is always simple assertion. But assertion – many times just ridicule – does not constitute proof. Appeals to the historical doctrine of the church does not prove anything. Arguments based on creeds amount to nothing more than traditionalism.

So, what is the substantive, textual difference between the resurrection event in 1 Corinthians and Revelation 10-11?

Is it mere *coincidence* that the resurrection of Revelation occurs at the seventh, trumpet, which is the "last trumpet?"

Is the everlasting kingdom of 1 Corinthians 15 a different kingdom from that in Revelation 11:15f, which will endure "forever and forever"?

The resurrection of 1 Corinthians 15 occurs at the end of Torah, as we have seen. The resurrection in Revelation 11 occurs in direct connection with the destruction of the city, "Where the Lord was slain" (11:8). So, where are we to draw the distinction?

The resurrection of 1 Corinthians 15 occurs in fulfillment of the Old Covenant promises to Israel. Likewise, the resurrection at the seventh trumpet is in fulfillment of, "the mystery of God foretold by the prophets" (10:7).

In light of the previous point, it is undeniable that the resurrection in Revelation 11 is the fulfillment of God's promises to Israel – since it clearly echoes Daniel 12. This means it is parallel with 1

Corinthians 15 that would be in fulfillment of Daniel, Isaiah 25 and Hosea 13 – the hope of Israel.

Note again how Revelation 11:15f so clearly echoes Daniel 7 as well. The motif of martyr vindication is obvious in both passages. The martyrs are vindicated at the judgment of the persecutor. That vindication is, per Daniel, in the days of the Roman empire and in Revelation 11 it is at the judgment of the city where the Lord was slain.

Not only does Revelation 11 echo Daniel 7, it also clearly reflects Daniel 12. Beale recognized this and made the following remarkable comment: "The OT and Jewish writings expected the judgment of all dead unbelievers at the conclusion of history (Daniel 12:2). The parallel of Revelation 20:12-13 makes this interpretation explicit" (1999, 614).

So, according to Beale, there is no difference between the resurrection in each of these texts. Of course, what Beale *completely ignores*, or overlooks, is that both Daniel 12 and Revelation 11 undeniably posit their predictions of the resurrection at the time of judgment of Israel, *which demands that Revelation 20 must also be seen as fulfilled at that time.*[139] Neither Daniel, Corinthians or Revelation speak of the end of time. Needless to say, this is fatal to his Amillennial view. It is also devastating to the Dominionist eschatology.

So, the Postmillennialists admit that Daniel 12 and Revelation 10-11 were fulfilled in AD 70. However, in order to maintain their

---

[139] Dr. Beale, (along with Kenneth Gentry and three other speakers) was on the dias at Criswell College in October of 2012. He presented the Amillennial view of the Millennium. I presented the Preterist view. Although the sponsors of the symposium specifically told all of the speakers to engage with each other where we differed, Beale (nor any of the others speakers) never engaged my comments at all. I even cited Beale in support of my position. A CD of that presentation is available from me.

futurist, literalistic, physical and earthly kingdom theology, they then turn around and claim that Revelation 20 must be a different judgment, a different end of another age, a different resurrection, even a different set of martyrs, from that set forth in Daniel and Revelation 10-11. But this is clearly untenable.

Notice that Daniel was told that the time of the resurrection would be the fulfillment of "all of these things" inclusive of the Tribulation, the resurrection, the end of the age and the kingdom. One cannot get more "eschatological" than that! All would be fulfilled at the destruction of Old Covenant Jerusalem.

In Revelation 10-11 we are told that in the sounding of the seventh trumpet the mystery of God foretold in the prophets would be fulfilled. This is the fulfillment of all prophecy, is it not? And it would take place when the city "where the Lord was slain" was destroyed.

It is all but universally admitted that the resurrection of 1 Corinthians 15, at the sounding of the seventh (last) trumpet when the mystery of God foretold in the prophets would be fulfilled, *is the time of the fulfillment of all prophecy.*

Then, we have the Great Judgment of Revelation 20 which, again, is the resurrection of 1 Corinthians that would take place *at the end of Torah.*

We should not miss the fact that *just like Daniel 12*, the resurrection of Revelation 20 also takes place as the climax of the Great Tribulation. At the end of the millennium we have the release of Satan and the great battle of "the war." This significant term is taken directly from Isaiah 3 and Daniel 9, which both posit the Day of the Lord as the time of the vindication of the martyrs. It is the time of the consummation of YHVH's covenant dealings with Israel.

Beale is correct therefore, to see the direct connection between Daniel 12 and Revelation 20. However, his failure to connect the

Great Tribulation - and thus the resurrection - with the first century judgment of Old Covenant Israel at the end of her age is misplaced.

Notice Luke 21:22. As Jesus predicted the impending judgment and destruction of Jerusalem, he said: "These be the days of vengeance when all things that are written must be fulfilled." This is a definitive and comprehensive statement that must be honored. Take note of some key facts.

#1 - As we have shown, Daniel 12, 1 Corinthians 15, Revelation 10-11 and, since Revelation 20 is the same as 1 Corinthians 15, then all of these texts posit the resurrection at the time of Israel's final judgment.

#2 - All of these texts either explicitly or implicitly teach that all prophecy would be fulfilled at the time of the resurrection and judgment of which they speak.

#3 - Jesus, in Luke 21:22 is speaking of the very time foretold by Daniel 12, 1 Corinthians 15 / Revelation 10-12 / Revelation 20 – the time of the end of Old Covenant Israel. It is the *Telos*, the eschatological goal.

#4 - Jesus emphatically said that in that judgment, "all things written must be fulfilled." This agrees perfectly with what those other prophecies said.

Kenneth Gentry has felt the pressure and power of Luke 21:22 and wrote an article in which he claimed that the preterist application of Jesus' words is misguided and wrong.

Gentry claims to make "one deadly argument" against the true preterist take on Luke 21:22. He says:

> "The grammar of the passage (Luke 21, DKP) limits the declaration. Jesus speaks of 'all things which are written' by employing a perfect passive participle: 'gegrammena' ('having been written'). This refers to prophecies already written - when he speaks in AD 30. Yet we know that more

> prophecies arise later in the New Testament revelation.
>
> Once again we see a limitation on Jesus' statement. Furthermore, technically it does not even refer to any prophecy which Christ speaks. For these are not prophecies that have already been written. That being the case, the final resurrection (for instance) is outside of this declaration (Jn 5:28-29). Thus, Jesus is referring to all things written in the Old Testament. At this stage of redemptive history those are the only prophecies that had already been written."[140]

I must confess that *I could hardly believe what I was reading* from Dr. Gentry. I wrote a response to Gentry and will give an excerpt here.

"I will only make two points in response to Dr. Gentry's amazing argument.

Argument #1– The New Testament prophecies of the resurrection are simply the reiteration of the Old Testament prophecies *(things already written in AD 30).*

Proof of this argument: I need only refer to the words of Paul. The apostle affirmed in the most unambiguous manner that his doctrine of the resurrection was *nothing* but that found in the Old Testament, i.e. *in that which had already been written.*

Acts 24:14-15: "But this I confess to you, that according to the Way which they call a sect, so I worship the God of my fathers, believing all things which are written in the Law and in the Prophets. I have hope in God, which they themselves also accept, that there will be a resurrection of the dead, both of the just and the unjust."

---

[140] Gentry's comments can be found in his book, *He Shall Have Dominion*, (2009, 542f).

Paul said his doctrine of the resurrection of the dead, for which he was on trial, was found in Moses and the Law and the prophets. That certainly qualifies as that which was written before AD 30.

Acts 26:21-23 – "Having therefore obtained help of God, I continue unto this day, witnessing both to small and great, saying none other things than those which the prophets and Moses did say should come: That Christ should suffer that he should be the first that should rise from the dead should shew light unto the people to the Gentiles."

Paul said he preached nothing, *nothing* but the hope of Israel found in Moses and the prophets. *Do you catch the power of that?*

Paul taught of the resurrection of the dead.

But Paul did not preach anything but the hope of Israel found in Moses and the prophets.

Therefore, the doctrine of the resurrection of the dead was found in Moses and the prophets.

So, the resurrection hope expressed by the New Testament writers was nothing other than a reiteration of what had already been written long ago in the Old Testament scriptures! This is *fatal* to Gentry's eschatology and theology and it is irrefutable.

You cannot truthfully say that the New Testament prophecies of the resurrection are not grounded in and based on the Old Covenant prophecies. This is to deny Paul who said he preached *nothing but the hope of Israel found in Moses and the prophets*. 1 Corinthians 15 is not different from Isaiah 25 or Hosea 13:14 or Daniel 12, for Paul says that when the resurrection occurred, it would be the fulfillment of those prophecies. To say 1 Corinthians 15 is the *explication* of those prophecies is not the same as saying that Corinthians is different from those prophecies.

You cannot say that all Old Testament prophecies were fulfilled at the AD 70 parousia of Christ, therefore, without admitting to the fulfillment of all New Testament eschatology. There is no "new" eschatology in the New Testament. *All New Testament eschatology is the anticipation of the imminent fulfillment of Old Testament promises. Period.* This falsifies Gentry's specious argument.

So, consider what this does for Dr. Gentry:

All Old Testament prophecy would be fulfilled by the time of and in the events of the fall of Jerusalem in AD 70 (Kenneth Gentry).

But the Old Testament predicted the general resurrection of the dead (Gentry applies Isaiah 26 to the end of time).

Therefore, the general resurrection of the dead occurred in the events of the fall of Jerusalem in AD 70.

This point alone destroys Gentry's attempt at refuting Covenant Eschatology. And, notice how Gentry's admission on Luke 21:22 impacts another key eschatological text, one that historically is all but foundational to Postmillennialism, and that is Romans 11:25-27.

Gentry believes that in Romans 11:25f Paul was anticipating a yet future time, when "all Israel" will be saved at the parousia (2009, 254). Yet, Paul's expectation of the salvation of Israel was that it would be the fulfillment *of Isaiah 27, Isaiah 59, Jeremiah 31, and Daniel 12* - i.e. Old Covenant prophecies. Yet, Gentry says all OT prophecy was fulfilled by AD 70! Thus, Romans 11:25f was fulfilled in AD 70. Once again, Dr. Gentry has entrapped himself in his desperate attempt to refute Covenant Eschatology.[141]

Argument #2 – I will gladly accept Dr. Gentry's own summary statement: "Thus, Jesus is referring to *all things written in the Old Testament.* At this stage of redemptive history those are the only prophecies that had already been written." (My emphasis, DKP)

---

[141] For more on Gentry's fatal self-contradiction on Romans 11, see my article: Gentry -V- Gentry, at: http://donkpreston.com/kenneth-gentry-v-kenneth-gentry-post millennialism-against-itself/.

Consider then the following argument:

> **"All things written in the Old Testament," i.e. all Old Testament prophecy, was fulfilled by the time of and in the events of the fall of Jerusalem in AD 70. (Kenneth Gentry).**
>
> **But the Old Testament prophesied the resurrection of the dead (Acts 24:14f; 26:6f; 26:21f, Romans 8:23-9:1-4, 1 Corinthians 15:55-56).**
>
> **Therefore, the prophecies of the resurrection of the dead were fulfilled by the time of, and in the events of, the fall of Jerusalem in AD 70.**

This argument is *prima facie* true.

It is *incontrovertibly true* that the Old Testament foretold the resurrection of the dead. Gentry agrees.

It is *irrefutably true* that all New Testament prophecies of the resurrection are drawn from and are the reiteration of the Old Testament prophecies.

It is *undeniable* that Jesus said that all things written would be fulfilled by the time of, and in the events of, the fall of Jerusalem in AD 70.

Gentry is correct in affirming that *all Old Testament prophecies* would be fulfilled at / in AD 70. And this proves, *beyond refutation*, that the resurrection of the dead came at the dissolution of the Old Covenant age of Israel in AD 70.

So, since Jesus in Luke 21:22 was referring to the fulfillment of all OT prophecies, he was in effect referring to the fulfillment of all NT prophecy. There are no "new" eschatological prophecies in the New Testament. Coupled with the fact that the resurrection prophecies we have examined very clearly do posit the resurrection at the very time Jesus was discussing in Luke, it becomes logically compelling to see the time of the judgment of Jerusalem in AD 70 as the fulfillment of the "final" resurrection.

What we find in our examination of Daniel 12, 1 Corinthians 15 and Revelation 10-11 is that they all agree with each other thematically, verbally and temporally. There is no disparity between these texts. There are no contrasts between the resurrection discussions. All points agree.

How much more perfect of correspondence would one need or demand to acknowledge that Corinthians and Revelation do in fact rely on and predict the same end time resurrection foretold in Daniel? What more evidence would be needed?

The evidence in these comparisons is overwhelming, unless we are controlled by presuppositional theology. Thus, we have established that Daniel 12 = 1 Corinthians 15 which = Revelation 11 which = Revelation 20. Thus, I would suggest that in light of the perfect correlations between all of these texts, that Frost's "objections" and his attempt to divorce Daniel 12 from Corinthians, Revelation 20 and the "real and final" resurrection are exposed as illogical and specious and should be rejected by serious students of the Bible.

Point #8

DANIEL 12, REVELATION 6 AND THE END OF THE INTERMEDIATE STATE

I want to return now, briefly, to a topic I discussed earlier and that is the Intermediate State of the Dead. To say that there is confusion in futurist eschatology about the "Intermediate State of the Dead" is to make a huge understatement.

There are, so far as I can discern, three views of what happens to man after he dies:

1.) Man (the spirit of the righteous) goes directly to heaven. There, they await the parousia, judgment and resurrection when they leave heaven and return to earth where their bodies and spirit are reunited. They then return to heaven. See the WCF citation above.

2.) Man (his spirit) goes to Hades, Abraham's bosom, either Paradise, or *Tartarus*, (2 Peter 2:4) a place of torment. This is primarily based on Luke 16 the story of the Rich Man and Lazarus. This is common among many Amillennial groups.

3.) The view often called "Soul Sleep" in which man has no consciousness after death. Man does not possess an eternal soul / spirit in this view. They are wholly in the grave / dirt. At the second coming, those decomposed bodies are raised and once again given sentience and life, in incorruptible bodies. This view is common among Adventists and some other groups.[142]

To keep this examination to a reasonable length, I will simply reiterate some of the points made above and try to drive home the points a bit stronger.

---

[142] Some scholars deny an intermediate state, *per se*, yet do not affirm what is called soul sleep. (Middleton, 2014)227+.

Consider again the power of Matthew 8:11 in light of Daniel 12. And we want to again focus on the hope of Abraham as it relates to these two texts particularly.

What was the hope of Abraham? It was the heavenly city, the heavenly country. It was the better resurrection. It was, to express it another way, eternal life.

Abraham's hope, expressed in Matthew 8, was the Messianic Banquet which was foretold in Isaiah 25. This was the "Banquet" to be established on Zion in the day that YHVH destroyed death. Thus, Abraham's hope of the "city" was the hope of resurrection life, the life promised in 1 Corinthians 15.

Abraham did not receive the fulfillment of his eschatological hope while he was alive and he did not receive it after he died (Hebrews 11:13, 39: "These all died in faith, not receiving the promise"). This means that Abraham, when in Hades,[143] was not in the kingdom. He had not sat down at the table in the kingdom.

Abraham and the Worthies realized that the fulfillment of their eschatological hope of the better resurrection was "far off" (Hebrews 11:13f). But they longed to see Jesus' day, "he saw it and was glad" (John 8:56).

All of this means, of course, that Abraham and the Worthies were in the Intermediate State of the Dead – no matter our concept of that state – from the time of their death onward.

But Matthew 8:11 undeniably posits the fulfillment of the eschatological hope of Abraham and the OT Worthies, not to

---

[143] For an in-depth and challenging study of Luke 16– the story of the Rich Man and Lazarus - and whether it is a parable, and whether it actually discusses the issue of "life after death," see Sam Dawson's book, *Essays on Eschatology*, (Bowie, Tx, SGD Press, 2013)305f. The book is available from my websites.

mention those who would come from the east and the west[144] to join them in the kingdom. In Matthew 8, Abraham sits at the Kingdom Banquet table promised in Isaiah 25. But again, this is the resurrection promise of 1 Corinthians 15 – the end of the Intermediate State of the Dead.

Keep in mind that we have documented that the leading Dominionists of the day affirm that Matthew 8:11 was fulfilled in AD 70.

If Matthew 8:11 is fulfilled, then Isaiah 25 is fulfilled. If Isaiah 25 is fulfilled, the resurrection of 1 Corinthians 15 is fulfilled. If the resurrection of 1 Corinthians 15 is fulfilled, the Intermediate State of the Dead no longer exists. (Keep in mind that both Jordan and McDurmon affirmed "a fulfillment" of 1 Corinthians 15 in AD 70).

Simply stated, if Abraham and the Worthies now sit at the Messianic Banquet the resurrection of the dead has taken place. After all, there is no Biblical warrant to suggest that the OT Worthies are sitting at the Resurrection Banquet *while still in Hades!*[145]

---

[144] The gathering from the east and the west is an eschatological motif found many times in the Tanakh. It has to do with both the re-gathering of the diaspora and the inclusion of the Gentiles as they are gathered to Zion at the time of the end. See for instance Isaiah 27:13; 43:5; 49:12f; Jeremiah 3, etc.. This time of gathering from the four winds / directions is directly related to the resurrection (Isaiah 27:13).

[145] Middleton (2014, 139f) and others deny an Intermediate State. But to deny that Abraham and the Worthies are now sitting at the Messianic Banquet denies Jesus' words. *How could being unconscious in the dirt be described in any sense as sitting at the Table in the Kingdom?* If the "sons of the kingdom" were cast out in AD 70, as Luke 13:28f demands, then Abraham and the Worthies are no longer in "the grave" or "the dirt" but sitting at the Table! Jesus' statement that Abraham and the Worthies would sit at the Kingdom

The Hadean realm was the Intermediate State of the Dead. It is not the kingdom. It is not the place of eschatological Zion. It is not the heavenly country. It is not the place of resurrection. Would anyone seriously argue that Abraham and the Worthies sat down at the Messianic Kingdom Banquet *in Hades*?

It is specious therefore, for Gentry, DeMar, McDurmon, Mathison, etc. to say, as they do, that Matthew 8 was fulfilled in AD and yet, we are still waiting for the resurrection. How can Matthew 8 be fulfilled and the resurrection not be fulfilled?

If the Abrahamic promise has been fulfilled the resurrection has occurred (Heb. 11:35f) - Abraham is in the Heavenly city / country.

And let me drive home a point we made earlier: if Abraham and the OT Worthies are now sitting at the Messianic Kingdom table as Dominionists affirm - the only way they could be doing so is if they are *resurrected from the dead*. But if Abraham and the Worthies are sitting at the Messianic Banquet table by being resurrected from the Hadean realm (death) then it is *prima facie* evident that *they were not raised out of the literal, dirt, in reconstituted, resuscitated, restored human bodies of flesh and blood!*

Let me put it like this:

Let's say that Abraham and the Worthies were taken out of Hades at Christ's ascension and took their place as martyrs under the altar in Revelation 6. Were they, at that time, taken into the Most Holy Place - The New Heaven and Earth of Revelation 21-22 - in fulfillment of the Messianic Banquet and the resurrection of Isaiah 25 / 1 Corinthians 15? Patently not according to Revelation 15:8 which clearly shows that there could be no entrance into the MHP (The New Heavens and Earth) until the wrath of God was fulfilled in the judgment of Babylon. Furthermore, according to Hebrews 11, those Worthies had not yet received the better resurrection and the heavenly City and "fatherland." The Dominionists have to agree

---

Table when the sons of the kingdom would be cast out is a powerful rejection of Middleton's eschatology.

with this, since they say that the Worthies did not sit at the Banquet until AD 70, when the sons of the kingdom were cast out.

The Dominionists agree that Babylon was Old Covenant Jerusalem, destroyed in AD 70. Thus, the Worthies could not and did not enter the New Creation - the MHP - at Christ's ascension. That means that neither the pre-ascension condition of the Worthies in the Intermediate State, nor the post-ascension condition meets the requirements of Matthew 8:11. Again, the Dominionists (ostensibly) agree with this, but that agreement demands that Matthew 8 was predictive of the fulfillment of the "final resurrection" promise of Isaiah 25 and 1 Corinthians 15. It means that Matthew 8 is the full realization of the Abrahamic promises, no matter what we perceive them to be.

Entrance into the MHP, Resurrection and the New Creation are all postmillennial realities.

So, it cannot be argued that the Worthies entered the full enjoyment of the Most Holy Place at the ascension of Jesus. They did not sit at the Messianic Banquet. They were not resurrected to enjoy eternal life in the kingdom. They did not enter the New Creation.

So, even if one wants to argue that the Worthies were removed from Hades at Jesus' ascension, it still cannot be argued that they had entered the Most Holy Place. They had not sat down at the Messianic Resurrection Banquet. Being "under the altar" in the heavenly realm (Revelation 6) was not entrance into the eternal kingdom, the New Creation, the Most Holy Place. (It was also not the time of the vindication of the martyrs which would only take place at the parousia (Luke 18:8 / Revelation 6:12-17) which Dominionists themselves posit at AD 70. I will not take the space to develop that here, but it is important).

Entrance into the New Creation, reception of resurrection life around the Messianic kingdom Banquet are all "post-millennial" realities. *Dominionists agree that the Resurrection Kingdom Banquet was bestowed on the Worthies in AD 70.* This is an admission that the full scope of the promises to Abraham, the

-149-

heavenly City, the heavenly "fatherland" and the better resurrection, of logical necessity, were fulfilled in AD 70. The Dominionists cannot logically deny this. By their own admission and position on Matthew 8, they have falsified their postmillennial theology.

These irrefutable facts refute the idea of Dominionists that Abraham and the Worthies will be resurrected to rule on a restored earth. McDurmon affirmed this view repeatedly in our debate. Frost claims the same thing: "God promised Abraham *land*" (2012, 47). But again, if Matthew 8 is fulfilled, then Abraham has been resurrected. So, where is he? Should he not be on earth... *somewhere*, ruling and *reigning over dirt*? The Dominionist admission of the fulfillment of Matthew 8:11 in AD 70 is nothing less than a dagger to the heart of their futurist eschatology. And let me drive home the point made above.

McDurmon affirms that the Abrahamic promise of Hebrews 11 (the City and the Fatherland) is the ultimate resurrection promise given to him. He says also, as demonstrated, that Matthew 8:11 was fulfilled in AD 70. But as we have shown, the resurrection promise of Isaiah 25:8 / Matthew 8:11 is the identical promise found in Hebrews 11. Therefore, by admitting the fulfillment of Matthew 8:11, McDurmon and the Dominionists thereby surrender their entire argument about Abraham and dirt! If Abraham received what was promised in Isaiah 25, *that is the promise of the "final" resurrection*. McDurmon has overthrown Dominionist eschatology.

Consider the connection between Daniel 12, Revelation 6, Revelation 11-16 and Revelation 20. Daniel 12 foretold the resurrection, the end of the Intermediate State of the Dead. Daniel foretold the kingdom and the rewarding of the prophets which is the end of the Intermediate State of the Dead.

In Revelation 6, we find the martyrs under the heavenly altar, awaiting vindication and their reward at the Great Day of the Lord. They are awaiting the end of the Intermediate State of the Dead and entrance into the Most Holy Place - the New Creation of chapter 21-22 which is patently the promise made to Abraham in Hebrews 11.

In Revelation 11, we have the Great Day of the Lord – at the judgment of the city where the Lord was slain (in fulfillment of Daniel 12). In that judgment the dead are judged, the everlasting kingdom arrives and the prophets are rewarded - the end of the Intermediate State of the Dead.

In Revelation 15-16, we find the vision of the Ark of the Covenant in the Most Holy Place of the Heavenly Temple. The declaration is made that no man could enter that Most Holy Place (The New Creation of chapter 21-22) until the wrath of God would be finished in the outpouring of the seventh bowl (15:8).

It is axiomatic that entrance into the Most Holy Place is the end of the Intermediate State of the Dead. So, the question therefore becomes, when, more precisely, could man enter the Most Holy Place? Be sure to read our response to Frost above. He insists that the "Sheolic" aspect of death has been destroyed. But the Sheolic aspect of death was the Intermediate State of the Dead!

Revelation 15:8 answers our question: "The temple was filled with smoke from the glory of God and from His power and no one was able to enter the temple till the seven plagues of the seven angels were completed."

So, there could be no entrance into the Most Holy Place – the Intermediate State of the Dead would not end – until the completion of the outpouring of the wrath of God. When was that to be?

The seven plagues of the seven angels were contained in the seven vials / bowls. So, when was that seventh bowl, completing the Wrath of God, to be poured out allowing man to enter the Most Holy Place, thus bringing to an end the Intermediate State of the Dead? Once again, Revelation gives us the answer:

> "Then the seventh angel poured out his bowl into the air and a loud voice came out of the temple of heaven, from the throne, saying, "It is done!" And there were noises and thunderings and lightnings; and there was a great earthquake, such a mighty and

great earthquake as had not occurred since men were on the earth. Now the great city was divided into three parts the cities of the nations fell. And great Babylon was remembered before God, to give her the cup of the wine of the fierceness of His wrath" (Revelation 16:17-19).

So,

Entrance into the Most Holy Place (the end of the Intermediate State of the Dead) would be at the completion of the Wrath of God in the pouring out of the seventh bowl / vial.

The seventh bowl of God's wrath was poured out in the judgment of Babylon.

Therefore, the Wrath of God was completed, allowing man to enter the Most Holy Place (bringing to an end the Intermediate State of the Dead) in the judgment of Babylon.

Following this, we would offer these thoughts:

The Wrath of God was completed, allowing man to enter the Most Holy Place (and thus bringing to an end the Intermediate State of the Dead) in the judgment of Babylon.

Babylon was Old Covenant Jerusalem (McDurmon, Gentry, DeMar, et. al).

Therefore, entrance into the Most Holy Place (bringing to an end the Intermediate State of the Dead) occurred in the judgment of Old Covenant Jerusalem (In AD 70).

Let me express it yet another way:

The reception of the Abrahamic promise of the New Creation, the New Jerusalem and the heavenly fatherland of Hebrews 11 and Revelation 21-22, would be at the completion of the Wrath of God in the pouring out of the seventh bowl / vial.

The seventh bowl of God's wrath was poured out in the judgment of Babylon.

Babylon was Old Covenant Jerusalem (McDurmon, Gentry, DeMar, et. al).

Therefore, Abraham, Isaac, Jacob and all the Worthies received and entered into the New Creation, the New Jerusalem and the heavenly land of Hebrews 11 and Revelation 21-22, at the AD 70 judgment of Old Covenant Jerusalem.

It is critical to realize that the majority of the Dominionists we have cited in this work, Gentry, DeMar, Leithart, McDurmon, Seriah, etc., *all agree that Babylon of Revelation was Old Covenant Jerusalem.*[146] *Do you catch the power of that?* You cannot admit that Babylon of Revelation was Old Covenant Jerusalem without thereby admitting that the "ultimate" land promise given to Abraham was fulfilled in AD 70.

In addition, remember that almost all of these same men likewise posit the vindication of the martyrs and the judgment of Revelation 6 and Revelation 11:15f in AD 70. And of course, don't forget that they affirm the fulfillment of Matthew 8:11 at the same time.

So, consider the following:

☞ Revelation 6 is the vindication of the dead at the Great Day of the Lord.

☞ That Great Day would be AD 70 (Isaiah 2 – Luke 23; Malachi 3 – Revelation 6, so say most of the leading Dominionists of the day).

---

[146] Mathison has vacillated. In his *Postmillennialism*, (1999, 153) book, Mathison identified Babylon as Jerusalem. However, in his *Age to Age* book (2009,689), he now says Babylon was Rome. Frost has clearly rejected the Babylon = Jerusalem identification, but has not been forthcoming with a clear-cut identity for who Babylon must be.

☛ That day of vindication and rewarding of the dead is the time of the *resurrection* (Revelation 11).

☛ That day of vindication (AD 70) is when man could enter the Most Holy Place (Revelation 15-16; *the end of the Intermediate State of the Dead*).

☛ The time of the end of the Intermediate State of the Dead is the time of the general resurrection.

☛ Therefore, the general resurrection - at the end of the Intermediate State of the Dead - was in AD 70.

Notice the correspondence between this and Hebrews 9:6-10. There, we are informed that man could not enter into the Most Holy Place as long as Torah remained valid.

So, entrance into the MHP (*the end of the Intermediate State of the Dead*) is posited at *the end of Torah* (This is clearly *Torah To Telos*).

Entrance into the Most Holy Place *(the end of the Intermediate State of the Dead)* would be in the judgment of Babylon, i.e. Old Covenant Jerusalem.

Of course, we would remind you again how the Dominionists cited in this work say that Abraham and the Worthies sat down at the Messianic Kingdom Banquet – (Which demands the fulfillment of Isaiah 25 / 1 Corinthians 15) – when, "the sons of the kingdom" were cast out, in AD 70.

So, the Dominionists have the resurrection of Daniel 12 fulfilled in AD 70. But that was to be *the resurrection to eternal life, which is nothing but the end of the Intermediate State of the Dead.*

They have the Messianic Kingdom Banquet promise, *which is nothing but the end of the Intermediate State of the Dead,* fulfilled in AD 70.

They have the Old Covenant Worthies, from Abel onward, receiving what was promised to them, i.e. the heavenly city, the heavenly fatherland, the better resurrection – *which is nothing but the end of the Intermediate State of the Dead* – *in AD 70*. It is likewise the "ultimate" fulfillment of the Abrahamic "land promise."

They have the vindication of the martyrs at the Day of the Lord, the time of the resurrection and rewarding of the prophets, *which is nothing but the end of the Intermediate State of the Dead* – in AD 70.

They have the judgment of Babylon – and thus, entrance into the MHP – *which is nothing but the end of the Intermediate State of the Dead and the consummate state of Revelation 21-22* - in AD 70.

All of these admissions, individually or collectively, are fatal to the futurist eschatology of Dominionism. You cannot *logically* affirm the past fulfillment of all of these prophecies which are patently related to the end of the Intermediate State of the Dead and at the same time say that there is a yet future coming of the Lord to put an end to the Intermediate State of the Dead. These admissions demand that the Abrahamic "land promise" that McDurmon and Frost place so much emphasis on, is fulfilled. That is undeniable.

If the (righteous) dead have received eternal life through resurrection, in fulfillment of Daniel 12, what more do they need?

If the righteous dead are sitting at the Messianic Kingdom Banquet by being resurrected in fulfillment of Isaiah and Corinthians, what more do they need? They have received immortality and incorruptibility.

If the dead entered into the heavenly City, Country and the "better resurrection," what more do they need? They surely don't need "dirt."

If the dead have been judged and received their reward of the everlasting kingdom – through the resurrection - what more do they need?

If Abraham and the Worthies have entered into the Most Holy Place and dwell there in the Presence, what more do they need? Why would they need *dirt*?

Of course, the Dominionists would respond by saying that the true end of the Intermediate State of the Dead occurs at the end of the millennium in Revelation 20. But this is simply a desperate attempt to avoid the power of the admissions they make about these other texts, which logically demand that Revelation 20 - the end of the millennium - was actually fulfilled in AD 70.[147]

Was there an *Intermediate*, Intermediate State of the Dead that was destroyed in AD 70, but we are still waiting the destruction of the "real" Intermediate State? Just how "intermediate" was the sitting down at the Messianic Kingdom Banquet, when Abraham and all the Worthies sat down there? Where do they get the idea of an Intermediate Resurrection to eternal life? Do the Worthies only get to participate a little bit in the blessings of that Banquet until some yet future time?

There is much, much more that could be offered on this subject, but this is sufficient to expose the utter fallacy and self-contradictions of the Dominionist view. All of the evidence brought forth here firmly establishes the truth that Daniel 12 foretold the "final" resurrection and the end of the Intermediate State of the Dead. This firmly establishes the truth of *Torah to Telos* - Torah endured until AD 70.

---

[147] An in-depth study of the millennium is clearly outside the limits of this book. However, for an excellent study and vindication of the idea that Revelation 20 was fulfilled in AD 70, see Joseph Vincent's *The Millennium, Past, Present or Future*, (Ardmore, Ok., JaDon Management Inc., 2012). Also, see my book *Who Is This Babylon?* for an excellent discussion.

The Dominionist admissions concerning what took place regarding Abraham and the OT Worthies (i.e. the dead) in AD 70 constitutes a *prima facie* falsification of the Dominionist's futurist eschatology.

The assertion of the fulfillment of Daniel 12, the entrance into the kingdom, the sitting at the Messianic Banquet, in the heavenly City, all constitute an admission that the end of the Intermediate State of the Dead - and the full reception of the Abrahamic "land promise" - was in AD 70

But if the Intermediate State of the Dead came to an end in AD 70 and if the ultimate Abrahamic land promise of Hebrews 11 is fulfilled - there cannot be - Biblically - any futurist eschatology.

Point #9

DANIEL 12 – RESURRECTION AND THE GREAT TRIBULATION: THE GREAT TRIBULATION IMMEDIATELY PRECEDES THE RESURRECTION

This is a particularly significant point and one that is all but ignored by many commentators - particularly the Amillennial and Postmillennial ones. Simply stated, in Jewish expectation, *based on the OT prophecies*, the resurrection of the dead was to come *immediately after and as the climax of the Great Tribulation*. The reality of this truth is fatal to both of these schools of thought.

The Great Tribulation was also known as the Messianic Suffering, the Birth Pangs of Messiah, the Footprint of Messiah and other terms. There is a well established pattern of events in the Jewish literature about the chain of events for the last days. Significantly, when one considers both the OT and the NT texts, that very same pattern and time line is clearly reflected there. That pattern may be briefly outlined in the following:

♣The Abomination of Desolation would initiate the Great Tribulation, a time of unparalleled horror on Israel - Daniel 9, 11, 12. Take note that Daniel 12 played a key role in the end times drama.

♣ There would be familial conflict – cf. Micah 7 – family members turning on family members. Compare with Jesus' statement that he came to set children against parents, etc. in Matthew 10.

♣ The tribulation would severely test Israel as a refiner's fire – cf. Malachi 3. In rabbinic literature the idea of refining is employed repeatedly as purifying the remnant for the kingdom.

♣ Only a remnant of Israel would successfully pass through the Tribulation and inherit the kingdom – Compare Isaiah 10:20; Amos 5:1-3; Isaiah 65; Zechariah 13-14.

♣ Elijah would appear before the Great Day of the Lord and prepare the people for the kingdom - Malachi 4.

❖ The resurrection, the Great Judgment, the arrival of the Kingdom and Messiah in glory would be the climax of the Tribulation.

Shurer, considered one of the greatest authorities on early Jewish history and beliefs, said that in Jesus' day, "Reference to the last things is almost always accompanied by the notion, recurring in various forms, that a period of special distress and affliction must precede the dawn of salvation...In Rabbinic teaching, the doctrine therefore developed of the birth pangs of Messiah which must precede His appearance (the expression is from Hosea 13:13; cf. Matthew 24:8)."[148]

Dubis[149] chronicles this pattern well and what sticks out in my mind as I read the literature is how well the NT epistles reflect these tenets.

Pitre also develops the theme of the Tribulation very well and more extensively than most commentators. He particularly shows the relationship between the Tribulation and the eschatological consummation, the resurrection: "According to the OT, the resurrection itself would be preceded by a period of great tribulation"... Daniel 12, which is the most explicit prophecy of resurrection in the Hebrew books of the Old Testament. Strikingly, this description of the resurrection is preceded by the Great Tribulation" (*2005*, 187).

Another critical point that is often overlooked, is that the Abomination of Desolation, which would be the direct cause of the Great Tribulation, *"always refers to a profanation of the Jerusalem Temple"* (Pitre, 2005, 304, his emphasis). He continues, "In the

---

[148] Emile Schurer, *History of the Jewish People in the Age of Jesus Christ*, Vol. II, (London, T and T Clark, 1979)514.

[149] Mark Dubis, *Messianic Woes in First Peter, Suffering and Eschatology in 1 Peter 4:12-19*. Studies in Biblical Literature, 33, (New York, Peter Lang, 2002).

book of Daniel, the 'abomination of desolation' not only refers to a profanation of the Temple that leads to the cessation of sacrifices, but also to the destruction of the sanctuary and the holy city that accompanies it." (2005, 305).

The connections here are profoundly important. If, as Pitre convincingly argues, the Abomination of Desolation[150] and the Great Tribulation are tied directly to the destruction of the Jerusalem Temple and city, then since *the resurrection is the consummation of the Tribulation,* this ties the resurrection to the judgment of the Temple and Jerusalem. Such is the importance of properly identifying the time and context of the Great Tribulation.

> **The Abomination of Desolation and the Great Tribulation are tied directly to the destruction of the Jerusalem Temple and City. Since *the OT ties the resurrection to the consummation of the Tribulation,* this ties the resurrection to the judgment of the Temple and Jerusalem.**

Russell notes, "The time period of distress before God's final triumph is 'the travail of the Messiah.'"[151]

Wright discusses the disciples' questions about the end of the age and Jesus' parousia in response to Jesus' prediction of the impending judgment of Jerusalem: "The start of Jesus' answer to

---

[150] See also: Timothy Gray, *The Temple In The Gospel of Mark,* (Grand Rapids, Baker Academic, 2008)141. He says the, "'Desolating sacrilege' literally means 'the sacrilege that causes desolation.' It causes desolation." It causes desolation because the profanation of the temple incurs God's judgment which ultimately leads to the destruction of the temple."

[151] D. S. Russell, *The Method and Message of Jewish Apocalyptic,* Westminster Press, 1964)272.

the disciples' question is a classic piece of reworked apocalyptic. Completely consistent with his whole approach to the events that were about to take place, he is predicting that the 'Messianic Woes', the birth pangs of the age to come, are about to occur in full force, this is how Israel will be reborn." (1996, 346).

Likewise, Dale Allison presents some excellent resource material on this subject.[152] He agrees with all of the other citations given here concerning the story line of Jewish eschatology.

The bottom line is that there was a widespread belief among the Jews of Jesus' time and well before, that immediately before the resurrection, the arrival of the everlasting kingdom and the appearing of the Messiah, the Abomination of Desolation would be set up leading to the Great Tribulation. This is not some fanciful theory. It was taken directly from Torah, as we shall see.

Do you see the power of this? Unless the Jewish expectation was totally wrong, *the Great Tribulation was immediately before the resurrection.*

Unless the scriptures of the OT did not in fact posit resurrection immediately after and as a climax to the Great Tribulation, *then the Tribulation and the resurrection are temporally tied together.* (So, when Jesus said, "immediately after the tribulation of those days, the sun shall be darkened... and they shall see the Son of Man coming," this was nothing less than a statement that the resurrection - at the parousia - was to be in that generation (Matthew 24:30-34).

This is a *devastating* point for the Amillennialists and Postmillennialists, both of whom admit that the Great Tribulation was in the first century leading up to the fall of Jerusalem. Furthermore, the majority of Dominionists and many Amillennialists say that not only was the Great Tribulation in the

---

[152] Dale Allison Jr., *The End of the Ages Has Come*, (Philadelphia, Fortress)1985.

first century, *they deny that there is another, yet future Great Tribulation.* Consider the import of this.

Reformed Amillennialist Jordan writes, "It is perverse for commentators to continue to insist that the Great Tribulation is still in the future."[153]

Mathison, as we have seen, rejects the idea of another, future Tribulation: "There is no end time tribulation. Jesus' prophecy about tribulation in Matthew 24 was fulfilled between AD 30 and AD 70. That fulfillment should give us confidence that His promise to return again is true." (1995, 144).

Gentry adds his voice: "Copious, clear and compelling evidence demonstrates that the great tribulation occurs in the first century." (2009, 356). DeMar likewise rejects a futurist application of the Great Tribulation (*Madness*, 1999, 117+).

Let me state again that if the OT taught, as we will show that it did, that the resurrection would climax the Great Tribulation, then if the Great Tribulation was in the first century as the Postmillennialists and Amillennialists believe, then the resurrection was to be in the first century.

So, unless one can demonstrate that the resurrection was not linked to the Great Tribulation in scripture, the fact that Jesus emphatically posited the Tribulation for the first century generation is powerful evidence that the resurrection was supposed to be in the first century.

What we need to do then, is to document from scripture that the Abomination of Desolation and the Great Tribulation were inseparably tied to the resurrection. And there is another element that is vitally important here. We will only mention it in passing, because I am currently working on a book on John the Baptizer as

---

[153] James Jordan, *Hand Writing On the Wall, A Commentary on Daniel*, (Powder Springs, GA. American Vision, 2007)619.

Elijah. Not only did the Jews believe and scripture teach that there would be a time of tribulation before the Kingdom arrived in power and glory, *they believed that Elijah would appear just before that Great Tribulation.*

Pitre shows how in Jewish expectation and in Malachi, *Elijah was to come in or immediately before the Tribulation period and the resurrection* (2005, 181f). This perfectly matches what we find in Matthew 3. John heralded the imminent coming of the kingdom, but he also warned that the judgment was about to fall. We thus find judgment and kingdom in the message of John, who was the fulfillment of the Elijah prophecies. Kingdom, judgment, the Tribulation and Elijah are all key tenets of the eschatological drama. Since John, as Elijah, said the judgment and the kingdom were at hand, this means the resurrection was at hand.

As we begin, don't forget that we have already seen that Gentry, DeMar, McDurmon, etc., now openly say that Daniel 12 foretold the resurrection for AD 70. Likewise, they admit that Matthew 8, Hebrews 11, 1 Peter 4 and Revelation 11 all speak of the first century judgment, the time of the end and resurrection. When one couples these resurrection texts with Jesus' prediction of the Tribulation for the first century, we have a harmonious picture.

I want now to demonstrate the undeniable fact – although commonly overlooked in the literature[154]– that the OT posited the Tribulation as *leading directly to the resurrection* and the establishment of Messiah's kingdom at his coming in judgment. There is no need – or space - to give all of the OT prophecies that in one way or another allude to the Messianic Woes, the Birth Pangs of Messiah, the coming of the Kingdom and resurrection. We will simply list some of the most pertinent passages, those that either

---

[154] Pitre comments in his book that the pattern of Abomination –> Tribulation –> Resurrection, *while very clear in the prophetic texts*, has not been generally recognized by scholarship. In Amillennial and Postmillennial literature this connection is virtually unknown and unexplored.

specifically mention resurrection, or, they discuss eschatological tenets that are undeniably tied to the resurrection, i.e. the New Creation, the redemption of Zion, etc..

Isaiah 24-27

We have already established that the "little apocalypse" foretold the end times resurrection and kingdom, so I need not go back over that material. Just take note that in chapter 24 we find the judgment of the "city of confusion," the fortified city and the Temple, followed by the reign of YHVH on Zion and the resurrection (24:19-25:8). We thus have the pattern of the judgment on Jerusalem followed by the resurrection.

Notice also that we have the specific language of the *birth pangs* in 26:16f, followed directly by the resurrection at the coming of the Lord in vindication of the martyrs. This text is one of the many that the Jewish writers cited when they spoke of the Messianic Birth pangs and resurrection.

Since Isaiah serves as the source for Paul's resurrection doctrine in 1 Corinthians 15 and since Paul in several of his epistles alluded to the time of tribulation before the parousia and resurrection (E.g. 1 Thessalonians 1; 3:1-3; 2 Thessalonians 1), we are on solid ground to say that Paul accepted the story line of Tribulation –> parousia –> resurrection –> kingdom. This being true, it demands a first century resurrection. Not a "typological" or "foreshadowing" resurrection, but "the resurrection."

Riddlebarger recognizes this: "Like Daniel, the prophet Isaiah (25:6-9) saw the resurrection occurring after a period of horrible anguish, a time when salvation will come to God's people" (2003, 132).

Yet, while admitting that there was a great tribulation in the first century, like some other Amillennialists, he posits another, real Great Tribulation at the end of the Christian age. He does this to salvage a futurist eschatology, for it is admitted for a moment that the "real resurrection" is inseparably tied to the Great Tribulation and it is then admitted that the Tribulation was in the first century, this would nullify any futurist resurrection doctrine.

Isaiah 65-66

When we are attuned to "seeing" the Biblical pattern of Tribulation –> Resurrection, the prophecies of Isaiah 65-66 become a shining example of that narrative. Furthermore, they firmly posit those events in the context of the judgment of Old Covenant Israel. I can only briefly examine these two texts.[155]

❖ - Israel's sin - Israel would fill the measure of her sin and be repaid at the Day of the Lord (65:8f; 66:3f).

❖ - Salvation of the remnant (65:8; 66:18f) - A key element of the doctrine of the Tribulation.

❖ - Judgment on Israel – "The Lord God will slay you!" (65:13f; 66:3f, 17f – "I will bring their delusions on them, the thing that they fear" (66:3f; 15f).

❖ - The New Creation – Does anyone seriously doubt that the New Creation – The New Heaven and Earth – is a resurrection motif?

So, in the foundational OT prophecy of the New Creation, the text that Peter and John draw from for their doctrine of the New Creation to arrive at the Great Day of the Lord, we find the pattern of Tribulation leading directly to the resurrection (New Creation) firmly established.

Jeremiah 30:5f

> "For thus says the Lord: 'We have heard a voice of trembling, Of fear not of peace. Ask now and see,

---

[155] See my *The Elements Shall Melt With Fervent Heat,* and my, *Who Is This Babylon?* for an in-depth discussion and exegesis of Isaiah's critical prophecies. Those books are available from my websites, Amazon, Kindle and other retailers.

Whether a man is ever in labor with child? So why do I see every man with his hands on his loins Like a woman in labor and all faces turned pale? Alas! For that day is great, So that none is like it; And it is the time of Jacob's trouble, But he shall be saved out of it. 'For it shall come to pass in that day,' Says the Lord of hosts, 'That I will break his yoke from your neck will burst your bonds; Foreigners shall no more enslave them. But they shall serve the Lord their God and David their king, Whom I will raise up for them. 'Therefore do not fear, O My servant Jacob,' says the Lord, 'Nor be dismayed, O Israel; For behold, I will save you from afar and your seed from the land of their captivity. Jacob shall return, have rest and be quiet and no one shall make him afraid."

While there was an immediate, contemporary application of this prophecy, it was almost certainly typological and Messianic. Further, the promise here cannot be limited to the return from Babylon, because it included both houses of Israel and this is a major, consistent Messianic kingdom and *resurrection* motif (Ezekiel 37).

→ The motif of the birth pangs is set forth to describe the time of suffering before the deliverance. This is the Great Tribulation leading to the Kingdom of Messiah!

→ Notice it describes this time of the birth pangs as a tribulation that "none is like it" (v. 7).[156] While one must certainly consider

---

[156] Compare also the parallel text in Ezekiel 5:8-14. We will not discuss the text extensively, but simply note that it contains the identical motifs of "unparalleled" Tribulation and "birth pains." It should also be noted that this Tribulation would be aimed directly at Israel for her violation of Torah. In fact, in v. 10, the language is taken directly from the Law of Blessings and Cursings of Deuteronomy 28-30, (28:56f).

whether this is hyperbole, it nonetheless reminds us of Daniel 12:1. Since the result of this time of tribulation would be the kingdom of David – Messiah – we should see a direct link with Daniel who saw the kingdom as the result of the tribulation and the resurrection.

→ Jeremiah sees the end of the tribulation as the time of *the redemption of Zion*, a key Messianic motif (v. 17, cf. Isaiah 52, 60-66). In Isaiah 25:6-8, the redemption of Zion is tied directly to the resurrection of the dead.

→ It is significant that this promise of the kingdom after the tribulation is, in the context, not only of the redemption of "Zion," but of *the New Creation*. The promise of the New Covenant in chapter 31 is, according to Kiwoong Son, tied directly to the New Creation: "Israel's return to Zion is connected with God's new creation (Jeremiah 31:21-22).[157] There can be little doubt of the connection between the redemption of Zion, the New Covenant, the New Creation – and thus, resurrection.

Micah 7

This entire chapter describes a time of horrible conflict, judgment on Jerusalem and the people. It reflects the book of Malachi in several ways.

☛ Verses 1-4 – "The faithful man has perished out of the land." As Dubis shows, this is one of the key markers in the rabbinic concept of the Messianic Birth Pangs of the Great Tribulation. There would be a dearth of righteous men, even rabbis (2002, 12).

YHVH said that when Israel apostatized, He would bring the foreign nations on them and besiege them. In the sieges, Israel would eat their own children (cf. Zechariah 11 also, a prediction of the AD 70 catastrophe, when YHVH would finally break His covenant bond with Israel).

[157] Kiwoong Son, *Zion Symbolism in Hebrews*. (Waynesboro, GA., Paternoster,2005)49.

☛ Familial Conflict– "A man's enemies are those of his own household" (v. 6). Of course, Jesus cited this verse in Matthew 10 as he sent his disciples out with the message of the imminent kingdom (Matthew 10:36). *He clearly applied the prophecy of Micah to his day.* Pitre takes note that, "in ancient Jewish eschatology, inter-familial and interpersonal strife are not simply the result of societal breakdown in human relations. Rather, they function together as a very common sign of the arrival of the eschatological tribulation" (2005, 184).

These verses echo Malachi 4 in that Elijah would come before the Great Day of the Lord and, "turn the hearts of the fathers to the children." Thus, there is a direct connection between the work of Elijah and the horrible time before the arrival of the kingdom. In Jewish thought, Elijah would come during (or immediately before) the eschatological tribulation and the tribulation would precede the restoration of Israel and the resurrection of the dead.

It must not be missed that Jesus emphatically identified John the Baptizer as the prophesied Elijah (Matthew 17:10-12). And John, as Elijah heralded, "the wrath about to come" at the Great Day of the Lord.

Thus, the Biblical pattern of Inter-familial turmoil –>Elijah –> Tribulation –> Kingdom and Resurrection are clearly echoed in the ministry of John as Elijah.

☛ It is interesting that in Micah YHVH depicts Israel at this time *as His enemy* that will be covered with shame (v. 10; cf. Isaiah 27:10f).[158] It is worth noting that in Philippians 3, Paul contrasts

---

[158] See my discussion of how Israel is depicted as the enemy of YHVH and His Son in the last days in my book *Like Father Like Son, On Clouds of Glory* (p. 176+). Not only in the OT, when Israel sinned, but in prophecies of the last days, Israel would become the enemy of YHVH and be destroyed. This is an important motif that is totally ignored or denied by

Old Covenant Israel with the true circumcision, the true seed of Abraham by faith. He says Israel had become *the enemy of the gospel of Christ*, "whose glory is their shame" (3:18).

☞ In that last days period of turmoil, YHVH promised: "As in the days when you came out of the land of Egypt, I will show them wonders" (v. 15). This is a remarkable prophecy, especially in light of the NT emphasis on the "Second Exodus" taking place in the first century. Jesus, the Second and Greater Moses, performed greater miracles than Moses and his disciples, and the "judges" of the New Israel were given the Spirit to lead them to the Promised Land.

☞ **Daniel 7**

Daniel's vision of the Little Horn of the fourth empire who persecutes the saints in the last days is paradigmatic for much of the NT doctrine of the coming of the Son of Man, the tribulation and the kingdom. I will only note a couple of important elements.

1. The fulfillment of the prophecy cannot extend beyond the days of Rome, the fourth beast. Daniel's vision spans four beasts / kingdoms, the last being Rome. (Just as in Daniel 2).[159] So, no matter our concept of the tribulation or of the kingdom, Daniel's prophecy posits its bestowal on the saints at the coming of the Son of Man, in the days of Rome.

2. Daniel clearly has the outline of suffering - vindication - kingdom in mind. Wright says "The Danielic story always was one of vindication and exaltation and was retold as such in the first century" (1996, 361). The saints are given into the hands of the "little horn" and persecuted for, "a time, times and half a time"

---

the Dispensational world, but it is present in several key OT Messianic texts.

[159] I do not accept the view that the Greek empire of the Selucids and Ptolemys is the fourth empire, but cannot discuss that here.

(7:25), until the judgment is set. Then, the Little Horn is destroyed and the eternal kingdom given to the saints. This agrees perfectly with Jesus' teaching on the vindication of the blood of all the martyrs in the judgment of Jerusalem (Matthew 23).[160]

3. Daniel's prophecy serves as the source for much of Jesus' eschatology (and NT eschatology as a whole). He cites it in his Olivet Discourse and in his predictions of his coming on the clouds of heaven with power and great glory (and the kingdom, Luke 21:28-32).

4. It is clear that unless one can divorce the coming of the one like the Son of Man *from the days of the Roman empire*, that the tribulation -suffering - parousia - vindication – kingdom / *resurrection* was to take place during that time. There is no Biblical doctrine of a "revived Roman empire." Since Jesus said the vindication of all the martyrs and the arrival of the kingdom (Luke 21:28-32) would be at his coming in the judgment of Jerusalem in the first century, this posits the Great Tribulation, the parousia and resurrection at the judgment of Jerusalem.[161]

---

[160] Beale, (*Theology*, 2011, 937, n. 79) says Revelation 20 and the opening of the books, "are based on Daniel 7:10f." The implications of this are powerful: Revelation 20 is Daniel 7. But Daniel 7 cannot be extended beyond the days of the Roman empire (the fourth beast). Thus, Revelation 20 cannot be extended beyond the days of Rome.

[161] See my *We Shall Meet Him In The Air, The Wedding of the King of kings*, for an in-depth study of how Daniel is employed by the NT writers, especially Paul in Thessalonians.

☞ Daniel 9

While many commentators overlook it, the goal of the six blessings to be achieved at the end of the seventy weeks in Daniel 9:24 was the *resurrection*.[162]

Notice that the end of the seventy weeks would be the time of the "overwhelming flood" (The Great Tribulation) caused by the appearance of the Abomination of Desolation (v. 26-27).[163]

So, what we have in Daniel 9 is the Abomination of Desolation leading directly to the Tribulation which in turn reaches its climax in the arrival of the New Creation wherein dwells the "everlasting righteousness" of the Kingdom of Messiah.

While I cannot discuss it at length, I want to insert a thought or two here that I think is appropriate and significant; that is that in Rabbinic thought:

1. The kingdom, resurrection and Messiah were all supposed to come at the end Daniel's seventieth week. This is self evident from the list of blessings in Daniel 9:24.

2. Many rabbis posited the end of the seventieth week at the destruction of Jerusalem in AD 70. This is rather amazing and important, but mostly ignored.

---

[162] See my *Seventy Weeks Are Determined...For the Resurrection*, in which I carefully examine the promised blessings and show that they are indeed related to the resurrection and New Creation. The book is available on my websites, Amazon, Kindle and other retailers.

[163] One should not ignore the fact that the destruction of the city would be tied directly to the death of Messiah in verse 26. We thus have the New Creation at the end of the seventy weeks tied to the vindication of the martyrs anticipated by Jesus in Matthew 23-24.

3. There was a strong sense of disappointment that the kingdom did not come at that time![164]

The first two points are established by the third. Gaston documents this disappointment among the Jews following the catastrophe of AD 70: "The coming of the final redemption depended no longer on an apocalyptic plan but only on the repentance of Israel," Likewise, some of the Rabbis said: "All dates for the end have expired and the matter now depends solely on repentance and good works."[165]

So, in Jewish thought, AD 70 was supposed to have been the fulfillment of Daniel 9. Messiah, the kingdom and resurrection were linked with that time and event. The question is entirely appropriate to ask therefore: Were they wrong in their "calculations" of the end? One thing is certain, Jesus and John the Baptizer came saying, "the time is fulfilled, the kingdom of heaven has drawn near" (Mark 1:15; cf. 4:17). There was clearly an air of imminent expectation of the kingdom among the Jews at that time.

Thus, Jesus and the Jews agreed on the time line of the kingdom, i.e the fulfillment of Daniel 9 was near. But before that kingdom could arrive, Daniel foretold the suffering of Messiah[166] (See Luke 17:25)

---

[164] I suggest that the strong sense of discouragement stemmed from the false concepts of the *nature* of the expected kingdom. The Jews desired the restoration of the nationalistic polity and a conquering king. Jesus had flatly refused to be that kind of king, leading to his rejection by the nation. So, while the Jewish timing for the kingdom was correct, their concept of the *nature* of the kingdom was wrong. They failed to "see" what had actually happened.

[165] Lloyd Gaston, *No Stone Upon Another*, (Brill Academic, 1970)464.

[166] Even though Daniel clearly speaks of Messiah being "cut off", the idea of a martyred Messiah seems to have been a foreign – and abhorrent – idea to the Jews. Paul could speak of the "offense of the cross." Jesus was *crucified*. This

and the destruction of the city and the sanctuary (26-27). This was the outline contained right there in Daniel 9: Death of Messiah –> Abomination –> Desolation of the City and Temple –> kingdom of everlasting righteousness.

The martyrdom of Messiah is part of the reason for the Tribulation and the destruction of the City and the Temple. That destruction must be seen as the vindication of Jesus' suffering.

While he is commenting on Matthew 16:27f, I think Wright's comments are totally *apropos* to Daniel 9:24f as well:

> "The whole of the story, of judgement for those who had not followed Jesus and the vindication for those who had, is summed up in the cryptic but frequently repeated saying 'the first shall be last, the last first.' In other words, when the great tribulation came on Israel, those who had followed Jesus would be delivered; and that would be the sign that Jesus had been in the right and that in consequence they had been in the right in following him. The destruction of Jerusalem on the one hand and the rescue of the disciples on the other, would be the vindication of what Jesus had been saying throughout his ministry." (1996, 338).

Daniel 12:1-2:

> "At that time Michael shall stand up, the great prince who stands watch over the sons of your people; and there shall be a time of trouble, such as never was since there was a nation, even to that time. And at that time your people shall be delivered, every one who is found written in the book. And many of those who sleep in the dust of

---

was proof positive, it was thought, that he was a sinner and cursed by YHVH. After all, Torah itself said: "Cursed is everyone that hangs on a tree" (Deuteronomy 21:23).

> the earth shall awake, some to everlasting life, some to shame and everlasting contempt. Those who are wise shall shine like the brightness of the firmament and those who turn many to righteousness like the stars forever and ever."

As Pitre observes: "The most explicit Old Testament reference to the resurrection of the dead is preceded by the most explicit Old Testament reference to the tribulation of the last days." (2005, 187).

I would add the comment of McKnight, who effectively shows that to remove Jesus' ministry and message from one centered on the "restoration of Israel" is to ignore or misuse the Biblical data. Commenting on Luke 19:41-44 and Jesus' lament over the coming judgment of his beloved city, McKnight says: "In his vision of human history, Jesus saw no further than AD 70 and to this date he attached visions of the final salvation, the final judgment and the consummation of the kingdom of God in all its glory."[167]

Regrettably, McKnight believes that Jesus' vision failed: "That history took another course does not at all mean that Jesus was in error; rather, like the Hebrew prophets before him, he saw the next event as the end event, but that next event resulted in a series of unfolding events." To suggest that it is "okay" to say that Jesus' prophetic expectation failed and that this somehow, "does not mean that he was in error" is clearly specious. Jesus himself said: "If I do not do the things that the Father has given me, do not believe me" (John 10:35f; see also John 5:21-23). *Jesus staked his very identity on the fulfillment of his words.*

The fact that Daniel is focused on the end times, the resurrection and the kingdom makes the Dominionists claims that Daniel is a typological event, foreshadowing the "real" resurrection all that much more untenable. Why are we given not so much as a syllable

---

[167] Scott McKnight, *A New Vision for Israel*, (Grand Rapids, Eerdmans, 1999)12.

of a suggestion that there is another, greater event beyond what was being foretold?

Furthermore, just like Isaiah 24-27 and some other texts we have examined, Daniel follows the Biblical outline of the unparalleled tribulation as the climax of Israel's exilic sufferings that would precede the final restoration in the resurrection of the dead (Cf. Pitre, 2005, 321). In other words, if the Tribulation is not supposed to be seen by Bible students as directly connected to the resurrection, why is it that in the OT prophecies of the resurrection, we find the Tribulation preceding it?

> If the resurrection of the dead is not chronologically tied to the Great Tribulation, why is it that in virtually every OT prophecy of the resurrection, the Tribulation immediately precedes the resurrection?
> **Are we supposed to ignore this connection?**

There can be no doubt that the Tribulation is inextricably tied to the resurrection to eternal life at the end of the age. In fact, virtually every tenet of "traditional" eschatology and the resurrection is found here in Daniel 12. But of course, also found here is the emphatic temporal delimitation of when that resurrection was to take place: "When the power of the holy people has been completely shattered, all of these things must be fulfilled" (v. 7).

It is this emphatic temporal delimitation, along with the undeniable fact that the "power" of the holy people was Torah, the Temple and Israel's relationship with YHVH, that is now forcing those who insist on maintaining a futurist eschatology to abandon Daniel 12 as a prediction of the "real" resurrection.

So, we are finding a wholesale abandonment of the view of the "historical church," the creeds and the patristics. We are now hearing that we should not be concerned that church history and the creeds got Daniel wrong! As long as a futurist eschatology can somehow, some way, be maintained, it seems that it matters little that the text that historically has been one of the foundational pillars of that futurist view is now being summarily and flippantly dismissed.

Solid exegesis however, falsifies such desperate attempts. As we have been demonstrating, the "historical church" did get it right in assigning Daniel 12 to the "final" resurrection, the resurrection to eternal life in the kingdom. The fact that the church completely and totally missed the timing and framework of the resurrection is lamentable, but it is a powerful example of how preconceived ideas can blind the minds of even the greatest of exegetes.

So, Daniel 12 not only predicted the eschatological resurrection, it undeniably posited that resurrection directly in the context of the Great Tribulation. The fact that Jesus, citing Daniel, said the Great Tribulation was to be in his generation serves as *prima facie* proof that the ultimate, final resurrection was to be in the first century. The fact that Daniel placed that resurrection to eternal life at the consummative judgment on Israel and the indisputable fact that Jesus did the same with the Tribulation, is definitive and final proof that the resurrection of the dead was to occur – and did – at the end of the Old Covenant age of Israel in AD 70. It had - and has – no relationship to the end of the Christian age or the end of time.

Hosea 13:12-14:

> "The iniquity of Ephraim is bound up; his sin is stored up. The sorrows of a woman in childbirth shall come upon him. He is an unwise son, for he should not stay long where children are born. "I will ransom them from the power of the grave; I will redeem them from death. O Death, I will be your plagues! O Grave, I will be your destruction!"

Exactly like in Isaiah 24-27 and Daniel 12, where we find the Tribulation, i.e. the Birth Pangs followed by the resurrection, Hosea describes the coming Birth Pangs that would lead directly to her "resurrection."

It is important to make the following observations:

Paul uses both Isaiah 24-27 and Hosea 13 (and, I suggest, Daniel 12) as the source of his resurrection doctrine in 1 Corinthians 15.

Each of those OT texts emphatically posit their prophecies of the resurrection at the time of the Tribulation / Birth Pangs.

All three of these texts clearly speak of those Tribulations as related directly to *the judgment of Israel* and particularly of Jerusalem.

So, since the OT prophecies of the resurrection *that serve as the source of Paul's resurrection doctrine* link their predictions of the resurrection to the Tribulation, upon what hermeneutical principle do we divorce the Tribulation from the resurrection?

What is the hermeneutic that separates the doctrine of the resurrection from the time of the judgment on Israel and Jerusalem?[168]

Zechariah 11-14

---

[168] As I have noted in other places, this is a tremendous problem for the Dispensational paradigm. Dispensationalists say that it is national Israel that experiences the Great Tribulation, essentially as an innocent victim of the Man of Sin. While the OT prophecies certainly do posit Israel as undergoing the Tribulation, Jesus interpreted those prophecies as predictive of his followers, the True Israel, as being persecuted by Old Covenant Israel! The righteous remnant of Old Covenant Israel would and did accept Jesus as the Messiah, and would be delivered, purified, as Malachi 3 foretold. But the indisputable fact is that Jesus posited Old Covenant Israel as the last days persecutor and his followers as the ones to be persecuted then vindicated at his parousia. See Matthew 10; Mark 13:8f; Galatians 4; 1 Thessalonians 2:15f; 2 Thessalonians 1, Revelation 3, etc.

I will not give the full text of these chapters but simply observe that the pattern of Tribulation leading to the Kingdom / resurrection is clearly set forth in these chapters.

✪ 11:9f – The Lord would, "break the covenant which I have made with all the people." As a result those who are left would, "eat each other's flesh." Of course, anyone familiar with Josephus knows well of his graphic description of the siege of Jerusalem and how the inhabitants of Jerusalem did in fact eat the flesh of their own children!

✪ 12:10 - The land would mourn as for an only son. Of course, this verse is cited by Jesus in Matthew 24:30 and by John in Revelation 1:7, to speak of the time of judgment coming on Jerusalem and Judea. The ones who pierced him would look on him and mourn.

✪ 13:7f - The "shepherd" would be smitten and the sheep scattered, "and it shall come to pass that in all the land, says the Lord, that two-thirds in it shall be cut off and die, but I will bring one third through the fire." Here is the Great Tribulation, but the salvation of the remnant.

✪ 14: 1-8 - The coming of the Lord, the establishment of YHVH over the land, the River of Life flowing from the throne, the nations coming to worship the God of Life. Here is the kingdom and resurrection, i.e. the River of Life, immediately following the judgment against Jerusalem.

Throughout these last few chapters of Zechariah, the pattern of coming judgment / tribulation followed by the time of salvation is presented. It is the same pattern found everywhere in the Tanakh.

As we stated at the out-set of this brief overview, we cannot examine every OT prophecy that sets forth the last days drama and scheme of Abomination –> Tribulation –> Judgment –> salvation of the remnant –> kingdom/judgment/resurrection. What we have shared however, is more than sufficient to establish the case. Of course, not every text contains every single tenet explicitly, but all of these texts do present sufficient information to know without doubt that the pattern is in the mind of the author.

With this in mind, let me say this: If Jesus and the NT writers followed the OT schema just presented, positing the resurrection and coming of the Lord in direct, inseparable connection with the Great Tribulation, then since both the Amillennial and the Postmillennialists posit the Great Tribulation for the first century (*exclusively*)[169] this serves as *prima facie* proof that – at least for those two schools – they must agree and admit that scripture posits the resurrection for the first century.[170] It is logically inconsistent to say the Tribulation occurred in the first century but then say that the resurrection, which would come at the climax of the Tribulation (cf.

---

[169] Of course, as we have seen, the Dominionists and Amillennialists are increasingly claiming that the events of the first century were typological of the "real" end time events. Thus, some, e.g. Riddlebarger, claim that there will be another, the "final" Great Tribulation in the future. Dominionists, as we have seen, reject this. But this logically demands that the resurrection did occur in the first century, in connection with the judgment of Jerusalem – just like Daniel 12 says. See my book: *AD 70 A Shadow of the "Real" End?* for a refutation of the idea that AD 70 was typological.

[170] Of course, the Dispensationalists claim that the Tribulation is yet future, but both Amillennialists, Postmillennialists and true preterists, would all respond that Jesus and the NT emphatically posit the Tribulation for the first century.

> **Amillennialists and Dominionists posit the Great Tribulation for the first century, tied to the judgment of Israel and Jerusalem.**
>
> **The Bible irrefutably links the Great Tribulation to the end time resurrection.**
>
> **Therefore, the Amillennialists and Dominionists must now reject their view of the Tribulation – or admit that the resurrection was in the first century.**

Daniel 12:1-2) has not yet taken place. The only question that remains is whether Jesus and the NT writers did follow the OT pattern of events. And they did. However, before proceeding to that examination, there is an important element of the Abomination / Tribulation that is almost totally ignored – especially by the Dispensational writers. That fact is that no matter what else we might think of the entire doctrine of the Abomination / Tribulation, we must honor the fact that Biblically, the Tribulation must be seen *as a judgment of Israel*, brought on her by YHVH as a direct result of her violation of the Law of Moses. In other words, *the Tribulation would be the application of Mosaic Covenant provisions for national judgment on Israel for her violation of that covenant.*

If the story of the Tribulation –> Resurrection –> Kingdom is the story of Israel and her promises then one cannot divorce eschatology from Israel. This is an important idea, for it challenges the dominant futurist views. Let me illustrate in our next chapter.

THE (TRIBULATION) & RESURRECTION
AS THE HOPE OF ISRAEL

In Amillennial and Postmillennial eschatologies Israel is all but dismissed as irrelevant when it comes to eschatology. After all, God was through with Israel no later than AD 70, we are told.[171] So, in the long term story of eschatology, Israel is all but forgotten. That is, until these commentators come to Romans 11. Then, all of a sudden Israel becomes, somehow, some way, important again.[172]

Noted Postmillennialist Lorraine Boettner says: "For information concerning the first coming of Christ, we go to the Old Testament. He came exactly as predicted and all those prophecies were fulfilled or were forfeited through disobedience. But for information concerning his Second Coming and what future developments will be, we go only to the New Testament."[173]

Amillennialists, among whom I once counted myself, have an equally misguided eschatology when it comes to Israel, eschatology and the Law of Moses. Prominent Amillennialist Kim Riddlebarger has written:

---

[171] The dominant view in the Amillennial world in which I was raised is that God was through with Israel and Torah at the Cross. It is all but anathema to deny this.

[172] To say that there is *massive* confusion, even consternation among the Amillennial and Postmillennial writers in regard to Romans 11:25f would be a huge understatement. I do not have the space here to chronicle all of the different views in these two schools. Just like in regard to Daniel 12, tremendous changes have been taking place in the Dominionist school. A growing number of teachers are openly espousing the idea that Romans 11:25f referred to events leading up to and consummating in AD 70.

[173] Lorraine Boettner, *Four Views of the Millennium*, (Downers Grove, InterVarsity,1977)102.

> "Because of Jesus Christ and his coming, the Christian possesses the complete fulfillment and blessings of all the promises of the messianic age made under the old covenant. But the arrival of the messianic age also brought with it a new series of promises to be fulfilled at the end of the age. The fulfilled promises pointed to a more glorious and future fulfillment. This is called the 'not yet' or future eschatology. It is this already/not yet tension which serves as the basis for understanding much of the New Testament eschatological expectation."[174]

Significantly, for all of the emphasis put on Israel by the Dispensationalists, it is nonetheless maintained that: "Eschatological studies are not concerned with...the Mosaic Covenant made by God with man, inasmuch as all these are temporary and non-determinative in respect to future things, but only with the four eternal covenants given by God, by which He has obligated Himself in relation to the prophetic program."[175]

What is so contradictory, however, is that while claiming that Biblical eschatology is unrelated to *the Mosaic Covenant*, the Dispensationalists *appeal directly to the Mosaic Covenant* to find their predictions of the Abomination of Desolation, the Tribulation, the restoration of Israel, and even the resurrection etc., i.e. their entire eschatological paradigm.

Make no mistake, Deuteronomy is undeniably "the Mosaic Covenant" and if the Dispensationalists see there the "prophetic roadmap" of Israel's last days destiny, then it is totally wrong to say that eschatology is unrelated to the Mosaic Covenant. It is in fact, vitally related to it.

---

[174] Kim Riddlebarger, *A Case for Amillennialism*, (Grand Rapids, Baker, 2003)61.

[175] Dwight Pentecost, *Things to Come,* (Grand Rapids, Zondervan, 1980)67.

Thomas Ice says: "As significant as Deuteronomy 4 is in establishing the Tribulation and its purpose, an expanded narrative of Israel's future history is provided in Deuteronomy 28-32. 'The last seven chapters of Deuteronomy (28-34),' says David Larsen, 'are really the matrix out of which the great prophecies of the Old Testament regarding Israel emerge."[176] He then gives Leviticus 26 as parallel to the Blessings and Cursings of Deuteronomy 28-32.

There is nothing more "Mosaic Covenant" than these texts. So, if these passages are about the end time eschatology, then since they are fundamentally the Mosaic Covenant, eschatology is inseparably tied to the Mosaic Covenant, thus falsifying Pentecost's claim.

Similarly, Ice, in his comments on Luke 21:22 says:

> "Those first century days are called the 'days of vengeance' for Jerusalem is under the divine judgment of covenantal sanctions recorded in Leviticus 26 and Deuteronomy 28. Luke notes that God's vengeance on His elect nation 'is in order that all things that are written may be fulfilled.' Jesus is telling the nation that God will fulfill all the curses of the Mosaic Covenant because of Israel's disobedience. He will not relent and merely bring to pass a partial fulfillment of His vengeance. Some of the passages that Jesus says will be fulfilled include the following: Leviticus 26:27-33; Deuteronomy 28:49-63; Deuteronomy 32: 19-27; 1 Kings 9:1-9; Jeremiah 6:1-6; 26:1-9; Daniel 9:26; Hosea 8:1-10:15; Micah 3:12; Zechariah 11:6" (*Tribulation debate*, 1999) 98.

---

[176] Thomas Ice (Kenneth L. Gentry and Thomas Ice, *The Great Tribulation Past or Future?*, (Grand Rapids, MI: Kregel Publications, 1999)75-76. In that debate Ice called Deuteronomy 4 Israel's "prophetic road map of the last days."

Take note that Ice posits AD 70 as the full expression of *Mosaic Covenant wrath*. Of course, this contradicts his other writings in which he affirms that the Mosaic Law was removed at the cross. Ice recognizes that the destruction of Jerusalem was the direct result of Israel's sin, *her violation of Torah.*

How in the name of reason can it be that AD 70 was the full outpouring of Mosaic Covenant wrath, yet the Mosaic Law ostensibly passed at the cross?[177] How can it be that the story of eschatology has nothing to do with the Law of Moses? This is totally untenable.

With these things in mind (however brief, yet critical they have been) let's explore the idea that the Great Tribulation would be the outpouring of Covenant Wrath on Israel for violating the Law of Moses. This examination will confirm the concept of *From Torah to Telos.*

---

[177] This is a problem for Amillennialists and Postmillennialists alike, who commonly claim that Torah ended at the Cross. How could the Law of Blessings and Cursing be applied in AD 70, if the Law of Blessings and Cursings "died" i.e. was nailed to the cross? This is part of the reason why we must see the concept of *Torah to Telos*. Torah would endure until the eschatological consummation.

THE GREAT TRIBULATION WOULD BE A COVENANT CURSE ON ISRAEL RESULTING FROM THE ABOMINATION OF DESOLATION

The Abomination of Desolation is one of the most feared – yet, paradoxically – anticipated prophetic events. It is feared because its appearance is part of the projected Great Tribulation period. It is anticipated because, while a horrible event, it is posited by Jesus as one of the definitive signs of his coming at the end of the age (Matthew 24:15f).

While volumes have been written about the Abomination (hereafter AoD) this section will focus on correcting some of the more popular misconceptions about that horrific event in order to demonstrate that the AoD occurred in the first century during the Jewish War of AD 66-70. We will do this by focusing on who was to "set up," or to express it differently, who was to *commit, or perpetrate* the Abomination. We will demonstrate that the popular definition and understanding of the Abomination is wrong and based on misguided interpretation of the critical texts.

The Abomination of Desolation is widely outlined in Dispensational scheme in the following:

After the rapture of the church, the Man of Sin appears in what seems an almost miraculous set of circumstances and convinces Israel to sign a peace treaty with him and their enemies.

The temple in Jerusalem is rebuilt and, "Judaism is revived and traditional sacrifices and ceremonies are re-instituted in the rebuilt temple in Jerusalem."[178]

---

[178] Thomas Ice and Timothy Demy, *Prophecy Watch*, (Eugene, Ore., Harvest House, 1998)60.

At the middle of the seven year period of time known generally as the Tribulation period, the Man of Sin breaks the peace treaty with Israel: "Antichrist will not only break his own covenant with Israel, but he will also set himself up as God to be worshiped in the rebuilt Jewish temple at the mid-point of the tribulation. This defiling of the third temple is called 'the abomination of desolation.' This will be a sign for the Jews to flee Jerusalem." (*Watch*, 1998, 166).

As you can see, in the Dispensational scenario, the Abomination is set up in the temple *by a non-Jewish figure*, the Man of Sin. It is critical to note that in the millennial schema Israel is basically the "innocent victim" in the end times drama. She is betrayed by the Man of Sin then persecuted by him in the Great Tribulation. However, the Bible knows nothing of Israel's "innocence" in the last days. The Bible knows nothing of her innocence in regard to the Abomination or the Great Tribulation. In fact, to use the old term, she is "as guilty as sin."

As suggested above, Biblically speaking, the Tribulation would be

> Biblically, the Tribulation is directly related to, and the result of, *Israel's violation of Torah – she is the one guilty of the Abomination!*
>
> She is NOT the innocent victim, as portrayed by the Dispensational world.
>
> **This turns Dispensationalism on its head!**

an *expression of Mosaic Covenant Wrath on Israel*. The Abomination and Tribulation were proof positive that Old Covenant Israel was being judged by YHVH for their rejection of Messiah. Israel in this scenario is not the "innocent victim." She is the focus of God's covenant wrath!

I want to present two proposals for the Abomination:

First, the Abomination was something done *by Israel herself*, something so despicable, so abhorrently evil that it led to her desolation and destruction.[179] (Our purpose here is not to specifically identify what it was that Israel did, but to simply posit Israel as the party guilty of committing, "the abomination that leads to desolation.").

Second, as a direct corollary, according to the linguistic scholars the term Abomination of Desolation actually means, "the abomination that causes desolation." Gray says: "'Desolating sacrilege' literally means 'the sacrilege that causes desolation.' It *causes* desolation. It causes desolation because the profanation of the temple incurs God's judgment which ultimately leads to the destruction of the temple."[180] Gibbs agrees that the concept of *defilement leading to destruction* is at stake in the term Abomination of Desolation.[181]

Pitre adds: "The profanation of the Temple, 'brings about the destruction of the Temple and the city of Jerusalem (Daniel 9:27). It is such an egregious sacrilege that it calls down divine wrath and destruction on both the temple and the city" (2005, 304f). In fact,

---

[179] It was held by some Jews that Antiochus Epiphanes had committed an Abomination of Desolation, in defiling the temple. Gibbs notes this. He cites 2 Maccabees 8:17, to show that the Abomination was set up by Antiochus in "the holy place." "And on the fifteenth day of Chislev, the one hundred forty-fifth year, he set up an abomination of desolation upon the altar and in the cities of Judah surrounding they set up the high places." Jeffrey A. Gibbs, *Jerusalem and Parousia*, St. Louis, MO, Concordia Academic Press, 2000)230, n. 108.

[180] Timothy Gray, *The Temple In The Gospel of Mark*, (Grand Rapids, Baker Academic, 2008)141.

[181] Jeffrey A. Gibbs, *Jerusalem and Parousia*, (St. Louis, MO, Concordia Academic Press, 2000)230, n. 112.

Pitre offers three points about the Abomination in his discussion of Daniel 9:24-27:

1.) It always refers to a profanation of the Jerusalem temple and this profanation, "is carried out by means of the forced cessation of the sacrifices."

2.) The profanation is always carried out by a royal figure, "he shall cause the sacrifice to cease."

3.) "The profanation of the Temple that takes place is not simply tragic, but fatal, for it brings about the destruction of the temple and the city of Jerusalem." ... "Hence, in the book of Daniel, the 'abomination of desolation' not only refers to a profanation of the Temple that leads to the cessation of the sacrifice but also to the destruction of the sanctuary and the holy city that accompanies it" (2005, 305).

So, Biblically speaking *Israel's sin is the Abomination that leads directly to the desolation of the Temple* by the pagan forces.[182] In other words, if the AoD was a sin that would lead to the destruction of the Temple and the City, then *it was Israel that was guilty of that sin*! If the punishment fits the crime, then *the crime had to be committed by the guilty party*. To me, that powerfully suggests that the AoD could not have been committed by a pagan force. *(Was YHVH going to destroy the Temple because of the sin of pagans? This does not fit.)*

This is a well documented concept in scripture and in Israel's thought. For instance, Elliott shows that the siege of Jerusalem in BC 63 by Ptolemy was considered *a covenantal curse* by Israel. He cites the Psalms of Solomon 17-19, that in turn cites Deuteronomy 11:16-17 for what had happened: "Take heed lest... he shut up the heavens. so that there be no rain.' or 1 Kings 8:35 – "When heaven

---

[182] Perhaps we could say that even if a pagan actually set up the Abomination, it was Israel's sin that allowed the very presence of pagans in the Temple.

is shut up and there is no rain because they have sinned against thee."[183]

Elliott goes ahead to say that there is clear evidence that in Israel there was the understanding that covenantal violation would bring covenant curse, i.e. the desolation. This is based on scripture.

In 2 Chronicles 6:24, Solomon said, "If your people Israel are defeated before an enemy because they have sinned against you..." David said in Psalms 41:11 – "By this I know that you are well pleased with me, when my enemy does not triumph over me."

God even promised in Exodus 34:23 that if Israel was faithful in her observance of the feast days, that He would ensure that no one invaded them at those sacred times.[184]

So if, as the Dispensationalists say, the Abomination will be a pagan setting up an idol in the Jerusalem temple, this would prove beyond any doubt that Israel will be in rebellion against God in violation of Torah *and under covenant curse*. For YHVH to allow a pagan to set up such a sacrilege would demand that there was an antecedent violation of Torah by Israel. A pagan in the Temple would be a judgment within itself brought about by YHVH. There could be no other way to view that. This refutes the Dispensational paradigm, to say the very least.

---

[183] Mark Adam Elliot, *The Survivors of Israel*, (Grand Rapids, Eerdmans, 2000)284.

[184] See my book *Israel 1948 Countdown to No Where*, for an examination of this powerful concept. Israel was invaded and destroyed in AD 70 and that siege, lasting five months, *spanned the entirety of Israel's festal calendar!* Thus, on the principle of Exodus 34, this served as *prima facie* demonstration that AD 70 was the outpouring of *Mosaic Covenant wrath*. The book is available from my websites, Kindle, Amazon and other retailers.

Look again at the admission of Ice in this regard:

> "Those first century days are called the 'days of vengeance for Jerusalem is under the divine judgment of covenantal sanctions recorded in Leviticus 26 and Deuteronomy 28. Luke notes that God's vengeance on His elect nation 'is in order that all things that are written may be fulfilled.' Jesus is telling the nation that God will fulfill all the curses of the Mosaic Covenant because of Israel's disobedience. He will not relent and merely bring to pass a partial fulfillment of His vengeance. Some of the passages that Jesus says will be fulfilled include the following: Leviticus 26:27-33; Deuteronomy 28:49-63; Deuteronomy 32: 19-27; 1 Kings 9:1-9; Jeremiah 6:1-6; 26:1-9; Daniel 9:26; Hosea 8:1-10:15; Micah 3:12; Zechariah 11:6" (*Tribulation debate*, 1999)98.

Take note that Ice posits AD 70 as the full expression of *Mosaic Covenant wrath*. So, Ice recognizes that the destruction of Jerusalem was the direct result of Israel's sin, *her violation of Torah*. How then, in light of the Dispensational view of the Abomination and the Great Tribulation, can it be affirmed that Israel is the "innocent victim" during the seven year Tribulation? And to reiterate, how can it be said that Torah, the Law of Moses, passed away before AD 70?

Yet, Ice claims that in the attacks from the man of sin, resulting in the Great Tribulation: "Israel is not under judgment from God in the tribulation, but under threat from Gentiles, and rescued by God."[185]

So, according to Ice and LaHaye, the AD 70 cataclysm was an expression of Mosaic Covenant Wrath from God. However, in the

---

[185] Tim LaHaye and Thomas Ice, *End Times Controversy*, (Eugene, Or. Harvest House, 2003)168.

tribulation period Israel is not under judgment from God, but from Gentiles and God delivers Israel from that Gentile attack.

This is patently false. It is a rejection of the scriptures given above. It is also a rejection of one of the most fundamental tenets of all of Dispensationalism and that is that Israel remains God's covenant people.

If Israel remains God's *covenant people*, what covenant are they under that would (will) result in such a horrible thing as the Great Tribulation *for her violation of that covenant*? It will do no good to simply say as Ice does, that Israel is not under judgment in the Tribulation. Ice is whistling past the grave yard. If Israel is being threatened by the Gentiles, it could only be if they were in violation of Torah. It was only when Israel violated the Law of Moses that YHVH allowed them to be threatened by pagan nations. Yet, Ice says Torah has been removed!

If Israel remains as God's covenant people, then what happens to Israel must be viewed as inseparably linked to and flowing from that covenant. So, again, what covenant is Israel under that will result in the horrors of the Abomination of Desolation and the Great Tribulation? The choices are very limited.

It cannot be the Abrahamic Covenant; that covenant contained no provisions for the horrors such as the Great Tribulation.

It cannot be the Davidic Covenant. The Davidic covenant had no distinct provisions for covenant wrath on the temple, the city and the nation such as those contained in Deuteronomy 28-30.

The *only covenant* that YHVH had with Israel that contained provisions for the kind of wrath described as the Great Tribulation was the Mosaic Covenant. It was the Law of Blessings and Cursings. And note again the quotes from Ice given above to that very effect.

It is important to see that it is *the Mosaic Covenant* to which millennialists appeal for predictions of the Great Tribulation. *They never appeal to the Abrahamic or Davidic Covenants.*

A "Google" search of "The Abomination of Desolation" or, "The Great Tribulation," quickly reveals that Dispensationalists believe the Abomination and the Tribulation are indeed predicted in the Mosaic Covenant. This flatly contradicts Pentecost's claim that eschatology is unrelated to the Mosaic Covenant.

Do you see the problem?

The problem is that on the one hand the Dispensationalists say the Mosaic Covenant was abrogated in the first century (generally at the cross). On the other hand, they appeal to the Mosaic Covenant for proof of a yet future Abomination of Desolation and Great Tribulation.

Ice says of the Mosaic Covenant: "The Mosaic Covenant (Exodus 20-23; *the book of Deuteronomy*, my emp. dkp), which contains the law of Moses for Israel, was given to Israel's people after they were delivered from the land of Egypt to show them how they could please God as His redeemed people. *This was a conditional covenant.* The New Testament makes it very clear that the Mosaic Covenant was temporary until Christ would come. Many passages teach that the law was done away with in Christ."[186] (His emphasis).

Okay, so how could the Abomination and Tribulation prophecies found in the Mosaic Covenant still be valid if the Mosaic Covenant is no longer valid? This is a huge problem.

The second proposal suggested above, for the source of the Abomination is that a pagan figure sets up an idol in the Jerusalem temple. This idol is seen as the Abomination. Of course, this is the Dispensational view.

Demy and Ice say: "The newly proclaimed world dictator desecrates the temple in Jerusalem and begins a period of intense persecution

---

[186] Thomas Ice and Timothy Demy, *Fast Facts on Bible Prophecy*, (Eugene, Ore., Harvest House, 1997)135.

of Jews" (1998, 60). However, this scenario offers a strong confirmation of the point I made earlier.

If the Abomination is perpetrated by a pagan leader in the Jewish temple at Jerusalem, it confirms the fact that Israel has violated the Mosaic Covenant and that Mosaic Covenant Wrath is being applied to Israel! It completely falsifies Ice's claim that Israel is not under judgment from God, but simply being persecuted by the Gentiles. Throughout the OT, anytime Israel entered into a covenant with anyone but YHVH, that was considered as spiritual adultery and brought judgment.

We must reiterate this critical and yet ignored fact: *the only way God ever allowed pagans to desecrate and destroy the temple was because of Israel's violation of the Mosaic Covenant.* And, we must take a moment here to address the issue of the "times of the Gentiles" as it relates to the Abomination of Desolation, the Great Tribulation and related themes.

"JERUSALEM SHALL BE TRODDEN DOWN OF THE GENTILES, UNTIL THE TIMES OF THE GENTILES ARE FULFILLED." (Luke 21:24).

As a general rule, Dispensationalists define the times of the Gentiles as the period of Gentile domination and control over Jerusalem. Some date it from the Babylonian Captivity,[187] while others believe it began in AD 70 with the Roman destruction of the city. All commentators who posit the times of the Gentiles as Gentile domination over Jerusalem, whether from BC 586 or from AD 70 onward agree with Ice's assessment: "At the parousia the times of the Gentiles cease and the focus of history once again turns to the Jews" *(Prophecy Watch*, 1998, 264). But there is an elephant in the room for those holding this position.

What is overlooked by almost every futurist positing the end of the times of the Gentiles at some future parousia, is the indisputable fact that the linguistics of Luke 21:24 forbid their definition of the times of the Gentiles. Virtually 100% of those commentators seem unaware of the term "trodden down" and its impact on the definition of the times of the Gentiles.

The word translated "trodden" down is *pateo* and contrary to the Dispensational idea that it refers to the socio-economic, political

---

[187] Cf. Michael F. Blume, commenting on the vision of Daniel 2: "In essence, this awesome dream describes the fullness of the 'times of the Gentiles - that is, the 'times' and seasons when Gentile kingdoms, or Gentile-influenced kingdoms, would rule over the world, or vast sections thereof. In other words, from the time of king Nebuchadnezzar of Babylon, till the present time, today, the world has been living under or within the 'times of the Gentiles' - the times GENTILE KINGDOMS would dominate and have the supremacy over the nations of the world!" (His emphasis). (http://mikeblume.com/timesgen.htm)

domination and control of the city,[188] this word means *active warfare*, conquest and *active destruction*.

Ardnt and Gingrich says the word means to tread down, to trample, "of the undisciplined swarming of a victorious army through a captured city."[189] Virtually all lexicons agree on this definition. This linguistic fact alone destroys the Dispensational concept of the trodding down of Jerusalem for the last 2000 years.[190] There have been *long* periods of time when there was no active military war taking place in Jerusalem. In fact, even though there certainly have been times of active military action in Jerusalem, for the most part, active military "down trodding" i.e. active trampling of the city by a victorious army, has not characterized the last 2000 years. Not only does history demonstrate that Israel has not been actively "trodden down" by the Gentiles for the last 2000 years, a quick study of how the word *pateo* is used in scripture verifies what we are saying.

We will keep this brief, but it is important. While the LXX uses *pateo* in the same way as the NT, we will confine our study to the NT occurrences of the word. However, for one quick reference see Lamentations 1:17, where Jeremiah looks back at the siege and destruction of Jerusalem under the Chaldeans as the *treading down* (a cognate of *pateo*) of the city. He was living in the time of socio - economic - political *domination that followed that treading down*.

---

[188] Actually, I have yet to find a Dispensational commentator that even examines *pateo*. It is totally ignored.

[189] *A Greek English Lexicon of the New Testament*, (University of Chicago Press, 1979)635.

[190] The proper definition of *pateo* likewise falsifies the Amillennial view of Beale who posits the treading down of the holy city in Revelation 11 as reference to the persecution of the church throughout time, until the end of time (Beale, NIGTC, *Revelation*, 1999, 569f). This is a gross abuse of *pateo*. The church has not been actively, militarily trodden down for 2000 years.

But that subsequent time of domination was not the time of her *pateo*.

Pateo is only used five times in the NT and as just suggested invariably refers to a violent action – it *never* refers to a simple socio / economic / political, control over a people.

☛In Luke 10:19 – Jesus told his disciples, "I have given you authority to *tread* on serpents and snakes." It is easily seen that Jesus was not talking here of simple "domination" of snakes, but the active crushing.

☛Luke 21:24 - The context of Luke is clearly referent to the active war and siege of Jerusalem. It has no reference to a 2000 year period of political domination. Notice the reference to Jerusalem surrounded, and the men of Jerusalem falling by the sword. This is active warfare.

☛Revelation 11:1-4 – John was told that, "the holy city shall be trodden down for time, times and half time." Unless one can make this referent to be 2000 years, then the context certainly seems to be the active, military, war time conquering of the city. This is the city, "Where the Lord was slain" (Revelation 11:8). The parallels between Luke 21 and Revelation 11 define the, "times of the Gentiles" as the period of the Jewish War. It was "42 months." It was, to express it another way, the time appointed by God for the destruction of Old Covenant Jerusalem.

☛Revelation 14:20 – This text also describes the judgment of Babylon and she is "trodden down in the winepress of God's wrath." Imagery could not be clearer. The treading down is the time of destruction.

☛Revelation 19:15 - Just as in Revelation 11 and 14, here in chapter 19, Jesus is described as the one that makes war on Babylon: "He treads the winepress of the wrath of God." There is not a hint of an idea of simple geo-political, domination. It is the active, real time of war against Babylon – her time of destruction.

The impact of this linguistic fact is quite devastating on the Dispensational and Premillennial paradigm. In July of 2015, I had a formal YouTube debate with Dr. Michael Brown, a renowned apologist and debater. I made the point on *pateo*, with the scriptural support. Dr. Brown did not initially respond. Near the end of the debate, when I had no opportunity to respond, he quickly stated that Jerusalem had undergone several times of military conflict during the last 2000 years, therefore my point, said he, was negated. This is as false as can be. As just demonstrated, the fact that there have been several times of active military conflict, interspersed between long periods of peace, does not meet the linguistic demands of *pateo*. Not to mention the fact that some of those supposed times of conflict were times when the Israeli forces took control of Jerusalem.

The indisputable fact is that *pateo* in Luke 21:24 gives no support whatsoever to the Dispensational view that Jerusalem has been "trodden down" for the last 2000 years, but that at some future coming of Christ she will be restored. The Dispensational schema is a violation of the meaning of *pateo* and thus, it is false. But there is even more here than the meaning of *pateo*.

As we have suggested above, the Abomination of Desolation and the Great Tribulation must be viewed as the imposition of Covenant Wrath on Israel for violation the Law of Moses. The same can be said of the times of the Gentiles.

According to Leviticus 26 and the Law of Blessings and Cursings (Deuteronomy 28-30) the only way that YHVH allowed the Gentiles to control the land of Israel and Jerusalem was when / if Israel had broken Torah. The invasions of the land and the capturing of the City were invariably viewed – according to the prophets - as God's judgment on the people for violating the Mosaic covenant.

Consider again that as we have documented above, Dispensationalists and Historic Premillennialists affirm that the Law of Moses is not in effect today. In my debate with Dr. Brown, I asked if the Law of Moses was still in effect and he answered "No." However, one cannot affirm on the one hand that Israel and

Jerusalem has been in subjection to the Gentiles for the last 2000 years and at the same time say the Law of Moses passed away 2000 years ago. The only way that Jerusalem and Israel could be enduring the times of the Gentiles is if the Law of Moses - every jot and every tittle - remains in effect and binding today.[191]

If a law or a covenant has been annulled it is irrefutably true that the provisions of that covenant are no longer applicable. This is beyond dispute. So, it was the Law of Moses that made provision for "the times of the Gentiles" i.e the appointed times of judgment against Israel for violating the covenant. If therefore, the times of the Gentiles have been in existence since AD 70 this is *prima facie* proof that the Law of Moses has remained in effect - and remains in effect - to this very day.

The Dispensationalists and Premillennialists cannot have their cake and eat it too. If the Law of Moses passed away in the first century as they all claim, the times of the Gentiles ended in the first century. If the times of the Gentiles have been in effect since AD 70 – or BC 586 - then Torah remains in effect and will remain in effect until the end of the times of the Gentiles, at the Second Coming of Christ.

There is therefore no way, Biblically or logically, to divorce the topic of the Abomination, the Tribulation or the times of the Gentiles from the fundamental fact of Israel's violation of the Mosaic Covenant. And since even the millennialists insist that the Mosaic Covenant is no longer valid, (and, they likewise say the Mosaic Law will never be restored) this demands that the Abomination, the Tribulation and the times of the Gentiles had to

---

[191] A glaring inconsistency in this regard came to light in my debate with Dr. Brown. Even though he affirmed that the Law of Moses has been done away, he then tried to prove that the judgment and resurrection must be yet future *because we are still waiting for Israel's last three feast days, Trumpets, Atonement and Succot (Harvest) to be fulfilled!* How could the Law of Moses have been done away, yet the climatic feast days have not been fulfilled?

have occurred at a time *when the Mosaic Covenant was still in force*. This demands a first century fulfillment of these tenets including the Abomination and Great Tribulation and that is precisely what we find.

The Times of the Gentiles could only be imposed if and when Israel violated Torah, according to Leviticus and Deuteronomy.

The Dispensationalists tell us the Law of Moses was removed in the first century and is no longer valid.

Yet, the Dispensationalists then turn around and say that the times of the Gentiles will not end until the end of the Christian age at the Second Coming of Christ.

Logically and Biblically, this demands that the Law of Moses - every jot and every tittle, remains valid until the end of the Christian age at the Second Coming of Christ.

This is a fatal error in the Dispensational doctrine!

THE ABOMINATION OF DESOLATION AND GREAT TRIBULATION AS FIRST CENTURY EVENTS – AND PROOF THAT TORAH DID NOT PASS AT THE CROSS

When Hebrews was written, the Mosaic Covenant[192] was "obsolete and ready (*engus*) to vanish away" (Hebrews 8:13). The time of its fulfillment, its *complete* fulfillment, was to be at the fall of Jerusalem (Daniel 9:24-27; Luke 21:22).

Notice a few important thoughts in regard to the Great Tribulation and its first century fulfillment. The following is an edited excerpt from my *Who Is This Babylon* book:

Notice what is said of the 144,000 in Revelation 14:4, "These are the ones who were not defiled with women, for they are virgins. These are the ones who follow the Lamb wherever He goes. These were redeemed from among men, *being first fruits to God and to the Lamb.*" Did you catch the power of what is said? *The 144,000 were the first fruits of those redeemed by Jesus Christ, the Lamb of God.*

Notice that these were Christians. But these are not just Christians, they are *Jewish* Christians out of the 12 tribes of Israel. Further, these are not just Jewish Christians, they are *the first generation of*

---

[192] It was the Mosaic Covenant itself, not simply the external "ministration" of the covenant that was passing. In my written debate with Kurt Simmons he argued that the Law had already passed at the cross, but that Hebrews 8 is speaking of the passing of the ceremonial cultus. In a similar vein, McDurmon argued that it was the external "ministration" of the covenant that was passing, not the covenant. Notice that the text uses the word *covenant* four times explicitly and two times by *ellipsis*. Not one word is said of the external trappings, or the *ministration* of the covenant delineated from the covenant. The claims of these men are a desperate attempt to avoid the implications for their own theological paradigms. Be sure to read the books of those respective debates, available from my websites, Kindle, Amazon and other retailers.

Jewish Christians. The significance of the first fruits must not be missed, or dismissed, for it places the book of Revelation in an early context.

You and I are living many, many generations beyond the time of the first fruit of Christians. Furthermore, the longer time marches on the farther removed we are from the generation of the first fruits redeemed from among men.

James wrote early in the first century generation, "To the twelve tribes scattered abroad" (James 1:1). What did he have to say about the first fruit concept? Hear him, "Of his own will he brought us forth by the word of His mouth, that we might be a kind of first fruit (*aparche*) of His creatures" (James 1:18). Likewise, the writer of Hebrews said, "You have come to Mount Zion and to the city of the Living God, the heavenly Jerusalem, to an unnumerable company of angels, to the general assembly and church of the firstborn who are registered in heaven" (Hebrews 12:22).

There can be no doubt as to the meaning of "first fruits." When Paul wrote to the saints in Rome he gave greetings to Epaenetus, "who was the first (*aparche*) convert to Christ in the province of Asia" (Romans 16:5 NIV). Likewise, in 1 Corinthians 16:15, the same apostle sent greetings to the household of Stephanas that was, "the first (*aparche*) converts in Achaia." Paul was referring to the very first converts.

John did not say the 144,000 were the first fruit of some far distant time. He did not say they were to be the first fruit of a different preaching of a different gospel message. The idea of the term "first fruit" has a temporal significance that cannot be mitigated. The 144,000 were the first generation of Jewish Christians and this has profound implications for not only the dating of the Apocalypse, but for many of today's eschatological paradigms.

The 144,000 were to come out of the Great Tribulation (7:14). If the 144,000 were the first Christians and if they were to endure the Great Tribulation, then it follows undeniably that the Great Tribulation was to occur in the first century generation. Of course, this is precisely what Jesus predicted in the Olivet Discourse (Matthew 24:15-34) in spite of the Dispensational objections. You cannot divorce the 144,000 from the Great Tribulation. No other generation can ever be, "the first fruits unto God and to the Lamb" (Revelation 14:4), than that first century generation. Patently, the Great Tribulation was in the first century.[193]

Notice that every point we have made is drawn directly from the texts, not imposed on them.

It is Israel that would (did) commit the heinous crimes that brought about the temple's destruction.

It was Israel's sin that brought the presence of the Romans into the temple, totally destroying it and putting an end to the temple cultus.

Jesus said all of those things would occur in the first century (Matthew 24:34) and without manipulating the text, that is the normal and natural application of Jesus' words. Israel did sin (heinously). Israel did sin, in the temple. Israel's sin did lead to her destruction and the out-pouring of Mosaic Covenant Wrath in AD 70.

Israel was under the Mosaic Covenant curse for her sins and AD 70 was the consummative and climactic out pouring of that Wrath. In that judgment, "all things that are written must be fulfilled" and thus, Torah passed away. *There is no further application of Mosaic Covenant Wrath beyond that point.* This is *Torah to Telos!*

Consider the following:

Deuteronomy 28-32 is part and parcel of "the law."

Deuteronomy 28-32 contains the prediction of the last days judgment on Israel – the Great Tribulation.

---

[193] See my book *Who Is This Babylon* for a further discussion of the topic. The book is available from my websites, Kindle, Amazon other retailers.

Not one jot or one tittle could pass from the Law until it was all fulfilled – which would be inclusive of the predictions of "the law" of Deuteronomy 28-32.

The Tribulation occurred well after the Cross.

Therefore, not one jot or one tittle of the law (inclusive of Deuteronomy) passed until the occurrence of the Tribulation. (The law did not pass at the cross).

As we have seen, the Dispensational application of Deuteronomy to a proposed Abomination of Desolation and Great Tribulation is self-contradictory. On the one hand they say that the Mosaic Covenant was abrogated at the cross. Then they say Mosaic Covenant Wrath was completely (not partially) fulfilled in AD 70. Then they try to apply the Mosaic Covenant provisions of covenant wrath to a yet future time. To say the least, this is inconsistent, self-contradictory and unscriptural.

The Abomination of Desolation and the Great Tribulation were the final expressions and out-pouring of Mosaic Covenant Wrath. That ended in AD 70 with the final, consummative destruction of the Old Covenant world. In this regard, it is important to realize that even in the traditional Jewish eschatological narrative, it was well understood that the appearance of the Abomination and the Great Tribulation would give way to the New Covenant world of Messiah, the kingdom – what they referred to as the "age to come."

In other words, the point to be taken from this discussion is that in the Biblical narrative and the eschatological "Time Line" it is indisputably clear that the Abomination leads to the Tribulation *which climaxes in the Judgment, the Kingdom and the resurrection.* The Abomination and the Tribulation were not to be typological or anticipatory of the real end, far removed from those events. So, if the Abomination and Tribulation were first century events – and they patently were – then the eschatological consummation had to be in the first century as well.

What simply cannot be missed, but as we have seen, tragically seems to be all but lost in evangelical circles, is that the Abomination and the Tribulation are inextricably tied to Israel and the outpouring of covenant wrath on her, *due to her violation of the Law of Moses*. And this in turn is irrefutably tied to the Judgment / Kingdom / Resurrection. This connection proves two things:

1.) If the Abomination and Tribulation are still future, then Israel remains under the Law of Moses, because it is the Law of Moses that contains the Law of Blessings and Cursings.

2.) It proves that the Abomination and the Tribulation are tied specifically *to Israel* and *to the eschatological resurrection*. It is improper therefore, to posit the resurrection at the end of the Christian age.

If the Great Tribulation is a covenant Curse on Israel and if the resurrection comes at the climax of the Tribulation, then the resurrection is posited at the climax of Israel's covenant history – i.e. "When the power of the holy people is completely shattered" - when YHVH would finally break His (old) covenant bond with Israel (Zechariah 11:8-9). The resurrection in the texts examined undeniably posit the resurrection in the context of the judgment of Israel and as the climax of the Tribulation on Israel.

So, we have established the following:

In the OT prophecies of the end of the age, the coming of Messiah, the judgment and the resurrection, the Biblical "time line" is: Elijah —> Abomination —> Tribulation —> Parousia / Judgment / Resurrection.

We have demonstrated that the Tribulation is invariably posited as the time of judgment on Israel for violation of Torah.

We have shown that the resurrection – the focus of this study – is explicitly positioned by those OT prophecies at the end of Israel's covenant age – *never at the end of time.*

What we need to do now is to explore whether Jesus and the NT writers followed this narrative and time line, or, whether they radically "re-worked" that time line and divorced it from Israel, her judgment and the end of her age.

THE NEW TESTAMENT TIME LINE: ABOMINATION –> TRIBULATION –> PAROUSIA / KINGDOM / RESURRECTION

The NT writers undeniably agreed with and followed the OT pattern. Space will not permit a full discourse on this, but we will list some of the outstanding eschatological texts, taking note of the OT pattern found in them.

Matthew 16:21-28

Jesus warns his apostles that he was about to die and they will join him in martyrdom. However, he promises that he will come in judgment – clearly judgment in vindication of that suffering that was coming. He promised them that he was coming in the kingdom, in their lifetime.

McKnight commenting on Matthew 16:27-28 says;

> "It is reasonable, then, to argue that this vindication took place when Jerusalem was sacked by Rome as God's punishment for covenant faithlessness. Jesus therefore predicted a vindication of himself and his followers before the death of the disciples. This view fits admirably with the context (Mark 8:34-38) and gives adequate ground for Mark's insertion of the logion before his account of the transfiguration. In the previous context, Jesus promises the disciples that, though they would suffer like him, they would be vindicated by God. And just as Jesus was to suffer the ignominy of a humiliating death at the hands of the leaders in Jerusalem, so he would be vindicated. The disciples need to be assured of Jesus' vindication and this is precisely how the transfiguration ought to be understood – as proleptic vindication." (1999, 136).

Likewise, Wright says,

> "The whole of the story, of judgment for those who had not followed Jesus and the vindication for those who had, is summed up in the cryptic but frequently repeated saying 'the first shall be last, the last first.' In other words, when the great tribulation came on Israel, those who had followed Jesus would be delivered; and that would be the sign that Jesus had been in the right and that in consequence they had been in the right in following him. The destruction of Jerusalem on the one hand and the rescue of the disciples on the other, would be the vindication of what Jesus had been saying throughout his ministry." (1996, 338).

Matthew 16:27-28 is a direct echo of Daniel 7 – the suffering of the saints - the vindication of the martyrs at the coming of YHVH – the arrival of the kingdom. And, just as Daniel's prophecy is confined to the days of the Roman empire, Jesus delimited that prophecy and its fulfillment even more by saying it would be fulfilled in the lifetime of his audience.

Matthew 24

There is perhaps no clearer illustration of the validity of the eschatological pattern we have been setting forth than the Olivet Discourse. In powerful and challenging form, Jesus shares with us that there is no question about the pattern. *He lays it out precisely as the rabbinic authors viewed it!* He presents it exactly as the OT gave it.

Did Jesus have the same materialistic and nationalistic "take" on these themes and prophecies? No, but this does not in any way negate the fact that he followed precisely the outline of the last days schema that the Jews of his day accepted and taught.

Notice that the question posed by the disciples is focused on Jesus' parousia and the end of the age. Contra what seems to be the majority of commentators today, the disciples were not confused, nor were they mistaken. That is a myth, with no textual support.

So, the theme of the Discourse is the end of the age in the disciples' mind – steeped as they were in the OT prophecies – and they link that consummation with the judgment on the Temple.

As Jesus answers their questions, he specifically speaks of the, "wars and rumors of wars, pestilence, famine, etc.." These are all elements of the "birth pangs of Messiah"[194] discussed in the Jewish literature. Note how Jesus described those coming difficulties: "these are the beginning of birth pangs" (i.e. the Messianic Woes, Matthew 24:8).

As Hagner says,

> "All these terrifying events and presumably others like them, are indeed but *arxe odinon*, 'the beginning of birth pangs.' The imagery of 'birth pangs' (1 Enoch 62:4; 2 Esdr 4:42; cf. Strack-Billerbeck 4:2:977-86) points to the commonly expected period of suffering (the 'woes of Messiah'...that would immediately precede the birth of the Messianic age (cf. The imagery of Isaiah 26:17; 66:7-8; Jer. 22:23; Mic. 4:9; and in the NT 1 Thes. 5:3). Only such an extended period of trevail in birth could bring forth the 'new birth' of the created order (cf. 19:28). The sufferings awaiting

---

[194] Cf. W. D. Davies and D. C. Allison, *International Critical Commentary, Vol. III, Matthew 19-28* (London, New York, T and T Clark, 1997)340+ in which they show from numerous sources – in addition to what we have shared above - that what Jesus was predicting was the widely accepted eschatological pattern of the day.

the disciples were but the beginning of that trevail."[195]

Notice that in verses 15f, Jesus follows *precisely* the pattern of the last days scheme found in Judaism of the day. He posits the appearance of the Abomination, followed by the unparalleled Tribulation (v. 21; cf. Again Daniel 12:1), followed "immediately" by the coming of the Son of Man - the resurrection, in v. 29-31.

What we have in the Olivet Discourse, Jesus' most extensive and paradigmatic teaching on the end times, is that he follows *exactly* the prevailing thought as to *what* was to happen and the order of occurrence. As Hilyer, (although commenting on references to tribulation in 1 Peter 5) notes: "The sufferings of Christ" – Could be taken as reference to the 'messianic woes,' a time of suffering preceding Messiah's advent, which was expected in Judaism. The emphasis in the rabbinic teaching however, was not on the suffering of Messiah himself but on the experience of Israel during the years of distress and suffering for this is the period of Mother Zion's 'birth pangs' ushering in a new era. The parallels with the NT teaching about the second coming of Christ are patent."[196] They are indeed patently clear if we are willing to see these parallels.

But Jesus and the NT writers did not simply lay out the same chronological pattern of the last days. They emphatically said that all of these things would occur in his generation.

---

[195] Donald Hagner, *Word Biblical Commentary, Matthew 14-28,* (Dallas, Word, 1995)691.

[196] Norman Hilyer, *New International Biblical Commentary, 1 and 2 Peter and Jude,* (Peabody, Mass, Hendrickson, 1992)135.

> **The last days sequence of events set forth by Jesus in Matthew 24:4-34 is *precisely* the pattern accepted by the Jews of Jesus' day. That time line of events was to consummate, not in some typological "end of the age," not some "minor" consummation, not just another of many Days of the Lord.**
>
> **That pattern was to climax in the resurrection of the dead!**
>
> **The fact that Jesus posited the fulfillment of that last days blue print at the AD 70 judgment of Jerusalem demonstrates that AD 70 was the "final" resurrection.**

Jesus lays out his eschatological schema in Matthew 24:4-34. *This order of events is precisely what was expected in Jewish thought of the day*. This strongly establishes the fact that the events of AD 70 were the "final" eschatological events. In other words, what Jesus laid out in these verses shows that he was – in this regard – in agreement with the prevailing thought of the day as to the last days events.[197] Jesus was not anticipating another eschaton, another end

---

[197] Make no mistake, Jesus was *often* at odds with the Jews of his day as to the *nature* of their expectations of the kingdom and resurrection. But to anticipate an objection, just because he differed as to the *nature* of the events does not logically demand that he opposed their concept of *the order of events* or when those things were to occur. Jesus undeniably did agree with the last days pattern.

of the age, another parousia,[198] another resurrection or judgment, different from that to climax his current age.

We must point out - again - how incredibly important it is to see how Jesus agreed with the time line. Remember, Jewish thought - and as we have seen - the OT itself, undeniably outlined the last days events as Elijah –> Abomination –> Tribulation –> Parousia / Kingdom / Resurrection. We have shown from the OT that the Tribulation was to immediately precede the resurrection and kingdom. With that in mind, take a closer look at Matthew 24:15-34.

In verse 15, we have the appearance of the Abomination of Desolation (in fulfillment of Daniel 9 and 12). Remember, both texts posit the Abomination in the time of the end and in context of the resurrection.

In verse 21, we have the Great Tribulation, once again, taken from Daniel, and in Daniel 12:1, the Tribulation occurs immediately before the resurrection in v.2.

In verse 29, Jesus said, "immediately after the tribulation of those days," the sun would be darkened, and then, "they will see the Son of Man coming in the clouds of heaven with power and glory."

If Jesus followed the Jewish time line and that set forth by Isaiah, Hosea, Micah, Daniel, etc., this means that the resurrection was to occur in direct, inextricable connection to the Great Tribulation that virtually all Amillennialists and Postmillennialists agree took place in the first century. And remember, they deny that there will be another Great Tribulation in the future. If that is true, then the "real"

---

[198] Matthew 24:30 - the coming of the Son of Man - like Matthew 16:27f - clearly echoes Daniel 7. Just like in Daniel, in Matthew 16, Jesus was promising his coming in vindication of the martyrs, which he had discussed in 24:9f (cf. Mark 13:9f). This means fulfillment of Matthew 24:29f was confined to the days of Rome and more particularly, to Jesus' generation, just as Matthew 24:34 says.

resurrection must have been in the first century, for in those OT texts of the "real" resurrection (Isaiah 25-27 / Hosea 13, etc.) the Tribulation is posited immediately before that predicted resurrection.

Notice how this confirms that Matthew 24:29f is about the resurrection. In v. 31, Jesus said that at the sounding of the Great Trump the elect would be gathered from the four winds. Jesus is undeniably echoing Isaiah 27:13, a prophecy of the last days coming of the Lord for the resurrection.[199] More on this below. The point is that since Jesus was, without doubt, following the last days time line of the Tribulation immediately before the resurrection, then Matthew 24:21-34 is a resurrection text and undeniably posited to occur in the first century.

So, Jesus set forth the last days drama *exactly* in the way his contemporaries expected it to occur, as to order of occurrence. More importantly, he followed, *step by step*, the time line laid out in Torah. The climax of their expectation would be the kingdom, judgment and resurrection. This is *prima facie* proof that the resurrection of the dead was to occur at the time of the judgment of Old Covenant Jerusalem – which of course – is precisely what Daniel 12 foretold.

---

[199] Many commentators see Isaiah 27:13 as a prediction of the resurrection at the sounding of the Great (Last) Trump of 1 Corinthians 15:52. See Greg Beale, *Commentary on the NT Use of the OT,* (Grand Rapids, Baker Academic, 2007, 747). See also W. D. Davies and Dale Allison, who link Isaiah 27:13 to the resurrection at the time of the end *(International Critical Commentary, Matthew 19-28,* (New York, T and T Clark International, Vol. III, 1997)363.

Acts 14:22 - "We must through much tribulation, enter the kingdom."[200]

In this tightly compacted verse, we find strong eschatological overtones. And we find the divine end times drama in "Reader's Digest" form.

Notice Luke's use of "we *must.*" He uses the word *dei*, which means it was a divine necessity. As Peterson notes: "As in other contexts, the *dei*, as in Luke 24:46-47; Acts 17:3; Cf. 9:15-16) refers to the divine plan. The implication seems to be that the persecution of believers is to be understood as consistent with God's plan, not that it is an entrance requirement that believers must meet by virtue of their own conscious choice.'"[201]

Paul warned all of the new converts that their new found faith and life was not to be easy. As Witherington says: "The basic message to the new converts is summarized in v. 22b: 'We must go through many hardships to enter the kingdom of God.' The word *thlipsis* refers to the difficulties or sufferings, in this case sufferings that come from persecution for loyalty to ones' faith. This may in fact allude to the early Jewish notion that believers must suffer the messianic woes at the outset of the eschatological age before the kingdom will come."[202]

---

[200] Note the direct parallels between Acts 14 and 1 Thessalonians 1:10, 3:1-3; 2 Thessalonians 1:4f. The idea of suffering (This was *persecution*; not heart attacks, cancer, or financial difficulty!) before entrance into the kingdom permeates the NT, just like in the OT prophecies.

[201] David Peterson, *The Acts of the Apostles, Pillar New Testament Commentary,* (Grand Rapids, Eerdmans, Apollos, England, 2009)414.

[202] Ben Witherington, *The Acts of the Apostles, A Socio-Rhetorical Commentary,* (Grand Rapids, Cambridge, Paternoster, 1998)428.

The connection between Luke's tightly compacted statement of Paul's theology is, while brief, nonetheless a powerful echo of Daniel 7:21f. It is the divine pattern of Tribulation –> kingdom – resurrection. And of course, once again, that demanded fulfillment in the days of the Roman empire.

Romans 8:18f

"I reckon that the suffering of this present time is not worthy to be compared with the glory that is about to be revealed..."

This text exemplifies the concept of end time sufferings before the resurrection. Paul spoke of, "the suffering (*pathemata*) of the now time" (literal rendering).[203] That was Paul's first century "now time." Paul even uses "Messianic Birth Pangs" terminology as he speaks of his "now time" in which he and his contemporaries were experiencing that suffering. Let me just make a few brief observations.

1. The "sufferings" (from *pathemata*) that Paul discusses are not the turmoils and suffering of the normal human condition. As Dunn observes,[204] Paul is undoubtedly using the word as he normally does to speak of 'the sufferings of Christ' that belong to the eschatological narrative, the end time drama. It is not a reference to cancer, heart problems, family distress, job pressure. The word he uses is a powerful word to describe persecution for the cause of Christ.

---

[203] See Wright's discussion of "the now time" in Paul, as it stands in contrast to the OT prophecies of "in those days." While Wright emphasizes the first century presence of the "age to come" in fulfillment of those OT prophecies, he then ignores the objective imminence of the "not yet" in the "already but not yet" of the NT writers. Part of his discussion is found in *Paul and the Faithfulness of God*, Vol. I, 2013, 555f).

[204] James D. G. Dunn, *Word Biblical Commentary, Romans 1-8*, (Dallas, Word Publishers, 1988)468.

Perriman adds to this by commenting on the word "groaning": "The language of 'groaning' in Romans 8:23 (*stenazo, stenagmos*), strongly suggests the experience of those who are oppressed by the enemies of God."[205]

2. Paul said those sufferings were part of the birth pains that would lead to glory. He uses the word *sunodinei*, the very word Jesus used in Matthew 24:8 to speak of the birth pangs that would occur in that generation and lead to the parousia.

Unless Paul is using the terminology of the Birth Pangs of Messiah and applying it in a way contrary to the normal eschatological pattern, his reference to the then present birth pangs that were leading to the "glory about to be revealed" should be seen as perfectly consistent with the pattern we have seen throughout this investigation: Tribulation – parousia / judgment / resurrection.

3. What should not be missed is that Paul is drawing directly from Isaiah 26:16f, where Israel is depicted as laboring in child labor to bring forth salvation and righteousness, but availing nothing but *futility*.[206] And yet, as seen above in our discussion of Isaiah, the promise was that the resurrection would take place at the time

---

[205] Andrew Perriman, *The Coming of the Son of Man*, (London, Paternoster, 2005)110.

[206] A good commentary on the "futility" that Paul had in mind is found in the book of Ecclesiastes, where the key word is "vanity." Another important aspect of that vanity / futility to which "creation" was subjected, is found in Ezekiel 20:25, where YHVH said He gave Israel, "statutes that were not good and judgments by which they could not live." Here is futility exemplified! This distinctive word *mataiotees*, is never used to describe trees being in futility because they are not tall enough, green enough or not fruitful enough. The word is used to speak of *moral futility*, of man failing to reach the goal, of man failing to be what he is capable of being and doing! In other words *matiaiotees* is a moral word. It has nothing to do with. "bugs slugs and mosquitoes."

YHVH vindicated the blood of the martyrs, destroyed Leviathan and brought redemption.

In Romans, Paul is expressing the hope of Israel found in Torah. Dunn states it well: "Paul clearly intends for his audience to understand that the blessings they are receiving are Israel's promises" (1988, 467f). The promised "glory" of redemption would be in fulfillment of God's promises to Israel – and this is *Torah to Telos*. God's promises to Israel – found in the Law of Moses - would remain valid until the day that YHVH consummated His purposes with and for Israel. Torah would pass when "the glory about to be revealed" came into reality and not before.

This thought is expressed well by Mayer who has some excellent comments showing that in Romans 11:25-28, Paul uses two catch words from Romans 9, "covenants" and "fathers" to drive home the point that: "The Israelites possess the 'covenants' (9:4) and 'the fathers' (9:5). All Israel will be saved when God's 'covenant' becomes a reality (11:25-28) because Israel is beloved on account of the fathers."[207]

In other words, to express this simply:

Israel would be saved when God's (New) covenant became a reality.

Israel's salvation was yet future when Paul wrote.

Therefore, the New Covenant had not yet become a full reality – the Old Covenant had not yet passed.

This is clearly *Torah to Telos!*

4. Paul said the anticipated "glory" to come at the resurrection was "about to be revealed." As Dunn says, "It is natural to hear in *mello*

---

[207] Jason Mayer, *The End of the Law: Mosaic Covenant in Pauline Theology*, (Nashville, B & H Publishing, 2009)178.

the note not only of certainty (see 8:13) but also of imminence: on the point of being, about to be revealed" (1988, 468).[208] Moo agrees that Paul's use of *mello* indicates a belief in the imminence of the coming glory. He discusses Paul's use of *mello* and agrees that it, "might stress the imminence of the revelation of this glory."[209]

Paul also uses some other words that powerfully express his sense of the imminence of the coming resurrection.

He uses the word *apokaradokeo*. Of this word, Balz and Schneider say: "The majority of fathers understand *apokaradokeo* as an intensification of *karadokia* and thus, an especially strong expression of expectation." .... "it remains most probable that with *apokaradokia* Paul intends to give expression to the element of earnest and eager longing. The preposition *apo* thereby strengthens the intensive character of the expression."[210] He says the word, "expresses well the sense of eschatological tension – a straining forward for an eagerly (or anxiously) awaited event."[211]

---

[208] Of course Dunn, like Moo and most commentators, believe the imminent expectation of Paul and the first century Christians failed. This is a tragic situation for which only Covenant Eschatology provides the answer.

[209] Douglas Moo, *Epistle to the Romans, New International Commentary on the New Testament,* (Grand Rapids, Eerdmans, 1996)512, n. 19.

[210] Horst Balz and Gerhard Schneider, *Exegetical Dictionary of the New Testament,* Vol. I, (Grand Rapids, Eerdmans, 1978)132.

[211] Dunn (p. 469) agrees that Paul is using the well known concept of the Messianic Woes leading to resurrection. He says the elements of the eschatological pattern of suffering leading to glory / kingdom / resurrection "are all there" in Paul.

Paul also uses the word *apekdekomai*, which means eager expectation, or eager, expectant looking. See Hawthorne's comments on this word in his commentary on Philippians.[212]

So, in Romans 8 we find the following: the presence of the Messianic Birth Pangs and the emphasis on the "now" time which stood in stark contrast to the OT predictions of "the days are coming." And we have the incorporation of three powerful words of imminence and the glory that would come imminently.

It would be difficult to find a text that more graphically, or accurately, followed the standard apocalyptic narrative, or that more powerfully expressed that the consummation of that pattern was near.

Pate comments on Paul's concept of the then present sufferings as they related to the end time narrative:

> "It is probable that Paul, like other NT authors, believed that, since the coming of Christ signaled the arrival of the last days, the messianic woes must have been set in motion at the event of the cross. This period was expected to run its course and be replaced with the kingdom of God at the parousia (Matthew 24; Mark 13; Luke 21; 2 Peter 3:3-14; Revelation 6-19). Thus, Paul likely believed that the natural disasters his generation encountered would shortly give place to cosmic disturbances and that these would, in turn, herald the return of Christ (cf. Romans 8:22 with Mark 13:9). The apostle may have even interpreted the extensive famine in his day to be one of the signs of the end times (Romans 15:26; with Acts 11:27-30)."

---

[212] Gerald Hawthorne, *Word Biblical :Commentary*, (vol. 43), *Philippians*, (Waco, Word Publisher, 1983)171.

In a footnote on page 65 Pate says that Paul saw his ministry to the Gentiles as "eschatological in nature" (N. 40, page 65).[213]

A final note on Romans 8 and the end time narrative. A great commentary on the text is found in 1 Peter. We will look closer at the text below, but notice briefly that Peter was anticipating the coming of the incorruptible inheritance, just like Paul (1 Peter 1:3).

Like Paul, who spoke of the futility (*mataiotees*) of creation, Peter speaks of the futility (*mataiotees*) of life, "received by tradition from your fathers" (1 Peter 1:18).

Like Paul, Peter and his audience were in the midst of persecution and *suffering* (*pathemata*: Peter also uses the word *pathemata* - 1 Peter 1; 5:9).

Like Paul, Peter was looking for the glory "about to be revealed" (1 Peter 5:1- *mellouses*) at the parousia of Christ.

Like Paul who used the words of imminence, Peter said that Christ was, "ready (*hetoimos*) to judge the living and the dead." He said, "the end of all things has drawn near" (1 Peter 4:7). And he said, "the (*appointed* time, from *kairos*) time for (*the*) judgment has come" (1 Peter 4:17).

Do not miss the fact that both Peter and Paul were anticipating the arrival of "the glory" which was nothing less than the "incorruptible, un-defiled, that cannot fade" inheritance. In Romans 8, that inheritance was, the "redemption of the body"(v. 23). So, when we conflate Paul's language of imminence with Peter's

---

[213] C. Marvin Pate, *The End of the Age Has Come*, (Grand Rapids, Zondervan, 1995)65. The problem of course, is that Pate does not believe that Paul's expectation and his belief was fulfilled within the time frame that Paul expected it, i.e. in that generation. Needless to say, this is problematic. Was Paul's "interpretation" of the signs and the Messianic suffering, wrong? Has the church - or the world - been in "birth pangs" for 2000 years?

language of imminence, we have definitive proof that the "final resurrection" was truly, objectively near in the first century.

We thus have Peter and Paul in agreement in regard to the end time narrative, and both declaring in emphatic and undeniable terms that the consummation – the glory of the redemption of the body - was near.

1 Thessalonians 1:10; 3:1-3; 2 Thessalonians 1 & 2

Like Romans 8, one would be hard pressed to find passages that more clearly set out the eschatological pattern of suffering before the parousia. None of Paul's epistles are so eschatologically saturated, none more focused on persecution, none more explicit in promising imminent vindication, relief and glory at the parousia.

Paul said the Thessalonians had received the Word in joy and also in "much affliction" (*thlipsis*) as they waited for the parousia of Christ (1:6, 10). Paul said Christ, "delivers (literally, is delivering us) us from the wrath to come." This is a direct echo of the message of John the Baptizer - who was Elijah of Malachi 4:5-6. John warned of, "the wrath that is about to come" (Matthew 3:7). The Day of Wrath John was anticipating was judgment on Israel for violation of Torah, as Malachi 3:6 shows. From the time of John until Paul, that wrath had not yet fallen, but, according to 1 Thessalonians 2:14f, it was very near. Failure to honor the connection between Paul's eschatology in Thessalonians and the ministry of John as Elijah is a tremendous oversight, leading to a false eschatology.

Paul urged the Thessalonians not to be shaken or overwhelmed by the suffering they were enduring, reminding them, "you yourselves know that we are appointed to this. For in fact, we told you before when we were with you that we would suffer tribulation, just as it has happened" (1 Thessalonians 3:3). Several things stick out about this.

1. Paul said that the Thessalonians – and of course, himself (Colossians 1:24f) - were "appointed" to suffer. The word "appointed" is from *keimai* and means determined, appointed, just as the translation suggests. And why were they appointed to suffer that persecution?

They were appointed to suffer because just as Paul said, "we must (*dei*, a divine necessity) through much suffering enter the kingdom" (Acts 14:22). It is because the end time drama posited a period of suffering on the part of the elect / the remnant in order to purify them (cf. 1 Peter 1:5f– compare 1 Peter with Malachi 3). In other words, they were appointed to suffer because they were living in the eschaton, the last days foretold by the OT prophets.

2. They were appointed to suffer because Jesus had predicted that his disciples would be persecuted (Matthew 24:9f; Mark 13:9f).

3. They were appointed to suffer because the body of Christ had to partake of the "sufferings of Christ" (cf. Colossians 1:23ff; 1 Peter 5:13).

4. They were appointed to suffer in order to fill up the measure of the eschatological suffering and as a corollary, their persecutors would fill up the measure of their sin by persecuting them. This was just as Jesus foretold in Matthew 23:29f.

5. They were appointed to suffer because the OT prophecies of the kingdom foretold the persecution of the saints before the full manifestation and bestowal of the kingdom (Daniel 7) and those saints were suffering for that kingdom (2 Thessalonians 1:5).[214]

This dominant theme of persecution (*thlipsis*) is found in the context of Paul's affirmation of the imminent parousia in 2 Thessalonians 1. Language could hardly be clearer. The apostle promised that Christ was coming in the lifetime of the

---

[214] See my discussion of the connection between Daniel 7 and Thessalonians in my, *We Shall Meet Him In The Air, The Wedding of the King of kings*.

Thessalonians, to give *them* – not some future, unknown generation of Christians – "relief, when the Lord Jesus is revealed from heaven" (2 Thessalonians 1:7).[215]

It should be observed that Paul was anticipating the fulfillment of Isaiah 2-4 in his prediction of the coming of the Lord to avenge the blood of the martyrs. He appeals directly to Isaiah 2:9f, 19f (LXX) for his prediction of the coming of the Lord. Significantly, Isaiah 2-4 contains the end time pattern under consideration and serves as a strong demonstration that Torah would endure until the *Telos*.

Isaiah contains the prophecy of the last days, the days in which Paul was living (Galatians 4:4; Hebrews 1:1). In those last days it would be a time of famine (3:1f), and warfare and judgment on Israel (3:13-24). The Branch of the Lord would come, avenging the blood of the martyrs (4:4) and establish His Tabernacle among men. This is the end time pattern. It matches 2 Thessalonians perfectly. This is suffering to enter the kingdom, vindication of the saints (the elect, 2:13), the glorification of Messiah in his kingdom and the promise that the parousia was to occur in their lifetime.

James

Much like 1 Peter that comes after it, a powerful theme in James is that of suffering, but also the promise of the soon coming parousia in vindication and relief.

James urged his readers to, "count it all joy when you fall into trials" (1:12). The word for trial is *peirasmos*. While it can occasionally refer to the temptation to do wrong (cf. Luke 4:13) it is also used of the trials of persecution, and more specifically, to the end times trials.[216]

---

[215] See my *In Flaming Fire*, (Ardmore, Ok. JaDon Management, 2011) for an exegesis of 2 Thessalonians 1.

[216] James 1:12; 1 Peter 1:6; 4:12; Revelation 3:10.

James reminds his audience that the rich persecute them, but he likewise reminds them that the poor are to inherit the kingdom (2:5). We have once again the narrative: "we must through much suffering enter the kingdom."

James continues his discussion of persecution in chapter 5 where he urges them to be patient until the coming of the Lord. He even refers back to Jeremiah 12 and, "the day of slaughter" against the rich oppressors to encourage them (5:1-6). He promises them: "the parousia of the Lord has drawn near," and, "the judge is standing right at the door" (5:8-9).

From the beginning of this short epistle to the end therefore, the story is that they were in the midst of persecution. However, the parousia of Christ was near and they would inherit the kingdom. This is a powerful affirmation of the end time narrative found everywhere else in Scripture. It is in fact, the story of Daniel 7 and 12.

So, if James' audience was living in the time of the end of Daniel 7 & 12 and were suffering the end times "Birth pangs of Messiah," then the resurrection of Daniel 12 was near. This demonstrates the unity of the end time narrative.

There is not a word in James to suggest that he looked beyond those present trials and that imminent parousia / kingdom to something else, something better, something far off. The actual testimony of the text indicates that James was in full agreement with the well established end times outline of suffering leading to glory – the Tribulation leading to the Resurrection.

While we cannot develop it here, it should not go unnoticed that James is writing to "the twelve tribes scattered abroad." This is the "diaspora" of Israel. He is, to put it another way, writing to the righteous remnant who have accepted Jesus as the Messiah. They would come through the Great Tribulation and be led to the River of Life in the New Creation (Revelation 7; 22).

In Jewish thought, there was a widespread belief that although YHVH had brought them back from Babylonian captivity, they still somehow remained in "captivity."[217] It would be YHVH's great work of redemption in the kingdom and resurrection that would finally deliver them. It is this belief that contained the idea of the end time narrative of the Return from Captivity, the Tribulation, the purification of the remnant and the coming of the Lord in the resurrection and kingdom.

So, the story of James is the story of Israel's final deliverance from the "captivity." It is not the deliverance from Roman oppression envisioned by many of the "zealous" revolutionaries,[218] but the deliverance from their sin through the work of Messiah.

James, following his Master and perfectly consistent with 1 Peter that will follow, is, "reworking" the story of captivity, of deliverance and redemption. He clearly maintains the chronological narrative of the end time expectation and the reality of the events, but he rejects the nationalistic hopes that led the nation to disaster in a few short years.

1 Peter

Like the other epistles, the theme of suffering and imminent relief and vindication / glory / kingdom permeates the first epistle from Peter.

In 1 Peter 1:5f, Peter speaks of the presence of suffering in the midst of the "diaspora" Christians, but assures them that it will only

---

[217] For more on this important theme see Dubis, (2002, 46f) as well as N. T. Wright, *Climax of the Covenant: Christ and the Law in Pauline Theology*, (Minneapolis, Fortress Press, 1992)141.

[218] His exhortation to humble submission under suffering and injustice did not set well with the revolutionaries who wanted blood, and ultimately got it. But it did not turn out as they had hoped.

be for a little while. Clearly, this is Tribulation before "the Glory." This is Romans 8:18f - as we have seen.

Note that in chapter 5:10, Peter repeats the promise that their sufferings, which would be rewarded at the parousia, would only be for a little while. As Dubis notes, "The theme of suffering 'for a little while' in both 1:6-7 (*oligon lupethentes*) and in 5:10 *(oligon pathontas)* forms an *inclusio* across the entire book." (2002, 54).

For Peter then, his readers were enduring the eschatological suffering that would shortly terminate in the parousia and the reception of the eternal inheritance of v. 3-4 - the eternal life of Daniel 12. This is a promise of the imminent resurrection. This is the end time narrative of Suffering before the Kingdom.

Peter is likewise emphatic that the promised salvation at the parousia, at the climax of that end time suffering, would be in fulfillment of God's Old Covenant promises to Israel.

Peter says the Old Testament prophets foretold the coming salvation for the last days, but they did not understand either the timing or the nature of that salvation (1 Peter 1:9-12). However, Peter declares that God was – in the first century – revealing both the time and the nature of that promised salvation and that time was Peter's "now time." The nature of the salvation was that Israel's redemptive promises were being fulfilled in the body of Christ.

As Dubis says: "First Peter has transferred first century expectations of an eschatological temple to the Christian community (2:5). Thus, the OT images of a gloriously restored temple are ultimately realized in the church for 1 Peter." (2002, 55).

It should not be missed that Peter is drawing heavily on the book of Zechariah for his eschatology. We have the suffering of Messiah and the glory to follow. We have the salvation of the remnant of Israel. We have the purification of the remnant through the end times trials. We have the promise of salvation and cleansing. We have the Messianic Temple. And much, much more! Virtually every tenet of the last days drama expounded in Zechariah – including the end of Torah – is found in 1 Peter.

Peter's promises then, are undeniably a fine example of *Torah To Telos*. That is, Torah foretold that salvation would come at the Day of the Lord in the last days – and those were the last days of Israel. The *telos*, the consummation, would be the fulfillment of God's promises found in Torah. Those promises of salvation at the parousia were never posited at the end of human history in fulfillment of new eschatological promises made to the church divorced from Israel. The consummation belonged to the final end of Israel's covenant age: *Torah to Telos*.

Revelation

Dubis says Revelation, "Is the premier NT illustration of the early church's adaption of the concept of messianic woes. The calamities that comprise the seven seals, the seven trumpets and the seven bowls, represent unquestioned parallels with the notion of messianic woes as found in other apocalyptic texts. Thus, one commentator says, 'the main themes of chapters 6-16 of the Revelation is the messianic woes.' The ten-day tribulation (*thlipsis*) that the church of Smyrna must undergo (2:10), the worldwide 'hour of trial' in 3:10, as well as the 'great tribulation' of 7:14 are all concise references to the messianic woes upon which chapters 6-16 elaborate." (2002, 33).[219]

---

[219] Space forbids elaboration, but note that the presence of the Tribulation in the first century demands that *the end of the millennium resurrection was near*. Revelation 20: 8 has the tribulation *at the end of the millennium*. There is no Bible doctrine of two tribulations before the end. Thus, since Revelation posits the presence of the Tribulation and confines it to the first century, this demands that the end of the millennium was near. See my book, *Who Is This Babylon?* for a discussion of the millennium, as well as Joseph Vincent's excellent book *The Millennium: Past, Present or Future?* (Ardmore, Ok., JaDon Management Inc., 2012).

To put it another way, Revelation is a perfect outline of Israel's eschatological time line and narrative. The correspondence between Daniel 12, the Great Tribulation and the Resurrection is a common and even dominant theme in Revelation.

Note the perfect correlation between Daniel 12 and Revelation 10-11 as illustrated by the chart:

Daniel 12	Revelation 10-11
Time of the End	Time of the End
Time far off – Seal the Book	There shall be no more delay (10:7) - Cf. Revelation 22:10f- "Do not seal the book, the time is at hand."
Time of the Kingdom	Kingdoms of this world have become the kingdoms of our God (11:16f)
Time of the Resurrection	Time of the dead that they should be judged
Prophets Rewarded	Time for the rewarding of the prophets
When the power of the holy people is completely shattered	Judgment of the city where the Lord was slain

Of course, we cannot fail to mention that Daniel foretold the Great Tribulation and Revelation likewise speaks of the Great Tribulation demonstrating that it was to be a first century event.[220]

---

[220] See my *Blast From the Past: The Truth About Armageddon*, for proof positive that the Great Tribulation *was* in the first century.

As we have already seen, Daniel ties the resurrection from the dead directly to the Tribulation. In Revelation 7:14, the righteous remnant of Israel who have followed Messiah, experience the Great Tribulation and are led to the River of Life – i.e. resurrection. In Daniel, the Tribulation is followed by the resurrection. In Revelation 20, the Tribulation is followed by the end of the millennium resurrection and the New Creation. And this naturally raises the question: Since Daniel 12 and Revelation 20 posit the identical narrative, and since virtually no one denies that Revelation 20 is the "general resurrection" then how does one distinguish between the resurrection in Daniel and that in Revelation 20?

Interestingly, Beale, (*Theology*, 2011, 210f) says Daniel 11-12 serve as the source of Revelation 7 and the 144,000 who go through the Tribulation. He demonstrates several direct verbal and thematic parallels and correlates it all to the Messianic Woes. He then says, (p. 211, n. 41), that John 5:24-29 sees the resurrection of the saints predicted in Daniel 12:2 as, "inaugurated in Jesus' ministry." Just how Beale fails to see the consummative fulfillment in Daniel 12:7 he does not tell us, except to posit it at the proposed "end of time."

In each of the texts we have examined above, we find the motif and theme of the saints undergoing intense persecution in the first century and the promise of imminent relief and vindication at the coming of the Lord, the time of the resurrection.

It may be helpful to visualize the fact of how dominate this theme is in the NT corpus. We will give here a sampling of texts, some a repeat from above, that focus on that theme:

➡ Acts 14:22 - Suffering to enter the kingdom.

➡ Romans 8 - Sufferings Of Present Time - The glory about To be revealed.

➡ 2 Corinthians 4:16f - Paul calls their present persecution "light affliction" and promises that it will only be "for a moment."

➡ 2 Thessalonians 1:7- "To you who are troubled, rest, when the Lord Jesus is revealed."

➻ Hebrews 10.34f - "You took joyfully the spoiling of your goods" – "In a very, very little while *the one who is coming will come and will not tarry (v. 32-37).*

➻ James 5.6f - "Be patient therefore, brethren, until the parousia..." "The parousia has drawn nigh!" "The judge is at the door!"

➻ I Peter 1:5f - You must suffer *a little while* - Salvation ready to be revealed. "The end of all things has drawn near."

➻ Revelation 6.9-11 - Martyrs had suffered - They were told to rest for a *little while*, until the Day of the Lord. In fact, the theme of martyr vindication, the doctrine of the Great Tribulation, the Great Judgment, the salvation of the remnant, are all found in the Apocalypse.

What we have in all of these texts, and there are others, is first century suffering, with the promise of imminent relief and vindication at the coming of the Lord.

What all of this proves – definitively in my view – is that there is little doubt whatsoever that the inspired NT writers did teach that the end times had arrived.[221] Further, they tied the time of tribulation that they were experiencing to the imminent Day of the Lord, the time of the resurrection.

Since Jesus and the NT writers restricted the Great Tribulation to the first century and since the resurrection is invariably tied to the Tribulation, this demands a first century fulfillment of the resurrection.

There is no justification therefore, for claiming that Daniel 12 foretold a different resurrection from that in 1 Corinthians 15, or Thessalonians or Revelation. The connection between the

---

[221] No NT writer ascribed to the idea that, "God does not see time like we do", or, "time does not mean anything to God." They believed in and expressed the objective imminence of the end.

Tribulation and the Resurrection demands that Daniel's prediction of the resurrection was the prophecy of the "final" consummative resurrection.

When the Amillennialists and the Postmillennialists teach, as we have documented that they do, that the Great Tribulation was in the first century and that there is not another Great Tribulation coming,[222] they are thereby admitting that the final resurrection occurred in the first century.

> The connection between the Great Tribulation and the resurrection of the dead is clear, firm and undeniable.
>
> This means that when the Amillennialists and the Postmillennialists teach that the Great Tribulation was in the first century and that there is not another, yet future Great Tribulation, *they are thereby admitting that the final resurrection occurred in the first century.*
>
> This falsifies the Amillennial and Postmillennial eschatology.

---

[222] See Jerry Johnson's "AD 70, The Destruction of Jerusalem" DVD, available from www.nicenecouncil.com. The DVD contains a good bit of very helpful historical information and posits the first century as the fulfillment of the Great Tribulation prophecy.

POINT #10

WAS DANIEL 12:2 FULFILLED IN MATTHEW 27:51-52

"And many of those who sleep in the dust of the earth shall awake, Some to everlasting life, Some to shame and everlasting contempt" (Daniel 12:2).

"Then, behold, the veil of the temple was torn in two from top to bottom; and the earth quaked the rocks were split the graves were opened; and many bodies of the saints who had fallen asleep were raised" (Matthew 27:51-52).

There are some who believe the resurrection prophecy of Daniel 12 was fulfilled in the awesome events recorded in Matthew 27. I think this is untenable and will offer a few reasons why I reject that suggestion.

☞What Daniel Foretold As Opposed to Matthew

Those who claim that Daniel foretold the events surrounding Jesus' resurrection must explain why there is nothing else in the entire chapter of Daniel 12 that comports to this view. If verse 2 is a prediction of the resurrection of the saints, why is there no mention of Jesus' death and resurrection?

The chronological flow of the predicted constituent elements of Daniel 12 forbids application of v. 2 to Matthew 27.

☞ The Great Tribulation And the Resurrection

Notice that Daniel 12 contains the statement "at that time" there was to be the Great Tribulation. Then, in verse 2 is the prediction of the resurrection. Thus, sequentially, one has the right to say, as we have emphasized above, that *the resurrection would follow or climax the Tribulation.* If this is so, then clearly verse 2 did not predict the resurrection of the saints in Matthew 27:52. As we have shown, in Jewish thought and in scripture *the resurrection was to follow the Tribulation.* Patently, the Great Tribulation did not precede Matthew 27:52.

In Matthew 24, Jesus gave the following sequence of events: The appearance of the Abomination of Desolation, which of course was foretold by Daniel 9 and 12:9f. *As a direct result* of the appearance of the Abomination, the Tribulation would follow.

Note then that in Matthew 24:31 we find the prediction of the resurrection at the sounding of the Great Trumpet. This is a direct reference back to Isaiah 27:13, which in turn is based on the prediction of the resurrection of those "in the dust" (26:19-21) at the coming of the Lord.

Is the resurrection "out of the dust" in Isaiah 26 a different resurrection from the resurrection "out of the dust" in Daniel 12? Commentators do not suggest such a thing. Those who would delineate between them bear the burden of proof to demonstrate that they are different. And what is important is that in Isaiah 27, that resurrection is specifically posited at the time when God would spurn the people He had created, destroy the temple and make the fortified city a desolation (27:9-11). This clearly is not a prediction of the time of the passion and Jesus' resurrection in Matthew 27.

Likewise, to get ahead of ourselves just a bit, Daniel posits the fulfillment of his resurrection promise at the time, "when the power of the holy people has been completely shattered." Thus, just as Isaiah 26-27 gives a sequence of events, Daniel follows that exact pattern.

Once again, we have this sequence of events: Abomination -> Tribulation —> Resurrection. This alone falsifies the application of Daniel 12 to the resurrection of the saints in Matthew 27. Those who apply Daniel 12 to Matthew 27 are taking Daniel completely out of the chronological flow of events by saying that the resurrection of Daniel 12:2 happened and then, later, the Abomination and Tribulation occurred. There is not a word in Daniel (Or Isaiah 26-27) to justify this.

The resurrection of Daniel 12 was to be at the time of the Tribulation. There is no way to say that the events of Matthew 27 were the Great Tribulation, or the climax of it.

Let me express some of the issues here:

The resurrection "out of the dust" of Isaiah 26-27 is the same resurrection as in Daniel 12:2.

The resurrection "out of the dust" of Isaiah 26-27 would take place at the sounding of the Great Trumpet – *at the time of the destruction of OT Israel* (27:10-13).

Jesus said the sounding of the Great Trumpet (the time of the resurrection) would be at his coming in judgment, power and great glory (Matthew 24:29-31) - at the time of the judgment of Jerusalem.

Therefore, the resurrection "out of the dust" of Daniel 12 – being the same resurrection as in Isaiah 26-27 – was to be at Christ's coming in *judgment*, power and great glory (Matthew 24:29-31).

This falsifies any application of Daniel 12 to Matthew 27:52. The resurrection of the saints in Matthew was patently not at the time of Christ's coming in judgment of Old Covenant Israel. But let me build on this.

The coming of the Lord at the time of the resurrection in Isaiah 26-27 would be when the Lord would come in judgment and *vindication of the blood of the martyrs* (Isaiah 26:21).

The resurrection of Isaiah 26 is the same resurrection as in Daniel 12.

But the coming of the Lord in judgment and vindication of the blood of the martyrs was to be in the judgment of Old Covenant Jerusalem – Not at the cross – Matthew 23:29-37.

Therefore, the resurrection of Daniel 12 was to be at the coming of the Lord in judgment and vindication of the blood of the

martyrs in the judgment of Old Covenant Jerusalem – not at the time of Matthew 27:52.

(It is important to note that Isaiah was not predicting an individualized "coming" of the Lord at their conversion or death. This is the prediction of an objective historical event related to the corporate judgment of Israel. This is what Jesus foretold in Matthew 23. This is *corporate eschatology*, not *individualistic* eschatology).

Again, the events of Matthew 27, no matter how intriguing they might be, are not what was predicted in Daniel 12.

So...

The order of events in Daniel 12 prohibits application to Matthew 27. The resurrection is inextricably tied to the Great Tribulation – and that was irrefutably not at the time of Matthew 27.

Unless one can delineate between the resurrection foretold in Isaiah 26-27 and that of Daniel 12 then since Isaiah clearly posits the resurrection at the time of the judgment of Israel, then Daniel 12 must be applied to that time as well. And of course, this is precisely what Daniel 12:7 teaches.

Just like Isaiah, Daniel was told that the resurrection would be fulfilled, "when the power of the holy people is completely shattered" (12:7). This agrees perfectly with Isaiah and forbids application of Daniel to Matthew 27.

Isaiah posited the resurrection at the coming of the Lord in judgment of Israel for shedding innocent blood (26:20f). Again, this agrees perfectly with Daniel and Matthew 23 and forbids application of Daniel to Matthew 27.

Notice now Daniel 12:3. Clearly, verse 3 is tied to verse two thematically as well as contextually. What happens in verse 3? It is the arrival of the kingdom, per Jesus' interpretation and application of verse 3.

Daniel 12:3 tells us that at the time of the resurrection, "those who are wise shall shine like the brightness of the firmament... like the stars forever." Notice the direct correlation of the resurrection to everlasting life in verse 2, to the shining as, "the brightness of the firmament and stars forever."

So, the resurrection of verse 2 leads to the righteous shining forth. Notice now Jesus' application of Daniel's prophecy. In his famous parable of the wheat and tares, Jesus gave his interpretation of the parable, as well as lending his comment on Daniel 12: 41-43: "The Son of Man will send out His angels and they will gather out of His kingdom all things that offend and those who practice lawlessness and will cast them into the furnace of fire. There will be wailing and gnashing of teeth. Then the righteous will shine forth as the sun in the kingdom of their Father."

Jesus directly cites Daniel 12:3 in v. 43. He says Daniel would be fulfilled at the coming of the Son of Man at the end of the age, the time of the harvest. Without doubt, the harvest at the coming of the Lord at the end of the age is the time of the resurrection of Daniel 12:2.

So, that leads us to this:

The harvest of Matthew 13:41-43 is the resurrection at the end of the age of Daniel 12:2.

But the harvest of Matthew 13:41-43 occurs at the coming of the Lord at the end of the age (Matthew 13:41-43).

Therefore, the resurrection of Daniel 12:2 occurs at the coming of the Lord at the end of the age.

This answers the suggestion by some that Jesus' teaching in Matthew 12 was fulfilled in Matthew 27. Jesus said the men of Nineveh would rise in the judgment against the men of his generation (Matthew 12:41-42). That would be at the end of the age judgment. But the resurrection of the righteous in Matthew 27 did not occur at the Lord's coming at the end of the age as demanded. Matthew 12 and Matthew 13 both speak of the end of the age, the coming of Christ and the judgment. Matthew 27 does not fit those contexts.

Jesus said that at the time of the harvest, the kingdom would be present and the righteous would shine in the kingdom. Did the kingdom arrive in Matthew 27:52? Did those who were raised in Matthew 27 begin to shine in the kingdom? If so, how? Again, per Jesus, that kingdom would arrive in power and great glory at his parousia (Matthew 16:27-28; 25:31f).

Patently, the events of Matthew 27:52 did not occur at the coming of the Lord with the angels at the end of the age.

Those who claim that Daniel 12 foretold the events of Matthew 27 must provide some powerful, substantive, contextual evidence to show that Daniel 12:2 can be cut out and divorced from verse 1 and verse 3 temporally. There is no contextual support for doing so and when we accept Jesus' application of Daniel 12 to his parousia at the harvest, this falsifies any application of Daniel 12 to Matthew 27.

Daniel 12:2 specifically says that those to be resurrected would be raised to everlasting life – or, in the case of the wicked, everlasting shame. Those who suggest that Daniel was fulfilled in the events of Matthew 27:52 are putting the horse before the cart. Here is why.

Daniel was told that he would not receive his reward until the time of the end. He and the rest of the prophets would receive that reward, according to Revelation 11:15f, at the time of the resurrection. Likewise, the time of the rewarding of the prophets was to occur at the end of the age (Daniel 12:2-4, 13). So, when we put these pieces of the puzzle together we find the following:

The resurrection is the time when the prophets – Daniel included – would receive their reward (Daniel 12:2-13).

The prophets would receive their reward at the time of the resurrection (Revelation 11:15-18).

The time of the resurrection and the time of the rewarding of the prophets was to occur at the judgment of the city, "where the Lord was slain" (Revelation 11:8-18).

Therefore, the resurrection for the rewarding of the prophets – Daniel 12:2 - occurred at the judgment of the city, "where the Lord was slain" (Revelation 11:8-18).

This is driven home even more strongly in Luke 13:28-30:

> "There will be weeping and gnashing of teeth, when you see Abraham and Isaac and Jacob *and all the prophets* in the kingdom of God, and yourselves thrust out. They will come from the east and the west, from the north and the south, and sit down in the kingdom of God. And indeed there are last who will be first, and there are first who will be last." (My emphasis).

The language here is graphic and undeniable. It parallels Matthew 8:11 which, as we have noted, is posited by the Dominionist as fulfilled in AD 70. Notice that Jesus posited the arrival of the kingdom, the time of weeping and gnashing of teeth on the part of those (cast) outside the kingdom as the time when "all the prophets" would sit down in the kingdom in their reward. This is patently a reflection on Daniel 12:13.

Jesus excludes any possibility of saying that he was speaking of some "end of time" event, when he told those Jews standing there that they would not only see the Worthies of Abraham, Isaac and Jacob in the kingdom, along with the prophets, but they would also see, "you yourselves cast out."

The language here is emphatic. Jesus was not speaking of some far distant future generation. He was speaking to and about his living audience! *They* would see the kingdom established. *They* would see Abraham, Isaac and Jacob sit down in the kingdom meaning *they* would see the resurrection! And *they* would see themselves cast out of the kingdom!

What Jesus said here agrees perfectly with his parabolic teaching in Matthew 21, where he told the recalcitrant Jews: "The kingdom shall be taken from you." This would be at the coming of the Master of the Vineyard to utterly destroy those who persecuted His servants and His Son.

This also agrees perfectly with what Jesus said in Matthew 23 about when all of the blood, of all the martyrs would be vindicated - in the judgment of Jerusalem.

This agrees perfectly with Galatians 4:22f where Paul said the children of the flesh - Old Covenant Israel - were about to be cast out for persecuting the New Covenant Seed of Abraham.

This agrees perfectly with 2 Thessalonians 1 where Paul said that those who were, at that very time, persecuting them would be cast out of the presence of the Lord at the parousia. He identifies their persecutors as the Jews in 1 Thessalonians 2:15f.

The rewarding of the prophets at the time of the casting out of "you yourselves" is undeniable. Just as Daniel was told that he and the prophets would be rewarded at the end of the age when the power of the holy people was completely shattered, Jesus said the kingdom and resurrection would be when "you yourselves" would be cast out of the kingdom.

Some might attempt to delineate between the resurrection in Daniel 12:2 and v. 13. But Luke 13 and Revelation 11 falsifies that idea. The resurrection of Daniel 12: 2 would be at the time of the end; the resurrection of v. 13 would be at the time of the end. Daniel 12 does not contain a prediction of two different "ends" and two different resurrections. Scripture consistently teaches *one* resurrection at the time of the end for the rewarding of the prophets. Luke 13 and Revelation 11 posits that at the judgment of Old Covenant Jerusalem. Matthew 27:52 does not satisfy the demands of the text.

Daniel 12 predicted the resurrection to eternal life. So, if the saints that were raised in Matthew 27 were the fulfillment of Daniel 12 it logically demands that they received eternal life when they were raised at the time of Christ's resurrection. This is where the problem arises.

The consistent testimony of the NT writers is that salvation would arrive at the parousia of Christ (cf.1 Peter 1:9f). Salvation would be given at Christ's appearing, to consummate the atonement (Hebrews 9:28). Some, in their desperation to avoid the significance of this text, have resorted to the wild claim that the "salvation" to be revealed at Christ's parousia in Hebrews 9:28 was deliverance from the physical horrors of the war of 66-70. Kurt Simmons made this unsubstantiated claim in our written debate.[223] This is specious.

Frost, before abandoning the truth of Covenant Eschatology, expressed it well:

> "Further, they exclaim, "The nations were angry and your wrath has come. The time for judging the dead and rewarding your servants the prophets and your saints" (11:18). Now, we have seen that 22:12 is entirely something John saw as "near," and Gentry concurs. We have also seen that the "rewarding" was near as well. Is this "rewarding" different from the "rewarding" and "coming" in 11:18, which is connected to the destruction of Jerusalem? Both David Chilton and Jay E. Adams see Revelation 11 as fulfilled. Chilton, before he became a preterist, tried to dodge this by dividing this "judgment/rewarding/ resurrection" from the "final judgement at the Last Day" of the whole world. Thank God, before he passed away, he saw that such a division is a desperate attempt to separate what cannot be separated.
>
> The basic reason why I call myself a "consistent" preterist is because I don't divide and piecemeal the

---

[223] You can order a copy of the debate in book form from my websites, from Amazon, Kindle and other retailers.

> Bible together to make it fit with the erroneous historical creeds on this point. I am not obligated to the creeds, but to Scripture. Creeds are fine they are logically necessary, but they "may err" as the Westminster Confession of Faith states (33:3). Some, however, have settled for man's word over God's it is this that I contend for."[224]

Personally, I have not seen one word from Frost (or anyone else) since he wrote those words that can even begin to negate the logic and force of what he said. It is a tragedy that he abandoned this well stated, well reasoned, position.

Daniel 12 predicted the resurrection to eternal life. So, if the saints that were raised in Matthew 27 were the fulfillment of Daniel 12 it logically demands that they received eternal life when they were raised. This is where the problem arises, as we suggested above. But take a closer look.

As we have seen, in Hebrews 11 the author chronicles the lives of the great men and women of faith under the Old Covenant, even extending to creation, i.e. Abel. He speaks of their eschatological hope of the heavenly country (fatherland) and city (i.e. Zion) as well as, "the better resurrection" (v. 35).

The author then says that those Worthies all died in faith, "not having received the promises" given to them.

Hebrews is clearly positing the fulfillment of their hope as something about to be fulfilled. Note that their hope was the "heavenly Jerusalem" (Zion) and he says, "you have come to Mount Zion!" (V. 21). They stood on the very cusp of the "better resurrection"!

Notice now what he says back in 11:39-40 concerning the OT Worthies and their hope: "they, without us, cannot be made

---

[224] http://www.restorationgj.com/id45.htm

perfect." Do you catch the power of that? Hebrews is affirming that the OT saints and the last days, New Covenant saints would receive fulfillment of their eschatological hope *at the same time!* The OT saints would not receive eternal life, the Heavenly Zion, resurrection, etc. *before or without that critical, last days generation of New Covenant saints.* (As we noted above, this is precisely what Paul affirms in 1 Thessalonians 4:13f – see my *We Shall Meet Him In The Air, the Wedding of the King of kings*, for more on this critical issue).

Do you see the problem for the view that Matthew 27 is the fulfillment of Daniel 12?

Daniel 12 says those resurrected would be raised to eternal life. So, if those in Matthew 27 were the fulfillment of Daniel, then it must be true that:

✪ They received eternal life before Jesus ascended to the Father into the Most Holy Place there to offer his sacrifice (Hebrews 9:24).

✪ But if they were raised to eternal life then they received their reward *before the church was even established.*

✪ They received eternal life before the gospel was even preached.

✪ They received eternal life before the Day of Redemption, the day of Salvation.

✪ They received eternal life before that inheritance was revealed and given at the parousia (1 Peter 1:3-7).

✪ They received their salvation before the appearing of the Lord, "a second time, apart from sin for salvation" (Hebrews 9:28).

In other words, they received their reward before the New Covenant saints would receive eternal life, redemption and salvation. Indeed, they received their reward of eternal life in the kingdom before there were even any New Covenant saints! This is a clear violation of what Hebrews 11:39-40 says. Thus, the idea that Matthew 27:52 was the fulfillment of Daniel 12 is falsified.

Daniel 12:3 speaks of the righteous shining forth in the kingdom at the time of v. 2 - the time of the resurrection. So, the righteous would shine in the kingdom of the Lord at the time of the resurrection of v. 2. Here is where another problem arises for those who posit fulfillment of v. 2 in Matthew 27 – the end of the age did not arrive at the cross.

In Matthew 13:39-43, Jesus spoke of the end of the age, when the angels would be sent out to gather the elect and cast the wicked into the fire. Jesus then said, "Then shall the righteous shine forth in the kingdom" directly citing Daniel 12:3.

So the time for the fulfillment of Daniel 12:3 would be at the end of the age harvest and the parousia of the Son of Man. To state it simply, there is no way to make the events of Matthew 27 to be the coming of the Son of Man, at the end of the age harvest and the sending forth of the angels. That did not happen in the events of Matthew 27, no matter how awesome that event might appear to us.

The motifs of Matthew 13 are purely eschatological. And while it is certainly to be noted that Jesus' Passion is part of the end time drama, *it was not the time of the harvest at his parousia* - it was not the end of the age.

Note also, very briefly, that Jesus and his disciples undeniably posited the end of the age at the time of the destruction of the temple at Christ's parousia (Matthew 24:1-3). This confirms what we have just seen.

So, Daniel 12 posits the resurrection at the end of the age (v. 4), when the righteous would shine in the kingdom. Jesus said the harvest at the end of the age would be at the time of his parousia, in judgment, at the time of the destruction of Jerusalem (Matthew 13 / 24).

When we consider all the facts concerning the chronological flow of Daniel, the constituent elements of his prophecy and the NT application of Daniel, there is no way to substantiate the idea that the resurrection of some of the saints in Daniel 12 was in any way the fulfillment of Daniel's prophecy. But there are additional questions.

Is the resurrection in Matthew 27 related to the resurrection in Revelation 20? That has been suggested to me, but I remain unconvinced. Here are a few of the reasons why.

I see no evidence that those raised in Matthew 27 were in any way different from Lazarus when he was raised. Yet, Lazarus could still die. In John 11, the Jews conspired to put him to death (John 12:10). However, those in Revelation 20 were in the heavenly realm, and patently not subject to physical death. To suggest that those in Revelation 20 were the saints that had been raised in Matthew 27, who had been taken into the heavenly realm truly has no solid exegetical support. It is mere speculation.

If those in Matthew 27 truly were still subject to physical death after their resurrection, then they had to lay off those mortal bodies to be "raptured" at the ascension, did they not? Would they not have to receive at least some form of "eternal life" to enter the heavenly realm? That would seem apparent from the (admittedly) highly wrought language of Revelation 6:9f.

The limited number of those raised does not seem to comport with Revelation 6 or 20. While the text does say that "many" were raised, nonetheless, in Revelation 6 and 20 the language suggests that it was all the martyrs that received that initial vindication of their suffering. Revelation 6:9 mentions, "those who had been slain for the word of God." There is no contextual qualifier to suggest that it was only a limited number of the martyrs. To suggest that the "many" of Matthew 27 includes all the Old Covenant Worthies who had been martyred (Hebrews 11) *which goes all the way back to creation* finds no support in the text of Matthew.

The resurrection of Matthew 27 should be best understood as one of the series of signs that were performed to point the Jews to Jesus and to the pivotal time they were living in. John 20:30-31 informs is that the resurrection of Lazarus (still mortal, as just suggested) and all of the other miracles of Jesus, including Jesus' own physical resurrection, were signs pointing to Jesus as the Son of God. When Matthew 27 tells us that those individuals went into the city and appeared to many, I think it is safe to say that they had plenty to say to their fellow Jews!

This may well be part of the reason that we then find in the book of Acts, that thousands were turning to Jesus as Messiah. After all, if you had seen with your own eyes and heard with your own ears, the raising of those people and had the opportunity to hear their testimony, would you not listen to them? And I think it safe to say that they were not talking about the latest sports scores or the weather!

The fact is that the incredible event in Matthew 27 is not positively and undeniably referred to in any text subsequent to that narrative. To create any kind of doctrinal position based upon the story of Matthew 27, in light of this significant silence, is tenuous at best.

POINT #11

IS THE RESURRECTION OF DANIEL 12

THE RESURRECTION OF JOB 19?

In my debate with Joel McDurmon (2012) he made the claim that the Abrahamic promise of the resurrection was different from the resurrection promises made to Israel. Similarly, he argued that the promise of the resurrection of Job 19:25 is different from the resurrection prophecies made to Old Covenant Israel.

Once again, we are in an area in which the Dominionists are at severe odds with tradition, church history and the creeds. McDurmon (and one wonders how many other Postmillennialists would even agree with McDurmon's arguments) - and the Dominionists would be hard pressed indeed to document such a distinction either in church history, the creeds and most especially from scripture. Such a distinction is unknown.

McDurmon's attempt at dichotomization of Israel's hope and Job flies in the face of the NT fact that there was but one eschatological hope. Paul said that "one hope" (Ephesians 4:4f) was, "nothing but the hope of Israel" found in the Moses and the prophets (Acts 24:14f; 26:21f). I drove this point home repeatedly in the debate and McDurmon had no definitive answer for it other than his presuppositional theology that demands a physical resurrection.

McDurmon's attempt to delineate between the Abrahamic / Jobian (is that a word?) resurrection raises a significant question, especially in light of the issues just raised. If the resurrection of Job 19 is the real, ultimate goal, *why does not one NT writer quote the resurrection hope of Job as the eschatological goal?*

Why is there no expression of the resurrection hope of Israel as an "addendum" or an addition to the real resurrection hope of Job? Why are we not, *somewhere*, told that the resurrection hope of Israel foreshadowed the "real" resurrection foretold by Job or Abraham?

When McDurmon sought to delineate between the Abrahamic resurrection promise and that of Israel, I took note, *repeatedly*, that in Hebrews 11 the writer discusses the *one* eschatological hope that extended from Creation (Abel) all the way up through his own time including of course, Abraham, Isaac, Jacob, etc.. There is an unbroken chain of "one hope" from creation onward and that one hope was "the better resurrection" that we have been discussing in this work. *There was but one hope.*

What this means is that although the Abrahamic resurrection hope – like that of Job (probably) - pre-dated the nation of Israel. The promise given to him was incorporated into and became the hope of Israel. There was no distinction therefore between the resurrection hope of Abraham and the resurrection hope of Israel. Nor was there a difference between the resurrection hope of Job and that of Israel. If the resurrection hope of Abel was carried through all the way from Abel through Israel, then that included the hope of Job for sure.

> **It is impossible to over-emphasize the central role of Israel in the eschatological narrative. Yet, Dominionists and Amillennialists alike virtually ignore - even deny - that relationship. This betrays a fundamental and fatal flaw in those paradigms.**

Another question to ask: If the resurrection of Job is the true eschatological goal, distinct from the hope of Israel, why does Paul say the fulfillment of *Israel's hope* would be the solution to the *Adamic death curse* (1 Corinthians 15:22)? Instead of saying the solution to that problem would be when Job would see the Lord in his flesh, he says it would be when Isaiah 25:8 and Hosea 13:14 – promises to Israel – were fulfilled. This is a total repudiation of any attempt to find a Jobian / Abrahamic resurrection promise divorced from the hope of Israel. McDurmon made no attempt to answer this.

The final question to ask, related to the above discussion, is: If Job is the "real" resurrection, then why is Paul concerned with nothing but the hope of Israel? Why in the name of reason does Paul never so much as cite Job, instead, citing the OT promises made to *Israel*, if two kinds of resurrection at two different times are found in Job and Israel's promises? This issue of Israel, eschatology and Israel is critical, but very clearly the Dominionists (nor the Amillennialists) do not want to deal with it. McDurmon certainly ignored this issue.

Like McDurmon, Frost, in his attempt to justify departing from the full preterist view, focuses on the land promise and the resurrection promise to Abraham. *He says literally not one word about the centrality of Israel in the eschatological narrative.* This is inexcusable, Biblically speaking. It is also particularly distressing since when he was a preterist, Frost recognized, preached and emphasized the centrality of Israel in the eschatological narrative.

Frost's refusal to even mention Israel's eschatological role is not surprising of course, since Frost tutored McDurmon in preparation for his debate with me. Frost, like McDurmon, says: "God promised Abraham *land*" (2012, 47, his emphasis). McDurmon, following Frost's lead, argued that Abraham never received the land, thus, he must be raised out of the dust biologically to receive the land promise.

Frost and McDurmon are patently desperate here, as I noted in my debate with McDurmon. I will return momentarily to an examination of McDurmon's arguments on Job, but I want to give here just a point or two in refutation of the view that there is a distinction between the Jobian / Abrahamic resurrection promises versus the resurrection promise to Israel. This is an un-Biblical view that is specious in the extreme.

☞ We just posed the question, and neither McDurmon or Frost have offered a syllable of answer: If Job is the "real" resurrection, then why is Paul concerned with *nothing but the hope of Israel*? Why does Paul never so much as cite Job in contrast to directly citing the OT promises made to Israel. This is critical. If there are two kinds of resurrection at two different times with Job being the true, final eschatological resurrection why does Paul never speak of that Jobian promise?

It should be noted here that (accepting the Pauline authorship of Hebrews) Paul does mention the Abrahamic resurrection promise, but he is emphatic that it was about to be fulfilled. He chronicles the "one hope" from Adam, through Abraham and posits fulfillment of that "one hope" at Zion, affirming, "you have come to Mt. Zion!" (12:18f). The critical thing to note here is that Paul no where delineates between the resurrection hope of Adam, Noah, Abraham or Moses and Israel. He never says that Adam, Noah, or Abraham looked for "better resurrections" or that he longed for two cities, or two heavenly countries. It was *one* hope.

☛ I noted in my debate with McDurmon that his claim that the land promises to Abraham were never fulfilled flies in the face of the Biblical data. God's promises to Abraham of the land were fulfilled in a two-fold manner, both literally and ultimately in Abraham's Seed.

You must understand how important the land promise to Abraham is to Frost and McDurmon. Their argument goes like this:

✔God promised to give the land to Abraham, to Abraham *personally*.

✔According to Acts 6, Abraham never received the land.

✔For Abraham to receive the land, he must (since he is dead) be raised from the dead, in a fleshly resurrection.

McDurmon claims that this is, "the most airtight and irrefutable argument for a bodily resurrection" (2012, 75). Unfortunately for him, the argument has gaping holes in it.

    1. The land promise was fulfilled in and to Abraham's seed, and this was, after all, the very promise that was made. Read Deuteronomy 34:1-4:

"Then Moses went up from the plains of Moab to Mount Nebo, to the top of Pisgah, which is across from Jericho. And the Lord showed him all the land of Gilead as far as Dan, all Naphtali and the land of Ephraim and Manasseh, all the land of Judah as far as the Western Sea, the South, and the plain of the Valley of Jericho, the city of palm trees, as far as Zoar. Then the Lord said to him, "This is the land of which I swore to give Abraham, Isaac, and Jacob, saying, 'I will give it to your descendants.' I have caused you to see it with your eyes, but you shall not cross over there."

Take careful note of the wording here. YHVH was showing Moses the land that He promised to give to Abraham. He reiterates that promise and says, "This is the land of which I swore to give Abraham, Isaac, and Jacob, *saying*, 'I will give it to your descendants.'"[225] Thus, Frost's claim: "Abraham, Isaac and Jacob never saw this fulfilled" (2012, 47) is specious and flies in the face of the emphatic words of YHVH in Deuteronomy.

YHVH here *explains the land promise to Abraham*. What He meant, when discussing the literal land promise, was not that Abraham was to personally receive it, but that he would receive it *through his descendants*. That is what is meant by, "This is the land of which I swore to give Abraham, Isaac, and Jacob, *saying*, 'I will give it to your descendants.'" So, He promised to give the land to Abraham, and what He meant was that Abraham's descendants would receive it - and of course - they did. Promise fulfilled.

This is confirmed when we look at the "Jewish perspective" of Abraham and the land promise. Read Ezekiel 33:24: "Abraham was

---

[225] For a discussion of the representative fulfillment of the literal land promise being fulfilled, see the book of my debate with McDurmon. I presented clear-cut proof of the Hebraic view of representative fulfillment, and McDurmon offered not a word of rebuttal.

only one, *and he inherited the land*. But we are many; the land has been given to us as a possession." (My emphasis). From this, it is undeniable that in one way, in some way, at least to the Jewish mind, the literal land promise to Abraham was fulfilled.

2. The greater promise to Abraham that he would "inherit the world" (Romans 4:13) was likewise *fulfilled representatively in Christ*, the "Seed" of Abraham, *through whom the world is blessed*! Jesus, the Seed of Abraham, said: "All authority is given to me in heaven and on earth..." (Matthew 28:18f). Has not Abraham inherited the world through this Seed?

It is important at this juncture to remember that, as we have documented, most Dominionists believe Revelation 11:15f was fulfilled in AD 70. Well, at that time, "The kingdoms of this world have become the kingdoms of our God and of His Christ, and He shall reign forever and forever."

Take note that in his temptation, Jesus was offered, "all the kingdoms of the world" if he would offer illicit worship to Satan. He refused that offer just as he later rejected the Jewish offer of a physical kingdom and a physical kingship (John 6:15).[226]

---

[226] In a stunning moment in the debate with McDurmon, he said Jesus and the Jews agreed on the nature of a physical, earthly kingdom, but that they just disagreed on the timing! (Shades of Dispensationalism!) McDurmon claimed: "But Jesus knew it wasn't time for that yet because he had to suffer and die bodily. ... So Jesus had a dispute not over the nature of the earthly rule, but over the time texts. *(End Times Dilemma* debate book p. 134). So, Jesus and the Jews ostensibly agreed on nature, but not time - begging the question of *why they then killed him for rejecting what they offered*? Did they not offer him the kind of kingdom he wanted? Why did Jesus not say, as on other occasions, "My time is not yet"? John and Jesus said, "the time is fulfilled, the kingdom has drawn near" (Matthew 4:17; Mark 1:15). Furthermore, in front of Pilate, Jesus unambiguously rejected the idea that his kingdom is earthly: "My kingdom is not of

Notice that in Romans, Abraham would inherit the "world" (Greek, *kosmos*). In Revelation 11, Jesus, the Seed of Abraham, inherited the "kingdoms of the world" (Greek, *kosmos*)! He took the kingdom and rules "forever and forever." He rules - right now - over the world.

Thus, even in the Dominionist view, *the Abrahamic promise was fulfilled in AD 70!* Do not fail to catch the power of this! How much more dominion would Abraham need to receive - through his Seed - than what the Dominionists agree he received in AD 70? After all, don't forget that Mathison himself said the OT Worthies have received all that was promised them.

The Dominionist admission that Revelation 11 was fulfilled in AD 70 is absolute refutation of any appeal to an eschatology, a resurrection, an inheritance different from that proclaimed by Paul who preached, "nothing but the hope of Israel."

As N. T. Wright cogently noted about Paul and his ministry:

> "His message for the world was the message that the God of Abraham, Isaac and Jacob had done at last what he had promised, providing the world its rightful Lord... Paul did not have to turn his back on engagement in the wider world in order to reaffirm his fundamental Jewishness. Genesis, Exodus, Isaiah and the Psalms, to look no further than some of Paul's favorite books, already affirm the whole world is to be claimed by Israel's God and is addressed by him precisely *through* what he is doing in and through and for Israel" (Vol I, 2013, 46f).[227]

---

this world" and Pilate accepted that denial.

[227] In spite of his clear-cut affirmations here, as is well known, Wright insists that we are still waiting on the full manifestation of the fulfillment of the "redemption of

The information above is enough to demonstrate the fallacy of ignoring the centrality of Israel in the eschatological narrative. When Frost, McDurmon, the Dominionist and Amillennial world as a whole ignore the fundamental, critical, indispensable role of Israel in the story of resurrection, this is a sure fire guarantee of a false eschatology. But let me turn back now to the examination of McDurmon's claim that Job foretold a different resurrection hope from that of Israel.

Translational Problems in Job

In McDurmon's presentation he *briefly* acknowledged the translational issues related to Job 19. However, he then tried to mitigate the severity of the issue by claiming that the translational issues are in fact "a piece of cake" compared to the issues in other texts, Daniel 9 for instance. (In his post-debate book, McDurmon spends considerable time trying to defend his view of Job 19).[228]

I must admit that I was somewhat taken aback to hear Joel claim that the translational issues are "a piece of cake." To suggest that the translation of Job is "a piece of cake" is to basically discount the entire history of what some of the greatest Hebrew scholars who have ever lived - (and current scholarship) - have had to say about those translational difficulties. In short, McDurmon attempted to run a bluff on this entire issue.

Time constraints prevented me from discussing the translational issues on Job 19. I did present an argument however, twice over, that McDurmon totally ignored. I will give that argument below. For the moment, let me present some material on the translational issues on Job and let the reader decide if Joel's claim that the problems are "a piece of cake" is valid.

---

creation."

[228] Joel McDurmon, *We Shall All Be Changed*, (Powder Springs, Ga., American Vision, 2012)87+.

Keil and Delitszch are still recognized as some of the finest Hebrew scholars in church history. Here is what they had to say about Job after discussing the translational difficulty: "We cannot find in this speech that the hope of a bodily recovery is expressed."[229] They take note, by the way, that Chrysostom (fourth century AD) was the first Christian commentator to apply Job as a prediction of a bodily resurrection. This is somewhat amazing, but McDurmon ignored this evidence.

What is interesting, to say the least, is that McDurmon tries to give the impression that it is only "some modern scholars" (2012, 88+) who posit the translational difficulties. In truth, church history from ages past is replete with commentators who have acknowledged the troublesome translation. It is disingenuous therefore, when McDurmon claims that only "modern scholars" see a translational difficulty. That is simply not true.

So, while McDurmon claims that the Hebrew translation is "a piece of cake," Keil and Delitszch disagreed. By the way, Joel gave no documentation for his claim that the translation of Job is "piece of cake." He simply asserted it. That hardly comprises any kind of proof.

The Jewish Translation – (Masoretic text, 1917) renders Job as: "When after my skin this is destroyed, then without my flesh I shall see God."

So, the Jewish translation, based on the Masoretic text, does not accept Joel's claim that the translation supporting a physical resurrection is a "piece of cake." They reject his desired translation.

Albert Barnes is likewise recognized as a great Hebrew scholar. Commenting on Job 19 he said: "The literal meaning is 'from, or out of, my flesh shall I see God. It does not mean in his flesh, but there is the notion that from, or out of his flesh he would see him;

---

[229] Keil And Delitzsch, *Commentary on the Old Testament,* Job, Vol. 4, (Grand Rapids, Eerdmans, 1975) 356f.

that is clearly, as Rosenmuller has expressed it, 'though my body is consumed and I have no flesh, I shall see him....without a body.'"[230]

So once again, one of the most highly regarded Hebrew linguists rejects Joel's "piece of cake" translational rendering and says Job "clearly" was not predicting a fleshly, physical resurrection.

In modern times, N. T. Wright, commenting on Job 19 says, "few scholars today" see Job as a reference to "bodily life after death."[231]

So N. T. Wright says there are few scholars today that would accept Joel's rendering of Job, as predictive of a physical, bodily resurrection. Yet, Joel says Job is "a piece of cake"and proves just that! It should be noted that McDurmon is forced to acknowledge that "linguistically" the case can indeed be made that, "Job meant 'out of my flesh.' In this case, he would have been replying in essence, 'Even after my flesh is destroyed, I know I will still see my Redeemer *even without it."* (2012, 92 - his emphasis). This is a significant admission.

There is something else here that is troublesome. After presenting his case for the "in my flesh" rendering of Job, McDurmon then addresses the preterist objection: "The preterist opponents, of course, cannot let these verses speak as clearly as I have interpreted them. The main tactic for countering this clarity is to exalt the alleged textual difficulties. But in exalting these beyond their warrant, these guys are engaging in more obfuscation than debate, and this is wholly undesirable in any discussion, let alone purported Christian scholarship" (2012, 95). I must say that this is rather condescending.

Let it be noted first of all, that it was not modern preterists that called attention to the linguistic and translational difficulties. That

---

[230] Albert Barnes, *Barnes on the Old Testament, Job* Vol. 1, (Grand Rapids, Baker, 1978)327f.

[231] N. T. Wright, *The Resurrection of the Son of Man*, (Minneapolis, Fortress, 2003)98.

goes back *centuries*. Once again, McDurmon is misrepresenting the history of the difficulty in regard to Job.

Second, the rejection of McDurmon's position was made by men who accepted and believed in a physical resurrection just like McDurmon. Yet, they realized that the text is not "a piece of cake" as McDurmon tries so desperately to convince his readers that it is.

Third, it is in fact, *true scholarship* to consider the textual and linguistic difficulties. That is not obfuscation, nor is it presuppositional. *This is scholarship at work*. It is really quite stunning, and a sign of desperation, to claim that one should not consider such evidence. What scholar in their right mind would suggest that we ignore all relevant evidence?

If calling attention to the textual, linguistic difficulties is, "wholly undesirable in any discussion, let alone purported Christian scholarship" then perhaps McDurmon should contact N. T. Wright and tell him he wasted his time and effort when he took note of those difficulties. Were Keil and Delitszch,[232] were Rosenmuller, Barnes, etc. and a vast array of other linguists not truly scholars when they took note of the difficulties? McDurmon's comments impugn the scholarship of history's greatest Hebrew linguists. His comments in this regard are truly unbecoming. They are in the truest sense unscholarly.

I could multiply these kind of quotes many times over. The indisputable fact is that the translational issues surrounding Job are, according to the top Hebrew linguistics, *extremely* difficult, to say the least. And remember, this is a matter of *translation*, not a matter of Biblical interpretation.

---

[232] McDurmon tries to impugn the weight of Delitszch's testimony by claiming, in essence, that he was not a conservative scholar - at least not as conservative as McDurmon. So, since he was not conservative, this must mean that when he took note of the linguistic difficulties he was not being a good conservative (2012, 96)! This is bad logic.

When some of the church's greatest Hebrew linguists, *men who actually believed in a physical, bodily resurrection,* nonetheless admitted that Job cannot be used to support such a doctrine, then it is patently clear that McDurmon was attempting to "run a bluff" to convince the audience otherwise. This is disingenuous to say the least. But these are not the only issues within Job that pose a serious - I would say fatal - problem for McDurmon's view of Job. The indisputable fact is that in the book of Job, there is a clear-cut affirmation by Job, that he would not rise from the dead as McDurmon claims! Read the words of Job:

> "Are not my days few? Cease! Leave me alone, that I may take a little comfort, Before I go to the place from which I shall not return, To the land of darkness and the shadow of death, A land as dark as darkness itself, As the shadow of death, without any order, Where even the light is like darkness'" (Job 10:21f).

Here is Job affirming in the clearest of terms that he was not going to return from the physical grave to which he was - like all mankind - going.

Notice that Job was not denying the possibility of life after death, which he pondered in chapter 14, "If a man die, will he live again?" Nor was he denying faith in his God! He was simply stating that he was going to grave *and would not return.* This virtually demands that we understand chapter 19:25 as an affirmation that he would see the Redeemer, out of his flesh - not in the flesh.

The Time Issue of Job 19

Job posits the fulfillment of its "prophecy" at the time of the end; "at the last." (There is contextual reason to believe that Job was anticipating his imminent vindication by the Lord, which he did receive. McDurmon ignores this possibility. We will not discuss that idea here. Instead, we will accept "for argument sake" the idea that Job was anticipating the last days resurrection).

So, Job anticipated his vindication at the time of the end, i.e. in the last days. With that in mind, take note of the following:

The resurrection of 1 Corinthians 15 is the resurrection foretold by Job 19. (McDurmon and Dominionists agree with this, at least ostensibly).

The Resurrection Of Job Would Be In The Last Days (Job 19:25).

The resurrection of 1 Corinthians 15 would be at "the end."

Now take note of this: The Last Days Were The Last Days Of Israel - Ending In AD 70 – (McDurmon, 2011, 47).

Therefore, The Resurrection Of Job / 1 Corinthians 15 Was No Later Than AD 70.

There is not another "last days" resurrection!

Of course, McDurmon, like all Dominionists, seeks to dichotomize between the last days and the last *day*. Joel was insistent that Jesus' prediction of the last day in John 6 must refer to a future event. But what proof did he (or they) offer? Nothing but presuppositions.

Did the last days (of Israel) not have a "last day"? Of course. McDurmon affirms this as we have seen. Commenting on Hebrews 8, he says: "As he wrote, in his time, the Old was becoming obsolete and was ready to vanish away. It has not yet been completely wiped out, *but was certainly in its dying moments.* It died in AD 70, when the symbol and ceremonies of that Old System – the Temple and the sacrifices – were completely destroyed by the Roman armies. *This was the definitive moment when "this age' of Jesus and Paul ended and completely gave way to their 'age to come.'* This, of course, is exactly why Jesus tied 'the end of the age' to His prophecy of the destruction of the Temple." (2011, 47- My emphasis).

So, the Old Covenant age of Israel had "last days." It had a "last day" - in fact, a "definitive" last "moment." Could that definitive last moment of the Mosaic Age not be "the last hour" that John said had arrived (1 John 2:18)?[233] When Frost argues (2012, 23f) that "the last day" has to be the end of time, he refutes his own claim that there have been many ages in the past and that each of them came to an end. If there have been many ages in the past and if all of those ages had a terminus, *then each of those past ages had a last day* - yet time did not end.

Not only did the Mosaic Age have "last days" and a definitive last moment, (per McDurmon and the Dominionists) but it had resurrection to eternal life at that last, definitive moment. Not only that, Daniel 12 – which our Dominionists friends now agree predicted the resurrection in AD 70 – emphatically posits the resurrection at, "the end of the days."

Notice the translation of Daniel 12:13: "But you, go your way till the end; for you shall rest will arise to your inheritance at the end of the days."

Notice that term, "the end of the days." Now, lest it be argued that the term here actually refers to a different time of the end from that in v. 2-4, it must be kept in mind that verses 2-4 are speaking of the time of the end, the resurrection and the rewarding of the dead. This is precisely what verse 13 is predicting. Not only that, the time of the end is the end of the 1335 day countdown, which cannot be divorced from the time of the Abomination of Desolation or the Great Tribulation. The time of the end, the "end of the days" is, in the context, *the last day*. We thus have the time of the end, the end of days and a 1335 day countdown, when all would be fulfilled. If the end of that 1335 day countdown is not the "last day" what, pray tell, was it?

---

[233] McDurmon was asked this very question in the Q & A session and had major difficulty giving a satisfactory answer. See the book of that debate.

You Must Catch the Power of the following:

We have documented how McDurmon, DeMar, Gentry and a growing number of other Postmillennialists agree that Daniel 12:2 predicted the AD 70 resurrection to eternal life. With that in mind, consider the following:

✦ Dominionists agree that Daniel 12:2 foretold the AD 70 resurrection.

✦ Dominionists agree that Daniel 12 foretold the resurrection to eternal life / condemnation.

✦ Dominionists agree that Daniel 12 was fulfilled at the time of the end - AD 70.

✦ Dominionists agree that Daniel 12 was fulfilled in the last days.

✦ Dominionists agree that the resurrection of Daniel 12 occurred at the "definitive moment," i.e. a last day – in AD 70. They even correlate it with Revelation 11 as we have seen.

✦ Dominionists seem oblivious to the fact that Daniel 12 undeniably posited the resurrection at "the end of days" and gave the 1335 days as the *terminus*. Thus, as just shown, it is indisputably true that, "the end of the days" would be "the last day." If not, why not?

The real question is, what is the difference between the Daniel 12, AD 70 resurrection to eternal life in the last days, at the last "definitive moment" (the last day) of that age and the proposed resurrection of 1 Corinthians 15?

During the debate, I asked McDurmon this very question. I put up a chart comparing Daniel 12 with 1 Corinthians 15 and challenged Joel to demonstrate exegetically what the differences are. I took note of *the perfect correspondence* between the Daniel 12 resurrection, when Israel's power (Torah) would be shattered, and 1 Corinthians 15 that posits resurrection at the end of "the law" which was the "strength of sin." That is Torah, without dispute. Be sure to see my discussion of those parallels above.

I received no answer to my question and my challenge.

Stunningly, Joel did say, as James Jordan did in my debate with him, that he could admit / agree that 1 Corinthians 15 and Revelation 20 had "a fulfillment in AD 70." However, there is another, consummative fulfillment in the future. When I asked for exegetical proof, Joel simply said that his belief system allows this. His "belief system" may allow it, *but scripture doesn't*. There is not a Dominionist alive that can demonstrate the difference. But let's take a closer look at this claim.

If Job = 1 Corinthians 15, keep in mind that McDurmon said there was "a fulfillment" of 1 Corinthians 15 in AD 70. If that is true, then there was "a fulfillment" of Job 19. But that means that there must have been a physical resurrection of fleshly bodies coming out of the graves in AD 70! After all, per McDurmon, Job posited resurrection *of the flesh* (not a spiritual resurrection). So, again, since Job = 1 Corinthians 15 and since there was "a fulfillment" of 1 Corinthians 15 in AD 70, of logical necessity, *there was "a fulfillment" of Job. This demands that there was a bodily, physical, fleshly resurrection in AD 70 – and that must have included Job. Job was to be raised in the "last days" and the first century was the last days time!*[234] If there was "a fulfillment" of Job's "in the flesh" resurrection hope in AD 70, *what is he still waiting for*? (Not to mention the question, 'Where is he?") After all, if there was "a fulfillment" of Job / 1 Corinthians 15, then of necessity:

---

[234] Don't forget that we have proven from Dominionist writings that many of them believe that the Biblical term "last days" refers to the last days of Old Covenant Israel. Thus, if / since Job's resurrection was to be in the last days, then of necessity, the resurrection of Job was to be in the last days of the Old Covenant age of Israel in AD 70. Once again, the Dominionists have falsified their own eschatology.

☛ There was a deliverance from the Adamic Curse (1 Corinthians 15:22). How many times does the Adamic Curse need to be destroyed?

☛There was a deliverance of "all men" i. e. all those in Christ, from that Adamic Curse. So, why did all of those living, breathing Christians who lived beyond that time still have to experience physical death, i.e. the Adamic Curse, per McDurmon, Frost, etc.? Even more to the point, why do men of faith today, redeemed by the Atoning work of Christ, still have to die physically? If death comes through sin, and Christ has finished that work of Atonement, why do Christians still die physically? Frost admits that "this is a fair question" (2012, 59). Indeed it is. Unfortunately, neither Frost, McDurmon, Gentry, et. al., have a satisfactory answer for this. In fact, Frost's attempt to answer the question is one of the more confusing bits of writing that you will find.

☛ If there was "a fulfillment" of Job and 1 Corinthians 15, then there was a resurrection to incorruptibility and immortality. This once again raises the issue of how many resurrections to eternal life are there?

☛ If there was "a fulfillment" of Job and 1 Corinthians 15, then there was a "bodily resurrection" (and McDurmon insists that the "body" of Job and Corinthians must be of human corpses). This emphasizes the question: Since Job 19 = 1 Corinthians, and since Job has nothing in it but the promise of a fleshly, bodily resurrection (Per McDurmon) then of necessity, there was a resurrection of human corpses, out of the dirt, to receive immorality and incorruptibility. As noted above, *it virtually demands that Job himself was raised in a fleshly body, in AD 70*. Neither Frost, McDurmon or any other Dominionist believes in such at thing, but *logically*, their affirmation of "a fulfillment" of Job / 1 Corinthians 15 in AD 70 demands it. This is inescapable.

☛ If there was "a fulfillment" of Job and 1 Corinthians 15, then there was "a victory" over sin and "the law" (Torah). If there is yet another, *real* fulfillment of Job / Corinthians in the future, then of necessity, either Torah remains valid until that time, or, the Gospel of Jesus Christ will one day be annulled and removed! (In McDurmon's view the gospel must now be identified as "the strength of sin" to be annulled at the end. Has the Gospel replaced Torah as, "the strength of sin"?).

Part of the irony here is that in admitting that there was "a fulfillment" of Job / 1 Corinthians 15 in AD 70 McDurmon is acknowledging the imminence factor found in 1 Corinthians 15:51 - "We (which McDurmon agrees referred to the first century saints and the "a fulfillment" in AD 70) shall not all sleep." But then, the title of his book rejects and refutes his own admission when he claims that Job and 1 Corinthians have not been fulfilled! The "We" is not the Corinthians after all, but some royal "we" of some future, unknown generation that will not die until the resurrection. So "We" was *them*, but not really. It is "us" that will not die before the resurrection. Oh, wait, perhaps - and probably - it refers to some future, *"they* will not sleep!" McDurmon's view turns the language of Corinthians on its head. McDurmon gives and McDurmon takes away.

If there was no resurrection of the flesh in AD 70, even though there was "a fulfillment" of 1 Corinthians 15 at that time, then this proves that 1 Corinthians 15 is not a prediction of a resurrection of flesh. Job, per McDurmon is a prediction of the resurrection of the flesh and did not include a "spiritual resurrection." So, once again, if that "a fulfillment" of 1 Corinthians 15 in AD 70 was not "in the flesh" then clearly, Job does not equal 1 Corinthians 15, or, there was not "a fulfillment" in AD 70. (Keep in mind our discussion of the end of the Intermediate State of the Dead).

I should also observe here that in his book, McDurmon says not one word about his debate admission that there was "a fulfillment" of 1 Corinthians 15 in AD 70. (Little wonder!) As I note just below, he likewise says not one word about his admission that there are imminence factors in 1 Corinthians 15 that demand a first century fulfillment. He fails to type even one syllable in response to my arguments below, in which I show that whatever the resurrection of Job, 1 Corinthians 15, 1 Thessalonians 4, etc., it was truly, objectively imminent in the first century, and there is not so much as a hint, of a clue, of a suggestion that there was to be, or that there will be another "final" fulfillment.

The Response I Gave to Joel

I offered the following argument from 1 Peter – with some current additions and emendations - in response to McDurmon's argument on Job 19. The reader needs to know that in his book, in his entire discussion of Job, McDurmon says not one word, *literally not one word*, about the argument that I gave from Peter.

☛ Peter was writing about the imminent revelation of the eternal inheritance (1 Peter 1:3-5. This is, of course, the "eternal life" of Daniel 12:2, is it not? If not, what is the difference? Would the resurrection of Job be a different resurrection? If so, what is the evidence to support such a claim?

☛ That eternal inheritance was promised by the OT prophets (1:10f).

☛ The OT prophets knew that fulfillment was not for their days, but Peter affirms it was for his day and was being revealed through the Spirit (1:10-12). Note how Daniel did not understand his vision of the end time resurrection but he was told it was not for his day (Daniel 12:9f). We would observe that Job - accepting that he predicted the final resurrection - saw it for "the end" or "at the last." That means that Peter was affirming that what was not near in Job's day was near when he wrote 1 Peter.

☞ To emphasize then, Job's "resurrection prophecy" was for the last time. Peter said he was in the last time (foretold by the prophets) and Christ was about to be revealed (Acts 2:15f; 3:23; 1:5-6; 20).

☞ Peter said Christ was "ready" (from *hetoimos*) to judge, "the living and the dead" (1 Peter 4:5).

☞ Peter said, "the end of all things has drawn near" (4:7).

☞ Peter said the appointed time for "the judgment" had arrived (4:17).

In the debate, I took note of Peter's use of the *anaphoric article* in 4:17 when he spoke of "the judgment." See my discussion of this above. Peter's use of the anaphoric article in v. 17 *demands* that the time had arrived for the judgment of the living and the dead in v. 5.

I made this argument at least twice during the debate. I took note that the judgment of the living and the dead is undeniably the time of the resurrection; *the time of the resurrection in Job* (cf. Matthew 25:31f; 2 Timothy 4:1). I also took note of Revelation 11 and the prediction of the judgment of the nations and the living and the dead, pointing out that Joel applies that prophecy to AD 70.

Joel never responded, in any way, to the connection between Job, 1 Peter and Revelation 11. He never commented on Peter's affirmations of the nearness of "the end of all things." He ignored Peter's use of the anaphoric article and his undeniable statement that the time for the judgment of the living and the dead had arrived. He ignored all of my arguments on Revelation 11. And then, in his follow up book in which he sought to explain what he did not explain in the debate, McDurmon once again said *not one word*. He typed not a single syllable to deal with Peter's undeniable, emphatic and explicit statements about the resurrection. To say that this is revealing is a huge understatement.

What all of this means is that while McDurmon tried to run a bluff on the translational issues of Job, we have divine commentary on the timing of the resurrection. Unless a person can substantively delineate between the time of the end in Job and Peter, then Peter establishes the time for the resurrection foretold in Job as the first century.

Let me add a bit more to all of this by another look at Matthew 8:11 and McDurmon's admission of its fulfillment in AD 70.

The promise of sitting at the Messianic table in the kingdom in Matthew 8 is the promise of Isaiah 25:6.

The promise of the Messianic Banquet in Isaiah 25:6 is the promise of the resurrection (25:8).

The resurrection – and the Banquet – of Isaiah 25 is the promise of the resurrection in 1 Corinthians 15 (15:54f).

The resurrection of 1 Corinthians 15 was the resurrection promise of Job (So says McDurmon and the Dominionists).

The resurrection Banquet of Matthew 8 was fulfilled when Abraham and the OT Worthies were given the kingdom, in AD 70, (So says McDurmon and the Dominionists).

Therefore, the resurrection promise of Job, being the same promise of 1 Corinthians 15 and Isaiah 25, was fulfilled in AD 70.

Once again, the Dominionist admission that Matthew 8 was fulfilled in AD 70 serves to falsify their futurist eschatology.

Unless the Dominionists are willing now to abandon their view of the fulfillment of Matthew 8:11 in AD 70, then Job 19 was fulfilled at that time (even admitting that Job spoke of the final resurrection).

Unless the Postmillennialists can prove definitively that the AD 70 fulfillment was a type or shadow of the "real" resurrection, the "real" kingdom, the "real" Messianic Banquet, then their admission that Matthew 8 was fulfilled in AD 70 falsifies their eschatology.

Unless Dominionists can prove that the resurrection to the eternal inheritance - which they ascribe to the resurrection of Job 19 - and the eternal inheritance that was about to be revealed in Peter's day are different, then Peter settles the issue of Job 19.

Unless someone can prove that Peter had a different judgment of the living and the dead, at the end of all things, from the supposed resurrection and judgment of the living and the dead, at the end of all things in Job, then Peter settles the issue of Job. The time for that resurrection had arrived.

Of course, if it is affirmed that Job spoke of a different resurrection to eternal life from that of Daniel and perhaps even from 1 Peter, it would have to be proven that there is such a distinction. There is none. We ask again: How many resurrections to eternal life are there in scripture? McDurmon, Frost, Gentry, DeMar, etc. all fail to tell us.

Let me drive this point home with a comparative chart, showing the parallels with 1 Corinthians 15 and 1 Peter. I believe any fair assessment of these parallels will show that Paul and Peter were speaking of the same time and the same event.

1 Corinthians 15	1 Peter
Coming of Christ ✔	Coming of Christ (1:5f) ✔
Resurrection ✔	Resurrection (1:3f) ✔
Incorruptibility ✔	Incorruptibility (1:3f) ✔
Hope of Israel ✔	Hope of Israel (1:10f) ✔
Time of the end ✔	Time of the end (1:20; 4:7,17)✔
We Shall Not All Sleep ✔	"the end of all things has drawn near"; "the time has come" (4:7; 4:17) ✔

I did not present this chart in the debate, but I did present the material on 1 Peter and McDurmon did not offer a syllable of response. The emphatic declarations in Peter leave us no room - the time for the resurrection to incorruptibility - the resurrection of Job and 1 Corinthians 15, per McDurmon, had arrived.

While McDurmon sought to dismiss the daunting translational issue of Job 19 as a "piece of cake," it is far from that. As demonstrated, there is no indisputable proof that Job even foretold the "end time resurrection."

On the other hand, if one does say that Job foretold the end time resurrection to eternal life, Peter's unequivocal, unambiguous declaration that the time had arrived for the resurrection foretold by the prophets, at the time of the end, truly is a "piece of cake."

Furthermore, if Job foretold the end time resurrection to eternal life, when the prophets such as himself would be rewarded, then Daniel 12 and Revelation 11 positively posits that resurrection in AD 70.

Job 19 offers no support for the raising of human corpses out of the ground and McDurmon did not (could not and cannot) prove otherwise.

Point #12

DANIEL 12, THE VINDICATION OF THE MARTYRS AND THE MILLENNIUM

The following is from a paper I delivered at Criswell College in Dallas, Texas, in October 2012. The theme of the conference was, "The Meaning of the Millennium." Other speakers on the dias were Craig Bloomberg, H. Wayne House, Craig Blaising, Ken Gentry and Greg Beale. Each of these men presented their respective view of the Millennium. I presented "The Preterist (Fulfilled) View of the Millennium." I have added some additional material to the MSS below. The original MSS was published in the Criswell Theological Review, Fall of 2013.

I want to discuss a theme that is admitted by almost all scholars and certainly by the text of Revelation 20, to be absolutely central to Revelation 20. That theme is the doctrine of the avenging of the martyrs. Revelation 20 and the millennium begins with the martyrs, those who had been slain for the word of God and it is consummated with the destruction of Satan who is the persecutor of the seed of the man child (Revelation 12).[235]

---

[235] Riddlebarger, (2003, 201) describes "the obvious parallelism" between Revelation 12 and chapter 20 and says that if they both speak of the same time and events, "this is a serious blow to all forms of Premillennialism, which place the events of Revelation 20 chronologically after the return of Jesus Christ described in chapter 19." I would suggest that a closer look at the theme of *martyr vindication*, in light of Matthew 23, also falsifies Riddlebarger's futurist take on these chapters. Since Revelation 6 is based on Jesus' promise of the vindication of the martyrs in AD 70 and Revelation 12 / 20 are parallel, this demands a first century fulfillment of Revelation.

Gentry, commenting on Revelation 20, says, "The martyrs' deaths not only demand vindication, but explain and justify the judgments to follow."[236] I fully concur.

Likewise, Blaising, commenting on Revelation 20 says, "Revelation chapter 6 introduced the expectation that some justice would be executed by God on their behalf and they wait for that justice even as they are joined in waiting by subsequent martyrs. What John sees in Revelation 20 is the just vindication of believers slain for their faith, the fulfillment of them, or of the promises made by Christ himself."[237]

I suggest that these comments are destructive not only to both men's paradigms, but to *any* futurist eschatology. The vindication of the martyrs is one of, if not *the* most pervasive motifs in the entirety of Revelation and the totality of scripture. Note the following from Revelation.

Revelation 1 – "Behold he comes with the clouds, every eye shall see him and they shall look upon him whom they have pierced, even those who pierced him."

Revelation 6 – The souls of those under the altar crying out for vindication, "How long, O Lord?"

Revelation 7 – Tells us of the 144,000 who come out of the Great Tribulation. They are martyrs.

Revelation 12 - The persecution of the seed of the man child and the destruction of Satan coming in just a little while.

---

[236] Kenneth Gentry, *Three Views of The Millennium and Beyond*, Stanley Gundry, Ed., (Grand Rapids, Zondervan, 1999)251.

[237] Craig Blaising, *Three Views of The Millennium and Beyond*, Stanley Gundry, Ed., (Grand Rapids, Zondervan, 1999)222.

Revelation 14 – Combines references to the martyrs, Babylon and the fullness of God's wrath, all elements linked with martyr vindication.

Revelation 16-19 - The destruction of Babylon, the persecuting power, guilty of shedding all the blood of all the righteous shed on the earth, including that of the prophets.

Revelation 20 is a recapitulation, a reiteration of the martyr theme of all of these chapters. Revelation 20 does not contain a separate promise of another vindication, of another body of martyrs different from that promised earlier in the apocalypse, and I might add, throughout the entire corpus of scripture. That motif – this is very critical – is inextricably tied to the end of the millennium resurrection. It is tied to the judgment. And, the motif of martyr vindication is inextricably tied to the judgment of Old Covenant Israel.

Follow closely. The resurrection and the vindication of martyrs was the Old Covenant salvation hope of *Israel after the flesh*. It was not a promise given to the church, divorced from Israel.

In Romans 8:17f, notice what Paul says in verse 18, "I reckon that the sufferings of the now present time," – that's Paul's present time – "are not worthy to be compared with the glory that is about to be revealed in us." This is martyr vindication for the suffering (*pathemata*) they were experiencing at that very time. <u>Pathemata</u> is not the everyday experience of the human experience. It is not financial distress. It's not job insecurity. It's not even teenage kids! It has to do with suffering for the cause of Christ. That vindication would come at the adoption, what Paul calls the redemption of the body (v. 23).

Paul explicitly says the covenant promise of the adoption belonged to Israel "after the flesh." What that means, therefore, is that until God's covenant with Israel was completely fulfilled, that covenant would remain valid. Israel would remain as God's covenant people. Thus the entire millennium, martyr vindication, the end of the millennium are all inextricably tied to Israel and her story. Most eschatologies fail to properly honor the connection between Old Covenant Israel, the end-of-the-millennium resurrection and martyr vindication.

For instance, Riddlebarger, noted Amillennialist says, "Because of Jesus Christ and his coming, the Christian possesses the complete," (notice his wording here, DKP), "the complete fulfillment and blessings of all of the promises of the messianic age named under the Old Covenant. But the arrival of the messianic age also brought with it a new series of promises to be fulfilled at the end of the age."[238] By the end of the age, he means the end of the Christian age.

Lorraine Boettner, noted Postmillennialist said, "For information concerning the first coming of Christ, we go to the Old Testament, he came exactly as promised or predicted all of those prophecies were fulfilled," or notice this, "*or were forfeited* through disobedience; but for information concerning his second coming and what future developments will be, we go only to the New Testament."[239] (My emphasis). I would suggest that nothing could be farther from the truth.

Let me give what I consider to be an axiomatic statement. The resurrection of Revelation 20 is the resurrection of 1 Corinthians 15. Paul said his gospel was nothing but the hope of Israel - *Israel after the flesh* – again, Romans 8 and 9.

Contra Dispensationalism, Paul knew *nothing* of a scheme and a hope for Old Covenant Israel versus or different from, a gospel, a message and a hope for the church. Paul said there was but *one hope*.

---

[238] Kim Riddlebarger, *A Case for Amillennialism, Understanding the End Times*, (Grand Rapids, Baker, 2003)61.

[239] Lorraine Boettner, *Four Views of the Millennium*, (Downers Grove, InterVarsity,1977)102.

In Acts 24:14f, as he preached about the resurrection, Paul said, "I believe all things contained in the law and the prophets; there is about to be a resurrection of the just and of the unjust." He stood on trial, he said, for the hope of the promise of the resurrection, the hope of the twelve tribes (Acts 26:6f).

In Acts 26:21f, Paul said, "I say no other things than what Moses and the prophets said should come to pass, that Christ would be the first to be raised from the dead and to show light and life to the Gentiles." Paul said, my gospel, my one hope, is nothing but the hope of Israel found in the Old Testament.

With this in mind, I will now focus on five key Old Testament prophecies of the end times, the end-of-the-millennium resurrection and the vindication of the martyrs. I will show how the consistent, Biblical testimony, both Old and New Testament, posits the eschatological vindication at the AD70 judgment of Old Covenant Israel, the city guilty of shedding all the blood shed on the earth. (Note: This will demonstrate, along the way, that all attempts to divorce Daniel 12 from the end of the millennium resurrection are futile. DKP).

#1 - The first passage is Deuteronomy 32, called the Song of Moses. In the preamble to the Song, Deuteronomy 31:29, Moses said to Israel, "I know that after my death, you will become utterly corrupt in the last days." I want you to grasp the motif. This is known as the filling the measure of sin.

In this Song, Moses said that this was for many generations to come, many generations in the future (32:7f) Yahweh said, "I will see what their last end shall be." This would be a time in which Israel would provoke God to "jealousy, by that which was not God," and as a result, He would "provoke them to jealousy," and call the Gentiles to him. In verse 29, as God continues to speak of Israel's last days apostasy. The Lord lamented that condition saying, "Oh, that they were wise, O, that they would consider what their last end will be."

Now, notice verse 32. In this last days scenario, Israel would become the "vine of Sodom." We will return to this below. Now verse 43: "Rejoice, O Gentiles, with his people, for He will avenge the blood of his servants." Thus in Israel's last days, Yahweh would avenge the blood of the martyrs. This is patently not *historical* eschatology, i.e. the end of history. This is not Christian eschatology, i.e. the end of the Christian age. This is about *Israel's last days*.

Now look at the New Testament application of the Song. Many scholars have noted the paradigmatic use of not only Deuteronomy, but of the Song itself. Ross Wagner wrote a great book, *Heralds of the Good News*.[240] He noted that with the exception of Isaiah and the Psalms, Paul quotes from Deuteronomy more than any other Old Testament book. Wagner does a great job of showing how many times Paul incorporates the Song into his eschatological teaching. And Paul specifically applies the Song to the issue of persecution and martyr vindication. We could take note of several passages, but time doesn't permit.

In Hebrews 10:26f, however, Paul speaks of the persecution they were then experiencing at the hands of the Jews. He twice, *twice*, quotes Deuteronomy 32, to promise vindication at the very, very soon – (*hoson, hoson, micron*) - coming of the Lord in vindication of their suffering. The context is Jewish persecution of the church, which is comprised, of course, of the righteous remnant of Old Covenant Israel now being joined by the Gentiles. Very clearly, Paul's citation of Deuteronomy is a citation of prophecy fulfillment.

As an interesting, although not determinative side note, Josephus believed that the Song of Moses was being fulfilled in his day: "Moses recited to Israel a poem of hexameter verse, which he has moreover bequeathed in a book preserved in the temple, containing a prediction of future events, in accordance with which all has come and is coming to pass, the seer having in no whit strayed from the

---

[240] J. Ross Wagner, *Heralds of the Good News*, (Boston, Brill Publishing, 2003).

truth." (*Antiquities*, 4:303). Josephus was patently not making a "Christian" application of the Song. The fact that he believed that Moses foretold the events of his day are nonetheless significant. Josephus also believed that the prophecies of Daniel 2, 7, 9 were being fulfilled in his day as well.

I agree with Beale that Paul was not simply citing these prophecies analogically. Paul was saying, here is what was predicted, here is what is coming true.[241] What was coming true and what was about to come true, was the very, very soon vindication of the suffering of the martyrs.

#2 - The next prophecy of the five – Isaiah 2-4, predicted the last days (Isaiah 2:2) and the establishment of the Messianic temple. Beale has done a great job in his book on the temple and the church. I recommend that book. Isaiah likewise predicted the Day of the Lord (Isaiah 2:10, 19f).

Notice verses 19f, when men could run to the mountains, cry to the rocks, "fall on us." Robinson said in his 1979 book, "exhortations or statements about fleeing to the hills and crying to the rocks, fall on us," hardly comports with the idea of a Day of the Lord in an earth-burning, time-ending, over-in-a-moment, in the twinkling-of-an-eye event,"[242] and I fully concur.

Notice in chapter 3, as the writer continues, Isaiah predicted that Jerusalem "declares their sin like Sodom. They declare it and they hide it not." This is a direct echo back to the Song of Moses (Deuteronomy 32:32). Deuteronomy 32 - Israel's last days; Isaiah 2-4 - Israel's last days. Israel will become like Sodom; Israel will declare her sin like Sodom.

---

[241] Greg Beale, *A New Testament Biblical Theology*, (Grand Rapids, Baker Academic, 2011)772.

[242] John A. T. Robinson, *Jesus and His Coming*, (Philadelphia, Westminster Press, 1979)74.

In chapter 3:18f, it speaks of the time of *the* war – definite article in the LXX - and it is a time of *the* war when Israel's men would fall by the edge of the sword. Jesus directly echoes that in Luke 21:24, when he said, speaking of the fall of Jerusalem in AD70, that Israel's men would fall by the edge of the sword. Not only that, it was this time of *the* war, the <u>polemos</u> in Revelation 16:14, 19:19, 20:8f, we find reference to the gathering of the kings of the earth.

So, Isaiah predicted the last days, the Day of the Lord, the vindication of the martyrs – and in Revelation 16:19-20, we have the motif of the vindication of the martyrs at the time of the gathering of the nations and the kings of the earth for *the* war. A different "*the* war"? No. It is the identical motif, the vindication of the martyrs.

But this event, this Day of the Lord, when Israel's men would fall by the edge of the sword in *the* war, is likewise the time of the appearing of the glorious Branch (Isaiah 4:1-2). It's either the appearing of the glorious Branch or the glorious appearing of the Branch, whichever you prefer there. But it's the glorious appearing of Yahweh's Branch and notice – **in that day** - God would avenge the blood guilt of Jerusalem. It's not the church. The blood guilt of Jerusalem would be avenged by the spirit of judgment and the spirit of fire.

I want you to notice an incredible set of correspondences.

Isaiah 2-4, foretold the last days and the Day of the Lord when Yahweh would judge Jerusalem for her blood guilt. This is the vindication of the martyrs.

In Luke 23:28f, Jesus was being led to his death. The women were weeping over him when he turned to them and he said, "Daughters of Jerusalem, do not weep for me, weep for yourselves and for your children for the time is coming in which they will... run to the hills and they will cry to the rocks, fall on us." This is a direct citation of Isaiah 2:19 and of course, the parallel of Hosea 10:8.

Scholars almost universally acknowledge that Jesus was referencing the coming AD70 judgment of Israel. But watch this:

In 2 Thessalonians 1:9, Paul writes to the Thessalonians being persecuted for their faith. He promised them imminent vindication of that suffering and relief from that persecution at the Day of the Lord. And, he quotes from the identical verse from Isaiah (2:19) that Jesus himself applied to AD70. He quoted it to promise the imminent vindication for Thessalonian martyrs.

But that's not all. In Revelation 6:9f, the souls under the altar had been slain for the word of God and the testimony which they held. They cried out for vindication, "How long, O, Lord, holy and true, do you not avenge us on the earth?" They were told to "rest for a little while." They were not told to rest for thousands of years. They were told to "rest for a little while," and the answer to their prayer is the Great and Awesome Day of the Lord.

Note that John quotes from Isaiah 2:19, the identical verse from Isaiah that Jesus applied to AD70 in his, John's, prediction of the imminent Day of the Lord for the vindication of the martyrs.

My question is, therefore, what is the hermeneutic of distinction? If Jesus applied Isaiah 2- 4 to AD70 and Paul and John quoted from the identical verse, what is our hermeneutic of distinction to say that John and Paul were applying Isaiah to something totally different?

#3 - The third text I want to look at is Isaiah, chapters 24-27, known as the Little Apocalypse. Beginning with verse 7 in chapter 25, the Lord said, "He will destroy on this mountain" – that's Zion. I would like to have a lot to say about that, but I can't – "the veil that is spread over all nations. He will swallow up death forever and the Lord God will wipe away tears from all of the faces...and it will be said **in that day**, behold this is our God; we have waited for Him; He will save us.... We will be glad and rejoice in His salvation."

This is very clearly the end-of-the-millennium resurrection. It's the very verse that Paul quotes in 1 Corinthians 15:55 when he said, "when this mortal has put on immortality... the corruptible has put on incorruption, then shall be brought to pass the saying, death is swallowed up in victory." That's Isaiah. Therefore, Isaiah is the end-of-the-millennium resurrection.

This is patently the salvation hope of Israel. But let's look a little closer at the Little Apocalypse. Let's move into chapter 26. Now by the way, most of these men agree that the Little Apocalypse is speaking of the eschatological consummation, not a typological consummation. Isaiah predicted the end-of-the-millennium resurrection (Isaiah 25:8). Likewise chapter 26:19f, "the earth shall give up its dead." But notice, it would be in the day in which the Lord shall descend out of the heavens and tread on the tops of the mountains (26:20).

But notice this. It is also the time of the vindication of the martyrs – the earth shall disclose its blood. Meredith Kline wrote a great article demonstrating this not too long ago.[243] But notice this. *In that day*, in what day? The day of the vindication of the martyrs, the day of the coming of the Lord, the day of the end-of-the-millennium resurrection. *In that day*, Leviathan shall be destroyed (27:1).

Note that in 27:10-11, it is at the time of the salvation of Israel which Isaiah 25:8-9 told us is the resurrection, the salvation of Israel. Significantly, it is likewise the time of the *destruction* of Old Covenant Israel, because *in that day* would be the time when He turns the stones of the altar into chalk stone, He destroys the fortified city, "the one who made them will no longer have mercy on them."Why? Well, it tells us. It is because, "this is a people of no understanding," a direct citation or allusion to Deuteronomy 32:28.

Deuteronomy 32:28 that said in Israel's last days, here is what will happen: They will become like Sodom; I will destroy them. So, in

---

[243] Meredith G. Kline, "Death, Leviathan and Martyrs: Isaiah 24:1-27:1" A Tribute to Gleason Archer, ed. by Walter C. Kaiser Jr. And Ronald Youngblood, Chicago, Moody Press, 1986, pp. 229-249.

Isaiah 24-27, we have Israel's last days, the vindication of the martyrs at the destruction of Old Covenant Israel.

#4 - Isaiah 59. As universally acknowledged, Isaiah 27 and Isaiah 59 serve as Paul's source for his prediction of the salvation hope of Israel in Romans 11:25-27. Just like Deuteronomy 32, just like Isaiah 2-4, just like Isaiah 26-27, Isaiah 59 predicted the vindication of the martyrs at the Day of the Lord and also at the judgment of Old Covenant Israel. Isaiah 59 breaks itself down easily into three headings:

Number 1 – *Accusation* – four times in verses 3-7 God accuses Israel of shedding innocent blood, of being quick to violence. That leads to point #2.

Number 2 – Israel *Acknowledges* her guilt. Notice what she says, "our transgressions are multiplied before you." This is Deuteronomy 31:29: "You will fill up the measure of your sin." So Israel even admits her transgression, "our transgressions are multiplied before you."

And so, Number 3- Yahweh decides to take *Action* in verses 16f: "He put on the garments of vengeance for clothing, he was clad with zeal as a cloak, according to their deeds, accordingly he will repay, fury to his adversaries, recompense to his enemies...so shall they fear the name of the Lord...the redeemer will come to Zion and to those who turn from transgression in Jacob, says the Lord. As for me, says the Lord, this is my covenant with them."

Romans 11:25-27 anticipated the parousia for the salvation of Israel in fulfillment of Isaiah 27 and Isaiah 59. That is abundantly clear.[244]

---

[244] As this book prepares to go to press, I am finalizing a book on Romans 11:25-27. This book will present an all but unprecedented examination of the relationship between the ministry of John the Baptizer as *The Voice* of Isaiah 40, *The Messenger* of Malachi 3 and *Elijah* of Malachi 4 - and Romans 11:25f. After extensive searches, I have not found a single commentary that addresses these connections

However, Isaiah 27 and Isaiah 59 foretold the coming of the Lord to be sure, for the salvation of Israel, i.e., the salvation of the remnant. And, that would be at the end-of-the-millennium resurrection (Isaiah 25-26).

Remember, that would be at the destruction of Leviathan, Satan. When does the destruction of Leviathan take place? All you have to do is read Revelation 20:10-12 – at the end of the millennium. When would that be, however? According to Isaiah 26:21 and Isaiah 59:16, it would be at the coming of the Lord *for the vindication of the martyrs*. But that is not all. It would be when the fortified city would be destroyed, the altar crushed and the people whom Yahweh had created would be forsaken. That is not the church.

Thus, Romans 11, being the anticipation of the fulfillment of Isaiah 27 and 59, would be fulfilled at the end of the millennium, at the avenging of the blood of the martyrs, at the time of the destruction of Old Covenant Israel. But I want to look a little closer.

I suggest that there is no futurist eschatology that properly honors what Isaiah 27 and Isaiah 59 actually says.[245]

Amillennialists redefine Israel in Romans 11 as the church, or they posit the salvation of ethnic Jews throughout the entire span of the

---

and yet, I believe that John's message lies directly behind Paul's prediction of the salvation of Israel.

[245] At the time of the writing of this book, I have not yet found a single commentator who discusses the prophetic context and content of Isaiah 27 and 59 and what impact an understanding of that context might have on our understanding of Romans 11. While virtually all commentators take note that Paul cites the two prophecies from Isaiah, they do not exegete the Isaianic texts and discuss the judgment aspect of them. They do not so much as mention the motif of martyr vindication found in both texts. This is an unfortunate oversight.

Christian age. Greg Beale does this.²⁴⁶ But these positions ignore the vindication of the martyr motif and *the judgment of Israel* motif explicitly found in Isaiah 27 and 59.

Post-millennialists (e.g. Kenneth Gentry,²⁴⁷ DeMar²⁴⁸) likewise ignore the judgment of Israel and the martyr vindication specifically and explicitly found in Isaiah 27 and Isaiah 59.

Pre-millennialists posit unbelieving Israel as the *victim* of a foreign persecuting power, not the persecutor as Isaiah clearly says.²⁴⁹ I would suggest, therefore, that none of these truly honors what Isaiah says.

---

²⁴⁶ Greg Beale, *A New Testament Biblical Theology*, (Grand Rapids, Baker, 2011)706+.

²⁴⁷ While Gentry spends time discussing Romans 11 in his *He Shall Have Dominion*, (Draper, VA, Apologetics Group, 2009)254, he ignores the prophetic background and does not so much as mention the themes found in Isaiah 27 / 59. He posits the traditional Postmillennial view that Romans 11:25f speaks of a yet future "massive, world-wide conversion" of national Jews

²⁴⁸ In a radio interview with Dr. Michael Brown, July 13, 2010, DeMar affirmed his belief that Romans 11 predicts a yet future time when a great majority of ethnic Jews will be converted: http://www.lineoffireradio.com/2010/07/13/dr-brown-discusses-preterism-with-dr-gary-demar/.

²⁴⁹ I have not found a single Dispensational author who honors the prophetic source of Romans 11:25f and the proper identification of *Israel as the persecutor*. Invariably, Premillennialists posit Romans 11 as predictive of a future time when Israel, being persecuted by the anti-Christ, cries out to the Lord and is saved at the parousia. This is a distortion of what the texts actually say.

This raises a serious hermeneutical question. Isaiah 26 and 27 predicted the end-of-the-millennium resurrection, the Day of the Lord, the destruction of Satan and the vindication of the martyrs at the time of the salvation of the righteous remnant, as well as the judgment on Old Covenant Israel, not the church.

Isaiah 59 likewise foretold the Day of Lord, the vindication of martyrs, the salvation of the remnant, the judgment on Old Covenant Israel as the persecuting power. Romans 11 anticipated the fulfillment of Isaiah 27 and Isaiah 59. What then, is the hermeneutical principle for saying Romans 11 anticipates a future salvation of the church or deliverance of Israel from a foreign persecuting power divorced from the context of judgment on Old Covenant Israel for her blood guilt for shedding innocent blood?

Inserted note: In my aforementioned debate with Dr. Michael Brown, he attempted to escape the force of Paul's use of Isaiah 27 and 59 and my appeal to the judgment context of those prophecies, by saying that Paul was speaking of Israel's salvation, whereas Isaiah was speaking of Israel's judgment. I responded by noting that throughout the Scriptures, judgment and salvation go hand in hand.

Dr. Brown acknowledged that fact and never raised the objection again. This is an important issue, for many commentators try to make the same false distinction between a time of judgment and the time of salvation, when in fact, as noted, salvation and judgment are siamese twins.

#5 - The fifth passage I want to examine is Daniel 12. Daniel 12, when compared to 1 Corinthians 15 and Revelation 20, very clearly contains the following constituent elements:

Number one is about the salvation hope of Israel, as we have demonstrated. It's the time of the end. Daniel foretold the Great Tribulation. Where does Revelation 20 posit the tribulation? *At the end of the millennium.* Again, we're dealing with the resurrection to eternal life (Daniel 12:2) just as 1 Corinthians 15 is talking about the resurrection for eternal life Revelation 21 as well.

Notice that Daniel 12 is about the vindication of martyrs, the time of the rewarding of the prophets. Likewise, Revelation 11 is the time of the dead that they should be judged and the time of the rewarding of the prophets. This is a direct allusion back to Daniel 12. Daniel 12 explicitly tells us that the resurrection would be fulfilled, "when the power of the holy people is completely shattered" (v. 7). Likewise, Paul said the resurrection of 1 Corinthians 15 would be when *the* law that is the strength of *the* sin would be fulfilled.

Here is a significant fact. The only law in scripture that is ever labeled as, described as, the "strength of sin" was *Torah*. Patently, the gospel is not the strength of *the* sin. Thus Paul agrees with Daniel in positing the end-of-the-millennium resurrection at the end of Torah, the strength of sin, when Daniel posits the end-of-the-millennium resurrection as a time when Israel's power would be completely shattered.

My argument here is simple.

Daniel 12 is the resurrection of 1 Corinthians 15, the end-of-the-millennium resurrection of Revelation 20. (To my knowledge, every man on the dais today agrees with that except Kenneth Gentry. He once took that position, but he now believes that Daniel 12 was in fact fulfilled in AD70).[250]

---

[250] As we have seen, Gentry once applied Daniel 12:2 to the "end of the world" (Kenneth Gentry, *The Greatness of the Great Commission*, (Tyler, Tx., Institute for Christian Economics, 1993)142). He now says, "Daniel appears to be presenting Israel as a grave site under God's curse; Israel as a corporate body is in the dust (Daniel 12:2; cp. Ge. 3:14, 19). In this he follows Ezekiel's pattern in his vision of the dry bones, which represents Israel's 'death' in the Babylonian dispersion (Ezekiel 37). In Daniel's prophecy many will awaken, as it were, during the great tribulation to suffer the full fury of divine wrath, while others will enjoy God's grace in receiving everlasting life" (*He Shall Have Dominion*, (Draper, VA., Apologetics Group, 2009) 538.

But the resurrection of Daniel 12 would be accomplished, "when the power of the holy people was completely shattered."

Therefore, the end-of-the-millennium resurrection of 1 Corinthians and Revelation 20, was, or will be, accomplished when the power of the holy people is completely shattered.[251]

Let me summarize my examination of these Old Testament texts.

Number one - They foretold the eschatological consummation, not a typological fulfillment.[252] They foretold the end-of-the-millennium resurrection, the parousia and the destruction of Satan.

In every one of these texts, Israel, Old Covenant Israel after the flesh, is the persecuting power, not a foreign Gentile power. It is Israel therefore, that is guilty of shedding all the innocent blood.

Furthermore, vindication is posited in Israel's last days when Yahweh would judge Israel for her internecine guilt, when He would no longer have mercy on the people that he created.

Notice something very important. Jesus' teaching on martyr vindication definitively confirms this analysis. Standing in the

---

[251] It is critical to realize that Daniel emphatically tells us that the kingdom of Messiah would never be destroyed (2:44; 7:13f). Similarly, Jesus said his word will never pass away. It cannot therefore, be suggested that the resurrection of Daniel 12 anticipates the resurrection at the end of the Christian age. Only one age was to come to an end that is the age represented by the Jerusalem Temple (Matthew 24:1-3).

[252] See my *AD 70: A Shadow of the "Real" End?* for a full discussion and refutation of the claim often made by both Amillennialists and Postmillennialists, that the events of AD 70 were typological of the coming end of the Christian age. The book is available on Kindle, Amazon, my websites and other retailers.

temple in Matthew 23, delivering the seventh of seven woes on Jerusalem and Israel, Jesus said,

> "Woe to you scribes and Pharisees, hypocrites, because you build the tombs of the prophets and you adorn the monuments of the righteous you say, if we had been alive in the days of our fathers, we would not have been partakers with them in the blood of the prophets; therefore, you are witnesses against yourselves that you were the sons of those who murdered the prophets, fill up then the measure of your father's guilt. Therefore, behold, indeed, I send you prophets, wise men and scribes, some of them you will kill and crucify, some of them you will scourge in your synagogues and persecute from city to city that on you may come all the righteous blood shed on the earth from the blood of righteous Abel to the blood of Zechariah, son of Berechiah, whom you slew between the temple and the altar." (Now notice,) "Assuredly," <u>*amen lego humin*</u>, "assuredly, I say to you, all these things will come upon this generation."

But this is not all that Jesus had to say about martyr vindication. During his ministry martyr vindication was, in fact, a major theme. In Matthew 21, he told the parable of the vineyard servants sent to the gather of the harvest, the servants were persecuted and the master sent out his armies. He came and miserably destroyed those evil men.

Matthew 22 – A man made a great wedding feast for his son. He sent out the servants to call those who had been invited. They were mistreated and killed. The master sent out his armies and destroyed those wicked men and burned their city.

Luke 13:33-34 - Jesus, being warned not to go to Jerusalem because Herod would kill him, said, "It is not possible that a prophet perish outside of Jerusalem."

In Luke 18:1-8, Jesus tells the parable of the importunate widow who cried out for vengeance, *ekdikeesis*, which is the key word for martyr vindication. And Jesus poses the question, "Will not God avenge his servants who cry out to him day and night?" Mattill said some time ago, "It's impossible to read Revelation 6:9f, without hearing the echo of Luke 18."[253] I agree with that assessment.

Notice that Jesus said, "Assuredly I say to you He will avenge them *speedily*. The Greek term, *en tachei* is used here and never – let me emphasize this– *en tachei* never emphasizes rapidity of action as opposed to imminence of occurrence. Never, in some seven occurrences in the New Testament. Thus, Jesus affirmed the objectively imminent vindication of the martyrs at his coming.

With Jesus' emphatic teaching on martyr vindication echoing in our hearts and minds therefore, notice what Paul says as he wrote to the Thessalonica church being persecuted for their faith. He said to them,

> "It is a righteous thing with God to repay with tribulation those who are troubling you and to give to you who are being troubled, rest *(anesis)* when the Lord is revealed from heaven...in flaming fire taking vengeance on those who do not know God on those who do not obey the gospel of the Lord. These shall be punished with everlasting destruction from the presence of the Lord and from the glory of His power."

You might ask yourself, who is the only people who ever dwelt in the presence of the Lord, but who would be cast out for persecuting the true seed? It's a relevant question.

I want you to notice some firm facts. Jesus said the Jews would persecute his followers, his apostles and prophets, filling up the

---

[253] A. J. Mattill, *Luke and the Last Things*, (Dillsboro, NC, Western North Carolina Press, 1979)94.

measure of their sin, and filling up the measure of suffering on the part of his followers. Judgment would fall on the Jews in the first century.

Paul said Christ was about to come in judgment of, "those who are troubling you." That was the Jews. Go back to 1 Thessalonians 2:14-16. Who was, through that persecution, filling up the measure of their sin by persecuting the Christians? It was undeniably Old Covenant Israel. And note that they were persecuting Jesus' *apostles and prophets*, just like Jesus said in Matthew 23.

Now watch. Clearly, Jesus could not give the Thessalonian church relief from their then ongoing persecution, if the Thessalonians would not be alive at the time of Christ's coming. You cannot give somebody relief from something at your coming if they are not enduring that pressure at the time of your coming. It is impossible.

2 Thessalonians 1 is about the fulfillment of Matthew 23. And, I suggest, as many of these men agree, by the way, Jesus did come in judgment of Israel for persecuting Christ and the "True Seed" in AD70 in vindication of all of the blood of all of the martyrs shed on the earth.

Remember that Paul said his gospel was nothing but the hope of Israel found in the law and the prophets. And Paul's promise of martyr vindication and judgment of the persecutors in 2 Thessalonians 1:10 is a direct citation, a direct quote, of the Septuagint of Isaiah 2:19, which predicted what? The last days, Day-of-the-Lord judgment of Jerusalem for her blood guilt, just like Isaiah 26 and 27 predicted the vindication at the end-of-the-millennium resurrection when God would destroy the persecuting city, the altar and the people that he had created.

Now notice this. The Old Testament foretold that Israel would fill the measure of her blood guilt in her last days, as we have seen. In Matthew 23, the measure of Israel's sin and the martyrs' suffering was to be filled in the first century in the killing of Jesus' apostles and prophets.

In 1 Thessalonians 2, Paul said Israel was filling up the measure of her sin by killing the apostles and prophets.

In 1 Corinthians 4:9, a text that has perplexed scholars for forever, Paul said, "I think that God has set forth us, the apostles last of all, as men condemned to death."

Johanne Munck said Paul was an ego-maniac.[254] He was crazy. No, he wasn't. He understood Jesus' prediction that the measure of eschatological suffering had to be filled up in that generation. This is why he said in Colossians 1:24, "I now rejoice in my sufferings for you fill up in my flesh what is lacking in the afflictions of Christ." You mean to tell me Jesus didn't suffer enough? No, Jesus suffered enough, but there was a measure of sin and suffering to be filled up.

Notice this. Revelation perfectly carries through all of these motifs. The measure of sin and suffering is a central theme of the book of Revelation that was to be filled. How? By the killing of the apostles and prophets of Jesus. This is the "rest of the dead" of Revelation 20. I suggest that this definitively delimits the end of the millennium to the first century.

Our Old Testament texts posited vindication at the judgment of Israel in *her* last days. Likewise, Jesus emphatically posited vindication for his generation and the judgment of Jerusalem. I suggest that Matthew 23 is normative and paradigmatic. Paul agreed with Matthew 23.

To suggest, therefore, that the end-of-the-millennium resurrection, the filling up of the measure of sin and the martyr vindication, is yet future, it is necessary to divorce Revelation 20 from all prior discussions of the vindication of the martyrs. I find no justification for that. Jesus' "this generation" delimits all of the "at hand" and "a little while" statements; it means we can't take "a little while" in

---

[254] Johannes Munck, *Paul and the Salvation of Mankind,* (Richmond, John Knox, 1959)38+.

some vague, nebulous elastic, plastic sense of, "Well, that's God's time and not ours." No, it's Jesus' "this generation."[255] Look very carefully.

Jesus said Old Covenant Jerusalem killed the prophets, they would kill him, they would kill *his* apostles and prophets. In fact, in Jerusalem was to be found all of the blood shed on the earth in killing the apostles and prophets. That would fill up the measure of sin and Israel would be judged in his generation.

What did Paul say in 1 Thessalonians 2? It was Jerusalem that had killed the prophets in the past and they had now killed Jesus. They were killing Jesus' apostles and prophets. In doing so, they were filling up the measure of their sin. Judgment was about to fall. The language of 1 Thessalonians 2:16 is very graphic.

Now notice Revelation. Babylon is the *harlot*. In an excellent book, Steven Temple points out that in the Bible, a harlot is not simply an immoral woman. It is a wife who has broken a covenant bond, a covenant relationship.[256] Well that excludes literal Babylon in Iraq. It excludes Rome. It excludes the Roman Catholic church.

Babylon the harlot had done what? She had killed the Old Testament prophets (Revelation 16:6). It is where the Lord was slain. And, she had killed the apostles and prophets of Jesus: "And

---

[255] See my *Who Is This Babylon?* for one of the fullest discussions of the temporal statements of imminence to be found. In this study, I examine all of the major arguments that are offered to negate the objective imminence of the "at hand" statements show them to be untenable. Biblically, when God communicated time words, those words were used in a concrete, objective sense. Don K. Preston, *Who Is This Babylon?,* (Ardmore, Ok., JaDon Management Inc. 2007).

[256] Steven Temple, *Who Was The Mother of Harlots Drunk With the Blood of the Saints?* (Ardmore, Ok., JaDon Management Inc., 2012).

in her was found all the blood shed on the earth," a direct echo of Matthew 23. And, of course, judgment was near.

I suggest, therefore that to identify Babylon as Rome, as does Beale,[257] or, "the present evil age" as Strimple does,[258] one must divorce John from Jesus and Paul– not to mention the Old Testament prophetic source of Revelation. Babylon was Jerusalem. I recommend Kenneth Gentry's book, *Before Jerusalem Fell*[259] and my, *Who Is This Babylon* for more on that.

Look now at how Revelation incorporates the key Old Testament prophecies that we've examined.

Deuteronomy 32:32, says that in Israel's last days, she would become the vine of Sodom. In describing the city that killed the two witnesses, i.e., the prophets of God, she is spiritually called Sodom.

Likewise, at her destruction and demise, in Revelation 19, the paean of victory is sung and that victory is what? It is a direct echo of Deuteronomy 32: 43 that said He *will* avenge the blood of his saints. But in Revelation 19:2 we find, He *has* avenged the blood of his saints.

Isaiah 2-4 predicted the last days vindication of the martyrs at the coming of the Lord. Yet, men would flee to the hills. Well, Revelation 6:12f, as we have seen, is a direct citation of Isaiah 2:19.

---

[257] Beale identifies "Babylon" as Rome, the pagan powers that persecuted (persecutes) the faithful, and even throws in Old Covenant Jerusalem. Greg Beale, *New International Greek Testament Commentary*, (Grand Rapids, Paternoster, 1999)884+.

[258] Robert Strimple in, *Three Views of The Millennium and Beyond*, Stanley Grundy series editor, Darrel Bock, general editor. (Grand Rapids, Zondervan, 1999)271.

[259] Kenneth Gentry, *Before Jerusalem Fell*, (Fountain Inn, SC, Victorious Hope Publishing, 1998).

Isaiah 27 foretold the destruction of Leviathan at the time of the vindication of the martyrs. In Revelation 20:8f, we find the destruction of Satan *at the end of the millennium.*

Isaiah 59, we have the salvation of the remnant. Revelation 7 and 14, is the salvation of the 144,000, the righteous remnant.

Daniel chapter 12 foretold the resurrection and the rewarding of the prophets. Revelation 11:15f is the time of the dead that they should be judged, the time to reward the prophets – once again a direct echo of Daniel 12. When would it be? At the fall of that city where the Lord was slain.

This raises another hermeneutical question. Each of these Old Testament prophecies posited martyr vindication in Israel's last days, at the end of the millennium and the destruction of Satan at the judgment of Old Covenant Israel. Revelation incorporates these Old Testament prophecies of the vindication of martyrs to promise imminent vindication at the judgment of *Babylon.* Revelation likewise incorporates Jesus' promise of imminent vindication of the martyrs, the Old Testament prophets and Jesus' apostles and prophets.

Remember Blaising's quote that Revelation 20 is about the fulfillment of Jesus' promises? Well, if Revelation 20, the end of the millennium judgment, is about the fulfillment of Jesus' promise of the vindication of the martyrs, *then the end-of-the-millennium resurrection had to be in Jesus' generation.* That is inescapably true. All of these things would come upon Jesus' generation. Jesus undeniably posited vindication of the martyrs, all the blood shed on the earth, all the way back to creation, in AD70.

So a great hermeneutical question is raised: What is the justification for rejecting the Old Testament prophecies, Jesus' emphatic promise, Paul's perfectly corresponding theology and then applying Revelation to a different persecuting power, a different set of martyrs, a different judgment, at the end of a different age, in fulfillment of a different set of promises, i.e., promises made to the church divorced from Israel? I suggest that there is no justification.

Inserted note. What is interesting about the situation at Criswell is that prior to the beginning of the lectures, in a back room, the president of Criswell encouraged each of the speakers to address what they considered to be error on the part of the other speakers. And yet, not one of them dealt with the undeniable fact, demonstrated in my presentation, that the consummative, *not typological*, but the consummative avenging of the martyrs is inextricably tied to Israel and *her* blood guilt in *her* last days, not the church divorced from Israel.

Not one of them even mentioned my emphasis on Jesus' emphatic statement about when all of the blood of all of the righteous would be vindicated.

Not one of them addressed Paul's promise that the Thessalonian Christians who were being persecuted by the Jews at that time would be given a relief "when the Lord Jesus is revealed."

Not one of them addressed the relationship between Thessalonians and Jesus' promise of vindication in that generation, thus delimiting the end of the millennium to that time.

What made this a bit more interesting and intriguing is the fact that I was the very first speaker on the schedule. Thus, all of the other speakers knew full well what I said. So, in spite of the fact that the speakers were encouraged to interact with the content of the other speakers and address what they perceived to be error and in spite of the fact that my presentation was the very first, not one of them addressed anything I said.

As I demonstrated in my presentation, any interpretation of Revelation 20 that excludes Old Covenant Israel, *her* covenant promises and *her* blood guilt, thus *her* judgment, at the end of *her* covenant age ignores Jesus' and Paul's emphatic teaching on martyr vindication is *prima facie* false. (End of insert).

Continuation of Criswell presentation. We have demonstrated therefore that the vindication of the martyrs is inextricably tied to the end of the millennium and to Israel, not the end of the church age.

Once again, Jesus emphatically posited vindication of all the martyrs, all the way back to creation, not just a small, isolated group, but all the martyrs all the way back to creation for his generation at the judgment of Jerusalem in AD70.

This agrees perfectly with all of the Old Testament prophecies, with what we have seen in Thessalonians and in Revelation. This definitively establishes my view. Does it raise all sorts of other questions? Indeed! But all of the evidence points to the fact that the end-of-the-millennium resurrection was, "when the power of the holy people was completely shattered." And no other time, no other event, better matches the Biblical datum than the end of the Old Covenant age of Israel that arrived with the destruction of Jerusalem in AD70. This is when all of the blood shed on the earth all the way back to creation was vindicated, i.e., at the end of the millennium. (End of my Criswell presentation).

Final thought on my Criswell presentation. Since the presentation of this material, in spite of the fact that I have personally distributed a great number of audio CDs of that lesson and even though the lecture was printed in the official journal of Criswell College, there has not been, to my knowledge, a single attempt to answer what I presented.

Point #12

JOHN 5:24-29 - THE HOUR IS COMING AND NOW IS...

THE HOUR IS COMING - TWO "HOURS"; TWO RESURRECTIONS?

We have noted above how Beale and others agree that in John 5:24f the prophecy of Daniel 12 began to be fulfilled. We have likewise observed that Gentry, DeMar and others now agree that Daniel 12 was fulfilled in a corporate resurrection of Israel in AD 70. However, those same commentators approach John 5:28-29 and divorce it from verses 24-25 and from Daniel 12.

The supposed justification for such a distinction is that in verses 24-25, Jesus spoke of, "the hour is coming *and now is*," but in verses 28-29, he spoke only of "the hour is *coming*." This means, we are assured, that Jesus had to be speaking of two different time periods and two different kinds of resurrections. This argument is untenable, especially in light of Jesus' prior use of that exact same language.

Read what Jesus said in John 4:21-23:

> "Jesus said to her, "Woman, believe Me, the hour is coming when you will neither on this mountain, nor in Jerusalem, worship the Father. 22 You worship what you do not know; we know what we worship, for salvation is of the Jews. 23 But the hour is coming now is, when the true worshipers will worship the Father in spirit and truth; for the Father is seeking such to worship Him."

Let's be very clear here. I know of no commentator that suggests Jesus was speaking of two totally different times, two different kinds of worship. This means that Jesus' referent to the hour that is coming and the hour that now is, *were the exact same hour and the same event.*[260] But if that language of the hour that *is* and the hour that is *coming* did not suggest two totally different times in chapter 4, why does it mean that in chapter 5?

What Jesus was saying is that the time of the resurrection had arrived.

There is something else here that is most often overlooked or ignored.

Take note that this argument turns God's historical *modus operandi* on its head. Here is what I mean.

God has always operated from the "physical" to the spiritual! For instance, Israel and everything about her was typological. Her physical land, her physical city, her physical temple, her physical sacrifices, her physical priesthood, her physical circumcision, etc., all pointed to *spiritual realities*– not physical!

This is confirmed over and over in the NT. For instance, Peter cites and echoes the promise of Hosea of the last days restoration of Israel to the land, with her temple, priesthood and ephod. And yet, Peter unequivocally interpreted that prophecy spiritually (1 Peter 2:4f).

Likewise, Paul was emphatic that these things foreshadowed spiritual realities (Colossians 2; Hebrews 10:1f).

So, in God's dealings with Israel, He had invariably gone from the physical realities to the spiritual realities that those things foreshadowed. I am unaware of a single example in which YHVH went from the physical shadow to the physical! Nor am I aware of a single instance in which the Lord took a spiritual reality and pointed toward a physical reality.

---

[260] I suggest that this terminology of the hour is coming and the hour that is, was nothing but a Hebraism, a common form of expression.

But per the futurist view of John 5, we find the spiritual resurrection that in fact (supposedly) foreshadows and anticipates the physical resurrection. This is the view of Gentry, Frost, McDurmon, etc., all who say that the events of AD 70– spiritual events - foreshadowed the physical land promises to be received at the end of the Christian age! To say that this turns God's method of operation on its head is an understatement. What is interesting is, I have yet to read a single article, or argument, that in any way sought to demonstrate *exegetically* that this argument is valid. All I have seen is presuppositional argumentation with no actual exegesis. And the reason is simple. There is no support for this "first the spiritual then the physical" argument. It is specious and false.

One of the key arguments offered by our Dominionist and futurist friends is that the hour of John 5:28f is the last day of John 6.39-40. Of course, it is the same time period. However, does this connection indicate (or demand, or even suggest) a literal, physical resurrection of human corpses? No not one thing in these texts suggests this.

But the argument is made that "the last day" must be the last day of time or of human history. But we ask, how so? See our earlier discussion of this, but let me briefly reiterate those thoughts.

Did not Daniel 12 predict the resurrection of the just and unjust at the "end of days"? Of course. So, what is the difference between "the end of days" and "the last day"? There is none.

Remember, Dominionists admit that the Old Covenant age had a definitive "moment" when "this age" gave way to "the age to come" and, "This, of course, is exactly why Jesus tied 'the end of the age' to His prophecy of the destruction of the Temple." (McDurmon, 2011, 47).

So, Dominionists agree – the last days of Israel had a last day and that last day was the end of "this age." And, we note, they even agree that Daniel 12 – the prophecy of the resurrection – occurred at that last day! To say that this is troublesome for their view is a huge understatement.

Did the last days have a last day? Of course. Did that last day not have a "last hour"? If not, why not– and, where is the proof?

In John's writings there is a constant thread concerning the consummative time, the last day, the last hour John was emphatic – that last hour had arrived. In fact, notice the NT progression of time and references to "the end."

✔ We find references, somewhat generic, to the "last time" (1 Peter 1:20) but even in this generic statement, Peter said the last times were present.

✔ Then we have references to "the last days." This is significant, because in the Tanakh, it was to be in the last days that the eschatological drama would take place and be consummated (Isaiah 2-4; Hosea 3:4f; Joel 2:28f, etc.). Once again, the NT writers are emphatic that they were living in the anticipated last days (cf. Matthew 13:17; Hebrews 1:1; Acts 2:15ff; 3:21-23; 1 Peter 1:10-12).

✔ Then, we find reference, particularly in John's gospel, to "the last day" (John 6:39f; 44, etc.). According to futurists, particularly the Dominionists, this reference must refer to the last day of human history, the end of the Christian age. This is truly an arbitrary claim and the reason that they do this is because of the presuppositional concept about the resurrection. It is claimed that the resurrection must be the raising of corpses out of the ground. As we have seen, however, this is totally unjustified.

✔ Then, we find referent to the last hour. Of course, any way you wish to look at it, the last hour is, just as the "last day" tied directly to resurrection (John 5:24-29). We need only to point out that in Dominionist and Amillennial circles it is common for the commentators to acknowledge 1 John 2:18 had a first century fulfillment.

Let me remind the reader of DeMar's comments:

> "In AD 70 the 'last days' ended with the dissolution of the temple and sacrificial system. A similar

pronouncement is made in 1 Peter 1: 20... "Gordon Clark writes of the meaning Peter gives to the 'last days'; 'The last days,' which so many people think refers to what is still future at the end of this age, clearly means the time of Peter himself. 1 John 2:18 says it is, in his day, 'the last hour.' Acts 2:17 quotes Joel as predicting the last days as the life time of Peter." (*Madness*, 1994, 28).

Likewise, Gentry, commenting on the significance of the appearing of John, as Elijah, alludes to 1 John 2:

"The evidence is really quite clear that Malachi's Elijianic prophecy was fulfilled during the ministry of Christ. This fulfillment is counter-indicative to both Dispensationalism's hermeneutic and its eschatology, as well as being supportive of the preteristic hermeneutic and postmillennial eschatology."[261]

Gentry then says: "The appearance of these anti-Christs was not a harbinger of a future coming AntiChrist, for their presence was the signal that 'the last hour' had already 'come' (*gegonasin*). The 'even now' emphasizes the presence of that which they feared ('as you heard')" (*Dominion,* 1992,367).

We must take note of the huge problem that Dominionists present for themselves. As we noted above, they believe that, "the hour is coming" of John 5:28f was "the last day" of John 6:39f. Then, they

---

[261] Gentry, like most Dominionists, fails to see the incredible implications in admitting that John was the fulfillment of Malachi 4:5f - the prophecy of Elijah. John, as Elijah, was the herald of the Great Day of the Lord – the day of the *resurrection*. Thus, John's declaration of the imminence of the judgment was nothing less than a positive affirmation that the time of the resurrection was near. See my DVD series on Acts 1 for a discussion of the eschatological role of John as Elijah.

agree that 1 John 2:18 and John's positive asservation that "the last hour" had arrived was referent to the last days, the last hour, of the Old Covenant age of Israel. What then is the distinction between "the hour" that was coming of John 5 that belongs to "the last day' of John 6? Exactly where does John delineate between the coming hour of John 5:28f, the last day, and "the last hour" that was upon them? All we get from the Dominionists are empty claims for that distinction. But John gives no support for such a difference.

Amillennialist Kim Riddlebarger agrees that John believed the presence of the anti-Christs proved that the "end" was near. However, he espouses the idea that the events of the time in which John was living pointed to a "Double Fulfillment" at the end of human history. He says of those then present events:

> "John's purpose in writing is, in part, to inform his readers about the fact that many 'antichrist's' (note the plural) have already come (1 John 2:18). He's also letting his readers know just who these people are and what they are teaching. 'Many deceivers, have gone out into the world.' Any such person is the deceiver and the antichrist' (2 John 7). Therefore, the presence of these individuals in the first century church is taken by the apostle to be an important indication that it is already the 'last hour' (1 John 2:18). This is another way of speaking of 'the last day' (John 6:40; see also John 5:25) or of the 'last times.'"[262]

Riddlebarger is clearly correct to see that the "last hour" is tied directly to the "last day." However, his claim that the events of the first century foreshadowed the "real" end and that those first century anti-Christs typified the true anti-Christs that are yet to come has no merit.

---

[262] Kim Riddlebarger, *The Man of Sin*, (Grand Rapids, Baker, 2006)738. The Double Fulfillment hermeneutic is critical to Riddlebarger's eschatology.

As we have seen, Dominionists as a general rule reject Riddlebarger's claims about the first century anti-Christs being typological of future anti-Christs. But then, in a strange, glaring bit of self-contradiction the Dominionists claim that (at least some) of the first century end of the age events were typological of the true end that is yet future. But to say that this presents problems for their view is, to say the very least, an understatement. Take a look at some of those problems.

The Dominionists arbitrarily pick and choose what is or is not typological. They condemn the Amillennialists and Dispensationalists for suggesting that John the Baptizer was a foreshadowing of the real, still future Elijah. Yet, they fail to realize that John / Elijah was the precursor and herald of the *resurrection*. Thus, if John was Elijah, as they admit, and if John / Elijah did not foreshadow another Elijah, then *this demands a first century fulfillment of resurrection*.

Postmillennialists castigate the idea of the first century anti-Christs anticipating the true last days antichrist, claiming there is no merit to such an idea. Yet, they ignore the fact that in the Jewish and Biblical eschatological story-line, the anti-Christ was to appear immediately before the parousia of Christ (2 Thessalonians 2). Thus, if the antichrist / man of sin appeared in the first century, the parousia of Christ must have been in the first century.[263]

Dominionists are insistent that the Abomination of Desolation and the Great Tribulation were strictly first century events, having nothing to do with our future. But then, they turn around and tell us that the coming of Christ, the judgment and the AD 70 resurrection in fulfillment of Daniel 12, all were, in fact, typological of the future. What is their evidence for this? There is no evidence; it is mere assertion.

---

[263] To avoid this glaring problem, Dominionist commentators such as Gentry, DeMar, Leithart, et. al. now admit that the parousia against the man of sin in 2 Thessalonians 2 occurred in AD 70!

Dominionists fail to see, or to acknowledge, the direct, inseparable connection between the Great Tribulation and the resurrection. So, if they admit that the Great Tribulation was strictly a first century event – and they do – then to suggest that the resurrection has not occurred is specious and un-Biblical. It is totally unjustified to posit the Great Tribulation in the first century and then rip the resurrection away from its connection to the resurrection. The bond between these two doctrines cannot be broken as we have demonstrated.

The harmony and consistency of the terminology in the New Testament in regard to the last times, the last days, the last day and the last hour all points to one consummation. The futurists' attempts to avoid this are arbitrary and capricious hermeneutical gymnastics that should cause all Bible students to take pause. The admission that Daniel 12 was fulfilled in AD 70 therefore falsifies all attempts to draw a distinction between these terms and those motifs.

The direct temporal connection between the end time events is categoric demonstration that there were not two resurrections in John 5, and even if there were, the last hour, the consummative time for the resurrection of John 5:28-29, had arrived when John wrote in 1 John 2, because the last hour, the consummation of the last day, was upon them.

This is evident in the closing words of Paul to the Roman churches: "And the God of peace will crush Satan under your feet shortly. The grace of our Lord Jesus Christ be with you. Amen" (Romans 16:20).

This incredibly powerful statement is nothing less than a statement that the solution to the Adamic death curse was at hand. This is an undeniable affirmation that the resurrection of 1 Corinthians 15 was near. It is a declaration that the end of the Millennium was at hand!

Gentry agrees, while ignoring the implications: "Romans 16:20 hearkens back to the Adamic Covenant" (*Dominion*, 1992, 113). Likewise, DeMar, commented on the work of Christ, accomplished through the cross and carried through to the passing of the Old

Covenant world of Israel in AD 70. He says that Christ has done the following:

"Satan has already been:

Defeated, disarmed spoiled by God (Col. 2:15; Rev. 12:7-17; Mark 3:27).

Fallen (Luke 10:18).

Thrown down: - (Revelation 12:9).

Crushed (Romans 16:20).

Lost all authority (Colossians 1:13).

Judged (John 16:11).

His works destroyed (1 John 3:8).

He has nothing (John 14:30).

He flees when resisted (James 4:7).

Is bound Mark 3:27; Luke 11:20; Revelation 20:2."[264]

I would ask the reader: How can anyone espouse the fulfillment of all of these eschatological actions of Christ and still affirm a yet future eschatology of any kind? The fulfillment of all of these actions by our Lord leaves nothing – *nothing* – undone and to be accomplished!

As Dunn well stated,

> "The hope of Satan being 'crushed under foot' is part of a larger eschatological hope for the final binding or defeat of the angelic power hostile to

---

[264] Gary DeMar, *End Times Fiction*, (Nashville, Nelson, 2001)212.

> God...That there is an influence from Genesis 3:15 is probable, but not necessarily direct and quite likely through the influence of Genesis 3:15 the entire strand of Jewish hope (Ps. 91:13). It is hard to diminish the strong eschatological note here and the note of imminence implied in the *en taxei*."[265]

It should be more than obvious - it is undeniable - that it is improper to posit two resurrections in John 5. The so-called distinction between the "hour that is coming" and the hour that "now is" is a false dichotomy.

It should likewise be emphasized that the Dominionist emphasis on the first century fulfillment of the Abomination of Desolation, the Great Tribulation, along with the presence of John as Elijah, falsifies any idea of a future resurrection. In scripture, those eschatological tenets are inseparably bound up with the "final resurrection." So, if those things were fulfilled, then "the hour is coming" was likewise fulfilled.

When the Postmillennialists point out Christ's imminent victory over Satan at the end of the Old Covenant age in AD 70, they are dealing a fatal blow to their own claims about another final victory. The NT writers knew nothing of a protracted delayed final victory. They believed in and proclaimed that Satan was about to crushed shortly - not two millennia and counting beyond their time. By admitting to the first century reality of Christ's victory and the imminent consummation, the Dominionists have entrapped themselves in their own claims.

---

[265] James D. G. Dunn, *Word Biblical Commentary, Romans 9-16, Vol. 38b*, (Dallas, Word Publishers, 1988)905.

Point #13

THE SALVATION OF THE REMNANT AND THE FINAL SALVATION

An issue that is critical to any discussion of the "final resurrection" has to do with the doctrine of the salvation of the remnant of Israel. This may strike many as strange, since both Amillennialists and Postmillennialists give so little time to discussing either Israel or the remnant. This oversight is truly sad since, as Wagner, citing several other scholars, including E. P. Sanders, notes: "The return of the remnant became an image and model of Jewish hope and thereby the concept of a remnant entered into a central position in Jewish eschatological hope."[266]

From Jesus' referent to the "little flock," to Paul's extensive discussion in Romans 9f, to Peter's epistle to the "diaspora," to John's references to the 144,000 out of the twelve tribes, the remnant theology is present throughout - and critical to any proper understanding of eschatology.

Thus, as just suggested, the remnant is a key eschatological doctrine. To ignore it, to deny it, to distort it, is to misconstrue the entire eschatological narrative.

Biblically, in both OT and New, God never promised to save the majority, or "all" – in the truly comprehensive sense. Just a few texts will illustrate this.

Isaiah 1:9 - "Unless the Lord of hosts had left to us a very small remnant, we would have become like Sodom, we would have been made like Gomorrah."

---

[266] J. Ross Wagner, *Heralds of the Good News*, (Boston, Brill Academic Press, 2003)108.

Set within the context of the impending Assyrian invasion and captivity, this text, along with several others in Isaiah, served as the source for the NT writers to speak of the salvation of the remnant in the first century. The significance of this should not be missed. There was both a physical and a spiritual side to the prophecies – even those OT prophecies.

The righteous – i.e. those in faithful covenant relationship to God – were the "spiritual remnant," and would be spared / delivered from the full force of the impending disaster. This does not mean they would not suffer to a certain degree. However, because of their faithfulness they would nonetheless be delivered from the full brunt of the horrors that were coming.

Isaiah 10:20-23 -

> "And it shall come to pass in that day That the remnant of Israel such as have escaped of the house of Jacob, Will never again depend on him who defeated them, But will depend on the Lord, the Holy One of Israel, in truth. The remnant will return, the remnant of Jacob, To the Mighty God. For though your people, O Israel, be as the sand of the sea, A remnant of them will return; The destruction decreed shall overflow with righteousness. For the Lord God of hosts Will make a determined end In the midst of all the land."

Needless to say, this text serves as the fountain for much of Paul's doctrine of the salvation of the remnant. He cites the text, verbatim, in Romans 9:27, just as he cited Isaiah 1:9 in Romans 9:29.

One thing that should not be missed yet, commonly is, is that the promise of the salvation of the remnant contains two interconnected motifs.

The first is the faithfulness of God to Abraham to bless the nations through his seed. Thus, Isaiah 1 echoes the Abrahamic promise and assures the reader that *the salvation of the remnant is YHVH's faithfulness to that promise.* And in Paul, the promise to Abraham is fulfilled in those who joined with Abraham in exhibiting the same faith as Abraham (Galatians 3:6f).

Second, lying just under the surface, but clearly present, is that the promise of the salvation of the remnant is in fact, a threat of impending judgment on the nation. That was the case in Isaiah and his contemporaries (cf. Hosea and Amos), Jeremiah and virtually every OT prophecy concerning the remnant. Wagner catches this well: "These two Isaianic prophecies of remnant (Isaiah 10:22-23) and seed (Isaiah 1:9) function *together* in Romans 9:27-29 not only to evoke the severe judgment of God on wayward Israel, but also to foreshadow God's ultimate restoration of his people." (Wagner, 2003, 116).

So, Paul's utilization of the Old Covenant promises of the salvation of the remnant was a two-edged sword. It manifested the marvelous grace of God, in spite of Israel's infidelity (Cf. Romans 10:18f). Nonetheless, the promise of the salvation of the remnant suggested that the "severity of God" (Romans 11:22) could not be totally mitigated by that grace if Israel continued in her recalcitrant ways. Justice would be served, but grace would be given – to the remnant.

Isaiah 11:10-12:

> "They shall not hurt nor destroy in all My holy mountain, For the earth shall be full of the knowledge of the Lord As the waters cover the sea. "And in that day there shall be a Root of Jesse, Who shall stand as a banner to the people; For the Gentiles shall seek Him His resting place shall be glorious." It shall come to pass in that day That the Lord shall set His hand again the second time To recover the remnant of His people who are left, From Assyria and Egypt, From Pathros and Cush, From Elam and Shinar, From Hamath and the islands of the sea. He will set up a banner for the nations will assemble the outcasts of Israel gather together the dispersed of Judah From the four

corners of the earth. Also the envy of Ephraim shall depart the adversaries of Judah shall be cut off; Ephraim shall not envy Judah and Judah shall not harass Ephraim."

This great prophecy contains a wealth of elements, motifs and promises that are picked up in the NT. Notice just a few of the doctrines contained in this prophecy:

☛The world mission – This promise that the word of the Lord would be preached into all the world is picked up by Jesus in Matthew 24:14. And by Paul, who said repeatedly that the Great Commission had been fulfilled.

☛The prophecy of the raising of the Ensign, for the re-gathering of Israel and the calling of the Gentiles. In Romans 15:8f, Paul cites this text for (partial) justification of his Gentile mission.

☛The salvation of the remnant gathered from the four winds. It is to be noted that on Pentecost, Luke all but quotes from this prophecy in his enumeration of the nations from which the attendees that day came.

☛The Second Exodus motif. This theme permeates the entirety of the New Testament.

So, in just three key OT Messianic prophecies (all of which the NT writers affirm were being fulfilled in the first century) of the last days and the eschatological consummation, it is the remnant that is the focus of those prophecies. There is no hint of a "total" salvation of every person of the lineage of Abraham, or even the salvation of every member of the twelve tribes. A brief march through Paul's discourse in Romans 9-11 demonstrates that Paul, unless he "jumped ship" from his entire discussion up to chapter 11:25-27, had one theme in mind, the salvation of the remnant.

9:1-3 - Not all Israel is actually Israel– "but in Isaac (i.e. in the promise), shall your seed be called." At the very outset of his discussion of his hope and love of Israel, Paul tells us that "all Israel" is not truly Israel.

9:27-33 - Paul appeals to Isaiah's prophecies of the last days salvation of the remnant. He then proceeds to speak of how Israel was not achieving her desired goal, because she was not seeking it by faith - unlike the Gentiles who were seeking the Lord in faith.

10:1f - Paul expresses his profound love for Israel. Nonetheless, he has to acknowledge that the corporate body of Israel was still in unbelief. Not only that, their unbelief was foretold by the prophets. Since Moses and the prophets spoke of Israel's last days unbelief and rejection of the Word of the Lord, they were without excuse. For Paul, Israel "knew" through those OT prophecies, that they were to obey the Lord in the last days and now that the last days had arrived, they were fulfilling those prophecies. Once again, we must note that Paul was speaking of the main body of Israel, the majority. Only a remnant was accepting the Word of the gospel.

This is confirmed also in the fact that in Romans 10:20-21, Paul quotes from Isaiah 65:1-2 which spoke of Israel's unbelief leading to the calling of the Gentiles, the salvation of the remnant (Isaiah 65:8) and judgment on the nation. So, the promise of the salvation of the remnant was also a tacit threat of judgment on the corporate nation (Isaiah 65:13f), which points us to Romans 11:22 – "the severity of God."

I think Wagner is correct therefore, to point out: "Paul's wish to be cut off from Christ for the sake of his people, which evokes images of Moses' intercession for idolatrous Israel, makes absolutely no sense unless Paul believes that a substantial part of Israel (cf. 9:24) currently stands under God's wrath." (2003,106).

11:1-15 - Paul says in no uncertain terms that the then present state of Israel's unbelief did not mean that God's promises had failed. His proof of that was the remnant, of which he was a part. The apostle adduces one of the great stories from Israel's past to prove his point, the case of Elijah and the battle of the gods. His point is that God's promises to Israel were being fulfilled in the remnant - just as foretold. Thus, he could confidently say: "Israel has not obtained what it seeks, but, the elect have obtained it the rest were blinded" (11:7).

Verse 7 is actually quite a stunning statement. What was it that Israel sought for? It was the kingdom. It was to be, "raised from the dead" (Ezekiel 37; Acts 26:6f). It was the New Creation (Isaiah 65). It was "eternal life" (John 5). One could make a long list of the constituent elements that comprised Israel's hope. But allow me to briefly digress here, to show how stunning Paul's statement in verse 7 is.

The Dispensational world tells us, as I have documented in other works, that neither the gospel of grace or the church was foretold in the Old Covenant promises. Israel's hope is to be kept totally distinct from the church and vice versa. They likewise tell us that Jesus came to establish the kingdom, but due to Jewish unbelief, the kingdom - the hope of Israel - had to be postponed. How then do we correlate that to Paul's statements that:

1. He preached nothing but the hope of Israel found in the Tanakh (Acts 24:14f; 26:21f; 28:16f)?,

2. In preaching nothing but the hope of Israel found in the prophets (Romans 16:25-26), Paul preached the mystery of God, Jew and Gentile equality in the one body of Christ. And,

3. So, Paul said he preached nothing but the hope of Israel found in Torah *and he interpreted that hope in the light of the work of Christ*. Thus, his statement that the remnant had and was obtaining the realization of the hope of Israel means that the Old Covenant did predict what was happening in the body of Christ, it means that there was no postponement of God's plans!

How could Paul say that the remnant was receiving the fulfillment of the hope of Israel if the hope of Israel was the inheritance of the land and the establishment of a physical kingdom with earthly Jerusalem as the political capital? This is especially pertinent in light of the fact that Paul well knew that earthly Jerusalem was about to be destroyed. He knew and predicted himself, that, "the kingdom of God is not in meats and drinks" (Romans 14:17) and that it was not geo-centric or physical (2 Corinthians 4:16-18, see Hebrews 12:21-28).

Gary Demar in 2015, debated Dr. Michael Brown. DeMar raised a similar question to what I am posing (similar but still somewhat different. DeMar did not appeal to Romans 11:7). DeMar noted that no NT writer appealed to a yet future return of Israel to the land. Dr. Brown sought to escape this argument by stating that Israel had not yet been dispersed. Thus, promises of a return were not appropriate. This is rather disingenuous to say the least and ignores three facts.

First, when the Babylonians were about to destroy Jerusalem and Judah, removing the Jews from the land, YHVH gave promises of their return to the land. Not only that, in Jeremiah 32, He instructed Jeremiah to bury the title to a piece of land as a sign that the people would return. There is no such event in the NT. In fact, the saints in Jerusalem and Judea sold their property in anticipation of the coming Roman invasion! Thus, Dr. Brown's objection fails.

Second, Dr. Brown believes that the Old Covenant foretold the last days re-gathering of Israel to the land! So, we have Israel ostensibly being promised, *centuries before the AD 70 dispersion* that they re-gathered in the last days! If those OT promises were appropriate to be given hundreds of years prior to the dispersion, then Dr. Brown's answer is misguided and DeMar's point is clearly pertinent. Unfortunately, DeMar did not point out this inconsistency in Brown's argument.

Third, Dr. Brown's objection divorces the then current reception of the hope of Israel from his proposed future hope of Israel. He is saying that Israel had two end times hopes, one to be fulfilled imminently in Paul's day, the other to be delayed for what is now two millennia. This is untenable and finds no support in the NT.

> Dispensationalists and Dominionists alike tell us that the hope of Israel was / is an earthly, physical kingdom.
>
> Paul said, 2000 years ago, that the righteous remnant of Israel was receiving the hope of Israel.
>
> It is patently undeniable, however, that the righteous remnant, inclusive of Paul, was not receiving an earthly, physical kingdom of any kind whatsoever!

So, when the Dispensationalists tell us that Israel's hope was the geo-centric, earthly and physical kingdom, this flies in the face of Paul's affirmation that the remnant was, when he wrote, receiving the hope of Israel! Likewise, when the Dominionists tell us that the hope of Israel - indeed - the hope of Christians, is an earthly, physical kingdom,[267] this hardly comports with Paul's comments. Why wasn't Paul ruling on a physical throne if such was part of the hope of Israel? Why wasn't he being given some prime real estate in Jerusalem or Palestine, or Rome, if "dirt" was an inherent element of the hope of Israel?

Consider also: how could the remnant be receiving the fulfillment of the hope of Israel if the hope of Israel had been deferred and postponed - the kingdom offer withdrawn? Paul set forth himself - of the tribe of Benjamin - and a member of the body of Christ, as proof positive that God had not cast off Israel (Romans 11:1-3). He was insistent that what he and the remnant was receiving was what Israel longed for. This is *prima facie* falsification of the

---

[267] This concept of a future physical kingdom was stated by Steve Gregg (Amillennialist), as well as Joel McDurmon and Harold Eberle, both Dominionists, in my formal debates with these men. All said the final fulfillment of prophecy will be a "physical kingdom on earth."

Dispensational view of the postponed kingdom. If Paul, as part of the remnant of Israel was receiving what Israel longed for and what had been promised to her, it is patently absurd to argue that those promises were not valid when Paul wrote.

Some point to Paul's mentioning of the blinding of Israel when he wrote and how he once again speaks of that blindness in chapter 11:25.[268] But then, it appears that he says that blindness would be taken away – from the corporate "all Israel" resulting in the salvation of the whole. Is this possible?

Theoretically, that is possible. However, it would be one of the strangest - not to say incongruous - things for Paul to say such a thing. Are we to believe that Paul emphasizes the salvation of the remnant when he knows that the "whole body" will ultimately be saved?

Why would Paul say that he was willing to be cut off from the Lord if it would ensure the salvation of Israel, if he knew Israel was going to be saved after all? Why would he even suggest his own cutting off in order to save all Israel, if he was going to say, just a short time later, that they were all going to be saved after all?

Why would Paul say that his mission to the Gentiles was to provoke Israel to jealousy "so that I might save *some*"? Paul realized that no

---

[268] The blindness motif referred to by Paul in Romans 11 is a *crux interpretum*, but is commonly overlooked. I cannot develop it here, but briefly, from Deuteronomy to Isaiah, to Jesus to Paul, God spoke of Israel's blindness. Almost invariably, when He did, it meant *judgment was imminent*! See Isaiah 6:9f Jesus' citation of Isaiah in Matthew 12 and 13, as well as Paul's citation in Acts 28. To make the application to Romans 11, Paul alludes to Israel's blindness, citing Deuteronomy 29, Psalms 69. And when in Rome, he quotes from Isaiah 6. In each of these prophetic texts, Israel's blindness would result in imminent judgment on the nation *and the salvation of the remnant*! Should this not help guide us in our understanding of "all Israel" in Romans 11?

matter how successful his ministry to the Gentiles was, the entire body of Israel would not be moved to "obedient jealousy" and thus be saved. Only "some" would be thus moved.

Why did Paul speak of the "severity of God" in reference to the cutting off of Israel, if in fact the "goodness of God" was going to finally prevail over that justice?

Why did Paul say - citing the OT examples and prophecies - that said: "A remnant shall be saved" (Romans 9:27f) if he knew that ultimately, "all" would be saved? This is critical. When Paul foretold the salvation of "all Israel" the OT prophecies that he cited actually foretold the salvation of the remnant - not "all Israel" in a comprehensive sense.

The solution, at least in part, it seems to me, to this "blindness" issue is found in 2 Corinthians 3 - and see my comments just above. The apostle spoke of the blindness of Israel in the reading of Torah without faith. However, he said that *some* would accept the testimony of Torah - the testimony that Jesus is Messiah - and when that realization came, the "veil" of unbelief was removed, resulting in salvation. Thus, while there was, when Romans and 2 Corinthians was written, an on-going blindness and hardness on the part of Israel, nonetheless, there was hope because "some" were accepting the testimony of the New Covenant and turning to Christ. We see here the consummation of the salvation of the remnant when the Covenantal transformation was completed.

There is no justification for the idea that in Romans 9-11:24 Paul discussed the remnant, but suddenly, without any evidence in support, he heralds the salvation of all Israel at some unknown future event. Thus, I think Wagner is correct in saying: "It is clear that although there is a clear progression of ideas in Paul's argument, there is no strong disjunction of thought between Romans 9 and Romans 11. Paul does not, as is often alleged, suddenly reject his remnant theory in Romans 11 (despite all the arguments he has advanced up to this point) in order to allow for the salvation of all Israel." (2003, 116, n. 238).²⁶⁹

Why is all of this pertinent to our discussion of Daniel 12 and the question of the "final resurrection?" There are several reasons.

Romans 11:25-27 predicted the salvation of Israel - the consummation of the salvation of the remnant - at the coming of the Lord. And make no mistake, the resurrection was the hope of Israel (Isaiah 25:8-9 / Acts 26:6f). If the hope of Israel was the resurrection - the end of the Millennium resurrection - then to posit the fulfillment of Romans 11 in the first century is to essentially settle the issue of the remnant and the question of whether Daniel 12 foretold the final resurrection. That is, unless one wants to suggest that the resurrection / salvation of Daniel 12 is totally unrelated to the climax and consummation of Israel's eschatological hope.

The parousia of Romans 11:25f would be in fulfilment of key OT prophecies of the eschaton – including prophecies of the resurrection out of the dust (Isaiah 26:10) which is very clearly the source of Daniel's prediction of the resurrection, "out of the dust." So, if, as is virtually unanimously agreed, Isaiah 26 is predictive of the end of the Millennium resurrection, then since Daniel is based on Isaiah, this demonstrates that Daniel 12 predicted the end of the Millennium, "final" resurrection.

Those OT prophecies of the resurrection serve as the source of Paul's resurrection doctrine in 1 Corinthians 15 – i.e. his doctrine of the "final" end of the Millennium resurrection.

So, the salvation of the remnant (Israel) is tied to the parousia and the resurrection, (the resurrection of 1 Corinthians 15). Thus, if

---

²⁶⁹ Interestingly, however, in spite of this comment, Wagner posits a yet future "massive" conversion of Israel, (*Heralds of the Good News,* (Boston, Leiden, 2003)279, n. 194.

(since) it can be shown that the finalization of the salvation of the remnant was imminent in the first century and was to be completed no later than the judgment of Jerusalem in AD 70, then this serves as definitive proof that the resurrection of Daniel 12 was a prophecy of the "final" resurrection.

Let me say this before proceeding. One could set aside the doctrine of the remnant for a moment and insist that Romans 11:25-27 was predictive, in fact, of the salvation of "all Israel." But *that admission would not negate the thesis of this work.* As we have shown, no matter what your definition of "Israel" and "all Israel" in Romans 11:25-27, that salvation would occur at the coming of the Lord, in fulfillment of Isaiah 27 / 59 / Daniel 9 & 12. And it is *prima facie* true that those prophecies foretold the salvation of Israel (and more correctly, the remnant of Israel) when the Lord would judge her for shedding innocent blood. According to Jesus in Matthew 23, that judgment / salvation came in AD 70. It is unfortunate that the commentators either overlook or ignore this connection.

The New Testament continues with the focus on the remnant – not on the whole. As Jesus foretold the coming catastrophe to fall on Jerusalem, he nonetheless gave instructions for the deliverance of the "elect" i.e. the remnant: "When you see the Abomination of Desolation, spoken of by Daniel the prophet, whoso reads, let him understand, then let those who are in Judea flee" (Matthew 24:15).

Just like in the days of Isaiah,[270] when only the faithful were delivered, in Jesus' day only his followers, so far as we know, were "wise" enough to heed his warnings and escape. But there was far more to this salvation of the remnant than the simple escape from physical death and the horrors of war. Jesus told his disciples that *after they would escape the physical horrors*, they were to look at the events of Jerusalem's demise and, "lift up your heads, for your

---

[270] We can also point to Jesus' comments regarding the "days of Noah" and how it relates to the salvation of a remnant (Matthew 24:37f).

redemption draws nigh" (Luke 21:28). Here is redemption / deliverance / salvation, *after escaping the siege and physical horrors of the war.*

I will skip over a good bit of territory now to focus on the Apocalypse and the doctrine of the remnant.

In Revelation 7 and 14, John saw the 144,000 that were out of the twelve tribes of Israel. In addition to that great number, which of course is highly symbolic - John saw a great host out of all nations.

For brevity, let me develop the doctrine of the 144,000 in the following manner:

✠ The 144,000 were out of the twelve tribes of Israel. The naming and enumeration of the tribes is highly suggestive, if not definitive, that it is in fact Israel in view. They are not, as some have suggested, "spiritual Israel" divorced from Israel. This is corroborated by Paul when, as he discusses the fate of Israel he asks if God had cast them off. He affirms that no such thing had happened. After all, he was of Israel, of the literal tribe of Benjamin and part of the remnant that was, when he wrote, entering into the hope of Israel (Romans 11:1-7). Just so, Revelation 7:4 specifically says that the 144,000 are, "of the twelve tribes of the children of Israel."

✠ These are therefore, Jewish Christians. They cleansed their robes in the blood of the Lamb, the Christ.

✠ The 144,000 experience the Great Tribulation (7:14).

✠ In chapter 7:15f, the Lord makes some marvelous statements about the 144K:

> "Therefore they are before the throne of God and serve Him day and night in His temple. And He who sits on the throne will dwell among them. They shall neither hunger anymore nor thirst anymore; the sun shall not strike them, nor any heat; for the Lamb who is in the midst of the throne will

shepherd them and lead them to living fountains of waters. And God will wipe away every tear from their eyes."

There are several things to be noted here, chief among them is that the "elder" speaking to John is offering a *pistache* of OT prophecies.

The promise of the coming time when there would be, "no more tears" is taken from several Old Covenant prophecies of the Messianic Kingdom. Isaiah 25, 35 and Isaiah 65, to name but a few of those prophecies, all foretold the time of no more tears.

For what it is worth, at least some of the early writers believed that the promise of "no more tears" had been fulfilled in Christ and the church. Read the following by Theodoret of Cyrus: "Let them (the Jews, DKP) show us their Jerusalem delivered from tears. For that city (Jewish Jerusalem) was handed over to many misfortunes, whereas for this city (the heavenly Jerusalem) alone enjoys life without grief and free of tears." (Commenting on Isaiah 65:19 and cited in Guinot, 3:324).[271] This citation is particularly suggestive since it echoes the story of Revelation which contrasts the Old Covenant Jerusalem (Babylon) with the New Jerusalem!

These prophecies all have some common elements with Revelation 7 and 14 indicating that John (i.e. the elder speaking to him) did not have a single Old Covenant promise in mind but a conflation of several prophecies.

The time of no tears would be the time of the salvation of Israel, the establishment of the Messianic Banquet and the resurrection (Isaiah 25:1-9). This is also when the city and the Temple would be turned over to foreigners (25:1-2).

The time of no tears in chapter 35 would be at the coming of the Lord in judgment and vengeance. Flowing from that Coming would

---

[271] Cited by Wilken in *The Land Called Holy*, (Yale University, 1992)324, n. 1 of chapter 11.

be the Highway for the righteous, the living waters, the glorification of Zion and salvation. While the word "remnant" is not used here, the limiting words that tell us the Highway would be for the righteous, while the unclean would not walk that way. This is the remnant concept.

In chapter 65, we find the destruction of the Old Covenant people, at the redemption of Zion, the New Creation, (which includes the creation of a New People) and, significant for our study, the salvation of the remnant (65:8).

While these texts clearly accord with Revelation, they are part of a "chain" of similar OT prophecies. And there is another prophecy in that chain that sounds the clearest echo in Revelation 7, that is Isaiah 49.

Isaiah 49:6-16:

> "Indeed He says, 'It is too small a thing that You should be My Servant To raise up the tribes of Jacob and to restore the preserved ones of Israel; I will also give You as a light to the Gentiles, That You should be My salvation to the ends of the earth.'" Thus says the Lord, The Redeemer of Israel, their Holy One, To Him whom man despises, To Him whom the nation abhors, To the Servant of rulers: "Kings shall see and arise, Princes also shall worship, Because of the Lord who is faithful, The Holy One of Israel; And He has chosen You." Thus says the Lord: "In an acceptable time I have heard You and in the day of salvation I have helped You; I will preserve You and give You As a covenant to the people, To restore the earth, To cause them to inherit the desolate heritages; That You may say to the prisoners, 'Go forth,' To those who are in darkness, 'Show yourselves.' "They shall feed along the roads their pastures shall be on all desolate heights. They shall neither hunger nor thirst, Neither heat nor sun shall strike them; For He

who has mercy on them will lead them, Even by the springs of water He will guide them. I will make each of My mountains a road, And My highways shall be elevated. Surely these shall come from afar; Look! Those from the north and the west these from the land of Sinim." Sing, O heavens! Be joyful, O earth! And break out in singing, O mountains! For the Lord has comforted His people and will have mercy on His afflicted. God Will Remember Zion. Lift up your eyes, look around and see; All these gather together and come to you. As I live," says the Lord, "You shall surely clothe yourselves with them all as an ornament and bind them on you as a bride does. "For your waste and desolate places the land of your destruction, Will even now be too small for the inhabitants; And those who swallowed you up will be far away. The children you will have, After you have lost the others, Will say again in your ears, 'The place is too small for me; Give me a place where I may dwell.' Then you will say in your heart, 'Who has begotten these for me, Since I have lost my children and am desolate, A captive wandering to and fro? And who has brought these up? There I was, left alone; But these, where were they?"

☞Isaiah foretold the salvation of the tribes of Jacob. This is the restoration of Israel.

☞ The work of Messiah would not be limited to the salvation of the tribes of Israel. Indeed, it would be "too small a thing" to simply restore the twelve tribes. He would also give light (Euphemism for "life") to the Gentiles. Since Isaiah 49 serves as the main source for Revelation 7/14, the innumerable multitude that would also partake of the salvation that was coming should be seen as the salvation of the Gentiles.

☞ Messiah himself would be the New Covenant (v. 8).

☞ The "earth" (*eretz*) would be restored in the Day of Messiah (v. 8). This is nothing less than the New Creation of Revelation 21-22, where the Tree of Life and the River of Living Waters would be enjoyed.

☞Messiah would deliver those in "darkness" (Euphemism for death) and the prisoners (cf. Isaiah 61).

☞ Restored Israel - and the nations - would no longer hunger or thirst (v. 10). They would be led to the rivers of living waters. Here is the water of life of Revelation 22.

☞ There would be the Highway of the Lord on top of the mountains for the Lord's people to come to Him (v. 11).[272] This Highway would be the continuation of the Voice in the Wilderness, John the Baptizer, who prepared the Way of the Lord in fulfillment of Isaiah 40.

☞Messiah's work of "restoration" would include the redemption of Zion (v. 13f). Although the children of Israel would lament her condition, the Lord promised to redeem Zion. It cannot be missed that in Hebrews the author told his suffering audience, "You have come to Mt. Zion!" (12:21f).[273] For a first century writer, addressing

---

[272] The motif of the Highway of the Lord is highly significant. In the book of Acts, there is a powerful development of this idea, as Luke tells the story of the restoration of Israel under Messiah. See my 51 lesson MP3 series, "Acts and the Restoration of Israel." In one of the lessons, I trace Luke's telling of the Highway of the Lord motif, as developed by Paul in his sermons.

[273] We cannot miss the fact that the language of Hebrews 12:21 is "festal" language, suggesting that they were gathered to Zion to celebrate the fulfillment of Israel's typological feast days. They clearly were not geographically gathered to literal Jerusalem. They were gathered to and in the

a Jewish Christian audience, to tell them they had arrived at Zion was a stunning and provocative claim.

It is not too much to say that the entire eschatological narrative is bound up in that one word, *Zion*. So, Revelation 7 speaks of the salvation of Israel, who would be led to the living waters in the day of the restoration of the "earth," - which is the time of the redemption of Zion. Likewise, Revelation 14 depicts the 144,000 standing on Mt. Zion, celebrating the Feast of Tabernacles (typological of resurrection). The significance of this cannot be missed. When Hebrews said they had arrived at Zion and when Revelation depicts them standing on Zion, the message was clear: the end time drama was being fulfilled.

☞ Notice that this is the time of the Wedding / Remarriage of Israel (v. 18f). Zion thought she was forgotten, abandoned and doomed. But Isaiah 49 and 54 gives the positive assurance that God would redeem her.[274] Revelation is likewise focused on the Wedding (Revelation 19:6; 22:17).

☞YHVH would create a New People (49:20). Israel would lose her children and be "left alone." Yet, she would stand in amazement at the children that God would cause to spring up. These verses should be read in conjunction with Isaiah 54:1f and then, in light of Paul's application of Isaiah in Galatians 4. There, the children that God was raising up were the spiritual seed of Abraham - barren Sarah's innumerable children - the children of God by faith.

☞The salvation prophesied in Isaiah 49, inclusive of all of the tenets listed above, was to occur in, "the acceptable time, the day of salvation" of Isaiah 49:8.

Heavenly Jerusalem, the City that Abraham longed for.

[274] It is significant that Paul, in Galatians 4, cites Isaiah 54 to speak of the casting out of the Old Covenant seed / Zion. Yet, he applies Isaiah 54 and the promise of the restoration of Zion as the *Bride, to the New Covenant seed of Abraham.*

With all of these elements from Isaiah 49 before us, when we come to Revelation 7 and its citation of Isaiah, several things become apparent.

First and foremost of course, is that John is clearly anticipating the fulfillment of Isaiah 49. That fulfillment would be in the New Creation of chapter 21-22, the locus of the promised living waters.

Second, John is reading and applying Isaiah typologically. The historical setting of Isaiah was the Babylonian captivity and the promise of restoration. However, just as Paul spoke of events in Israel's prior history and said: "they are types of us" (1 Corinthians 10:11[275]) John is applying those typological historical situations to the persecuted New Covenant saints.[276]

Third, John is clear that fulfillment is at hand. The imminence of Revelation cannot be ignored without doing grave injustice to

---

[275] See Richard Davidson, *Typology in Scripture*, (Berrien Springs, MI. Andrews University Seminary Doctoral Thesis Series, Vol. II, 1981)268: "Paul is not saying that the events can now be seen to be *tupikos*– as if they had *become tupoi* as a result of some later occurrence or factor. Rather, Paul insists that in their very happening, they were *tupikos*. The tupoi-quality of the events was inherent in their occurrence, not invented by the Pentatuechal historiographer or artificially given a 'typical' significance by Paul the exegete. The divine intent of the events clearly includes the tupos-nature of the event."

[276] Another classic example of this is found in Isaiah 60:14. There, YHVH promised physical Israel that He would vindicate them, by returning them from Babylon. But notice that in Revelation 3:9, Jesus speaks of the oppressor as, "the synagogue of Satan" (i.e. Old Covenant Israel) and applies the promise of vindication in Isaiah 60 to his followers as the true Seed! The Synagogue of Satan in Revelation 3 is none other than the Babylon of Revelation, Old Covenant Jerusalem. See my *Who Is This Babylon* for an in-depth presentation of this thesis.

proper exegesis. The imminence of fulfillment is seen when we examine the 144,000 a little closer.

Note that the 144,000 are emphatically said to experience the Great Tribulation (7:14). Revelation 14:2-4 tells us something about the 144,000 that definitively demands a first century fulfillment of John's prophecy:

> "And I heard a voice from heaven, like the voice of many waters like the voice of loud thunder. And I heard the sound of harpists playing their harps. They sang as it were a new song before the throne, before the four living creatures and the elders; and no one could learn that song except the hundred and forty-four thousand who were redeemed from the earth. These are the ones who were not defiled with women, for they are virgins. These are the ones who follow the Lamb wherever He goes. These were redeemed from among men, being first fruits to God and to the Lamb."

Did you catch it? The 144,000 were, "the first fruits to God and to the Lamb." This critical, determinative description is commonly overlooked or ignored (sometimes overtly distorted).[277] Yet, it is the *crux interpretum* for understanding the Great Tribulation and the salvation of the remnant in the New Creation where the living waters is located.

So, we have in Revelation 7 and 14 the prophecy of the salvation of the first generation of Jewish converts to Christ and the explicit link to the Great Tribulation. Not only that, but coming out of the Great Tribulation, in that they overcame, they were promised that they would be led to the living waters. This is a direct citation of Isaiah 49.

---

[277] For instance, I recently heard a TV preacher, whose name escapes me, say that we today can become a part of the first fruit 144,000! Such claims are staggeringly bad.

The thrilling and important prophecy of Isaiah 49[278] clearly serves as the key prophetic source of Revelation 7:14f. As you can see, it contains numerous eschatological elements that are key to understanding Revelation and our study of the salvation of the remnant, resurrection and Daniel 12.

Revelation 7 is not strictly limited to any one of these texts. It should be evident that the major tenets of each of these prophecies agree, however. They all speak of the climax of Israel's covenant history, the time of her salvation (cf. Romans 11!). Many of them are patently resurrection texts.

The point here is that the promise of the salvation of Israel found in Isaiah 49, cited in Revelation 7 & 14, is nothing other than the resurrection of Daniel 12. Isaiah 25 identifies the day of the resurrection as the time of Israel's salvation. Isaiah 49 is the time of Israel's salvation, when they (the remnant) would be led to the living waters. Daniel is the salvation of Israel, those written in the book (12:1-2).

The resurrection of Revelation 20:10f is when the books would be opened. Those in the books would be led to living waters. Likewise, Daniel 12 is about those written in the books and the resurrection to eternal life. This is demonstrable proof that Daniel 12 was a prediction of the "final" resurrection.

I must close this discussion with a few comments about the correlation between the salvation of the remnant in Revelation and the salvation of "all Israel" in Romans 11:25-27. Needless to say, this cannot be exhaustive. Romans 11 is such a gold mine and a mine field that one must be cautious and careful about making claims about it. Nonetheless, there are certain "nails" that we can hang our hat on - or at least it seems so to me - that help us place Romans 11 within its proper context.

---

[278] Isaiah 49 is cited numerous times in the NT and played a key role in Paul's discussion of the gospel of reconciliation in 2 Corinthians 5:18-6:1-4.

First of all, Revelation 7 and 14 are about the salvation of Israel. Thus, Revelation is John's contribution to our understanding of Romans 11. This being true, since Revelation depicts the salvation of the *remnant* (the 144,000) this suggests, does it not, that Romans 11 is about the salvation of the remnant and not, as many propose, the salvation of the numeric majority of Israel?

Unless Paul is expanding on the remnant motif in Romans 11, telling us that while throughout God's dealings with Israel it was invariably a remnant that was saved, but that now, at the eschatological consummation all of Israel would be saved, then we must view Romans 11:25f as a prediction of the consummation of the process that had already begun. After all, in chapters 9-11, up to verses 25f, his entire discussion has been focused on the salvation of the remnant. So, does he suddenly abandon that discussion to say that after all, the entirety of Israel would be delivered?

Contra such a suggestion, I propose that Romans 9-11 and Revelation present the same narrative, the same concern for the salvation of Israel. Furthermore, the correlation between Romans 11 with Revelation – particularly as Revelation develops the fulfillment of Isaiah 49 and the resurrection - proves that Daniel 12 foretold the final resurrection.

Since I am focusing a great deal in this work on the impact of Daniel 12 on the Postmillennial paradigm (with implications for all of futurism, of course) I want now to show how the correlation between Romans 11, Revelation, Isaiah 49 and Daniel 12 are so devastating to Postmillennialism. To do so, I will examine these connections as presented in the writings of Kenneth Gentry.

Gentry espouses what may be called the Classical Postmillennial view:

> "The Postmillennialist sees here (Romans 11:25f, DKP) the promise of world conversion as finally including Israel herself.".... "We must understand that since Israel's loss is almost total (only a remnant remains, 11:5), her 'fulfillment' (Gk,

pleroma) must be commensurate with her loss, which means it must be virtually total. Hence, postmillennialists believe in future, massive conversions among the Jews, not only due to general systematic requirements of world salvation, but also due to this exegetical evidence" (2009, 254).

We need only briefly to note that Revelation 7 & 14 are likewise patently about the salvation of Israel. After all, the 144,000 are out of the twelve tribes of Israel and they are redeemed to God from men. And, they are led to the "Postmillennial" world of the Water of Life in the New Creation (Revelation 7:14f– 22:1f).

I must note a stunning claim on the part of Gentry. Contra all church history and in stark contrast to all creeds,[279] Gentry now claims that: "Despite initial appearances, Revelation 21-22 does not speak of the consummate new creation order."[280]

The problem for Gentry and his new position is that it violates what Paul had to say. There is no support for the (stunning) claim that the New Creation of Revelation 21-22 is not, "the consummate new creation." To see how radical and groundless Gentry's new position

---

[279] I call attention to this amazing rejection of creedal theology because Gentry has often condemned the preterist view because it is "non-creedal." Yet now, Gentry is espousing a view that is *unknown* in all creeds and particularly in the Westminster Confession.

[280] Kenneth Gentry, *Navigating the Book of Revelation*, (FountainInn, SC., GoodBirth Ministries, 2010)177. It might be argued that a careful reader of Gentry could see this dramatic change coming. After all, he earlier took the view that the marriage of Christ depicted in Revelation 21 took place in AD 70 (2009, 367). The implications of Dr. Gentry's new position are staggering, but we cannot fully develop them here.

truly is, we need to develop how John anticipated that New Creation and how it relates to the consummative salvation of Israel.

As we have already seen, Revelation 7 & 14 are patently about the salvation of Israel. Their salvation would be the fulfillment of Isaiah 49 as evidenced by the fact that one of the elders before the throne describes the 144K and describes their reward:

> "Therefore they are before the throne of God and serve Him day and night in His temple. And He who sits on the throne will dwell among them. They shall neither hunger anymore nor thirst anymore; the sun shall not strike them, nor any heat; for the Lamb who is in the midst of the throne will shepherd them and lead them to living fountains of waters. And God will wipe away every tear from their eyes" (Revelation 7:15-17).

Take note of the constituent elements of the promise:

1. The 144K would be before the Throne of God.

2. They would be in the Temple of God. In Jewish thought and in scripture, the Temple of God would be fully established at the parousia – the postmillennial parousia - of Messiah.

3. They would no longer hunger or thirst. If Gentry sees this as a metaphoric, spiritual reality fulfilled in AD 70, where will he go to prove a yet future, literal reality and fulfillment?

4. They would be led to living waters. Needless to say, the living waters are in the New Creation (Revelation 22:1f). But once again, we ask, if Gentry posits this as spiritually fulfilled in Christ and his body in AD 70, what texts would he then appeal to for a literal fulfillment of the prophecy?

5. The Great Shepherd would lead them to these blessings.

6. There would be no more tears.

Now, if / since Gentry sees Revelation 7 & 14 fulfilled in Revelation 21-22 and that was in AD 70, he has a severe problem. Revelation 7 & 14 are prophecies that are drawn directly from Isaiah 49 as we have seen. But Isaiah 49 was a prophecy of the salvation of Israel - in other words, *the fulfillment of Romans 11:25f.*

So, if Isaiah 49 was fulfilled in AD 70 – as necessary in Gentry's application of Revelation 21-22 to AD 70 - then, unless Romans 11 foretold a different salvation of Israel from that foretold in Revelation, of logical necessity Romans 11 was fulfilled in AD 70.

If Isaiah 49 is a prophecy of the salvation of Israel and was fulfilled in AD 70, where is the delineation between Isaiah 49 / Revelation 7 & 14 and the salvation of Israel in Romans 11:25f? Did the Old Testament foretell two distinct last days, Messianic salvations of Israel, different in nature, separated in time by so far 2000 years?

There is strong contextual support for the argument we just made. In Romans 13:11f, Paul said, "and now is our salvation nearer than when we first believed." This salvation would arrive at the full arrival of "the day" which was imminent. The question is valid, is this not the salvation of Israel of chapter 11? In both chapter 11 and chapter 13 the promised salvation would arrive with the parousia - the Day of the Lord.

The salvation of Israel in Romans 11 and 13 is the salvation of Israel in Revelation 7 & 14,[281] which was likewise imminent. But if the salvation of Romans 13 is the salvation of chapter 11, then

---

[281] The salvation of Israel in Romans 11-13 and Revelation is the "salvation" to arrive at Christ's second appearance in Hebrews 9:28. After all, that salvation in Hebrews would, just as in Romans and Revelation, be in fulfillment of God's Old Covenant promises to Israel found in Torah (Hebrews 9:6f; 10:1-2). Hebrews 10:37 emphatically and dramatically says that Jesus' coming would be in a "very, very little while" and without delay. This demands that the fulfillment of Romans 11 was very, very near.

Gentry - (not to mention other Postmillennialists who agree that the salvation of the remnant in Revelation 7 / 14 occurred in AD 70) - has surrendered the creedal view of Romans 11. I fail to see how one can divorce the "salvation" of Romans 11 from the salvation of chapter 13.

Let me make a couple of closing points here.

If the salvation of the remnant – at the Living Waters – is after the millennium – and it is – and if the salvation of the remnant belongs to the first century – and it does, Romans 9:28 – then the end of the Millennium – final resurrection - belongs to the first century.

So, if the salvation of the remnant is an "end of the Millennium" event, then since the salvation of the remnant was unequivocally to be in the first century this demands a couple of things:

It is *prima facie* demonstration and validation of *Torah to Telos*.

It means that the Biblical story of eschatology is indeed Covenantally based and focused. Eschatology is not about the end of time, or the consummation of the New Covenant age. It is about the climax of the Old Covenant history of Israel.

It means that Daniel 12 cannot be predicting another resurrection beyond that first century, end of the Millennium salvation of the remnant.

Point #14

THE LAST DAYS PRESENCE OF THE SPIRIT AND THE RESURRECTION

It is widely recognized among scholars that the presence of the Spirit in the first century was an incredibly important eschatological reality. Let me briefly list some of the key eschatological tenets tied directly to the Old Testament prophecies of the out-pouring of the Holy Spirit in the last days.

❖ Joel 2:28-32 / Micah 7:15[282] - The Spirit would be poured out:

1. In the last days.

2. In miraculous manifestation.

3. As a sign of the Great Day of the Lord.

4. The result of the Spirit's work would be the salvation of the remnant of Israel and as well, the offering of salvation to anyone and everyone: "Whosoever shall call on the name of the Lord shall be saved."

❖ Isaiah 32 - The Spirit would be poured out to anoint the Messianic king and to restore Israel, bringing in the world of righteousness.

❖ Ezekiel 37:11-14 - The Spirit would be poured out to restore Israel - to raise Israel from the dead:

---

[282] Tom Holland, *Contours of Pauline Theology*, (Christian Focus Publications, Geanies House, Fearn, Ross-Shire IV20 1TW, Scotland, UK, 2004)21, comments on Micah 7:15. He says it was believed among the Jews that in the last days "second exodus": "There would be miracles like when they came out of Egypt." The "Second Exodus" motif as it relates to the last days work of the Spirit is incredibly important.

"Son of man, these bones are the whole house of Israel. They indeed say, 'Our bones are dry, our hope is lost and we ourselves are cut off!' Therefore prophesy and say to them, 'Thus says the Lord God: "Behold, O My people, I will open your graves and cause you to come up from your graves and bring you into the land of Israel. Then you shall know that I am the Lord, when I have opened your graves, O My people and brought you up from your graves. I will put My Spirit in you and you shall live and I will place you in your own land. Then you shall know that I, the Lord, have spoken it and performed it," says the Lord.'"

✤ Daniel 9:24-27 - It is important to realize that Daniel foretold *the cessation of the prophetic office*. The angel told Daniel that, "seventy weeks are determined... to seal vision and prophecy" which as we shall see, meant the cessation of the prophetic office through the fulfillment of all prophecy.[283]

We could add additional elements to this list, but take note of how the New Testament writers describe the work of the Spirit in their day:

1. He would reveal all truth reveal things to come – this is the prophetic office restored (John 14-16).

2. As the revealer of all Truth, the Spirit would confirm the word that was being revealed through the miraculous gifts of the Spirit (Mark 16:17-20 / Acts 14:2-3 / 1 Corinthians 1:4-8).

3. He would not only reveal the New Covenant, but the Spirit was the means by which the covenantal transformation from the Old to the New was accomplished (2 Corinthians 3:16f). And that was

---

[283] See my *Seal Up Vision and Prophecy*, for a full discussion and documentation. That book is available on Amazon, Kindle, my websites and other retailers.

specifically related to Paul's personal ministry (2 Corinthians 4:1-3).

4. He would "guarantee"[284] the fulfillment of the Old Covenant promises of the resurrection (Romans 8:18-23 / 2 Corinthians 5:5), the promise of the "redemption" (Ephesians 1:12-14).

I differ with Pate who says the Spirit was a "down payment" on the resurrection: "Judaism... assigned the resurrection of the body and the coming of the Spirit to the end of time (Ezekiel 37; Daniel 12:1-3; Enoch 62:15; 2 Enoch 22:8; 4 Ezra 2:39, 45)." - he then says (231) - "The age to come is not yet finished, for the presence of the Spirit within the believer is only the deposit or down payment of the resurrection body (Ephesians 1:13-14)" (1995, 231).[285]

5. The charismatic gifts of the Spirit served as a sign of the coming Day of the Lord (Acts 2:15f / 1 Corinthians 14:20f[286]). As the

---

[284] Paul uses the word *arrabon*, to speak of the work of the Spirit in regard to redemption and resurrection. This word denoted more of the idea of "guarantee" than it did (as Pate claims, (1995, 231) a down payment. See how the word is used in Genesis 38 (LXX) and the story of Judah and Tamar. Judah gave Tamar his signet ring and staff as the *arrabon* of his payment of her harlot price. He most assuredly was not promising to give her more of those things. Rather, by giving those items, he was guaranteeing that he would make payment of what was owed.

[285] I do not know if Pate is a charismatic, most Amillennialists are not, but from a logically consistent perspective, if Pate believes that we possess the Spirit today as the guarantee of the resurrection then he *must* be a charismatic. The *arrabon* that Paul posited as the guarantee of the resurrection was nothing other than the miraculous gifts of the Spirit.

[286] Gentry is correct when he says of the gifts and specifically that of the tongues in the NT: "is evidence of

Tanakh foretold, the last days outpouring of the Spirit was in fact a sign of the last days and the impending Day of the Lord.

Simply stated, the outpouring of the Spirit on Pentecost was proof positive that the last days were in process and that the Great and Terrible Day of the Lord, for the ushering in of the resurrection and kingdom was near.

There was a widely held and Biblical view in Israel that the Spirit had departed from Israel from Malachi onward. The prophetic office had ceased and would not reappear again until the last days as a precursor and sign of the Day of the Lord and resurrection.

David Aune says the, "Rabbis believed that 'when the last prophets died,– (Haggai, Zechariah, Malachi) - the holy spirit ceased in Israel."[287]

Russell says: "Jews believed the spirit of prophecy had ceased during the inter-testamental period."[288] Likewise, Ladd says: "Israel had a sense that the Spirit had departed after Malachi"[289] Pate is correct when he says: "From the post-exilic period on, Judaism complained about the cessation of the Spirit and prophecy, eagerly awaiting their return in the age to come (Ps. 74:9; Lam. 2:9; Zech. 13:4-5; Mal. 4:5)" (1995, 150). Wright acknowledges the absence of

---

God's judgment (Deuteronomy 28:49; Isaiah 28:11; Jeremiah 5:5; 1 Corinthians 14:21-22). Thus, the New Testament tongues experience serves as a sign of God's wrath on her." *(Four Views of the Revelation*, Gundry and Pate, editors, (Grand Rapids, Zondervan, 1998)89, n. 84.

[287] David Aune, *Prophecy in Early Christianity*, Eerdmans, 1983)103.

[288] D. S. Russell, *Method and Message of Jewish Apocalyptic*, (Westminster Press, 1964)78f.

[289] George Eldon Ladd, *A Theology of the New Testament* (Grand Rapids, Eerdmans , 1974)343.

the Spirit in the second temple period and the promise that in the last days, the time of the kingdom, the Spirit would return.[290]

Not only did Israel understand that the Spirit *and the attendant prophetic office* had departed, but they understood that the Spirit would come in the last days to usher in the resurrection, the judgment and the everlasting kingdom. Not only that, but the Old Covenant also foretold that the Spirit would only be given for a short duration in order to accomplish the resurrection. We will develop this below in our look at Daniel 9. In the meantime, consider the following.

The Spirit and John the Baptizer - The Prophet of God

The eschatological role of John the Baptizer is of critical importance.[291] According to Jesus, John was *Elijah*, the *Voice* and the *Messenger*. John was a *prophet* and John was *full of the Spirit*. When the angel spoke to Elizabeth about the son to be born to her, he said:

> "And you will have joy and gladness and many will rejoice at his birth. For he will be great in the sight of the Lord and shall drink neither wine nor strong drink. *He will also be filled with the Holy Spirit, even from his mother's womb.* And he will turn many of the children of Israel to the Lord their God" (My emphasis, Luke 1:14-16).

---

[290] N. T. Wright, *Paul and the Faithfulness of God*, Vol. I, (Minneapolis, Fortress, 2014)105.

[291] I am convinced that other than Jesus and Paul, John was the most significant eschatological figure in the NT. With him the prophetic office was restored. As the *Voice* (Isaiah 40) the *Messenger* (Malachi 3) and as *Elijah* (Malachi 4), he was the herald of the Day of the Lord, judgment and the resurrection. John's message of the imminent kingdom, the imminent judgment, cannot mean anything but that the resurrection was at hand.

To emphasize John's prophetic role and identity the angel continued: "He will also go before Him in the spirit and power of Elijah, 'to turn the hearts of the fathers to the children,' and the disobedient to the wisdom of the just, to make ready a people prepared for the Lord" (v. 17).[292] The fact that John was to operate in the spirit and power of Elijah was tantamount to saying that Israel's last days arrived with John. Look now at how Jesus spoke of John:

> "Now it came to pass, when Jesus finished commanding His twelve disciples, that He departed from there to teach and to preach in their cities. And when John had heard in prison about the works of Christ, he sent two of his disciples and said to Him, 'Are You the Coming One, or do we look for another?' Jesus answered and said to them, 'Go and tell John the things which you hear and see: The blind see and the lame walk; the lepers are cleansed and the deaf hear; the dead are raised up and the poor have the gospel preached to them. And blessed is he who is not offended because of Me.' As they departed, Jesus began to say to the multitudes concerning John: "What did you go out into the wilderness to see? A reed shaken by the wind? But what did you go out to see? A man clothed in soft garments? Indeed, those who wear soft clothing are in kings' houses. But what did you go out to see? A prophet? Yes, I say to you more than a prophet. For this is he of whom it is written: 'Behold, I send My messenger before Your face, Who will prepare

---

[292] John's function and role as described in Luke 1 is stunning - and eschatological to the core. When one examines what the angel said of John's role, it is undeniable that John was a true "last days" prophet to prepare for the eschatological consummation. The connection between John's message with Paul's eschatological message is a powerful testimony to this. Yet, it is one of the most ignored topics in the literature.

> Your way before You.' "Assuredly, I say to you, among those born of women there has not risen one greater than John the Baptist; but he who is least in the kingdom of heaven is greater than he. And from the days of John the Baptist until now the kingdom of heaven suffers violence and the violent take it by force. For all the prophets and the law prophesied until John. And if you are willing to receive it, he is Elijah who is to come. He who has ears to hear, let him hear!" (Matthew 11:1-15).

To ignore the role of John - as a last days *prophet full of the Holy Spirit* - is to miss the incredible eschatological significance assigned to him by the OT prophets and by Jesus. John was a prophet *full of the Spirit*. Thus, the last days had arrived. The Day of the Lord and the attendant resurrection was near.

Hagner caught a bit of this: "John symbolizes the breaking of centuries of prophetic silence recognized by the Jews themselves (cf. Macc 4:46; 9:27; 14:41). Here then is a new thing: a voice from God out of the silence, self-authenticating by its power and message, as well as by its unusual mediator. Prophecy appears again in the midst of Israel, the people of God."[293] Reiser also points to the eschatological tone of John's message: "The expectation of the final judgment in the immediate future was the basis of his call for repentance and the action that gave him his name: baptizer."[294] (1997, 167).

Drury shows that Elijah was expected to come before the Day of the Lord in judgment. He (John, DKP) is, "clearly an eschatological figure signaling the beginning of the end." He was to come,

---

[293] Donald Hagner, *Word Biblical Commentary on Matthew 11:14, Vol. 33*, (Dallas, Word Publishers, 1993)49.

[294] Marius Reiser, *Jesus and Judgment*, Fortress, English translation, 1997)167, 169.

"immediately before the coming wrath of God."[295] Pitre demonstrates that in Jewish eschatological expectation, the appearance of Elijah is inseparably tied to the resurrection. Elijah was to come in or immediately before the Tribulation period and the resurrection (1975,181f).

While there is a vast amount that could be said on this, suffice it to say that in both Jewish expectation and in the OT, The *Voice*, The *Messenger* and *Elijah*[296] was expected to appear immediately before the Day of the Lord, the resurrection and the judgment.[297] The prophetic office, long silent, would be revived in that last days prophet to prepare for the final eschatological event.

John's message was that the judgment and the kingdom was near. Since the resurrection is inextricably tied to judgment and kingdom, how do we extrapolate two millennia beyond John's ministry to

---

[295] John Drury, "The Elijah who was to come: Matthew's Use of Malachi" (Matthew 11:2-15) (2007) www.drurywriting.com/john/The%20who%20was%20%20to%20%0%come.htm

[296] Significantly, each of these designations indicates the return of the prophetic office. What cannot be missed is that in Isaiah 40, the *Voice*, would proclaim the coming of the Lord in *judgment* (v. 10-12). Likewise, the *Messenger* of Malachi 3 would give warning that the Lord was coming and no one could stand before Him (except the righteous), because He was coming in *judgment* (v. 6). Needless to say, that would likewise be the role of Elijah (Malachi 4). Thus, as the *Voice*, the *Messenger* and *Elijah*, John's role as eschatological prophet is undeniable.

[297] While many scholars comment on the relationship between John as Elijah and the end times, it has amazed me how few commentators then fully investigate the implications of that for a proper understanding of NT eschatology. And yet, we hear clear echoes of John's message in Paul, Peter, 1 John and Revelation.

another proposed coming of the kingdom, the judgment and the resurrection? John proclaimed imminent judgment on Israel (which was the specific role of The *Voice, The Messenger* and *Elijah*) and in Daniel 12 the resurrection and the kingdom are patently posited at the time of the destruction of the "power of the holy people" (v. 2, 7).

In John, the Spirit and the prophetic office was being restored. The message of the prophet John was that the Day of the Lord was near. To get another resurrection into the picture one must suggest that John was the herald of a "typological foreshadowing" judgment, kingdom and resurrection.

What is so significant is that the Dominionists who love to say that AD 70 was a type of the "real" Day of the Lord and judgment,[298] nonetheless deny that John was typological. They deny that there will be another *Voice*, another *Messenger*, another *Elijah*.

Gentry claims: "The evidence is really quite clear that Malachi's Elijianic prophecy was fulfilled during the ministry of Christ. This fulfillment is counter-indicative to both Dispensationalism's hermeneutic and its eschatology, as well as being supportive of the preteristic hermeneutic and postmillennial eschatology" (1992, 367). Gentry is clearly wrong in believing that John as Elijah supports his brand of preterism. If John was Elijah, as Gentry agrees, then the Day of the Lord proclaimed and "sign-i-fied" by the Baptizer was the "final" Day of the Lord and the resurrection.

Gentry makes a comment that logically destroys his Postmillennialism when he says of John: "Christ teaches his disciples that John the Baptist fulfills the Malachi prophecy covenantally, even though the Jews do not understand it. John

---

[298] See my *AD 70: A Shadow of the "Real" End?* for a thorough refutation of the claim that AD 70 foreshadowed an "end of time" coming of the Lord and the end of the Christian age. That book is available on Amazon, Kindle, my websites and other retailers.

introduces the restoration of all things, i. e. redemptive history's final phase in Christ's kingdom" (*Dominion*, 2009, 372). We will look at this momentarily.

In similar vein, Wright speaks of John in the role of Elijah. Speaking of Israel's expectation of the Day of the Lord, the time of the restoration of all things and her salvation, he says:

> "The promise of that return is stated most fully at the end of Ezekiel, balancing the dramatic story, and near the beginning of the book, in which the divine presence takes its leave. But the aching sense of absence, coupled with further promises – and warnings! – that this absence will not last forever, continue to echo through the post-exilic period, summed up vividly by Malachi. The priests, ministering in the renewed temple, are bored and careless. But, Israel's God is not finished. There will come a final messenger of warning and then 'the Lord whom you seek will come suddenly to his temple.' But, as with Amos several centuries earlier, so now, 'who can endure the day of his coming and who can stand when he appears?'"[299]

It seems not to have dawned on these men that if John was Elijah, "the last messenger," heralding the Day of the Lord, then the resurrection - the final resurrection - had to have been near, for John

---

[299] N. T. Wright, *Paul and the Faithfulness of God, Parts III & IV,* (Minneapolis, Fortress, 2013)1051.

had no message of delay.[300] And, he had no message of two Days of the Lord, two judgments, two resurrections.

Take note of the following facts concerning the restoration of all things:

☛John initiated the "restoration of all things" (Matthew 17:10 -12). Gentry and other Dominionists concur.

☛That restoration would be consummated at the Day of the Lord (Acts 3:21f - Gentry agrees).

It is more than noteworthy that when discussing the "restoration of all things spoken by the prophets" Peter was emphatic that those prophets "spoke of these days" (Acts 3:24). Those were Peter's first century days. Thus, like Paul who said that the goal of the previous ages had arrived - see our discussion of that below - Peter was clear that the time had come for the fulfillment of those long anticipated promises. To suggest that 2000 years later those promises are still not fulfilled does not agree with the sense of imminence of the consummation found on virtually every page of the NT. Neither the OT prophets or the New ever so much as hinted that the New Creation would be born, but that it would take over two millennia and counting to arrive at, "the end of all things."

☛John, as The *Voice*, The *Messenger* and *Elijah* was a sign and herald of the Great Day and *he said the Day of the Lord was near*.

---

[300] I find Wright's attempt to explain the long delay from John, Jesus and the first century until now tenuous at best. He says of the delay: "the present time is the time of the formation of truly human beings; this cannot be achieved at a stroke, precisely because of what a human being is" (2013, 1048). But neither John, Jesus or Jesus' disciples envisioned a long, two millennia, delay in the restoration of all things. They invariably said the end was near. Wright, with his insistence on a restored material universe, must therefore struggle with that imminence - to no avail.

This means that the consummative restoration of all things was near - and Postmillennialism is false.[301]

Notice that Gentry joins the appearance of John and the (later) appearance of the anti-Christs (1 John) together temporally: "The appearance of these anti-Christs was not a harbinger of a future coming Anti-Christ, for their presence was the signal that 'the last hour' had already 'come' (*gegonasin*). The 'even now' emphasizes the presence of that which they feared ('as you heard') (ibid).

So, for Gentry, neither John or the appearance of the anti-Christs was typological of other yet future events. But if that is true, how can the Day of the Lord that both John and the anti-Christ's presaged - that imminent, first century Day of the Lord - be a foreshadowing of another, greater Day of the Lord?

Mathison also rejects the idea of John being a type of yet another Elijah to come: "The promise of the coming of 'Elijah' ensures one more prophetic voice before the end came. (citing Baldwin). Before the coming of the great day of the Lord, God will send Elijah. Does this mean that God will send a reincarnation of the prophet Elijah or an Elijah-type prophet? The New Testament provides the answer by identifying John the Baptist as the one who fulfilled the prophecy (Matthew 11:13-14; 17:10-13). He is the one who prepared for the coming of Jesus the Messiah." (2009, 312).

The reason all of this is important (and we could give other quotes from Postmillennialists affirming that John was Elijah) is because John, as Elijah, was the "restoration" of the long silent prophetic office, the proof that the last days had arrived. The long anticipated Day of the Lord and the attendant resurrection and kingdom was

---

[301] See my discussion of the restoration of all things and John's role in that in my, *Like Father Like Son, On Clouds of Glory* book. In that book, I expose the inconsistency of Gentry in regard to the restoration and show from his own words that the Restoration of all things was to be consummated at the end of the Old Covenant age of Israel in AD 70.

near. John never, in any way, hinted or suggested that there was to be another, Great (or Greater) Day of the Lord, thousands of years beyond the focus of his message as Elijah. Prophetically, the restoration of the prophetic office, the renewed presence of the Holy Spirit, and the restoration of all things, were *never* presented as typological or foreshadowing events. If, as the Dominionists (rightly) argue, John was not typological of another Elijah, then it is illogical to argue that the Day of the Lord that John foretold was a type or foreshadowing of another Day of the Lord. John, as Elijah, was a sign that the eschatological consummation was near. Let me drive home the Postmillennial inconsistency in regard to the non-typological nature of the first century events.

The following list of eschatological events are admitted by Dominionists to have occurred in the first century as signs of the imminent Day of the Lord against Old Covenant Jerusalem. Not only do the Postmillennialists agree that these things happened in the first century as signs of the impending Day of the Lord against Jerusalem, *they vigorously deny that these events were typological* of yet future events. Strangely, however, those same Dominionists then turn around and claim that the AD 70 Day of the Lord did foreshadow a yet future Day!

☛Appearance of Elijah before the Great Day of the Lord – Fulfilled in John and not typological of another future "Elijah."

☛ Outpouring of the Holy Spirit and restoration of the prophetic office as a sign of the impending Day of the Lord against Israel. Fulfilled in the first century and not typological of another, future outpouring of the Spirit or another restoration of the prophetic office.

☛Appearance of anti-Christs. Fulfilled in the first century, before the fall of Jerusalem and not typological of future anti-Christs.

☛The Abomination of Desolation. Fulfilled in the first century and not typological of another, future Abomination.

☛ The Great Tribulation. Fulfilled in the first century and not a foreshadowing of another, future Tribulation.

So, Dominionists posit the "final fulfillment" of each of these eschatological tenets and deny that they were mere foreshadowings of future eschatological events. Yet, they nonetheless turn around and claim that the Day of the Lord that climaxed those events was a mere shadow of the real Day of the Lord to occur at the end of the (endless) Christian age. I will simply say that this is inconsistency exemplified in a desperate - but futile - attempt to hang onto "orthodoxy."

Acts 1-2 and the Fulfillment of Joel

When the disciples asked Jesus: "Will you at this time restore the kingdom to Israel?" it is widely held that: "Israel's desire for the restoration of that kingdom blinded their eyes to the Christ; and here it is evident that even the sacred Twelve themselves were contaminated with the earthly kingdom virus!"[302]

Williams shares Coffman's view:

> "There is a certain poignancy in their failure right to the end to understand that the kingdom was not of this world (cf. John 18:36) but of the Spirit, to be entered only by repentance and faith. It would be unjust to suggest that the apostles had learned nothing from Jesus. In some respects they had come a long way. But clearly they were wedded still to the popular notion of the kingdom of God as something political - and that its coming would see the gathering of the tribes of Israel, the restoration of Israel's independence and the triumph of Israel over her enemies. In this respect they had not progressed very far from their earlier hope of

---

[302] Burton Coffman, *Commentary on Acts*, (Austin, Firm Foundation Publishing, 1976)19.

occupying the seats of power in such a kingdom (Mark 10:35f; Luke 22:24f). But, given this hope and against the background of Jesus' resurrection and his statements concerning the Spirit, their question, though mistaken, was a perfectly natural one."[303]

Are we to believe that after having their minds opened, and then having the scriptures opened to them for 40 days that the disciples *still* did not understand the kingdom? Is that not disingenuous? I suggest that it was not those disciples that were confused but rather modern day commentators. As Pao says: "An understanding that suggests that the disciples misunderstood the nature of the kingdom must be rejected in light of Acts 1:3."[304]

Notice that in response to the disciples' question about the restoration of Israel, Jesus told them to go into Jerusalem and: "He said to them, 'It is not for you to know times or seasons which the Father has put in His own authority. But you shall receive power when the Holy Spirit has come upon you; and you shall be witnesses to Me in Jerusalem, in all Judea and Samaria to the end of the earth.'" (Acts 1:7-8). So, an eschatological question brought forth an eschatological answer; they would receive the outpouring of the Holy Spirit, which as we have just seen, is directly related to resurrection, to kingdom, to salvation, to the Day of the Lord, in just a few short days.

The stunning events of Acts 2 should not be seen as "just" the establishment of the church. They should not be seen as "just" an account of conversion. Those auspicious events must be viewed in

---

[303] David Williams *New International Biblical Commentary,* (Peabody, Mass, Hendrickson Press, Paternoster, 2002)23.

[304] David Pao, *Acts and the Isaianic New Exodus,* (Grand Rapids, Baker Academic, 2000)95, n. 141.

the context of the last days and the impending Day of the Lord. The events of Pentecost were eschatologically loaded.

Witherington speaks of Jesus' promise of the Spirit in Acts 1, when he told the disciples to wait for the promise of the Father: "Jesus identifies the Holy Spirit as 'the promise of the Father,' thus connecting it with the OT prophecy, which prepares us for what follows in Acts 2:16-22. ...it seems likely that in Luke's mind the coming of the kingdom or dominion of God is synonymous with, or at least closely associated with, the coming of the Holy Spirit in power (Cf. Luke 11:13, 20)." (1998, 109). This connection is undeniable since it was Jesus' promise of the Spirit that prompted the disciples' question about the restoration of Israel. The (return of) the Spirit and establishment of the kingdom are inseparable motifs in prophecy.

Frost makes the fatal mistake of commenting on the outpouring of the Spirit: "The Spirit, or the living waters' flows from the New Jerusalem. *There are not two outpourings of the Spirit.* The Hebrew Prophets envisioned one:[305] 'And it shall come to pass afterward, that I will pour out my spirit on all flesh'" (Joel 2:28f). (2012, 20, His emphasis). But this demands that Frost take some positions that he rejects - or at least that he has rejected in the past.

Frost has told me on more than one occasion that he once belonged to the charismatic movement. He came to realize that it was false and there are no genuine miracles being performed today. As a preterist, he affirmed that the miraculous gifts – *along with the revelatory and prophetic office* - ended in AD 70. However, he has now taken a position that logically demands that he return to the

---

[305] By "one last days outpouring of the Spirit" Frost means that the Spirit was poured out on Pentecost and continues to be operative throughout the Christian age, which he now identifies as the "last days." He clearly does not mean that the Spirit was only poured out on Pentecost and ceased to be manifested.

charismatic world. Not only that, his position demands the restoration - or the continuance - of the prophetic office.

Frost takes his current position based on the Reformed argument that it is the Holy Spirit that regenerates the heart of the sinner so that the sinner can then believe (2012, 21+). The Spirit was to be poured out in the last days. Frost then argues that if we are not in the last days the Spirit is no longer operative. Thus, there is no work of regeneration, meaning there is no salvation today. To say this is specious and presuppositional is to be kind.

First, let me take note again that Frost says there are not two outpourings of the Spirit, and I agree with that assessment.

Second, I would point out that the outpouring of the Spirit on Pentecost was not for the purpose of regeneration, *per se*, but rather to prove that the apostles were the spokesmen of Jesus, the Messiah and to serve as a *sign* of the coming Great Day of the Lord.

Third, I would point out that the outpouring of the Spirit was undoubtedly the miraculous manifestation of speaking in tongues. It was not some mysterious, unfelt, "inner working" of the Spirit, but the overt, external, visible manifestation of the miracle power of God. The opening of the hearts of that Pentecost audience *was through the evidence presented by the apostles' message* and the visible, audible miraculous outpouring of the Spirit.

Those tongues that resulted from the outpouring of the Spirit were not some "unknown language" but in the languages that the apostles had never learned before. Furthermore, that outpouring of the Spirit – that one time outpouring - would be the restoration of the prophetic office: "I will pour out My Spirit... and they shall prophesy" (Acts 2:18).

So, let me offer this to illustrate the logical implication of Frost's current view:

There is but one outpouring of the Spirit - Frost.

That outpouring of the Spirit was to take place in the last days and endure until the Day of the Lord (Acts 2 / 1 Corinthians 1:4-8).

We are in the last days.

(Frost, 2012, 23). In fact, he now says that "the last days" is, "descriptive of each generation since Paul wrote those words" and will be true for the entirety of the Christian age.

The outpouring of the Spirit was manifested in the miraculous gifts of the Spirit (Acts 2:15f) - including the office of inspired, authoritative, infallible prophets.

Therefore, the miraculous gifts of the Spirit - including the office of inspired, authoritative, infallible prophets - will continue to be manifested until the Day of the Lord.

So, Frost says the promise of the Spirit of Joel 2 / Acts 2 was a one time event. He says it is to be manifested during the span of the last days - i.e. the Christian age. Of necessity, then, he must now be, once again, a proponent of the miraculous gifts of the Spirit.[306] But not just the tongues, healings, etc.. He must be an advocate of the continuing office of *inspired, infallible, authoritative prophets*.

It should be apparent from a reading of Joel / Acts, that the outpouring of the Spirit was a *sign* of the imminent Day of the Lord.

---

[306] Some who call themselves preterists, and some who are "Idealists," espouse the continuance of the charismata in the church today. John Noe, Idealist, is one of them. In a private email, I asked Noe if he believed that there are living, authoritative, infallible, inspired prophets alive and operative in the church today. In his response of (12-29-15) he said "No." He added that this does not mean that the charismata have ceased. This is inconsistent, but, common among "preterist / Idealist" students.

The prophecy said the Spirit would be poured out, manifested by prophesying and tongues (tongues were a sign of impending judgment) as signs of the impending Great and Terrible Day of the Lord.[307]

It is hardly logical to argue that the outpouring of the Spirit was to be a sign of the Day of the Lord, and yet that Day still has not come after two millennia. When Peter urged his audience: "Save yourselves from this untoward generation" (Acts 2:40) echoing the Song of Moses, a prediction of Israel's last days, this essentially forces us to refrain from extrapolating that outpouring of the Spirit beyond that generation and the judgment that truly was imminent.

Frost's proper insistence that there are not two outpourings of the Spirit entraps him into likewise affirming that there is but one Great Day of the Lord. If there was but one outpouring, then that singular outpouring was a sign of *one Day (not Days) of the Lord.* This would strongly suggest then that "the last day" was the Day signified by those signs. As just noted, Peter believed that Day was coming in his generation. There is no warrant for divorcing that singular outpouring of the Spirit from a singular imminent Day of the Lord, the last day. Frost has thus falsified his own new found futurist eschatology.

Although Beale refuses to acknowledge and apply the imminence of the Day of the Lord signified by the outpouring of the Spirit, he nonetheless expresses well the implications of that incredible Pentecost and the subsequent "gifting" of the Spirit:

---

[307] This is acknowledged by numerous Postmillennialists, including Gentry, who says the presence of tongues in the NT, "is evidence of God's judgment (Deuteronomy 28:49; Isaiah 28:11; Jeremiah 5:5; 1 Corinthians 14:21-22). Thus, the New Testament tongues experience serves as a sign of God's wrath on her. Gentry in *Four Views of the Revelation,* Stanley Gundry and C. Marvin Pate, (Grand Rapids, Zondervan, 1998)89, n. 84.

"The purpose of this chapter (chapter 17, dkp) is to study the divine Spirit, not in all of His various roles, but, rather with a focus on his eschatological function, especially in the NT, particularly with respect to the giving of resurrection life. In line with the argument of the book and the core of the proposed NT storyline so far, we will see again that the Spirit is best understood as a key agent in bringing about the in-breaking eschatological new creation and kingdom."[308] (2011, 559).[309]

Barton points to the eschatological significance of Pentecost as a sign of the impending Day of the Lord: "The conviction seems to be widespread in early Christianity that the spirit of God had returned, a sign that the last day had arrived (a point stressed by the author of the Acts of the Apostles when he describes the events of the Day of Pentecost as a sign of the last days in Acts 2:17.")[310]

Pate also agrees that the outpouring of the Spirit points directly to the presence of "the age to come" and the eschatological climax, although he, as so many scholars do, extend that consummation into a future far removed from the first century audience: "That the Spirit was thought to be a sign that the New Age had arrived is evident from Isaiah 21:15; 34:16-44:3; Ezekiel 11:19; 36:26, 27; 37:4-14; Joel 2:28-32..." (1995, 47, n. 11). He continues: "The Spirit is proof that the age to come has dawned, though it is not yet completed." (1995, 150). He adds: "Though it is rarely noticed by

---

[308] Greg Beale, *A New Testament Theology*, (Grand Rapids, Baker Academic, 2011)559.

[309] In his commentary on Revelation, Beale says that the two witnesses of Revelation 11 represent the Christian church, gifted continually with the Spirit for a prophetic witness to the whole world. (1999,573+).

[310] John Barton, *The Biblical World, Vol 1,* (London and NY, Routledge Taylor and Francis Group, 2002)145.

commentators, the spiritual gifts Paul mentions are a sign that the age to come has dawned." (1995, 154).

There is an eschatological connection here that should not be missed. In Acts 1, Jesus promised that the disciples would receive the charismatic gifts of the Spirit and the Spirit would then empower them as they served as his witnesses: "You shall be my witnesses to Jerusalem, Judea, Samaria to the utter most parts of the earth" (1:8). Two things must be observed here:

First is the fact that the promise of the charismatic gifts of the Spirit would divinely, miraculously empower the apostles to fulfill the Great Commission. This is attested in Mark 16:17f where after Jesus gave the disciples the Great Commission, they went everywhere preaching the Word, the Spirit bearing witness to them "with signs following." (See also Acts 14:1-3).

This is the same promise found in the Olivet Discourse where Jesus told the apostles to preach the Gospel to the nations (Matthew 24:14). In the parallel text of Mark 13:9f, Jesus warned them that they would be persecuted and brought before kings, governors and sanhedrins. But Jesus promised:

> "But watch out for yourselves, for they will deliver you up to councils, (*Sanhedrins*, DKP) and you will be beaten in the synagogues.[311] You will be brought before rulers and kings for My sake, for a testimony to them. And the gospel must first be preached to all the nations. But when they arrest you and deliver you up, do not worry beforehand, or premeditate

---

[311] This text is harmful to the Dispensational paradigm that applies Matthew 24 / Mark 13 to the Tribulation period after the rapture. They claim that in that period it is Israel being persecuted by the Man of Sin, not the church. But this flies in the face of the text: Jesus' disciples would be brought before the Sanhedrins and Synagogues! This is Jewish persecution of Christians, not persecution of the Jews by some pagan Man of Sin.

what you will speak. But whatever is given you in that hour, speak that; for it is not you who speak, but the Holy Spirit" (Mark 13:9-11).

We find this promise being fulfilled even in Stephen, "full of faith and power" and performing, "great wonders and signs among the people" (Acts 6:8); "full of the Holy Spirit," (Acts 7:55), as he was tested by the enemies of Christ in Acts 6-7. His inquisitors, however, "could not withstand the wisdom and the spirit by which he spoke (Acts 6:10).

Jesus' promise of the Spirit for the empowerment of the Great Commission enabling his disciples to refute and confound their persecutors is manifested throughout Acts – but *it is not present today*. In the first place, the Great Commission was completed and fulfilled in the first century.[312] The end of the age, the terminus of the promise of those gifts (Matthew 28:18-20) arrived with the fall of Jerusalem in AD 70.

I am fully aware of the claims made by the charismatics in regard to this issue. However, history is replete with examples of zealous, but misguided, missionaries - with no training in the languages of the countries to which they were going - trusting in the "gift of tongues." Yet, they were totally embarrassed when it was indisputably true that they were not speaking in tongues as the first century disciples could do.

The "empirical fact" is that the divine empowerment promised by Jesus (Acts 1) for the completion of the World Mission does not exist today. The fact that charismatic missionaries spend considerable time learning the languages of the people to whom they are going demonstrates that there is a fundamental realization that the divine empowerment promised in Acts 1 is not operative in them.

---

[312] See my *Into All The World, Then Comes The End*, for a full discussion of this.

There is a tremendous irony here. Pentecostal missionaries spend considerable time learning the languages of the nations to which they will travel. Then, when there, they supposedly *speak in tongues*, a miraculous gift! Yet, even though they had to learn the language of the native people, the so called miraculous "tongues" *are still not the languages of those native people and have to be "translated!"* Why didn't the Spirit just inspire them to speak in the native tongues in the first place? This is a glaring inconsistency.

The second issue in Acts 1 is that in calling those disciples his *witnesses* (Acts 1) Jesus echoes Isaiah 43:10. What is so significant about *that* is that the witnessing would be the message of the coming in of the New Creation (Isaiah 43:18-21).

So, the promise of the Spirit in Acts 1 echoes the promise of Isaiah and the prophecy of the coming New Creation, which is nothing less than the time of the resurrection - the final resurrection. This means the disciples were to be witnesses of Jesus to proclaim the coming in of that promised New Creation - and the resurrection.

All of this is directly relevant to our question about Daniel 12 and whether it foretold the "final" resurrection. In Torah, there are not multiple prophecies of many different outpourings of the Spirit (as Frost concedes) to accomplish different kinds of resurrections. So, Daniel foretold the resurrection at the time of the end. The Spirit was to be the means of and the guarantee of the end time resurrection. Since the Spirit was poured out in the first century and served as the guarantee of that coming resurrection there is no justification to look for another, future resurrection.

Consider again that the charismatic gifts were to be a sign and warning of the Great and Terrible Day of the Lord (Acts 2:15f). Furthermore, the charismatic signs, inclusive of the prophetic office, the healings, the tongues, etc. were only temporary, until the Day of the Lord (1 Corinthians 1:6-8), the arrival of "that which is perfect" (1 Corinthians 13:8) and the, "measure of the stature of the fullness of Christ" (Ephesians 4:8-16). This is what Jesus meant in Matthew 28 when he said "I am with you always, even to the end of the age." The end of the age was to be the end of the miraculous outpouring of the Spirit.

Peter, in the context of the outpouring of the charismata, pointed out that what was happening was in fulfillment of Joel. He then warned the audience, "Save yourselves from this untoward generation" (Acts 2:40) indicating that the charismatic signs of that day were a sign of something coming soon.

When we consider the prophetic office we hardly need much evidence to know, without any doubt, that it has ceased. In the midst of all of the modern claims of the operation of the charismata, it is abundantly strange (and revealing) that the claims of living, inspired, authoritative, infallible prophets, or to their presence in the church, is strangely missing. To be sure, there have been and are fringe individuals who have made such claims, but none are able to pass the test (cf. Deuteronomy 18; Revelation 2:1f).

If there are *inspired, authoritative, infallible prophets* in the church today, then every effort should be made to find them in stark contrast to McDurmon's claims that we will examine below. But let's face it, if there are genuine prophets in possession of the Spirit as promised in Joel and by Jesus in John 14-16, then we should surely know without doubt- as the early church did - of individuals that possess and manifest the following:

Knows "all things" - John 14:26; 16: 13 - "The Helper, the Holy Spirit, whom the Father will send in my name, He will teach you all things..." "When the Spirit is come, He will guide you into all truth." There are no men or women in the church today who possess knowledge of "all things," and who possess "all truth," i.e. all spiritual knowledge. This is indisputably true.

Perfect remembrance of the words of Jesus - John 14:26 - "He will teach you all things and bring to your remembrance all things that I said to you." If we have anyone living in the church today that possesses the Spirit as promised here, then of necessity, they should have perfect memory, total recall, of every single word of Jesus. This would include the words not written in Scripture. John knew,

John *remembered*, that Jesus had spoken and done far, far more than what was recorded (John 20:30; 21:25). So, where are those, supposedly possessing the Spirit as promised in Joel or John 14-16, that have perfect knowledge and recall of everything Jesus did and said, including things not recorded?

"He will show you things to come..." - John 16:13 - Nothing could be more self-evident, so indisputably true, than to say that we have no living prophets who are able to infallibly tell the truth about "things to come." The lamentable history of the church in almost every generation, is that one false "prophet" after another has declared that the end is near![313] One has but to witness the recent debacle of Jonathan Cahn and his *Mystery of the Shemitah*, or, Harold Camping, Mark Blitz, and the embarrassment of John Hagee and his Four Blood Moon prediction that, "something big, something earth shattering is about to take place." (That, "something big, something earth shattering" was to occur no later than September, 2015).

Let me say this as kindly as possible, at the risk of offending my charismatic friends, but, this is self-evident: We know that the charismatic gifts of the Spirit have ceased because the office of inspired, infallible, authoritative prophets has ceased. We know this for the very same reason that we know psychics are charlatans. Psychics don't win the lottery. Charismatics in a similar fashion, do not go to the cancer wards of the hospitals and clean them out. So

---

[313] See Francis Gumerlock, *The Early Church and the End of the World* for documentation of the sad history of false predictions in the church (Powder Springs, Ga., American Vision, 2006). The evangelical community *must* come to grips with this issue! Either the first century apostles and prophets were right in their declarations that the end was near *then*, or, they were simply the first in a long, sad chain of false prophets. Sadly, Gumerlock seems at times to go out of his way to condemn the true preterist view as heresy, seeming not to realize that if preterism is not true, the Bible itself is falsified.

called prophets do not stand up and verify through the "signs following," that they are of God and, "show things to come." This is undeniable.

All of this is directly relevant to our discussion of Daniel 12 and the question of the "final resurrection." Everyone agrees, do they not, that the time of the final resurrection is the time of the fulfillment of all prophecy? I do not know of anyone that would deny this. But that means that if all prophecy is fulfilled at the time of the "final resurrection" then there would be no further need for the prophetic office after the final resurrection. So, if in fact the prophetic office has ceased - as all non-charismatics affirm - this serves as powerful evidence that the final resurrection has been fulfilled. And that

---

Everyone agrees that the time of the "final" resurrection is when all prophecy is fulfilled and the prophetic office ceases to function.

Almost all futurist eschatologies agree that the office of inspired, infallible, authoritative prophets has ceased and no longer functions.

This is tantamount to admitting - and logically demands - that the "final" resurrection has taken place!

---

brings us back to Daniel 9, since Daniel 9 gives us the time for the end of the prophetic office.

Daniel 9:24 - "Seventy weeks are determined... to seal vision and prophecy." In Daniel's great prophecy of the consummation of Israel's eschatological hope, we have a prediction of the time when all prophecy would be fulfilled[314] - including the resurrection.[315] Here is what that means.

If there are no living, authoritative, infallible prophets in the church today - and there aren't - then the seventy weeks have been fulfilled, terminated.

If the seventy weeks have been fulfilled then every constituent element of Daniel 9 has been fulfilled.

But the constituent elements of Daniel 9 are inseparably connected to the resurrection (i.e. the taking away of sin is related to the resurrection in 1 Corinthians 15:55-56), the making of the Atonement is consummated at the Second Coming / the time of the resurrection (Hebrews 9:28), the world of everlasting righteousness would arrive at the Day of the Lord, the time of the resurrection (cf. Galatians 5:5; 2 Peter 3).

Therefore, since there are no living, inspired, authoritative and infallible prophets in the church today, this is *prima facie* proof that the "final" resurrection has occurred.

This has a profound implications for the Dominionist and the wider non-charismatic world.

---

[314] There is widespread consensus among scholars that the term "seal vision and prophecy" refers to the cessation of the prophetic office through the fulfillment of all prophecy. I present a wealth of testimony on this in my book *Seal Up Vision and Prophecy*, available on Amazon, Kindle, my websites and other retailers. There really is little disagreement on the meaning of this term.

[315] As I demonstrate in my book, *Seventy Weeks Are Determined...For the Resurrection*, almost every constituent element in Daniel 9:24 is directly related to the resurrection. Thus, the resurrection - the final resurrection as the hope of Israel - would be fulfilled by the end of the seventy weeks. And that terminated in AD 70.

Frost, as noted above, at one time was part of the charismatic movement. Unless he has once again reverted to that, he told me several times that he no longer believes in the validity of modern gifts and certainly not the gift of prophecy.

Gentry wrote a book in response to Gundry and in that book Gentry affirmed that there are no charismatic gifts operative in the church today. He particularly focused on the gift of prophecy, insisting:

> "It has been pointed out by several evangelical scholars that also contained in Daniel is an important prophecy which seems to tie the close of the canon and all prophetic revelation to the AD 70 destruction of the temple. Daniel 9:24 reads, 'Seventy Weeks are determined... to make an end of sin, to make the atonement for iniquity, to bring in everlasting righteousness, to seal up vision and prophecy and to anoint the most holy place... after the sixty-two weeks the Messiah will be cut off and have nothing and the people of the prince that is to come will destroy the city and the sanctuary. And its end will come with a flood.' This seventy weeks of years period is widely held among conservative scholars to refer to the First Advent of Christ. The usefulness of this passage is enhanced by the fact that Christ draws from it in His Olivet Discourse which is clearly related to the AD 70 destruction of the Temple (Matthew 24:1-2)" (1989, 135).

Gentry does not limit the cessation of the charismata to the prophetic office. In his rebuttal of Wayne Grudem, Gentry correctly argued that if any of the gifts ended - which he affirms - then all ended and that if some were temporary, then all were temporary.[316] This is the Biblical view. There is no Bible evidence for claiming,

---

[316] Kenneth Gentry, *The Charismatic Gift of Prophecy A Reformed Response to Wayne Grudem*, (Fountain Inn, SC, Victorious Hope Publishing, 1999)59f.

as some do, that the prophetic office has ceased, but that the miraculous healing and tongues, words of wisdom, etc. continue. Yet, Paul believed that the prophetic office would end with the arrival of, "the perfect man, the measure of the stature of the fullness of Christ" (Ephesians 4:8-16).[317]

For Paul, tongues, miraculous knowledge and the prophetic office would all cease at the same time, at the arrival of, "that which is perfect" (1 Corinthians 13).[318] But this also means that if any of the gifts are operative today, then *all of them* are operative.

Pate says, "At the moment of faith, the sinner receives the gift of the Spirit" (1995, 151) and that, "Every believer possesses at least one gift" (1995, 153). This raises the relevant question of whether he also believes that there are living, inspired prophets operative in the church today, since he says, "Prophecy was of paramount importance to Paul" (1995, 154). If prophecy was of paramount importance to Paul and it patently was, then why would the office of prophecy cease and the "less important" gift of tongues continue?

---

[317] It is often argued that Paul's "perfect man" is the individual, given "perfection" upon death, or at the parousia, or that it refers to individuals reaching a point of spiritual maturity. That misses the point of 1 Corinthians 13 and Ephesians 4 where Paul is discussing the arrival of the *corporate* "fullness of Christ" through the completion of the mystery of Christ. I discuss this at length in my response to Joel McDurmon's article on "that which is perfect." I wrote a series of articles in response to McDurmon on this and the first article can be found here: http://eschatology.org/index.php?option=com_content&view=article&id=1268:joel-mcdurmon-on-1-corinthians-13-a-response-1&catid=131:uncategorised.

[318] I disagree with Gentry that "that which is perfect" was the completed canon of the NT, although I think that was included in that concept. I believe that term is more comprehensive and speaks of the New Covenant Creation as a whole. I cannot develop that here, however.

Would Pate affirm the presence today of divinely inspired, infallible, authoritative prophets? It is inconsistent to say that the gifts are present in the church, all the while denying the presence of inspired, authoritative, infallible prophets.

Gentry, commenting on, "that which is perfect" suggests that it means, "there is coming a time (from Paul's perspective, DKP) when will occur the completion of the revelatory process of God" (1999, 54). In the footnote of this comment (n. 4), he adds, "We even believe that this idea is contained in a proper understanding of the Daniel 9:24 statement regarding the 'sealing of the vision and prophecy.'" He cites A. Clarke and Matthew Henry in support of that view.[319] I agree that Daniel 9 predicted the cessation of the prophetic office - and the charismata - but this is deeply problematic for Gentry.

Gentry takes the position that "seal up vision and prophecy" is referent to the revelatory process - the close of the NT canon. If he then posits the completion of the seventy weeks in AD 35 (as he does), *the revelatory process must have been finished, sealed up through fulfillment, by AD 35!* Furthermore, if, as is true, the sealing of vision and prophecy means the fulfillment of all prophecy which brings the prophetic office to an end, then for Gentry to posit the termination of the prophetic office at the end of the seventy weeks demands that the resurrection - the final resurrection - occurred no later than AD 35. But the problem does not belong to Gentry alone.

Joel McDurmon, unlike Gentry, takes a confusing - and confused - position on the charismata.[320] He tells us that he was part of that

---

[319] I fully concur that "seal vision and prophecy" refers to the cessation – through the fulfillment - of the entire revelatory corpus, I agree that this was accomplished no later than AD 70. See my book, *Seal Up Vision and Prophecy* for a full discussion.

[320] See his full article on the American Vision website, under the heading: "An Exegetical Glance At

movement for over five years and yet never experienced or witnessed a genuine miracle. Yet he says, after discussing 1 Corinthians 13: "I realize the analysis given above opens the possibility that the revelatory gifts are still in operation. I have no problem with that, although in my personal experience – which includes at one time nearly five years as a Pentecostal – I can't say I have every (sic- ever) experienced a genuine undeniable case of tongues, prophecy, or interpretation of tongues. Even if I did, however, any such experience could not stand as an authoritative argument for anyone but the direct witnesses, seeing as it would be anecdotal only. This holds true, by the way, for any of the miraculous gifts."[321]

I must say, in all candor, but with due respect, this is simply *awful* – not to mention destructive of Biblical authority! To suggest that the revelatory process is - or could be - still functioning today is quite incredible. Does this not *at least potentially* open the door that more inspired scripture could be written by these unknown prophets? For

---

Revelatory Gifts in 1 Corinthians 13."
http://americanvision.org/?s=That+which+is+perfect#sthash.X wEyleWu.dpbs.

[321] McDurmon hedges where others openly affirm. Williams insists that: "Not all are apostles, but all are commissioned to witness the truth that they may established. To all, therefore, the promise is given: you will receive power when the Holy Spirit is come upon you. (V. 8). The statements of this verse should be understood as cause and effect. Effective witness can only be borne where the Spirit is and where the Spirit is, and effective witness will always follow, in word, in deed (miracle) in quality of the lives of those who bear it)" (David Williams *New International Biblical Commentary*, (Peabody, Mass, Hendrickson Press, Paternoster, 2002)24. For anyone to affirm such a position and not likewise posit the existence of divinely inspired, authoritative, infallible prophets in the church is surely disingenuous.

McDurmon to so flippantly say that he has no problem with the idea that the revelatory gifts may still be functioning today is staggering!

Where are the prophets? Where are the infallible ministers / prophets? Where are those exercising the revelatory gifts? Where are those with perfect understanding of "all things" and perfect recall of everything Jesus ever said and taught? Where are the prophets showing us, infallibly, "things to come"? Where are the prophets that can convene conferences - ala the Jerusalem council in Acts 15 - and authoritatively, by inspiration, settle perplexing theological issues? McDurmon's cavalier comments about the possibility of on-going inspired revelation are quite amazing in their implications.

When men such as Beale, Barton, Williams, Frost, etc. claim that the church is continually gifted today for prophetic witness to the world, do we not have the right to ask: Where are those prophets? Where are the prophets doing what Revelation 11 says, calling down fire from heaven, or, making it rain "on demand"?

When men such as Noe claim that the charismatic gifts of the Spirit are present today, what justification can be given for saying that the prophetic gift and office is absent? If the prophetic office has ceased, *all of the gifts have ceased*. If the church is continually gifted to witness to the whole world, as described in Revelation 11, then we should be able to identify those powerful, infallible, authoritative prophets. But, with all due respect to Dr. Beale, he is not an inspired prophet, and neither is Noe, Williams, Barton or Frost.

As a caveat, I will say that McDurmon's view *somewhat* allows him to maintain a futurist eschatology in contrast to Gentry and Frost. (At the time of this writing I am unaware if Frost would agree with McDurmon's comments about the possibility of the present day operation of the revelatory office).

Remember that the gifts of the Spirit – including the prophetic office - were *the guarantee of the resurrection* (2 Corinthians 5:5). They guaranteed the, "redemption of the purchased possession"

(Ephesians 1:12f). So, if the resurrection has not taken place then *most assuredly* (not in some "maybe," "could be," "who knows and it really does not matter," manner as expressed by McDurmon) the charismata, including the prophetic office, should be fully functional in the church today. But let me say again, it is *prima facie* true that this simply is not the case.

We have a perfect Biblical, (1 John 4:1-4) right to demand where the inspired, infallible, authoritative prophets are today, if the charismatic gifts are still operative and if the resurrection has not taken place. Not only that, when the cessationist commentators tell us there are no living prophets today, (as they all do!) and that the charismata have ceased, then we have the right, no, the *obligation*, to point out that this demands that the parousia, the judgment and the resurrection have been fulfilled (1 Corinthians 1:6-8). Those gifts were to continue until the Day of the Lord, serving as guarantee of the resurrection.

This cannot be over-emphasized! As we have shown, the OT prophecies were that the Spirit would return to Israel and the prophetic office would be restored as a sign of the impending Day of the Lord and the resurrection.[322] But the prophetic office would cease to function at the end of Israel's covenant age (Daniel 9). There is a direct connection between resurrection and the charismatic, prophetic function of the Spirit. This raises a severe problem for the Postmillennialists.

---

[322] According to Isaiah 32, Ezekiel 37 and in Joel 2, the Spirit would be poured out (the charismata) with a very specific purpose - the restoration of Israel. Thus, if Israel has been restored in Christ and the church, as posited by both Amillennial and Postmillennial writers, then the charismatic function of the Spirit for that purpose is no longer needed. Conversely, if Israel has not been restored (e.g. Romans 11:25f) then by all means, the charismata should be operative to accomplish that! A great deal could be said on this, but space forbids it.

We remind you once again of Frost's admission that there was but one outpouring of the Spirit. This being true, Frost must affirm the continuance of the charismata - *inclusive of the prophetic and revelatory gifts* - until the resurrection. It was the Spirit - the one miraculous outpouring of the Spirit which was to guarantee the resurrection.

Daniel 9 posited the cessation of the prophetic office (thus, all the charismata) by the end of the seventy weeks. The prophetic office and the presence of the charismata was tied directly to the resurrection work of the Spirit as we have seen. The Spirit guaranteed that resurrection. Postmillennialists by and large agree that the charismatic gifts of the Spirit and most assuredly the prophetic office, ended by AD 70. But if (since) that is true, it is patently illogical to say that the resurrection - the final resurrection - has not yet occurred. Since Frost is now positing the on-going presence of that one last days outpouring of the Spirit - which was indubitably miraculous - then of necessity that means that the seventy weeks of Daniel are not fulfilled. This in turn demands that Israel's covenant age is not consummated and Israel remains as God's covenant people.

The Postmillennialists are not alone in positing fulfillment of the seventieth week of Daniel circa 34-35 or by the time of the martyrdom of Stephen. Some Amillennialists do the same. They believe the seventieth week was finished no later than the conversion of the Gentiles. Denham places the beginning of the seventieth week at Jesus' baptism and the *terminus ad quem* (end) at the stoning of Stephen and/or preaching of the gospel to the Samaritans.[323] Wayne Jackson (Amillennialist) believes the seventieth week terminated with the conversion of Paul.[324]

---

[323] H. Daniel Denham, an eight part series on *Daniel's Seventy Weeks*, in "The Defender," (4859 Saufley Rd. Pensacola, Florida 32506).

[324] Wayne Jackson, "Christian Courier," (3906 E. Main St., Stockton, California. 95205, Vol. 15, number 7,

These writers fail to consider the fact that, "seal up vision and prophecy" means to give and to fulfill revelation. So, to say that the seventieth week of Daniel was completed no later than the conversion of the Gentiles about AD 35, *is to say that all revelation was given and confirmed no later than AD 35!* But that is not all. *It means that the resurrection occurred no later than AD 35*, because to, "seal vision and prophecy" meant not only the revelatory *process*, but the cessation of the prophetic function *through the fulfillment of all prophecy!* And that includes the prophecies of the "final" resurrection.

Consider the following.

> **If seal up vision and prophecy means the completion of the revelatory process and the end of the charismata, and if the seventy weeks ended in AD 35 as some suggest, then the revelatory process - and the charismata - ended in A.D. 35!**

If seal up vision and prophecy means to give and to fulfill, (or if, just for argument sake, it means simply the *giving of revelation*),

And,

If all vision and prophecy was to be given and confirmed (or just *revealed*) within the seventy weeks,

And,

If the seventy weeks ended with the conversion of the Gentiles (no later than AD 35),

Then,

It must be true that all vision and revelation was given and fulfilled (or at least *given*) by the time of the conversion of the Gentiles, no

---

November, 1979)25.

later than AD 35! To understate the case, this calls for a *radical* reevaluation of the time of the completion of the canon!

This dilemma is acute for anyone maintaining a late date for *any* book of the New Testament. Jackson, for instance, advocates the late date of the Apocalypse.[325] He believes seal up vision and prophecy relates to the revelation of God's will and its miraculous confirmation. Commenting on the term seal up vision and prophecy, Jackson says: "With the coming of the Savior to effect human redemption the completion of the NT record setting forth this glorious system, the need for visions and prophecies became obsolete. Accordingly, prophecy ceased (cf. I Cor. 13:8-13, Eph. 4:11-16) with the complete revelation of the gospel system."[326]

Jackson and others fail to see the implications of what they are saying. Daniel's seventy weeks were determined for the sealing of vision and prophecy. If there was *anything* written after the determined seventy weeks *it was not inspired*. Many of those who contend that the seventy weeks ended in 33-35 also believe the canon was not completed until at least AD 95. In fact, none of them would date *any* of the books prior to 33-35! Therefore according to their own interpretation none of the books of the New Testament can be inspired since they were written after the completion of the seventy weeks.

On the one hand they admit that seal up vision and prophecy is referent to the revelatory process. On the other hand they insist that the seventy weeks were fulfilled by AD 35, all the while not seeing that if vision and prophecy[327] were sealed (completely revealed,

---

[325] Wayne Jackson, "Christian Bible Teacher," (P. O. Box 1060, Abilene, Texas, 79604-1060, November, 1989).

[326] Jackson, "Christian Courier," September, 1979.

[327] Some try to avoid the problem here by saying that "seal vision and prophecy" means simply to fulfill the specific prophecy of Daniel 9. This is untenable. Hebrew scholars note

confirmed and fulfilled), that this demands that the revelatory process and all of eschatology was completed by AD 35! Not only that, let me say again: If prophecy ceased, the resurrection has been fulfilled. The presence of the charismata and the prophetic office was the guarantee of the resurrection.

We could say much more on this particular issue, but this will suffice. Let me summarize my thoughts on the presence of the charismata and the resurrection.

The Jews understood and Scripture taught - that the Spirit had departed from Israel and that there were no prophets after Malachi.

The Old Testament foretold the return of the Holy Spirit and revival of the prophetic office in the last days.

The return of the Spirit and the revival of the prophetic office was to serve as a sign and herald of the resurrection and the Day of the Lord.

Beginning with John, as *the prophet Elijah* and manifested by the incredible events of Pentecost, the Spirit returned and the prophetic office was restored to Israel.

The NT prophets, inspired by the Holy Spirit, proclaimed the imminence of the parousia, the end of the age and the resurrection.

The confusion in the evangelical world in regard to the charismatic gifts *and particularly the prophetic office*, is directly related to a confusion about eschatology. On the one hand, Postmillennialists, Amillennialists and even many Dispensationalists insist that the prophetic office has ended. *There are no living, inspired, infallible, authoritative prophets in the church today.* And yet, while affirming

---

that there is no definite article in Daniel 9:24. Thus, it is not "seal *the* vision and *the* prophecy." "Seal vision and prophecy" is comprehensive, not limited. Further, even if the referent was to "*the* prophecy" of Daniel 9, the reality is that *Daniel 9:24 is a prophecy of the resurrection!*

this truth, they then say the resurrection has not occurred. This is a contradiction, since the presence of the charismatic, inspired prophetic office, along with the other charismatic gifts, was the guarantee of the resurrection. To affirm the cessation of the prophetic office is to posit the fulfillment of the resurrection - the final resurrection.

When commentators such as Pate, Frost, Beale and others affirm that the Spirit continues to operate today, as they were manifested in the NT, and yet, they deny the presence of the inspired, authoritative, infallible prophets (as many do) they are exposing their own fatal self-contradictions.

When commentators say the "final" resurrection has not occurred, they must, of logical necessity, affirm the presence of inspired, authoritative, infallible prophets in the church until that proposed end of the age event. And yet, many of them try to deny this, once again exposing their inconsistency. The connection between the prophetic office and the resurrection is unbreakable.

To affirm, as do most futurists, the cessation of the inspired, infallible and authoritative prophetic office is to say that the resurrection of the dead has occurred.

The charismatic gifts of the Spirit, *including the prophetic office*, were the signs and the guarantee of the resurrection.

If there are no prophets, the resurrection work of the Spirit is fulfilled.

If the resurrection has not occurred, there should be - there *must be* - authoritative, infallible and inspired prophets in the church today.

Yet, it is *prima facie* evident that there are no such prophets today. Thus, the "guarantee" work of the Spirit failed, or,

The resurrection is fulfilled!

Point #15

WAS DANIEL 12 DESCRIBING THE TIME AND EVENTS OF ANTIOCHUS EPIPHANES?

I must offer here a *brief* discussion of whether Daniel 12 is actually an *ex eventu* (after the fact) description of the horrific events that fell on Israel during the reign of the Seluecid king Antiochus Epiphanes. This view is probably the dominant view in the higher critical world and those who deny it are often viewed as "fundamentalists" (in an almost pejorative sense, meaning ignorant and unlearned). Yet, there are serious problems with this view. Any in-depth discussion of all of the issues surrounding the dating and application of Daniel would expand this work far beyond tenability. So, I will keep my comments limited to a discussion of whether the prophecy was primarily applicable to the second century BC, or, if it was a prediction all along of the events of the first century and the fall of Jerusalem in AD 70.

As to the dating of the book of Daniel, I take the "early date" and believe that Daniel was written by the Daniel who was taken captive by the Babylonians in the siege and destruction of Jerusalem at the hands of Nebuchadnezzar.[328] I would argue that the early dating is not *necessary* to posit Daniel 12 as a prediction of the "final resurrection." But I do believe that in spite of some real challenges, the early dating is the preferred dating.

One bit of evidence, perhaps not logically coercive, but nonetheless definitely worth considering is this: The critical scholars tell us the book of Daniel was not penned until the time of Antiochus Epiphanes, *second century BC,* when some unknown scribe penned

---

[328] Take note of Ezekiel 14:14, where the prophet mentions Daniel as a very real person of note. Unless there was another exilic righteous "Daniel" in the days of Ezekiel, this is some good evidence that Daniel lived and worked at the early date.

this work under the pseudonym Daniel.[329] And yet, the Jews, who believed that there were no inspired prophets at that proposed time, *(seemingly) gladly accepted Daniel as an inspired prophetic book.* To say that this is troublesome for the later dating of Daniel is an understatement. How could the Jews accept Daniel as genuine - which they did - if they believed there were no inspired prophets when Daniel was written?[330]

With this said, here is my approach: Even if one grants that Daniel foretold – or described *ex eventu (a view I do not accept)* - the time and events of Antiochus Epiphanes (175- 164 BC) this does not in any way negate the fact that Jesus utilized Daniel in his predictions of the end.[331] Israel of Jesus' day believed that the events of their past history were typological of the last days events. Thus, even if one posited Daniel as "late" and initially descriptive of the second century BC events, that does not preclude Jesus or the NT writers from reading those events figurally, that is, reading the events of the OT "backward," to use Richard Hays' terminology, seeing those

---

[329] It is often claimed that the writing of books under pseudonyms was an accepted, if not honored, practice in the ancient times. But I have yet to see it effectively demonstrated that Daniel was such a work.

[330] Another interesting fact is that Eusebius, fourth century church historian, spoke of the book of Daniel and said that he and his contemporaries, "are now nearly a thousand years from the date of the prophecy" (of Daniel 9). (Eusebius, *Proof of the Gospel, Book VIII,* chapter 2, Grand Rapids, Baker, 1981)139). Critical scholars simply say Eusebius naively accepted the early date. But this claim does not constitute any kind of *proof* that Eusebius was in fact wrong.

[331] We need to keep in mind that Jesus definitely ascribed Daniel to "the prophet" (Matthew 24:15). One could, as some do, say that he was just consenting to the prevalent, misguided view of his day, but once again, this is not convincing.

events typologically but being now fulfilled in their day. Here is what Hays means by that:

> "Figural reading need not presume that the OT authors - or the characters they narrate - were conscious of predicting or anticipating Christ. Rather, the discernment of a figural correspondence is necessarily retrospective rather than prospective. (Another way to put this point is that the figural reading is a form of intertextual interpretation that focuses on an intertextuality of *reception* rather than *production*). The act of retrospective recognition is the *intellect spiritualism*. Because the two poles of a figure are events within 'the flowing stream of time, the correspondence can be discerned only after the second event has occurred and imparted a new pattern of significance to the first."[332]

R. T. France, discusses a similar idea:

> "The idea of fulfillment in NT typology derives not from a belief that the events so understood were explicitly predicted, but from the conviction that in the coming and work of Jesus the principles of

---

[332] Richard Hays, *Reading Backwards, Figural Christology and the Fourfold Gospel Witness*, (Baylor University Press, 2014)2-3. I do disagree with Hays' statement that the NT writers had to witness an event and then compare it with some past event. This would demand that when Jesus cited Daniel 12 in his prediction of the Abomination of Desolation, the Great Tribulation and the fall of Jerusalem, that those events were already past and that he was looking back, comparing those events with the days of Antiochus. However, Jerusalem and the Temple were not totally destroyed in the days of Antiochus and Jesus undeniably spoke of the impending destruction before it took place. Thus, the comparison breaks down.

God's working, already imperfectly embodied in the O.T., were more perfectly re-embodied thus brought to perfection. In that sense, the OT history pointed forward to Jesus. For the OT prophets the antitypes were future; for the NT writers they have already come."[333]

He also says typology is, "Grounded in history and does not lose sight of the events with which it is concerned. Typology may be described as 'theological interpretation of the OT history." (Ibid).

Wright *seems* to suggest this as well. He is clear that Jesus applied Daniel to his day. However, he also posits Daniel 9 as descriptive of the events of Antiochus:

"The date is 167 BC, the place is Jerusalem and the situation could not be worse. The warning of Daniel 9 has come true: a 'desolating sacrilege' has been placed on the altar of burnt-offering in the Temple by an arrogant king Antiochus Epiphanes, who makes havoc of Judea, putting people to death for daring to stick fast by the covenant and the law. (1 Macc. 1:41-64)." (2013, 87)."

The point then should be clear. Jesus and the NT writers cited, alluded to and quoted from Daniel, including chapters 9-12. Jesus referred to the coming Abomination of Desolation. He said the Great Tribulation was coming. He likewise anticipated the resurrection harvest at the time of the end. All of these eschatological tenets spring from Daniel 9 & 11-12. Jesus undeniably stated that those things would be fulfilled in his generation (Matthew 24:34). So, was Jesus wrong, naive or misguided to apply Daniel to his day? Was he just another in a long line of misguided prophets?

---

[333] R. T. France, *Jesus and the Old Testament*, (Regent College Publishing, 1992)40.

The fact that Jesus and the NT writers applied Daniel to their day puts to rest the idea that Daniel spoke *primarily or exclusively* of second century BC events. If there is an Antiochan application, it was, to restate the case, typological of the end time events. This was illustrated in my formal debate with Jason Wallace in Salt Lake City, September 12, 2015. The debate was sponsored by Shawn McCraney, of "The Heart of the Matter," and can be viewed on line.[334]

In my first affirmative presentation, I focused on Daniel 12:2, both in the immediate context and then, comparing it with several NT texts that are clearly reliant on Daniel's end of the age prophecy. In response, Mr. Wallace said that Daniel was dealing "specifically and explicitly" with the time of Antiochus. I responded with the following (I am abbreviating the discussion for space considerations):

1. The resurrection of Daniel 12 - no matter our concept of it - would occur when, "the power of the holy people" was completely shattered. I demonstrated that the "holy people" had to be Old Covenant Israel, for several reasons.

2. I proved that Old Covenant Israel's only power was her covenant relationship with God. Mr. Wallace never disputed this.

3. I took note of the following three facts:

    a. Israel's covenant relationship with YHVH was not shattered in the days of Antiochus. Mr. Wallace admitted - fatally - that this was true.

    b. I demonstrated that Israel's covenant with YHVH was terminated forever, in AD 70. Once again, Mr. Wallace actually agreed that this is true.

---

[334] https://www.youtube.com/watch?v=PjOMCLbPhvc

c. I then demonstrated, in response to Mr. Wallace's claim that AD 70 was a type of the yet future end of the age[335] resurrection, that if AD 70 was typological of a yet future event, that this demands that the church and the New Covenant will be shattered - in direct contradiction of the many texts that affirm that neither the church of the Lord will ever be shaken and that the Gospel can never be removed! Mr. Wallace agreed that neither the church nor the Gospel will ever be shattered.

So, the power of the holy people was not shattered in the days of Antiochus. It was shattered in AD 70. But the power of the body of Christ cannot ever be shaken in some future end time event. That means that *the only time* and the only event that fits Daniel 12 was in fact AD 70. But back to our examination of whether "Daniel" was written after the fact of the horrors of Antiochus.

The fact is that if some unknown "Daniel" was writing *ex eventu* of the events of his day, events that had already taken place, he was not a very good historian. Let me illustrate.

Daniel foretold the overwhelming, total destruction of Jerusalem and the Temple (Daniel 9:24-27). He likewise foretold the total shattering of the power of the holy people (12:7). *But the forces of Antiochus never totally destroyed the City or the Temple, and Israel's covenant relationship with YHVH was not ended in the time of Antiochus.* The forces of Antiochus desecrated the Temple to be sure, but they most assuredly did not destroy the Temple. So, if Daniel was describing those events – *post facto* – don't you think he would have gotten the facts right?

---

[335] In a telling moment in the debate, when I pressed the issue that the Christian age has no end, thus, falsifying Mr. Wallace's eschatological paradigm, Mr. Wallace vigorously stated that the Christian age, "this age" has no end. I immediately pointed out that in our email correspondence, he had stated specifically that he believes the resurrection does occur at the end of the current age.

Let me give again the citation from Pitre: "While the destruction of both the Temple and city is quite explicit in the text of Daniel, it is routinely downplayed by proponents of the "Antiochus Epiphanes" interpretation of Daniel 9 (since, I would suggest, it is the Achilles heel of that interpretation)" (2005, 304, n. 188).

So, to reiterate: Jesus cites Daniel 9 & 12 in the Olivet Discourse and said those things would be fulfilled in his generation. This means one of two things:

1. Daniel was not, in the ultimate sense, speaking of Antiochus.

2. If Daniel spoke of Antiochus, then Antiochus was typological. That would mean that Jesus was pointing to his generation as the final fulfillment of those typological events.

The conclusion to be drawn from this is that unless Jesus and the NT writers wanted us to think that there would be yet another (tertiary) fulfillment of Daniel 12, then since Antiochus (if we allow the Antiochan application) was *typological,* Jesus posited fulfillment in his generation. We must accept Jesus' application as final. What indication do we have that Jesus and the NT writers ever suggested a three-fold, or four-fold, or an on-going, unending series of fulfillments of the Old Covenant types and foreshadowings? What proof do we have for McDurmon's claim that there are "multiple fulfillments" of prophecy?[336] We have not a syllable of evidence to suggest such a thing. As a matter of fact, we have definitive proof to the opposite. Take a look at 1 Corinthians 10:1-11:

"Now all these things happened to them as examples they were written for our admonition, upon whom the ends of the ages have come."

---

[336] As noted above, in our debate, McDurmon said there are multiple fulfillments of prophecy. Of course, this is a blatant contradiction of his rejection of the "double fulfillment" hermeneutic of Dispensationalism, which he strongly condemned!

I have developed and discussed this text in-depth in other places so I will not do that here.[337] But take note of just a few thoughts:

Paul said (literally) that the events of Israel's past were typological of what was happening in the first century: "They were types of us" is the correct rendering of the text.

Paul did not say, "they were types of us and we are types of the real end." Paul's language in this text is very powerful, "the end (*telos*, goal, destiny) of the ages has come."

Frost (2012, 23+) in what is one of the most confused and confusing bits of writing imaginable on "the end of the ages" and "the last days" totally ignores the force of this text. He ignores the fact that Paul said the Old Covenant people and praxis were "types of us" i.e. the first century people and events. He ignores the force of Paul's statement that the goal (not simply "end") of the previous ages had arrived. Frost knows that if the goal of all previous ages was arriving in the first century there is no greater "goal of the ages" in the future. So, he obfuscates and throws out a lot of verbiage, none of which addresses the core message of the text.[338]

---

[337] See my *AD 70: Shadow of the "Real" End?* for a full discussion. That book is available on Amazon, Kindle and other retailers.

[338] Frost's claims of many ages to come, entraps him. Every previous "age" was characterized by the dominant covenant, and sometimes even the dominant personage, of that age. (We will not discuss here the fact that in the different "ages" which Frost seems to identify as "generations" that the over-arching singular covenant was Torah. This was the Rabbinic thought of the first century - and Jesus). Yet, even the dominant person, i.e. Abraham, David, etc., were identified according to the *covenant*. Thus, for Frost to suggest that there will be many ages to come logically demands that there will be *many more covenants*, or perhaps many more covenant personages. What then becomes of the Gospel of Christ, when those other "ages" (covenants) come into existence?

The force of this text cannot be missed!

Paul is saying that the events and time to which the typological events of the past pointed to were taking place in the first century. The goal of the previous ages was being achieved. This language would be entirely inappropriate if in fact, those types foreshadowed the arrival of another set of types and shadows - as demanded in the futurist paradigm. *Types were never the goal / destiny*. But if Frost is correct, the events of Torah were typological of the first century, but the first century events and personages were typological of other, greater events and people to come. There is not a syllable of proof for this. What those OT types foreshadowed and typified was the goal. So, for the apostle to say that the typological events - and people - of the Tanakh were being fulfilled, the goal being reached, is to eliminate any idea that other events were to be typified and foreshadowed.

Frost's claims of many ages also flies in the face of Jewish thought as well as scholarly consensus (that he likes to place so much emphasis on). In Rabbinic thought, there were not many ages, but two, even though they clearly understood that there were dominant personages within the ages.

Wright cites several primary Jewish sources showing that there were two ages: this age and the age to come. He offers this: "The Most High has made not one age but two." He also says,

> "By the time of the rabbis, the notion of 'two ages' had become well established, and the distinction between the 'present age' and the age to come - the present time when evil seemed to be triumphing, and the future time when it would be overthrown – was well known. But the distinction goes back well into the second-temple period, with its roots in

scripture themselves." (Wright, 2013, Vol II, 1059n. 71. He cites 4 Ezra 7:50).[339]

So, it is mere sophistry for Frost to speak of "many ages" when in fact, the dominant, overwhelming thought of Jesus' day, and that iterated in both the OT and the NT writings, was that there were only two, over-arching ages. There was "this age" and there was "the age to come."

This means that the end of the age events of Daniel 12 - the Great Tribulation, the Abomination of Desolation, the time of the end, the resurrection, all of which were to be fulfilled, "when the power of the holy people is completely shattered" were not typological foreshadowings of the "real end." They were not to occur at the end of "an age" among many ages. They were to be "the real thing," the end of "this age" and those events would usher in the full bloom of "the age to come." This falsifies all futurist eschatology.

---

[339] See my discussion of the two ages in my *The Last Days Identified* book. It is available on Amazon, Kindle, my websites and other retailers.

Point #16

MANY - OR ALL?

DOES DANIEL 12 PREDICT A SPIRITUAL AND "PARTIAL" RESURRECTION, OR THE "UNIVERSAL RESURRECTION?"

Frost, in an on-line article posted November 2011, attempts to negate the power of Daniel 12 by claiming that Daniel did not predict the "final resurrection." We know this, he says, because the resurrection of Daniel 12 is a limited resurrection. He argues that only "some - sometimes rendered "many" - of those who sleep in the dust shall arise" - and not all: "The first point is this: many does not mean all. Logic, anyone? Seems "plain" enough of a point. And, it would fit into any Logic textbook. "Many" does not mean "all.""

Frost believes this is definitive proof that Daniel is not referent to the general resurrection . But Frost's argument is weak at best.

It is lamentable that someone that has properly called for Bible students to understand the Hebraic modes of expression suddenly resorts to a Grecian literalism. Furthermore, it is interesting that someone that has resorted to an appeal to church history and creedalism, is so flagrantly at odds with church history and the creeds!

After acknowledging that church history testifies to the almost universal application of Daniel 12 to the "final resurrection" at the end of human history, Frost almost flippantly rejects that testimony: "So, it matters not whether Calvin or whoever believed that it refers to the general resurrection, or not. We can't fault expositors and commentators for getting details wrong to a complex idea of eschatology."

So, full preterists should heed the voice of history and the creeds. But wait! History and the creeds posit Daniel 12 as the final resurrection. Frost can't have that, because he acknowledges that Daniel 12 was fulfilled in AD 70. So, Frost says we should not be concerned that the "orthodox" view on Daniel 12 is, after all wrong!

Frost has rejected orthodoxy (while condemning preterists for doing so) and simply calls on Bible students not to worry that he has rejected the very authority that he calls on preterists to honor!

Frost tells us that we should not be overly concerned that the creeds missed his interpretation of Daniel. Do we not then, have the right to say that we should not be concerned that the creeds overlooked all of the emphatic time statements about *when the resurrection was to occur?* After all, that seems to be precisely what Frost is saying: "Hey, creeds and church history, you missed the temporal delimitations and the meaning of "some" in your view of Daniel 12, so let me set you straight. All of you creeds and church fathers missed those elements in Daniel 12, so I am okay to reject your testimony."

If we can reject the creedal view of Daniel 12 in regard to "some," can we not reject the creedal view of 1 Corinthians 15, which, as we have documented, Paul posits at the end of Torah? Why, other than a selective devotion to the creeds and "orthodoxy," should we overlook the errors of the creeds in some regards, but tenaciously cling to them in other matters?

The real issue is whether Daniel 12 foretold "a resurrection" in AD 70, but it simply foreshadowed the final resurrection at the end of time. So, does the language of "some" in Daniel demand that it cannot be the resurrection of "all"? Let's take a look.

Joyce Baldwin offers this:

> "Many of those who sleep appears to imply a limited resurrection and this is the view taken by those interpreters who think in terms of a setting in the Maccabean period. According to them it is essential that justice be done because in the general massacre good and bad alike perished. The resurrection is in that case a 'flash of inspired insight,' as Porteous calls it, a way of making possible God's vindication of the martyrs and his judgment on the opposition. But the use of the word

'many' in Hebrew is not quite parallel with its use in English. Hebrew *rabbim*, 'many' tends to be 'all', as in Deuteronomy 7:1; Isaiah 2:2, where 'all nations' becomes 'many peoples' in the parallel verse 3; and in Isaiah 52:14, 15; 53:11, 12, where this key-word occurs no fewer than five times, with an inclusive significance. As Jeremias points out, the Hebrew word *kol*, 'all' means either totality', 'sum'; there is no word for 'all' as a plural. For this *rabbim* does duty so it comes to mean 'the great multitude', 'all'." (Baldwin also believes, with a host of scholars, that Jesus cites Daniel in John 5:28-29).[340]

Baldwin is saying that the referent to "some" should be seen as a Hebraism, and not a woodenly literal restrictive term. (At one time, Frost accepted that Daniel 12:2 was a Hebraism, and did not demand a literal, limited "some").

I think Wright offers the best explanation of why "many" is the referent in Daniel 12: "There can be little doubt who these persons are: they are the righteous who have suffered martyrdom on the one hand and their torturers and murderers on the other. The rest – the great majority of humans indeed of Israelites, are simply not mentioned." (2003,110).

In other words, Daniel was not excluding "all" from the resurrection. In fact, Daniel 12:1 specifically says, *"everyone written in the book"*[341] would be delivered. Would Frost argue that

---

[340] Joyce Baldwin, *Daniel and Introduction and Commentary*, (Downers Grove, Ill., IVP Press, 1978)225.

[341] Deliverance of those written in the book and the books, in Revelation 20, is clearly - as historically attested - an echo of Daniel 12. And, historically and creedally, the church has said that Revelation 20 is the "general resurrection." So, if Revelation 20 = Daniel 12, that means that Daniel 12 was the

only some people are recorded in the books, for either salvation or damnation? I think not. *Would he not argue that in Revelation 20 we find the judgment of "all men"?* And are not those "all" judged for eternal life or condemnation - just as Daniel said? Where is there any delineation between Daniel and Revelation?

So, the "all" are in the background and in the text of Daniel. But the angel's words in v. 2 are focused specifically on the martyrs and those who persecuted them. It is not, in other words a limited resurrection, but rather a focus on a specific group involved in the "all" of the "final resurrection."

This is supported by the fact that in Scripture the time of the vindication of the martyrs is patently the time of the parousia (Luke 18:8), the resurrection and the judgment. The idea is pervasive in both Old and New Testaments. To put it another way, scripture knows nothing of a coming of the Lord for the vindication of the martyrs, called resurrection, at the time of the kingdom and judgment, and then, another, greater, Day of the Lord, another greater resurrection and another judgment. We have shown this in our comments above on Abraham, Isaac and the Worthies (classified as *martyrs* in Hebrews 11) sitting down at the Kingdom banquet, at the resurrection (Matthew 8:11). This was in fulfillment of Isaiah 25:6 which is the context of Paul's "final" resurrection prophecy of 1 Corinthians 15. Let me express it like this:

The resurrection of 1 Corinthians 15 is the "final," resurrection – Frost, Gentry, Dominionists and virtually all futurists.

The resurrection of 1 Corinthians 15 would be the fulfillment of Isaiah 25:8 according to Paul (1 Corinthians 15:54-56).

---

resurrection of "all those in the book" i.e. the general resurrection, thus falsifying Frost's objection. So, once again, Frost has to reject church history and the creeds to justify his new theology, all the while calling on his readers to follow the creeds and church history.

The resurrection of Isaiah 25 would be the time of the Messianic Banquet (Isaiah 25:6-8).

The time of the Messianic Banquet is, therefore, the time of the "final," resurrection.

But the time of the Messianic Banquet – when Abraham, Isaac and the Worthies sat down at the Table - was when, "the sons of the kingdom" were cast out – in AD 70 per many, if not most Dominionists.

Therefore, the "final," resurrection was in AD 70.

When we incorporate the idea of the vindication of the martyrs into the discussion, this brings Daniel 12 into full agreement.

The resurrection of Daniel 12 would be the time of the vindication of the martyrs and judgment of their persecutors.

The vindication of the martyrs – inclusive of Abraham, Isaac and the Worthies (Hebrews 11) - would be at the resurrection (Hebrews 11:35).

The vindication of Abraham, Isaac and the Worthies would be when they sat at the Messianic Banquet Table in the kingdom (Matthew 8:11).

The Messianic Banquet would be established at the time of the resurrection of Isaiah 25:6-8.

The resurrection of Isaiah 25:6-8 is the resurrection of 1 Corinthians 15 (v. 54-56) – which is the "final" resurrection.

But the Messianic Banquet, martyr vindication and the resurrection of Abraham, Isaac and the Worthies, would be when, "The sons of the kingdom are cast out" (i.e. AD 70 – Gentry, DeMar, McDurmon and most Postmillennialists, as well as many Amillennialists).

Therefore, the vindication of the martyrs in resurrection – the resurrection of Daniel 12 - is the time of the final resurrection and occurred in AD 70.

It is important to see that one cannot divorce martyr vindication from 1 Corinthians 15 (And Revelation 20) and the general resurrection.

Gentry, commenting on Revelation 20, says, "The martyrs' deaths, not only demand vindication, but explain and justify the judgments to follow." (1999, 251). Dispensationalist Greg Blaising agrees. Commenting on Revelation 20 he offers this,

> "Revelation chapter 6 introduced the expectation that some justice would be executed by God on their behalf they wait for that justice even as they are joined in waiting by subsequent martyrs. What John sees in Revelation 20 is the just vindication of believers slain for their faith, the fulfillment of them, or of the promises made by Christ himself." (1999, 222).

Aune concurs that Revelation 6 and 20 speak of the same vindication, noting that Revelation 6 and 20 form "a doublet" (1998, 1087f) in reference to the same time and same event - the vindication of the martyrs.

We could multiply this kind of quote many times over. The important thing to realize is that Revelation 20, the "final resurrection" is almost universally recognized as the time of the vindication of the martyrs. But since this is true the points above serve as *prima facie* proof that Daniel 12, being a prophecy of the vindication of the martyrs at the end of the age, was not some limited, spiritual resurrection as opposed to a yet future literal, bodily resurrection at the so-called "end of time."

Let me express it like this:

Daniel 12 is a prophecy of the end of the age vindication of the martyrs.

Revelation 20 - the prophecy of the "final resurrection" - is also a prediction of the end of the age vindication of the martyrs.

The end of the age vindication of the martyrs of Daniel 12 was when the power of the holy people was completely shattered (Daniel 12:7 - AD 70, Matthew 23:29f).

Therefore, the "final resurrection" of Revelation 20 was in AD 70 when the power of the holy people was completely shattered.

Unless one can completely divorce Daniel 12 and the vindication of the martyrs from Revelation 20 and its prediction of the vindication of the martyrs, this connection serves as irrefutable proof that Daniel 12 foretold the "final resurrection." This further establishes our premise of *Torah to Telos*, since Revelation 20 is the consummative resurrection and it would occur when the power of the holy people was completely shattered. Torah (the Law of Moses) would remain valid until all that it foretold was fulfilled, just as Jesus said.

Another text proves this beyond dispute. In Matthew 23:29f, Jesus castigated Israel for her bloody history of killing the prophets. He said that his generation of Jews would finally fill up the measure of their fathers guilt by persecuting his followers. Notice carefully the words that he used:

> "Therefore, indeed, I send you prophets, wise men and scribes: some of them you will kill and crucify some of them you will scourge in your synagogues and persecute from city to city, that on you may come all the righteous blood shed on the earth, from the blood of righteous Abel to the blood of Zechariah, son of Berechiah, whom you murdered between the temple and the altar. Assuredly, I say to you, all these things will come upon this generation."

Could words be any clearer, more graphic, more undeniable? I must confess that I once looked at Jesus' words here as a prediction of the "local" judgment on Jerusalem. Then, I looked closer at his words. Let me ask you: Were there any "Jews" around in the days of Abel? No? Well, Jesus said that all of the blood of all the righteous shed on the earth – all the blood, all the way back to Abel - was to be judged, avenged and vindicated in his generation! That is not a "local" judgment in any way, shape, form or fashion! That is the "universal" vindication of the martyrs, the vindication of Revelation 20![342] And so, once again:

☞ Daniel 12 is the prediction of the vindication of the martyrs.

☞ Revelation 20 is the vindication of the martyrs.

☞ Jesus posited the vindication of the martyrs at the judgment of Jerusalem in AD 70.

To refute this, one has to prove beyond doubt that Revelation 20 has nothing to do with Matthew 23. That cannot be done. So, since Daniel 12 is Matthew 23, and since Matthew 23 is Revelation 20, this proves that Daniel 12 predicted the "general resurrection." And there is more to consider.

The resurrection of Daniel 12 is described as the resurrection to eternal life. The resurrection of John 5:28-29, 1 Thessalonians 4, 1 Corinthians 15 and of course, the resurrection and New Creation of Revelation 20 are likewise the resurrection to eternal life, as all agree. This raises the question once again, how many resurrections to eternal life are there in scripture? With that question in mind, consider the following.

1. It is all but universally admitted that in 1 Corinthians 15, where Paul spoke of the resurrection to eternal life and incorruptibility, that he is speaking of the "general resurrection." Yet, he says not one word about the wicked. Does that mean that he was not speaking of the general resurrection, just because he was only

---

[342] See my extensive discussion of the parallels between Matthew 23, Hebrews 11 and Revelation in my book, *We Shall Meet Him In The Air, the Wedding of the King of kings*. Surprisingly few commentators develop these connections, but they are definitive. My book is available from Amazon, Kindle, my websites and other retailers.

speaking of "some of the dead" and not all of them? That would hardly be logical or textual. It would certainly not be historical or creedal.

2. The same is true in 1 Thessalonians 4:13f. Frost and virtually all futurists agree that Paul does not speak here of the resurrection of the wicked. He speaks only of the resurrection of "some" i.e. the righteous. Does that mean he did not believe in the resurrection of the wicked? Patently not. You cannot find that doctrine in the creeds.

As Wright suggested, in Daniel and these other texts, the focus is on a limited group, not because the "rest of the dead" are not in the background, but because the discussion is on a particular issue: vindication of the martyrs, or on only one side of the resurrection, i.e. the fate of the righteous.

As we demonstrated above, Hebrews 11:39 and 1 Thessalonians are emphatic in declaring that the entrance into resurrection life for the Old Covenant Worthies and the last days, terminal generation was to be synchronous: "They (the OT Worthies) without us, can not be made perfect" said the author of Hebrews 11. They could not enter into eternal life before that final climactic generation of saints. The first fruits saints and the Old Covenant saints would enter into the "eternal Inheritance" (Hebrews 9:15) *together*. But the view that Daniel 12 foretold a partial resurrection of some to eternal life, as opposed to the "general resurrection" of Thessalonians, Corinthians, Revelation when "all" would receive life flies in the face of this.

Where is such a delineation to be found in any of these texts? Where does Paul, or John, or any NT writer, distinguish between the impending, at hand resurrection to eternal life that Abraham and the Worthies were about to receive, and another, far off resurrection that is (ostensibly at least) better than the "better resurrection" that Abraham and the Worthies were about to receive - as posited by the Dominionists themselves? We have to ask again, in light of the claim by McDurmon that, "we are in a better position than they" i.e. the OT Worthies, *how this is true*? If those OT Worthies have been resurrected to eternal life in the kingdom, at the Messianic Banquet

– which is the resurrection of 1 Corinthians 15 - then what could be better than that? Eternal life, kingdom life; *what is better than that?*

How could some future "resurrection to eternal life" be better than "the resurrection to eternal life" that the Dominionists now agree occurred in AD 70?

What the Dominionists do, in their attempt to divorce Daniel 12 from the consummative resurrection, is to create two resurrections to eternal life and two resurrections to kingdom life, a doctrine totally unknown in scripture.

Furthermore, and this is critical, Dominionists and Amillennialists alike rip their proposed future resurrection to eternal life from its context of the fulfillment of God's Old Covenant promises made to Israel. As I shared above, McDurmon, in our public debate, argued that there was an Adamic / Abrahamic / Jobian resurrection, but that there was also an "Israel eschatology" if I many coin that term.

McDurmon tried, unsuccessfully, to say that the promise of the resurrection of Job 19 is not the resurrection promise given to Israel in Torah, since Job was written before Torah! Of course, as I argued repeatedly, this means that none of Paul's resurrection predictions can be applied to a "final (Jobian) resurrection" to eternal life, since Paul is emphatic that he preached nothing (do you catch the power of that? - "*Nothing*") but the hope of Israel found in Moses, the law and the prophets.

So, if the resurrection promise of Job is not the resurrection promise given to Israel in Torah, why don't we find Paul, in his *magnum opus* on the resurrection, even slightly alluding to, citing, echoing, Job's promise? When I pressed McDurmon to provide some documentation for his claimed dichotomy he offered not a word.

Paul is clear that the resurrection of 1 Corinthians 15, the resurrection to eternal life of Daniel 12 as we have proven above, would be in fulfillment of God's promises made to Israel. The refusal of McDurmon, Frost, Gentry and Dominionist apologists as a whole to honor this irrefutable Biblical fact is a fatal oversight in that paradigm.

Given that Daniel 12 was the resurrection to eternal life, eternal kingdom life, this proves that Daniel 12 was not a prophecy of some "minor" preliminary typological resurrection of only "some" as Frost and others claim. Rather, the *focus* is simply on martyr vindication and the judgment of their persecutors. There is no "exclusion" of the "all." It is simply a matter of "focus of attention." Daniel 12 was in fact a prophecy of the general resurrection.

All of this demonstrates the validity of our premise of *Torah To Telos*, since the resurrection of Daniel was when Israel's power - her covenant with YHVH (Torah) – was finally fulfilled and removed forever. Thus, all futurist eschatologies are falsified.

The claim that Daniel 12 foretold a "partial" resurrection is falsified in the text itself.

"All of those written in the book" - the book of Life, which is the Book of the general resurrection of Revelation 20 - would be delivered / resurrected.

Thus, it is wrong to argue that Daniel 12 only foretold a partial, typological resurrection.

SUMMARY AND CONCLUSION

We have covered a lot of ground in our investigation of Daniel 12 and the question of whether it foretold the "general resurrection." This was necessary in order to prove conclusively that the claims of an increasing number of Bible students, that Daniel 12 was fulfilled in AD 70 as a type of the true resurrection that is still future, is a false claim.

What we have seen is that the Bible posits, repeatedly and unequivocally, the truth of *Torah to Telos*. The consummative resurrection, judgment and full arrival of the kingdom of Messiah would be, not at some proposed end of time, but at the end of Torah. The Law of Moses did not pass away at the Cross.

We have shown that the Dominionists of the day, the leading advocates of the idea that AD 70 was typological of the real end, have ensnared themselves by the positions they have taken. Their conflation of Daniel 12 with Matthew 8:11f and the affirmation that Matthew 8:11f was fulfilled in AD 70 demands that the "final" resurrection, the resurrection of 1 Corinthians 15, was fulfilled in AD 70. If Abraham and the Worthies sat down at the Messianic Kingdom table in AD 70, when the sons of the kingdom were cast out, it is undeniably true that they were resurrected to eternal life at that time. After all, if Abraham and the Worthies were raised to the Messianic Kingdom Banquet, in fulfilment of Daniel 12, then they received everlasting life at that time.

If Abraham and the Worthies were resurrected to sit at the Messianic Kingdom table in AD 70 it is irrefutably true that they were not raised out of the literal dirt, in restored, resuscitated, human bodies to sit at that Kingdom Banquet on earth.

If Abraham and the Worthies "received what was promised to them" as affirmed by Mathison, DeMar, McDurmon, et. al., then they clearly were raised to the heavenly city and country in the "better resurrection." That is what they looked for and that is what was promised. Their reception of those promises falsifies the

Dominionist claim that they are still looking for an earthly, physical kingdom.

If Abraham and the Worthies, "received what was promised to them" in the resurrection of Daniel 12 (as affirmed by Mathison, DeMar, McDurmon, et. al.) and that meant they received everlasting life at the Messianic Kingdom table, this demands that the Intermediate State of the Dead has been abolished. After all, are we to believe that Abraham and the Worthies were delivered from Hades and the Intermediate State, but that faithful believers today are still destined to go there upon death? If Sheolic death is over, the final resurrection has occurred. If so, that means that they do not go to "Abraham's bosom" because Abraham is no longer in Hades.

With a wealth of exegetical evidence and argumentation, we have shown how the Dominionists point to Revelation 11:15f and claim it was, since it was based on and drawn from Daniel 12, fulfilled in AD 70. This is just another fatal admission by the Dominionists. If Revelation 11:15f was fulfilled in AD 70, then since Revelation 11 and Revelation 20 speak of the same resurrection for the judgment of the living and the dead, this serves as *prima facie* falsification of the claim that AD 70 was a mere foreshadowing of the real resurrection. You don't get more "real" than Revelation 11 and 20. And, you don't get more "final" than the resurrection to eternal life of Daniel 12 and Matthew 8.

Likewise, we have shown that the Dominionist admission that Revelation 11 was fulfilled in AD 70 is a powerful and fatal admission that the Abrahamic promise to "inherit the world" has been fulfilled. After all, Revelation 11 is a powerful declaration that, "the kingdoms of this world have become the kingdoms of our God and of His Christ." That is Romans 4:13 fulfilled.

Our study of the last days work of the Holy Spirit has shown that it is illogical and Biblically untenable to say that the Holy Spirit, as promised in Joel and Acts 2 - the charismatic gifts of the Spirit - have ceased, without thereby demanding that the resurrection has occurred. The direct, inseparable connection between the prophetic office, inspired by the Spirit, has been demonstrated. That prophetic, charismatic office, along with the rest of the miraculous gifts, served as sign and guarantee of the resurrection. According to Scriptures, the prophetic office and the gifts would cease at the time of the resurrection. It is, therefore, inconsistent for futurists to say, as many do, that the gifts have ceased (i.e. there are no inspired prophets today) and then turn around and insist that were are still looking for the resurrection. *The charismatic gifts of the Spirit and the resurrection are inseparable tenets.* As we have shown, this means that Daniel 12 foretold the final resurrection.

We have shown that any appeal to Daniel 12 as a foreshadowing of another, greater resurrection event is false and cannot be justified. The Old Covenant events were the types, fulfilled finally and consummatively in the first century.

Finally, we have effectively refuted what some consider to be definitive proof that Daniel did not predict the "general resurrection" and that is the argument that Daniel only speaks of "many" and not all being raised. By a careful analysis and comparison with other texts and comments from Hebrew scholars, we have shown that this argument is specious and false.

We began this study with the statement that if Daniel 12 foretold the "final" resurrection then all forms of futurist eschatology are falsified. We have proven, I think beyond reasonable doubt, that Daniel 12 did in fact predict that final resurrection.

> **We began by affirming that if Daniel 12 foretold the "final resurrection" then without doubt, all futurist eschatologies are falsified.**
>
> **With a wealth of exegetical and textual evidence, we have effectively proven that Daniel 12 did predict the "final" end of the age resurrection.**
>
> **Thus, all futurist views of eschatology are false.**

BIBLIOGRAPHY

Allison, Dale Jr., *The End of the Ages Has Come*, (Philadelphia, Fortress)1985.

Ardnt and Gringrich, *A Greek English Lexicon of the New Testament,* (University of Chicago Press)1979.

Arichea, Daniel and Eugene Nida, *A Handbook on the First Letter From Peter*, (United Bible Society, 1994)– referenced in the Logos Bible Program.

Aune, *David, Revelation,* Vol. #52, (Nashville, Thomas Nelson Word Biblical Commentary,1998.

Prophecy in Early Christianity, (Grand Rapids, Eerdmans)1983.

Baldwin, Joyce, *Daniel and Introduction and Commentary*, (Downers Grove, Ill., IVP Press)1978.

Balz, Horst and Gerhard Schneider, *Exegetical Dictionary of the New Testament*, Vol. I, (Grand Rapids, Eerdmans)1978.

Blass-DeBrunner, A Greek Grammar of the New Testament and Other Early Christian Literature, (Chicago, University of Chicago Press)1961.

Barnes, Albert, *Barnes on the Old Testament, Job* Vol. 1, (Grand Rapids, Baker)1978.

Barton, John, *The Biblical World, Vol 1,* (London and NY, Routledge Taylor and Francis Group)2002.

Beale, Greg, *Commentary on the NT Use of the OT,* (Grand Rapids, Baker Academic)2007.

New International Greek Testament Commentary, *Revelation*, (Grand Rapids, Paternoster)1999.

Commentary on the NT Use of the OT, (Grand Rapids, Baker Academic)2007.

A New Testament Biblical Theology, (Grand Rapids, Baker Academic)2011.

Blaising, Craig, in, *Three Views of The Millennium and Beyond*, Stanley Gundry, Ed., (Grand Rapids, Zondervan)1999.

Boice, James Montgomery, *An Expositional Commentary, Daniel,* (Grand Rapids, Baker)1989.

Boettner, Lorraine, *Four Views of the Millennium*, (Downers Grove, InterVarsity)1977.

Brooke, Canon A. E.(D. D.), *The International Critical Commentary, The Johannine Epistles*, (Edinburgh, T & T Clark)1957.

Bruce, F. F., *The Time is Fulfilled*, (Exeter, Paternoster Press)1978.

Carroll, John T., *The Return of Jesus in Early Christianity,* (Peabody, Mas, Hendrickson,)2000.

Coffman, Burton, *Commentary on Acts*, (Austin, Firm Foundation Publishing)1976.

Dawson, Sam, *Essays on Eschatology*, (Bowie, Tx, SGD Press)2013.

Davidson, Richard, *Typology in Scripture,* (Berrien Springs, MI. Andrews University Seminary Doctoral Thesis Series, Vol. II)1981.

Davies, W. D. and D. C. Allison, *International Critical Commentary, Vol. III, Matthew 19-28* (London, New York, T and T Clark)1997.

Denham, H. Daniel, an eight part series on *Daniel's Seventy Weeks*, in "The Defender," (Pensacola, Florida).

DeMar, Gary, (*Last Days Madness*, Powder Springs, GA., American Vision,)1994.

End Times Fiction, (Nashville, Nelson)2001.

Dubis Mark, *Messianic Woes in First Peter, Suffering and Eschatology in 1 Peter 4:12-19*. Studies in Biblical Literature, 33, (New York, Peter Lang)2002.

Dunn, James D. G., *Word Biblical Commentary, Romans 1-8*, (Dallas, Word Publishers)1988.

Word Biblical Commentary, Romans 9-16, Vol. 38b, (Dallas, Word Publishers)1988.

Elliot, Mark Adam, *The Survivors of Israel*, (Grand Rapids, Eerdmans)2000.

Eusebius, *Proof of the Gospel, Book VIII*, chapter 2, (Grand Rapids, Baker)1981.

France, R. T., *Jesus and the Old Testament*, (Regent College Publishing)1992.

Frost Samuel, *Why I Left Full Preterism*, (Powder Springs, GA, American Vision)2012.

Gaston, Lloyd, *No Stone Upon Another*, (Brill Academic)1970.

Gentry, Kenneth, *The Beast of Revelation*,(Powder Springs, Ga, American Vision)2002.

The Greatness of the Great Commission, (Tyler, Tx., Institute for Christian Economics)1993.

Four Views on the Book of Revelation, ed. C. Marvin Pate (Grand Rapids, MI: Zondervan)1998.

Before Jerusalem Fell, (Fountain Inn, SC, Victorious Hope Publishing)1998.

Kenneth L. Gentry and Thomas Ice, *The Great Tribulation Past or Future?*, (Grand Rapids, MI: Kregel Publications)1999.

The Charismatic Gift of Prophecy A Reformed Response to Wayne Grudem, (Fountain Inn, SC, Victorious Hope Publishing)1999.

Three Views of The Millennium and Beyond, Stanley Gundry, Ed., (Grand Rapids, Zondervan)1999.

He Shall Have Dominion, (Draper, VA., Apologetics Group)2009.

The Olivet Discourse Made Easy, (Draper, VA. Apologetics Group)2010.

Navigating the Book of Revelation, (FountainInn, SC., GoodBirth Ministries)2010.

Gibbs, Jeffrey A., *Jerusalem and Parousia*, St. Louis, MO, Concordia Academic Press)2000.

Gray, Timothy, *The Temple In The Gospel of Mark*, (Grand Rapids, Baker Academic)2008.

Gumerlock, Francis, *The Early Church and the End of the World*, (Powder Springs, Ga., American Vision)2006.

Hagner, Donald, *Word Biblical Commentary, Matthew 14-28*, (Dallas, Word)1995.

Word Biblical Commentary on Matthew 11:14, Vol. 33, (Dallas, Word Publishers)1993.

Hays, Richard, *Reading Backwards, Figural Christology and the Fourfold Gospel Witness*, (Baylor University Press)2014.

Holland, Tom, *Contours of Pauline Theology*, (Christian Focus Publications, Geanies House, Fearn, Ross-Shire IV20 1TW, Scotland, UK)2004.

Hawthorne, Gerald, *Word Biblical Commentary,* (vol. 43), *Philippians,* (Waco, Word Publisher)1983.

Hilyer, Norman, *New International Biblical Commentary, 1 and 2 Peter and Jude,* (Peabody, Mass, Hendrickson)1992.

Jackson, Wayne, "Christian Courier," (Stockton, California, Vol. 15, number 7, November)1979.

"Christian Bible Teacher," (P. O. Box 1060, Abilene, Texas, 79604-1060, November)1989.

Jordan, James, *Handwriting on the Wall*, (Powder Springs, GA., American Vision)2007.

Ironside, H. A., *Daniel the Prophet,* (Neptune, N. J., Loizeaux Brothers)1969.

Keil and Delitzsch, *Commentary on Ezekiel and Daniel*, Vol. IX, (Grand Rapids, Eerdmans)1975.

Kelly, J. N. D., *Black's New Testament Commentary, The Epistles of Peter and of Jude*, (London, A & C Publishers, Hendrickson)1969.

Ladd, George Eldon, *A Theology of the New Testament* (Grand Rapids, Eerdmans)1974.

LaHaye, Tim and Thomas Ice, *End Times Controversy*, (Eugene, Or. Harvest House)2003.

Lane, William, *Hebrews, Vol. 47, (Dallas, Word Publishers, Hebrews)*1991.

Mathison, Keith, *Postmillennialism: An Eschatology of Hope*, (Philippsburg, NJ, P & R Publishing)1999.

Age to Age: *The Unfolding of Biblical Eschatology*, (Philippsburg, NJ, P & R Publishig)2009.

Mattill, A. J., *Luke and the Last Things*, (Dillsboro, NC, Western North Carolina Press)1979.

Mayer, Jason, *The End of the Law: Mosaic Covenant in Pauline Theology*, (Nashville, B & H Publishing)2009.

McDurmon, Joel, *Jesus V Jerusalem,* (Powder Springs., GA, American Vision Press)2011.

We Shall All Be Changed, (Powder Springs, Ga., American Vision)2012.

McKnight, Scott, *A New Vision for Israel*, (Grand Rapids, Eerdmans) 1999.

Middleton, Richard, *A New Heaven and a New Earth*, (Grand Rapids, Baker Academic)2014.

Moo, Douglas, *Epistle to the Romans, New International Commentary on the New Testament,* (Grand Rapids, Eerdmans) 1996.

Munck, Johannes, *Paul and the Salvation of Mankind,* (Richmond, John Knox)1959.

Nanos, Mark, *The Mystery of Romans*, (Minneapolis, Fortress)1996.

Nicoll, Robertson, *The Expositors Greek Testament*, Vol. V, (Grand Rapids, Eerdmans)1970.

Pate, C. Marvin, *The End of the Ages Has Come, The Theology of Paul,* (Grand Rapids, Zondervan)1995.

Peterson, David, *The Acts of the Apostles, Pillar New Testament Commentary,* (Grand Rapids, Eerdmans, Apollos, England)2009.

Pitre, Brant, *Jesus, Tribulation and the End of Exile*, (Grand Rapids, Baker Academic)2005.

Pao, David, *Acts and the Isaianic New Exodus,* (Grand Rapids, Baker Academic)2000.

Pentecost, Dwight, *Things to Come*, (Grand Rapids, Zondervan)1980.

Perriman, Andrew, *Coming of the Son of Man*, (London, Paternoster) 2005.

Preston, Don K. *AD 70: A Shadow of the "Real" End?* (Ardmore, Ok., JaDon Management Inc.)2013.

Into All the World, Then Comes The End, ((Ardmore, Ok., JaDon Management Inc.)1996.

The Last Days Identified, (Ardmore, Ok., JaDon Management Inc.)2004.

Blast From the Past: The Truth About Armageddon, (Ardmore, Ok., JaDon Management Inc.)2005.

Seal Up Vision and Prophecy, (Ardmore, Ok., JaDon Management Inc.)2008.

We Shall Meet Him In The Air, The Wedding of the King of kings, (Ardmore, Ok. JaDon Management Inc.)2010.

Like Father Like Son, On Clouds of Glory, (Ardmore, Ok., JaDon Management Inc.)2010.

Seventy Weeks Are Determined...For the Resurrection, (Ardmore, Ok., JaDon Management Inc.)2010.

Who Is This Babylon? (Ardmore, Ok., JaDon Management Inc.)2011.

Israel 1948 Countdown to No Where, (Ardmore, Ok., JaDon Management Inc.)2011.

The Elements Shall Melt With Fervent Heat, (Ardmore, Ok., JaDon Management Inc.)2012.

Torah to Telos: *The Passing of the Law of Moses*, (Ardmore, Ok., JaDon Management Inc.)2012.

Preston v-McDurmon Debate, End Times Dilemma: Fulfilled or Future? (Ardmore, Ok., JaDon Management Inc.)2013.

In Flaming Fire, (Ardmore, Ok., JaDon Management Inc.)2015.

Reiser, Marius, *Jesus and Judgment*, (Fortress, English translation)1997.

Riddlebarger, Kim, *A Case for Amillennialism*, (Grand Rapids, Baker Academic)2003.

The Man of Sin, (Grand Rapids, Baker)2006.

Robinson, John A. T., *Jesus and His Coming*, (Philadelphia, Westminster Press)1979.

Russell, D. S., *The Method and Message of Jewish Apocalyptic*, Westminster Press)1964.

Schmisek, Brian, *Resurrection of the Flesh or Resurrection From the Dead*, (CollegeVille, Min. Liturgical Press)2013.

Schriener, Thomas, *New American Commentary*, 1, 2 Peter and Jude, Referenced in the Logos Bible Program.

Schurer, Emile, *The History of the Jewish People in the Times of Jesus Christ*, Vol. II, (Edinburgh, T and T Clark)1979.

Seriah, Jonathin, *The End of All Things*, (Moscow, Idaho, Canon Press)1999.

Son, Kiwoong, *Zion Symbolism in Hebrews*. (Waynesboro, GA., Paternoster)2005.

Strimple, Robert in, *Three Views of The Millennium and Beyond*, Stanley Grundy series editor, Darrel Bock, general editor. (Grand Rapids, Zondervan)1999.

Temple, Steven, *Who Was The Mother of Harlots Drunk With the Blood of the Saints?* (Ardmore, Ok., JaDon Management Inc.)2012.

Vincent, Joseph, *The Millennium, Past, Present or Future*, (Ardmore, Ok., JaDon Management Inc.)2012.

Wagner, J. Ross, (Heralds of the Good News, (Boston, Leiden)2003.

Wallace, Daniel B., *Greek Grammar Beyond Basics: An Exegetical Syntax Of The N.T.*, (Grand Rapids, Zondervan)1996.

Wilken, Robert, *The Land Called Holy*, (Yale University)1992.

Williams, David, *New International Biblical Commentary*, (Peabody, Mass, Hendrickson Press, Paternoster)2002.

Witherington, Ben, *The Acts of the Apostles, A Socio-Rhetorical Commentary*, (Grand Rapids, Cambridge, Paternoster)1998.

Wright, N. T., *Resurrection of the Son of God*, (Minneapolis, Fortress)2003.

Climax of the Covenant: Christ and the Law in Pauline Theology, (Minneapolis, Fortress Press)1992.

Paul and the Faithfulness of God, Vol. I, (Minneapolis, Fortress)2013.

Paul and the Faithfulness of God, Vol. 2 & 3, (Minneapolis, Fortress)2014.

Scripture Index

Genesis

Gen. 3.14, 19 8, 282

Exodus

Ex. 34.23 189

Leviticus

Lev. 26 197
Lev. 26.27-33 183, 190

Deuteronomy

Dt. 3.18f 275
Dt. 18 21
Dt. 21.23 173
Dt. 28-30 197
Dt, 28-32 202
Dt. 28.49 332
Dt. 28.49-63 183, 190
Dt. 28.53-57 134
Dt. 28.56f 167
Dt. 29 311
Dt. 31.29 272, 278
Dt. 32 272
Dt. 32.7f 272
Dt. 32.19-27 183
Dt. 32.20, 29, 43 74
Dt. 32.28 277
Dt. 32.32 274, 289
Dt. 32.43 289
Dt. 34.1-4 248
Dt. 43.19-27 190

I Kings

I K. 8.35 188
I K. 9.1-9 183, 190

II Chronicles

II Chron. 6.24 189

Job

Job 10.21 256
Job 19.23-27 64
Job 19.25 57, 245, 257

Psalms

Ps. 41.11 189
Ps. 69 311

Isaiah

Isa. 1.9 303
Isa. 2-4 296
Isa. 2.2 274
Isa. 2.9f, 19f 222, 274
Isa. 2.13 222
Isa. 2.19 275, 286
Isa. 3.1f 222
Isa. 3.13-24 222
Isa. 4.1-2 275
Isa. 4.4 222
Isa. 6 311
Isa. 6.9f 311
Isa. 10.20 158
Isa. 10.20-23 304
Isa. 10.22-23 305
Isa. 11.10-12 305
Isa. 24.1-5 59
Isa. 24.10 59
Isa. 24.10f 79
Isa. 24.13 59
Isa. 24.19-25.8 164
Isa. 24.20-25.8 77
Isa. 24.22-23 59
Isa. 24-27 164, 276-277
Isa. 25 22, 24
Isa. 25-27 212
Isa. 25.1-3 79
Isa. 25.1-9 316
Isa. 25.6 265, 380
Isa. 25.6f 77-79, 82
Isa. 25.6-8 25, 93, 167
Isa. 25.6-9 24, 164
Isa. 25.8 61, 150, 246, 277
Isa. 25.8-9 277, 313
Isa. 25.9f 61
Isa. 26.1-3 61
Isa. 26.10 313
Isa. 26.10-11 61
Isa. 26.12-19 2
Isa. 26.16f 61, 164, 215
Isa. 26.17 208
Isa. 26.19 64
Isa. 26.19f 277
Isa. 26.19-21 232
Isa. 26.20f 234
Isa. 26.21 233, 279
Isa. 26.50 65
Isa. 26.50-51 64
Isa. 27.1f 65
Isa. 27.9-11 232
Isa. 27.10-11 168, 277
Isa. 27.10-13 233
Isa. 27.13 147, 212, 232
Isa. 28.11 332
Isa. 32 329
Isa. 43.5 147
Isa. 43.10 351
Isa. 49.6-16 317
Isa. 49.8 320

Isa. 49.12f 147
Isa. 52.1f 63
Isa. 54 320
Isa. 54.1f 320
Isa. 59 278
Isa. 59.16 279
Isa. 61 319
Isa. 61.10 319
Isa. 61.11 319
Isa. 61.13f 319
Isa. 61.18f 320
Isa. 62 63
Isa. 65 14, 308
Isa. 65-66 165
Isa. 65.1-2 307
Isa. 65.8 317
Isa. 65.8f 165
Isa. 65.13f 165, 307
Isa. 65.13-19 79, 158
Isa. 65.19 316
Isa. 66.3f 165
Isa. 66.7-8 208
Isa. 66.15f 165
Isa. 66.17f 165
Isa. 66.18f 165

Jeremiah

Jer. 3 147
Jer. 5.5 332
Jer. 6.1-6 183, 190
Jer. 23.23 208
Jer. 26.1-9 183, 190
Jer. 30.5f 165
Jer. 31.21-22 167
Jer. 32 309

Lamentations

Lam. 1.17 195

Exekiel

Ezek. 5.8-14 166
Ezek. 14.14 368
Ezek. 20.25 215
Ezek. 33.24 249
Ezek. 37 2-3, 308, 331
Ezek. 37.11-14 329

Daniel

Dan. 2.44 283
Dan. 7.10f 170
Dan. 7.13f 283
Dan. 7.21f 80, 132
Dan. 9 232
Dan. 9.24 354
Dan. 9.24f 50, 87, 171, 173
Dan. 9.24-27 188, 200, 372
Dan. 9.26 183
Dan. 9.26-27 171
Dan. 9.36 190
Dan. 12 21, 227
Dan. 12.1 209, 211
Dan. 12.1-2 173
Dan. 12.1-3 3, 331
Dan. 12.2-3 14
Dan. 12.2-4 259
Dan. 12.2-4, 13 236
Dan. 12.2-7 126
Dan. 12.2-13 33, 236
Dan. 12.3 235, 242
Dan. 12.4 14, 46, 234
Dan. 12.6-7 57
Dan. 12.7 11, 31, 46, 228, 234, 372
Dan. 12.9f 232, 263
Dan. 12.12-13 68
Dan. 12.13 259
Dan. 12.41-43 235

Hosea

Hos. 2.3f 296
Hos. 8.1-10.15 183, 190
Hos. 10.8 275
Hos. 13 212
Hos. 13.12-14 176
Hos. 13.13 159
Hos. 13.14 141, 246

Joel

Joel 2.27f 296
Joel 2.28f 344
Joel 2.28-32 329

Amos

Amos 5.1-3 158

Micah

Mic. 3.12 183, 190
Mic. 4.9 208
Mic. 7.1-4 167
Mic. 7.15 329

Zechariah

Zech. 11-14 177
Zech. 11.6 183, 190
Zech. 11.8-9 134, 204
Zech. 11.9f 178
Zech. 12.10 178
Zech. 13-14 158
Zech. 13.7f 178
Zech. 14.1-8 178

Malachi

Mal. 3.6 220
Mal. 4.5-6 220, 297

Matthew

Mt. 2.15 314
Mt. 3.7 220
Mt. 4.17 250
Mt. 8 19-21, 91
Mt. 8.11 237, 265, 380
Mt. 8.11f 23, 80, 110, 128, 133, 146-147, 149-150
Mt. 10.23 100
Mt. 10.36 168
Mt. 12.41-42 235
Mt. 13.17 296
Mt. 13.28 19
Mt. 13.39-40, 49 46
Mt. 13.39-43 242
Mt. 13.40-43 45
Mt. 13.41-43 235
Mt. 16.21-28 206
Mt. 16.27-28 173, 211
Mt. 16.28 100
Mt. 17.10-12 168

Mt. 21.43 23
Mt. 22 284
Mt. 23 38, 73
Mt. 23.29f 71, 383
Mt. 23.29-36 81
Mt. 23.29-37 233
Mt. 23.36 74-75
Mt. 24 27, 207, 218
Mt. 24.1-3 242
Mt. 24.3 46
Mt. 24.4-34 210
Mt. 24.8 159, 208, 215
Mt. 24.9 211
Mt. 24.13 211
Mt. 24.14 306, 350
Mt. 24.15 370
Mt. 24.15f 15, 185
Mt. 24.15-21 62
Mt. 24.15-34 202, 211
Mt. 24.21 211
Mt. 24.21-34 212
Mt. 24.29 211, 233
Mt. 24.29f 211-212, 221
Mt. 24.30 100, 178, 211
Mt. 24.31 232
Mt. 24.32f 96
Mt. 24.34 202
Mt. 24.36 98
Mt. 24.37f 314
Mt. 24.53, 55, 50 98
Mt. 25.5, 19 83
Mt. 25.13 99
Mt. 25.31f 264
Mt. 26.64 100
Mt. 27.51-52 231
Mt. 27.52 241
Mt. 28.18f 250
Mt. 28.18-20 350
Mt. 28.20 46

Mark

Mk. 1.15 102, 172, 250
Mk. 3.27 301
Mk. 4.17 172
Mk. 8.34-38 206
Mk. 13.8f 177
Mk. 13.9f 211, 218, 221, 350
Mk. 16.17f 350
Mk. 16.17-20 331

Luke

Lk. 1.14-16 333
Lk. 4.13 222
Lk. 10.18 301
Lk. 10.19 196
Lk. 11.20 301
Lk. 12.40, 46 99
Lk. 13.27f 81
Lk. 13.28 22, 33
Lk. 13.28f 33, 78, 147
Lk. 13.28-30 237
Lk. 13.33-34 284
Lk. 17.25 172
Lk. 17.26-37 31
Lk. 18 31
Lk. 18.1-8 285
Lk. 18.8 149, 380
Lk. 19.41-44 174
Lk. 21.22 139, 143
Lk. 21.24 194, 196-197, 275
Lk. 21.25f 66
Lk. 21.28 315
Lk. 21.28-32 170
Lk. 23.28f 275
Lk. 24.46-47 213

John

Jn. 4.21-23 174, 293
Jn. 5.24f 14-15
Jn. 5.24-29 3, 130, 228, 293
Jn. 5.28 64
Jn. 5.28-29 2, 100, 297
Jn. 6.15 250
Jn. 6.39-40 295, 297
Jn. 6.44 296
Jn. 6.44, 54 96
Jn. 6.56 146
Jn. 10.35f 174
Jn. 12.10 243
Jn. 14.26 352
Jn. 14.30 301
Jn. 16.11 301
Jn. 16.13 352-353
Jn. 20.30 353
Jn. 20.30-31 243
Jn. 21.15 353

Acts

Ac. 1.3 343
Ac. 1.5-6 264
Ac. 1.7 83
Ac. 1.7-8 343
Ac. 2.15f 264, 331, 351
Ac. 2.15ff 296
Ac. 2.17 91, 297
Ac. 2.18 345
Ac. 2.40 347, 352
Ac. 3.21-23 296
Ac. 3.23 21, 264
Ac. 6.10 350
Ac. 9.15-16 213
Ac. 11.27-30 218
Ac. 14.1-3 350
Ac. 14.2-3 331
Ac. 14.22 213, 221, 228
Ac. 17.3 213
Ac. 17.30f 86
Ac. 17.31 100
Ac. 24.14 106
Ac. 24.14-15 86, 108, 113, 117, 140, 245, 272
Ac. 24.15 1
Ac. 24.24f 308
Ac. 26.6f 143, 272, 308, 313
Ac. 26.21f 245, 272, 308
Ac. 26.21-23 141
Ac. 26.31f 143
Ac. 28.16f 308

Romans

Rom. 3.21 122

Rom. 4.13 26, 124, 250
Rom. 8.1-3 127
Rom. 8.17f 270
Rom. 8.18f 86, 214
Rom. 8.18-23 331
Rom. 8.22 218
Rom. 8.23 215
Rom. 8.23-9.4 143
Rom. 9.1-3 109, 306
Rom. 9-11.24 312
Rom. 9.27 304
Rom. 9.27f 312
Rom. 9.27-29 305
Rom. 9.27-33 307
Rom. 9.41 135
Rom. 10-11 306
Rom. 10.1f 307
Rom. 10.18f 305
Rom. 10.20-21 307
Rom. 11.1-3 310
Rom. 11.1-7 315
Rom. 11.1-15 307
Rom. 11.7 307
Rom. 11.22 305, 307
Rom. 11.24-27 142
Rom. 11.25 311
Rom. 11.25f 181, 324, 327, 361
Rom. 11.25-27 10, 278, 306, 313-314, 323
Rom. 11.25-28 216
Rom. 13.11 99
Rom. 14.17 308
Rom. 15.8f 306
Rom. 15.26 218
Rom. 16.5 201
Rom. 16.20 300-301
Rom. 16.25-26 308

I Corinthians

I Cor. 1.4-8 331
I Cor. 1.6-8 351, 361
I Cor. 2.6-10 62
I Cor. 4.9 287
I Cor. 10.11 53
I Cor. 13.8 351
I Cor. 13.8-13 364
I Cor. 14.20f 331
I Cor. 14.21-22 332
I Cor. 15 10, 22, 118, 265
I Cor. 15.22 246, 261
I Cor. 15.23-24 96, 100
I Cor. 15.50f 118
I Cor. 15.51 133, 263
I Cor. 15.52 212
I Cor. 15.53-56 111
I Cor. 15.54-55 36, 60, 265
I Cor. 15.54-56 380
I Cor. 15.55 276
I Cor. 15.55-56 79, 125, 134, 143
I Cor. 16.15 201

II Corinthians

II Cor. 3.5f 125
II Cor. 3.16f 331
II Cor. 4.1-3 331
II Cor. 4.16f 228
II Cor. 4.16-18 308
II Cor. 5.5 331, 361
II Cor. 5.18-6.1-4 323

Galatians

Gal. 4 177
Gal. 4.4 222
Gal. 4.6-14 124
Gal. 4.20-21 127
Gal. 4.22f 125, 238
Gal. 4.24f 125

Ephesians

Eph. 1.12f 361
Eph. 1.12-14 331
Eph. 2.1f 37
Eph. 3.4-6 30
Eph. 4.4 12
Eph. 4.8-16 351
Eph. 4.11-16 364

Colossians

Col. 1.13 301
Col. 1.24 287
Col. 1.24f 221
Col. 2 294
Col. 2.15 301

I Thessalonians

I Thes. 1 164
I Thes. 1.10 213, 220
I Thes. 2.14f 81, 220
I Thes. 2.14-16 286
I Thes. 2.15f 177, 238
I Thes. 2.16 288
I Thes. 3.1-3 164, 213, 220
I Thes. 3.3 208, 220
I Thes. 4 43, 49, 74
I Thes. 4.13f 78, 241
I Thes. 4.15, 17 100
I Thes. 4.16 64, 100
I Thes. 5.2 100

II Thessalonians

II Thes. 1 164, 286
II Thes. 1-2 220
II Thes. 1.4f 213
II Thes. 1.5 80, 221
II Thes. 1.7 100, 2 22, 228
II Thes. 1.9 276
II Thes. 1.10 286

II Timothy

II Tim. 2.16-17 84
II Tim. 3-4 91
II Tim. 3.10, 14 83
II Tim. 4 89
II Tim. 4.1 85, 264
II Tim. 4.1-2 83
II Tim. 4.8 86

Hebrews

Heb. 1.1 222, 296
Heb. 1.1f 91
Heb. 1.2 84, 96
Heb. 7.10f 125
Heb. 8.13 125, 200
Heb. 9.6f 327

Heb. 9.6-10 154
Heb. 9.15 37, 385
Heb. 9.24 241
Heb. 9.28 126, 239, 241
Heb. 10.1-2 294, 327
Heb. 10-11 73
Heb. 10.26f 273
Heb. 10.33f 74
Heb. 10.33-37 74
Heb. 10.34f 17, 229
Heb. 10.37 76, 95, 126-127
Heb. 11 12-13, 16, 21, 89, 91
Heb. 11-12 17
Heb. 11.10, 16 88
Heb. 11.11-13 103
Heb. 11.13 146
Heb. 11.13f 146
Heb. 11.13-16 94
Heb. 11.14 12
Heb. 11.16 87
Heb. 11.35 240, 381
Heb. 11.35f 14, 75-78, 148
Heb. 11.39 146, 385
Heb. 11.39-40 41-43, 87, 89, 240-241
Heb. 11.40 18
Heb. 12.18f 248
Heb. 12.21f 24, 76, 319
Heb. 12.21-28 308, 320
Heb. 12.22 18, 201
Heb. 12.28 94

James

Jas. 1.1 201
Jas. 1.12 222
Jas. 1.18 201
Jas. 4.7 301
Jas. 5.1-6 223
Jas. 5.6f 229
Jas. 5.7-9 100
Jas. 5.8-9 223

I Peter

I Pet. 1.3 219
I Pet. 1.3-5 263
I Pet. 1.5f 221, 224-225, 229
I Pet. 1.5-7 95
I Pet. 1.6 222
I Pet. 1.9 95
I Pet. 1.9f 239
I Pet. 1.9-12 95, 225
I Pet. 1.10f 263
I Pet. 1.10-12 104, 263, 296
I Pet. 1.18 219
I Pet. 1.20 91, 296-297
I Pet. 2.5 225
I Pet. 4 55
I Pet. 4.5 96, 106, 264
I Pet. 4.5-17 94-95
I Pet. 4.7 98, 100-101, 219, 264
I Pet. 4.12 222
I Pet. 4.12-19 159
I Pet. 4.17 101, 103-104, 106, 219, 264
I Pet. 5.1 219
I Pet. 5.10 225
I Pet. 5.18f 225

II Peter

II Pet. 2.4 145
II Pet. 3 10
II Pet. 3.3-13 218
II Pet. 3.4-9 83

I John

I Jn. 2.18 28, 91, 96, 98, 258, 296, 298
I Jn. 3.2 100
I Jn. 3.8 301
I Jn. 4.1-4 361

II John

II Jn. 7 298

Revelation

Rev. 1.1, 3 89
Rev. 1.3, 7 100
Rev. 1.7 178
Rev. 2.10 226
Rev. 3.3 99
Rev. 3.9 322
Rev. 3.10 222, 226
Rev. 6.9f 243, 276, 285
Rev. 6.9-11 229
Rev. 6.12f 111, 289
Rev. 6.12-17 149
Rev. 6.19 218
Rev. 7.4 315
Rev. 7.14 228, 315, 322
Rev. 7.14f 323
Rev. 7.15f 315
Rev. 10-11 30, 92, 227
Rev. 10.5f 31
Rev. 10.7 136
Rev. 11.1-4 196
Rev. 11.5f 290
Rev. 11.8-18 237
Rev. 11.15f 30-31, 68, 135-137, 236, 250, 289
Rev. 11.15-18 32, 236
Rev. 11.15-19 33
Rev. 11.18 239
Rev. 12.7-17 301
Rev. 12.9 301
Rev. 14.2-4 322
Rev. 14.4 200, 202
Rev. 14.20 196
Rev. 15.8 110, 151
Rev. 16.6 288
Rev. 16.17-19 152
Rev. 16.19-20 275
Rev. 17.14 201
Rev. 19.2 289
Rev. 19.6 320
Rev. 19.15 196
Rev. 20 228, 291
Rev. 20.2 301
Rev. 20.8 226
Rev. 20.10f 111

Rev. 20.10-12 279
Rev. 20.11f 65
Rev. 20.11-15 114
Rev. 20.12-13 137
Rev. 21 10
Rev. 21.1-2 77, 88
Rev. 21-22 319
Rev. 21.2-5 89
Rev. 22.1f 326
Rev. 22.6, 10 89
Rev. 22.12 239
Rev. 22.17 320

Topic Index

A

A Case for Amillennialism Kim
 Riddlebarger 23, 182
*A Handbook on the First Letter from
 Peter*, Daniel Arichea and
 Eugene Nida 96
A New Heaven and a New Earth
 Richard Middleton 3
A New Testament Biblical Theology
 Greg Beale 5, 348
A New Vision for Israel Scott
 McKnight 174
A Theology of the New Testament
 George Eldon Ladd 332
abomination of desolation
 covenant wrath 197
 direct cause of 159
 first century event 200
 great tribulation a covenant curse
  on Israel resulting from 185
Abraham
 at messianic banquet 19
 the better resurrection of 123
Acts 1-2 and the fulfillment of Joel
 Ac. 1.3 343
 Ac. 1.7-8 343
 Ac. 2.15f 352
 Ac. 2.18 345
 Ac. 2.40 352
 Ac. 6.10 350
 Ac. 14.1-3 349
 Dan. 9.24 354
 discussed 342
 Eph. 1.12f 361
 Eph. 4.8-16 352
 Eph. 4.11-16 364

Frost, Samuel
 on miraculous spiritual gifts
  356
 on the last days 346
I Cor. 1.6-8 352, 361
I Cor. 13.8 352
I Cor. 13.8-13 364
II Cor. 5.5 360
I Jn. 4.1-4 361
Isa. 43.10 351
Jn. 14.26 352
Jn. 16.13 352-363
Jn. 20.30 352
Jn. 21.15 352
Joel 2.28f 344
Mk. 13.9f 349
Mk. 16.17f 349
Mt. 24.14 349
Mt. 28.18.18-20 350
Rom. 11.25f 361
seal up vision and prophecy 364
Acts and the Isaianic New Exodus
 David Pao 343
AD 70, postmillennialists posit
 resurrection in 11
AD 70: A Shadow of the Real End?
 Don K. Preston 53, 114
after death, the intermediate state 145-157
*Age to Age: The Unfolding of Biblical
 Eschatology* Keith Mathison 17
Allison, Dale Jr. *The End of the Ages
 Has Come* 161
An Expositional Commentary, Daniel
 James Montgomery Boice 3
anti-Christ, Pate thinks antichrists of I
 Jn. 2.18 are predictive of final 28
Antiochus Epiphanes
 Dan. 9.24-27 372

Dan. 12.7 372
figural reading 369
McDurmon on multiple fulfillments of prophecy 373
Preston's debate with Jason Wallace 371
was Dan. 12 describing 367-376
Apostles Creed affirms Dan. 12.2 is final, general resurrection 56
Aune, David *Prophecy in Early Christianity* 332

B

Babylon, postmillennialists inconsistent on identity of in Revelation 10
Baldwin, Joyce *Daniel and Introduction and Commentary* 379
Barnes, Albert *Barnes on the Old Testament, Job Vol. 1* 254
Barnes, Albert, on Job 18.25 254
Barton, John *The Biblical World, Vol. 1* 348
Beale, Greg
   comments on Rev. 10-11 31
   on Dan. 12.2 5
   on Jn. 5.24-29 130
Beale, Greg *A New Testament Biblical Theology* 5, 348
Beale, Greg *Commentary on the New Testament Use of the Old Testament* 31
Beale, Greg *New International Greek Testament Commentary, Revelation* 348
Before Jerusalem Fell Kenneth Gentry 31
better resurrection of Heb. 11.35 13, 76
Blass-DeBrunner, *A Greek Grammar of the New Testament and Other Early Christian Literature* 85
Blast From the Past: The Truth About Armageddon Don K. Preston 227
Blume, Michael F. on Daniel 2 194
body, natural doesn't mean physical 52
Boettner, Lorraine *Four Views of the Millennium* 181

Boice, James Montgomery *An Expositional Commentary, Daniel* 3
Boice, James Montgomery, on Dan. 12.2 3
Brooke, Canon A. E.(D. D.) *The International Critical Commentary, The Johannine Epistles* 99
Bruce, F. F. *The Time is Fulfilled* 102
Bruce, F. F., on I Pet. 4.17 102

C

Carroll, John T. *The Return of Jesus in Early Christianity* 67
church history, can postmillennialists reject but not preterists? 7
Climax of the Covenant: Christ and the Law in Pauline Theology N. T. Wright 224
Coffman, Burton *Commentary on Acts* 342
Coming of the Son of Man Andrew Perriman 31
Commentary on Acts Burton Coffman 342
Commentary on Ezekiel and Daniel John Peter Lange 2
Commentary on Ezekiel and Daniel Keil and Delitzsch 2
Commentary on the New Testament Use of the Old Testament Greg Beale 31
Commentary on the Old Testament, Job, Vol. 4. Keil and Delitzsch 253
Contours of Pauline Theology Tom Holland 329
Countdown to Nowhere Don K. Preston 189
creeds
   Gary DeMar on 7
   Kenneth Gentry and 5
   postmillennialists can reject but preterists cannot 7
   postmillennialists disagree with 9
   postmillennialists inconsistent adherence to creeds 9
   resurrection in the 5

cross, Torah didn't pass at the 200
crushing of Satan, postmillennialists and 65

D

Daniel 12
   describing Antiochus Epiphanes discussed 367-376
   figural reading 369
   historically viewed as general resurrection at end of Christian age 4
   history of interpretation 1-34
   postmillennialists and 1-34
   the creeds and 1-34
Daniel 12.2
   general resurrection on last day 1
   Keil and Delitzsch viewed as source of Jn. 5.28-29 2
   Matthew Henry on 1
Daniel and Introduction and Commentary Joyce Baldwin 379
Daniel called "the prophet" in Mt. 24.15 370
Daniel the Prophet H. A. Ironside 2
Davies, W. D. and D. C. Allison *International Critical Commentary, Vol. III, Matthew 19* 208
Dawson, Samuel G. *Essays on Eschatology: An Introductory Overview of the Study of Last Things* 146
Dawson, Samuel G., on Lk. 16 146
day of the Lord is "that day" of Isa. 26.20 65
dead of Heb. 11 looked for better resurrection 16
death, the intermediate state after 145
debates, Kenneth Gentry refuses 6
DeMar, Gary
   fate of Satan 301
   on creeds 7
   on double fulfillment in Mt.24 27
   rejects futurist application of the great tribulation 162
DeMar, Gary *End Times Fiction* 301
DeMar, Gary *Last Days Madness* 101

DeMar, Gary *The Olivet Discourse: The Test of Truth* 28
dominionism *See* postmillennialism
double fulfillment, Gary DeMar on in Mt. 24 27
Dubis, Mark *Messianic Woes in First Peter, Suffering and Eschatology in I Peter 4:12-19* 159
Dunn, James D. G. *Word Biblical Commentary, Romans 9-16, Vol. 38b* 301
Dunn, James D. G. on fate of Satan 301

E

Elliot, Mark Adam *The Survivors of Israel* 189
end of sin in I Cor. 15.55-56 134
End Times Contnroversy Thomas Ice and Tim LaHaye 190
End Times Fiction Gary DeMar 301
end, resurrection at the 129
Essays on Eschatology: An Introductory Overview of the Study of Last Things Samuel G. Dawson 146
eternal life, resurrection to
   discussed 129
   is the general resurrection 55-70
Eusebius *Proof of the Gospel, Book VIII* 368

F

Fast Facts on Biblical Prophecy Thomas Ice and Timothy Demy 192
figural reading 369
filling the measure of sin 273
Four Views of the Millennium Lorraine Boettner 181, 271
Four Views of the Revelation Gundry and Pate, editors 332
Four Views on the Book of Revelation Kenneth Gentry 27
France, R. T. *Jesus and the Old Testament* 370

Frost, Sam
  on correspondence of Dan. 12 and Ac. 24 114
  on Dan. 12.2 96
  on I Thes. 4 49
  on miraculous spiritual gifts 356
  on New Testament use of Old Testament 50
  on resurrection of Dan. 12.2 48
  on resurrection of the just and unjust 109
  on the last days 346
Frost, Sam *The Problem with Daniel 12:2* 14
Frost, Sam *Why I Left Full Preterism* 96

G

Gaston, Lloyd *No Stone Upon Another* 172
Gentiles, times of *See* times of the Gentiles
Gentry, Kenneth
  and Dwight Pentecost 8
  and the creeds 5
  hyper preterism 11
  on Dan. 12.2
    applies to AD 70 8
    discussed 5, 8, 113
  on Lk. 21.22 139
  refusal to debate 6
  rejects futurist application of the great tribulation 162
Gentry, Kenneth *Before Jerusalem Fell* 31
Gentry, Kenneth *Four Views on the Book of Revelation* 27
Gentry, Kenneth *He Shall Have Dominion* 8, 140
Gentry, Kenneth *Navigating the Book of Revelation* 325
Gentry, Kenneth *The Charismatic Gift of Prophecy: A Reformed Response to Wayne Grudem* 356
Gentry, Kenneth *The Greatness of the Great Commission* 8, 282
Gentry, Kenneth *The Olivet Discourse Made Easy* 46

Gibbs, Jeffrey A. *Jerusalem and Parousia* 187
Gray, Timothy *The Temple in The Gospel of Mark* 160
great tribulation, the
  and the resurrection 158-230
  covenant wrath 197
  first century event 200
  precedes the resurrection 158
Greek Grammar Beyond Basics: An Exegetical Syntax Of The N. T. Daniel B. Wallace 105
Gumerlock, Francis *The Early Church and the End of the World* 353

H

hades
  end of in Dan. 12 and Rev. 6 145-157
  messianic banquest in? 25
Hagner, Donald *Word Biblical Commentary on Matthew* 11:14, Vol. 33 335
Handwriting on the Wall, A Commentary on Daniel James Jordan 8, 162
harvest, the, when both Old Testament and the first New Testament saints entered the everlasting kingdom 89
Hays, Richard *Reading Backwards, Figural Christology and the Fourfold Gospel Witness* 370
He Shall Have Dominion Kenneth Gentry 8, 140
heavenly fatherland, martyrs of Heb. 11 longed for 12
Henry, Matthew on Dan. 12.2 1
Heralds of the Good News J. Ross Wagner 273
History of the Jewish People in the Age of Jesus Christ Emile Schurer 159
Holland, Tom *Contours of Pauline Theology* 329
Holy Spirit's presence in last days
  Ac. 2.15f 331
  Ac. 14.2-3 330
  D. S. Russell on 333

Dan. 9.24.27 329
Dan. 12.1-3 331
David Aune on 333
Dt. 28.49 332
Eph. 1.12-14 331
Eph. 1.13-14 331
Ezek. 37 331
Ezek. 37.11-14 329
Four Views of the Revelation Gundry and Pate, editors 332
George Eldon Ladd on 333
I Cor. 1.4-8 330
I Cor. 14.20f 331
I Cor. 14.21-22 332
II Cor. 3.16f 330
II Cor. 4.1-3 331
II Cor. 5.5 331
Isa. 28.11 332
Isa. 32 329
Jer. 5.5 332
Joel 2.28-32 329
John the Baptizer
    Ac. 3.21f 339
    Ac. 3.24 339
    Lk. 1.14-16 335
    Mt. 11.1-15 333
    Mt. 11.13-14 339
    Mt. 17.10-12 339
    Mt. 17.10-13 339
Lk. 1.14-16 333
Mic. 7.15 329
Mk. 16.17-20 330
N. T. Wright on 333
Preston on 330
resurrection and the 329-366
Rom. 8.18-23 331
hope of Israel
N. T. Wright on 120
resurrection and tribulation as the 181
resurrection as the 120
hour is coming, the, how many of them? 293
hyper preterism, Kenneth Gentry and 11

I

Ice, Thomas and Kenneth Gentry *The Great Tribulation Past or Future?* 182
Ice, Thomas and Tim LaHaye *End Times Controversy* 190
Ice, Thomas and Timothy Demy *Fast Facts on Biblical Prophecy* 192
Ice, Thomas and Timothy Demy *Prophecy Watch* 185
Ice, Thomas, on Lk. 21.22 182
in that day, the day of the Lord in Isa. 26.20 65
intermediate state, end of in Dan. 12 and Rev. 6 145-157
International Critical Commentary, Vol. III, Matthew 19 S. D. Davies and D. C. Allison 208
Into All the World, Then Comes the End Don K. Preston 46
Ironside, H. A. *Daniel the Prophet* 2
Ironside, H. A., on Dan. 12.2 2
Israel, salvation of remnant 303-328

J

Jerusalem
    Mt. 23.29f a universal vindication of the martyrs 384
    Mt. 23.29f not local judgment on 383
    new can come only after the resurrection 77
    trodden down of the Gentiles 194
Jerusalem and Parousia Jeffrey A. Gibbs 187
Jesus and His Coming John A. T. Robinson 275
Jesus and Judgment Marius Reiser 335
Jesus and the Old Testament R. T. France 370
Jesus called Daniel "the prophet" in Mt. 24.15 370
Jesus v Jerusalem Joel McDurmon 18
Jesus, The Tribulation and the end of Exile Brant Pitre 5, 15

Joel, Acts 1-2 and the fulfillment of
See Acts 1-2 and the fulfillment
of Joel
John the Baptizer
   Ac. 3.21f 339
   Ac. 3.24 339
   Holy Spirit's presence in last days 333
   Mt. 11.1-15 335
   Mt. 11.13-14 340
   Mt. 17.10-12 339
   Mt. 17.10-13 340
Jordan, James H*andwriting On the Wall, A Commentary on Daniel* 8, 162
Jordan, James, Dan. 12.2 applies to AD 70 8
judgment on Jerusalem
   Mt. 23.29f a universal vindication of the martyrs 384
   Mt. 23.29f not local 383
judgment, the, resurrection of the living and dead 71-107
just and unjust, the, resurrection of the 108-116

K

Keil and Delitzsch
   on Job 19.25 253
   viewed Dan. 12.2 as source of Jn. 5.28-29 2
Keil and Delitzsch *Commentary on The Old Testament, Ezekiel and Daniel* 2
Keil and Delitzsch *Commentary on the Old Testament, Job, Vol. 4.* 253
kingdom, the, and the resurrection 132

L

Ladd, George Eldon *A Theology of the New Testament* 332
Lange, John Peter *Commentary on Ezekiel and Daniel* 2
last day, the
   Dan. 12.2 is resurrection on 1
   resurrection on the *See* resurrection on last day
   vs. the end of days 260

Last Days Madness Gary DeMar 101
last days presence of the Spirit and resurrection *See* Holy Spirit in last days
last days, the, postmillennialists inconsistent on 10
Law of Moses did not pass at the cross 200
Like Father Like Son, On Clouds of Glory Don K. Preston 51, 168
local judgment on Jerusalem, Mt. 23.29f not a 384
Lorraine Boettner *Four Views of the Millennium* 271
Luke and the Last Things A. J. Mattill 285

M

martyr vindication
   and the millennium 268-306
   and the resurrection 384
   Heb. 11.35 381
   I Cor. 15 and Gentry, Blaising, and Aune on 382
   in Isa. 59 278
   Mt. 23 and 66
martyrs longed for a heavenly fatherland 12
Mathison, Keith
   destruction of temple finished the mystery 30
   on Hebrews 11-12 17
   on Heb. 12.21f 76
Mathison, Keith *Age to Age: The Unfolding of Biblical Eschatology* 17
Mathison, Keith *Postmillennialism: An Eschatology of Hope* 10, 17
Mattill, A. J. *Luke and the Lsst things* 285
McDurmon, Joel
   a fulfillment of I Cor. 15 in AD 70 36
   on Job 10.21 256
   on Job 19.25 252
   on messianic banquet 22
   on multiple fulfillments of prophet 373
   on Zion 18

on Matthew 8 22
McDurmon, Joel *Jesus v Jerusalem* 18
McDurmon, Joel *We Shall All Be Changed* 252
McKnight, Scott *A New Vision for Israel* 174
mello
   Blass-DeBrunner, *A Greek Grammar of the New Testament and Other Early Christian Literature* on 85
   inconsistency of postmillennialists on 85
   studies of the word 116
messianic banquet
   Abraham at 19
   in Hades? 25
   Jesus' reference from Isa. 25.6-9 24
   Joel McDurmon on 22
Messianic Woes in First Peter, Suffering and Eschatology in I Peter 4:12-19 Mark Dubis 159
Method and Message of Jewish Apocalyptic D. S. Russell 332
Middelton, Richard, on Dan. 12.2 3
Middleton, Richard *A New Heaven and a New Earth* 3
millennium, the
   martyr vindication and 268-306
   the meaning of 268
Mosaic law didn't pass at the cross 200
multiple fulfillments of prophecy 373
Munck, Johannes *Paul and the Salvation of Mankind* 287
mystery, the, when the destruction of temple finished 30

N

Nanos, Mark *The Mystery of Romans* 122
natural body doesn't mean physical 52
Navigating the Book of Revelation Kenneth Gentry 325
new creation of Rev. 21,
   postmillennialists inconsistent on 10

New International Biblical Commentary David Williams 343
New International Greek Testament Commentary, Revelation Greg Beale 348
New Jerusalem can only come after the resurrection 77
New Testament usage of Old Testament 50
Nida, Eugene and Daniel Arichea *A Handbook on the first Letter From Peter* 96
No Stone Upon Another Lloyd Gaston 172

O

Old Testament used by New Testament 50

P

Pao, David *Acts and the Isaianic New Exodus* 343
Pate, C. Marvin
   antichrists of I Jn. 2.18 are predictive of the final anti-Christ 28
   on Dan. 12.2 3
   on I Cor. 2.7-10 62
Pate, C. Marvin *The End of the Ages Has Come, The Theology of Paul* 3
Paul and the Faithfulness of God N. T. Wright 122, 333
Paul and the Salvation of Mankind Johannes Munck 287
Pentecost, Dwight *Things to Come* 182
Pentecost, Dwight, and Kenneth Gentry 8
Perriman, Andrew *Coming of the Son of Man* 31
Pitre, Brant *Jesus, Tribulation and the End of Exile* 5, 15
Pitre, Brant on Dan. 12.2 5
Postmillennialism: An Eschatology of Hope Keith Mathison 10, 17
postmillennialists

admit Dan. 12 foretold spiritual resurrection in 1st century 90
can reject church history and scholarship, but preterists cannot 7
Dan. 12 and 1
disagree with the creeds 9
inconsistent
    on adherence to creeds 9
    on early dating of Revelation 10
    on I Cor. 15 10
    on II Pet. 3 10
    on *mello* 85
    on new creation of Rev. 21 10
    on Rom. 11.25-27 10
    on the last days 10
    on wedding of Christ in AD 70 10
posit a resurrection in AD 70 11
say no one today has been raised to eternal life 16
Preston, Don K. *AD 70: A Shadow of the Real End?* 53, 114
Preston, Don K. *Blast From the Past: The Truth About Armageddon* 227
Preston, Don K. *Into All the World, Then Comes the End* 46
Preston, Don K. *Like Father Like Son, On Clouds of Glory* 51, 168
Preston, Don K. *Seal Up Vision and Prophecy* 330
Preston, Don K. *Seventy Weeks Are Determined... For the Resurrection* 171
Preston, Don K. *The Elements Shall Melt With Fervent Heat* 165
Preston, Don K. *The Last Days Identified* 376
Preston, Don K. *We Shall Meet Him In The Air, The Wedding of the King of Kings* 39, 170
Preston, Don K. *Who is This Babylon?* 165
Preston, Don K. *Countown to Nowhere* 189
Proof of the Gospel, Book VIII Eusebius 368

Prophecy in Early Christianity David Aune 332
Prophecy Watch Thomas Ice and Timothy Demy 185
prophecy, multiple fulfillments of 373

R

Reading Backwards, Figural Christology and the fourfold Gospel Witness Richard Hayes 370
Reiser, Marius *Jesus and Judgment* 335
remnant, salvation of 303-328
resurrection
    Apostles Creed says Dan. 12.2 is final, general 56
    better of Heb. 11.35 76
    Daniel and Isaiah compared discussed 59
    out of the dust 59
    fulfillment of Heb. 11.35 14
    Keil and Delitzsch viewed Dan.12.2 as source of Jn. 5.28-29 2
    New Jerusalem can only come after 77
    of Heb. 11 12
    of Isa. 26, characteristics of 62
    on last day
        John Peter Lange on 1
        Matthew Henry on 1
    out of the dust in Daniel and Isa. 26 63
    postmillennialists posit one in AD 70 11
    the better one of Heb. 11 13
    Westminster Confession of Faith on 35
    what Daniel 12.2 predicted 58
    without being raised out of the ground 16, 35, 40
Resurrection of the Flesh or Resurrection From the Dead, Brian Schmisek 2, 6
Resurrection of the Son of God N. T. Wright 13, 379

resurrection, the
- and end of Torah in Dan. and Rev 138
- and Holy Spirit's presence in the last days *See* Holy Spirit's presence in last days
- and the creeds 5
- and the end of Torah 133
- and the great tribulation 158-230
- and the kingdom 132
- are Dan. 12 and Job 19 the same resurrection? 245-268
- as the hope of Israel 120, 181
- at the end 129
- correspondence of Dan.12 and I Cor. 15 118-156
- Dan. 12 historically viewed as at the end of the Christian age 4
- dead of Heb. 11 looked for a better one 16
- did martyrs of Heb. 11 receive eternal kingdom? 45-54
- fulfillment of Job in I Cor. 15 262
- hour is coming, the 293
- is the judgment of the living and the dead 71-107
- Jn. 5.24-29 293
- martyr vindication and 384
- martyrs of Heb. 11 longed for 41-43
- of many or all? 377-390
- of the just and unjust
  - Ac. 24.14 108
  - discussed 108-116
  - Sam Frost on 109
- partial or universal
  - discussed 377-390
  - everyone written in the book 379
  - I Cor. 15.54-56 380
  - Isa. 25.6 380
  - Lk. 18.8 379
  - Mt. 23.29f 383
  - Mt. 8.11 380
- the better one
  - at the end of Torah 126
  - of Heb. 11 123
- the great tribulation precedes 158, 174
- the wicked not in I Cor. 15 384
- the wicked not in I Thes. 4.13f 385
- time issue of Job 19 257
- to eternal life
  - discussed 129
  - is the general resurrection 55-70
  - postmillennialists say no one has received 16
- translational problems in Job 252
- was Dan. 12.2 fulfilled in Mt. 27.51-52? 231-244

Revelation
- early dating of, postmillennialists inconsistent on 10
- identify of Babylon, postmillennialists inconsistent on 10

Riddlebarger, Kim *A Case for Amillennialism* 23, 182

Robinson, John A. T. *Jesus and His Coming* 275

Russell, D. S. *The Method and Message of Jewish Apocalyptic* 160

salvation of remnant 303-328

S

Satan
- Col. 1.13 301
- Col. 2.15 301
- crushing of, postmillennialists and 65
- fate of
  - DeMar on 301
  - discussed 301
  - James D. G. Dunn on 301
- I Jn. 3.8 301
- Jas. 4.7 301
- Jn. 14.30 301
- Jn. 16.11 301
- Lk. 10.18 301
- Lk. 11.20 301
- Mk. 3.27 301
- Rev. 12.7-17 301
- Rev. 12.9 301
- Rev. 20.2 301
- Rom. 16.20 301

Schmiesek, Brian *Resurrection of the Flesh or Resurrection From the Dead* 2, 6
Schmiesek, Brian, on Dan. 12.2 6
scholarship, postmillennialists can reject but preterists cannot 7
Schurer, Emile *The History of the Jewish People in the Times of Jesus Christ* 15, 159
Schurer, Emile, on Dan. 12.2 15
seal up vision and prophecy 364
Seal Up Vision and Prophecy Don K. Preston 330
Seraiah, Jonathin *The End of All Things* 9
Seraiah, Jonathin, on Dan. 12.2 9
Seventy Weeks Are Determined... For the Resurrection Don K. Preston 171
sin
　end of in I Co. 15.55-56 1
　filling the measure of 273
Son, Kiwoong *Zion Symbolism in Hebrews* 167
Strimple, Robert *Three Views of The Millennium and Beyond* 289

T

temple, destruction of finished the mystery 30
Temple, Steven *Who Was The Mother of Harlots Drunk With the Blood of the Saints?* 288
The Acts of the Apostles Ben Witherington 343
The Biblical World, Vol. 1 John Barton 348
The Charismatic Gift of Prophecy A Reformed Response to Wayne Grudem Kenneth Gentry 356
The Early Church and the End of the World Francis Gumerlock 353
The Elements Shall Melt With Fervent Heat Don K. Preston 165
The End of All Things Jonathin Seriah 9
the end of days vs. the last day 260
The End of the Ages Has Come Dale Allison Jr. 161

The End of the Ages Has Come, The Theology of Paul C. Marvin Pate 3
The Great Tribulation Past or Future? Thomas Ice and Kenneth Gentry 182
The Greatness of the Great Commission Kenneth Gentry 8, 282
The History of the Jewish People in the Times of Jesus Christ Emile Schurer 15
The International Critical Commentary, the Johannine Epistles Canon A. E. Brooke (D. D.) 99
The Last Days Identified Don K. Preston 376
The Method and Message of Jewish Apocalyptic D. S. Russell 160
The Millennium, Past, Present, or Future Joseph Vincent 156
The Mystery of Romans Mark Nanos 122
The Olivet Discourse Made Easy Kenneth Gentry 46
The Olivet Discourse: The Test of Truth Gary DeMar 28
The Resurrection of the Son of Man N. T. Wright 254
The Return of Jesus in Early Christianity John T. Carroll 67
The Survivors of Israel Mark Adam Elliot 189
The Temple in The Gospel of Mark Timothy Gray 160
The Time is Fulfilled F. F. Bruce 102
Things to Come Dwight Pentecost 182
Three Views of The Millennium and Beyond Robert Strimple 289
times of the Gentiles
　discussed 194
　only imposed if Israel violated Torah 199
tongues, Pentecostal missionaries learn languages of the nations to which they will travel 351
Torah
　did not pass at the cross 200
　resurrection and the end of 133

tribulation, the great
   and the resurrection 158-230
   as the hope of Israel 181
   covenant curse on Israel resulting from abomination of desolation 185
   DeMar rejects futurist application of 162
   directly caused by abomination of desolation 159
   Gentry rejects futurist application of 162
   immediately precedes the resurrection 174

V

Vincent, Joseph *The Millennium, Past, Present, or Future?* 156
vindication of martyrs *See* martyr vindication

W

Wagner, J. Ross *Heralds of the Good News* 273
Wallace, Daniel B. *Greek Grammar Beyond Basics: An Exegetical Syntax Of The N. T.* 105
Wallace, Jason, Preston's debate with 371
war, the of Dt. 3.18 275
We Shall All Be Changed Joel McDurmon 252
We Shall Meet Him In The Air, The Wedding of the King of Kings Don K. Preston 39, 170
wedding of Christ in AD 70, postmillennialists inconsistent on 10
Westminster Confession of Faith on resurrection 35
Who Is This Babylon? Don K, Preston 165
Who Was The Mother of Harlots Drunk With the Blood of the Saints? Steven Temple 288
Why I Left Full Preterism Samuel Frost 96

wicked, the
   resurrection in I Cor.15 not about 384
   resurrection in I Thes. 4.13f not about 385
Williams, David *New International Biblical Commentary* 343
Witherington, Ben *The Acts of the Apostles* 343
Word Biblical Commentary on Matthew 11:14, Vol. 33 Donald Hagner 335
Word Biblical Commentary, Romans 9-16, Vol. 38b James D. G. Dunn 301
Wright, N. T.
   on Dan. 12.2 13
   on Mt.16.27-28 and Dan. 9.24f 173
   on resurrection as the hope of Israel 120
   on Job 19.25 254
Wright, N. T. *Climax of the Covenant: Christ and the Law in Pauline Theology* 224
Wright, N. T. *Paul and the Faithfulness of God* 122, 333
Wright, N. T. *Resurrection of the Son of God* 13, 254, 379

Z

Zion Symbolism in Hebrews, Kiwoong Son 167
Zion, McDurmon on 18